BAD GIRLS DO IT!
An Encyclopedia of Female Murderers

by
Michael Newton

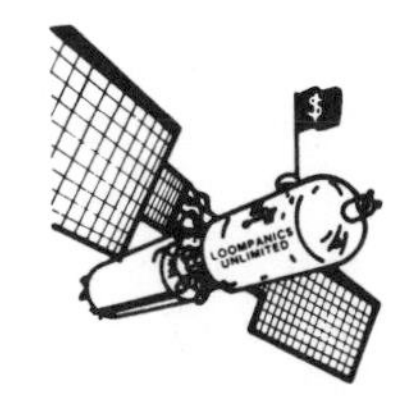

Loompanics Unlimited
Port Townsend, Washington

This book is sold for information purposes only. Neither the author nor the publisher will be held accountable for the use or misuse of the information contained in this book.

BAD GIRLS DO IT!
An Encyclopedia of Female Murderers

Published by:
Loompanics Unlimited
PO Box 1197
Port Townsend, WA 98368

Loompanics Unlimited is a division of Loompanics Enterprises, Inc.

Cover design by A

ISBN 1-55950-104-9
Library of Congress Catalog Card Number 93-79481

Contents

For Loretta... in the library, with the candlestick.

The female of the species is more deadly than the male.
Rudyard Kipling

Oh woman, woman! when to ill thy mind
Is bent, all hell contains no fouler fiend.
Homer, *Odyssey*

Acknowledgments

Few books — and none of this kind — are produced in a vacuum. Many cooks make contributions to the final stew, and they deserve acknowledgment. I owe a special debt of thanks to Michael Hoy, at Loompanics Unlimited, for suggesting the original concept, first as a short piece, later as a full-length book. Without his encouragement, ***Bad Girls Do It!*** would not exist. Others who contributed crucial information include:

Det. Donald Bradley, Cleveland (OH) Police Dept.

Dave Frasier, Indiana University Library

Eleanor Geheres, manager, Denver (CO) Public Library

Lt. R.L. Jenkins, Little Rock (AR) Police Dept.

Jon Jensen, Idaho Falls *Post-Register*

Steven Keeney, Louisville, KY

Melanie McElhinney, Federal Bureau of Investigation

Steve O'Keefe, Loompanics Unlimited

Chief James Vandiver, Little Rock (AR) Police Dept.

Introduction: Murder By Numbers

Feminists complain, and rightly so, that women's contributions have been largely overlooked and undervalued in the annals of American — and world — history. It is high time, they insist, that members of America's statistical majority receive full credit for their numerous achievements in such varied fields as politics and education, medicine and social activism, science and the arts. Ironically, a venue typically ignored is also one where modern females demonstrate a strong determination to succeed.

That field is crime.

In 1991 — the last year with complete figures available at this writing — female offenders accounted for 18.4% of America's total arrests. It comes as no surprise, perhaps, to learn that 64% of all arrested prostitutes and 56% of runaways were female, but what of the 44% locked up for fraud, 41% for embezzlement, 34.6% for forgery and counterfeiting, or 32% for larceny and theft? In the same period, American women also accounted for 19% of disorderly conduct arrests, 17.8% of crimes against family or children, 16.8% of all drug violations, 13.8% of gambling arrests, 13% of arrests for arson and aggravated assault, 10.4% for homicide, 10% of all reported auto thefts, and 8.3% of robbery arrests. Reversing the traditional view of women as victims, they further logged 7.7% of all arrests for sex offenses and 1.1% of arrests for forcible rape.

From all appearances, the ladies are no shrinking violets any more.

The work in hand is restricted, for reasons of space and convenience, to treatment of female multiple murderers. Sex offenses aside, these are the rarest of female offenders, their exploits frequently overlooked in the midst of headline-grabbing carnage perpetrated by the likes of John Wayne Gacy, George Hennard, and Jeffrey Dahmer. I have tried to make the survey comprehensive, but, inevitably, readers in the hinterlands will be aware of cases I have missed.

At that, the limitation has required deletion of some interesting specimens. Gertrude Baniszewski choreographed the torture slaying of teenager Sylvia Likens "to teach her a lesson," but Sylvia was Gertrude's only victim, and her case is not included here. Likewise Darci Pierce, whose obsession with motherhood led her to kidnap and murder a pregnant stranger, stealing her victim's unborn child in a crude Cesarean section performed with car keys in lieu of a scalpel. Fifteen months before Jeffrey Dahmer's arrest in Milwaukee, another local resident — 27-year-old Debrah Kazuck — lured a man to her apartment with promises of sex, then opened his scalp with a hatchet. Her aim was bad and her motive bizarre: Kazuck believed she was Jack the Ripper's mother, and she sought to resurrect her lethal "son" through human sacrifice.

Some "classic" cases of female multicide have also been omitted here. Lizzie Borden may have given her parents forty whacks with an ax, back in 1892, but Massachusetts jurors found her innocent, and I bow to their judgment. "Ma" Barker is likewise excluded, despite her notoriety as a mother of quick-trigger bandits, because there is no solid evidence of her committing any crime, much less repeated homicide. (Author Jay Robert Nash's description of "Ma" as a prolific lesbian serial killer is laughable on its face.) "Bandit Queen" Belle Starr was certainly a thief of cash and livestock, but the only murder she participated in appears to be her own, in 1889.

Defining multiple murder is no simple task, in itself. Criminologists have devoted much time and thought — in some cases, whole careers — to the task, without reaching any general consensus. Logic dictates that a multicide must claim at least two victims, but beyond that starting point the "experts" are in disarray.

The FBI's Behavioral Science Unit (BSU), world-famous for its criminal taxonomy, identifies five kinds of multiple murder. *Double* and *triple* slayings are self-explanatory, based on the number of victims killed at one time and place, but the others are more problematic. A *mass* murder, in FBI parlance, claims the lives of four or more victims in one continuous event, enacted at a single location. There are also subcategories of mass murder, described respectively as "classic" and "family" slayings. According to Robert Ressler, ex-BSU chief and author of *Sexual Homicide,* "A classic mass murder involves one person operating in one location at one period of time. That period of time could be minutes or hours, or even days." Family murders are further subdivided by the Bureau into "family killings" (with four or more persons massacred by a relative) and "mass murder/suicide" (in which a killer snuffs three victims and himself). Oddly, Ressler's published examples of "classic" mass slayers include Sylvia Seegrist, who killed *three* persons and wounded seven more in a 1985 shooting spree.

The two remaining types of multicide, according to the FBI, are *spree* and *serial* murder. As defined by Ressler, "A spree murder involves killings at two or more locations with no emotional cooling-off period between murders. The killings are all the result of a single event, which can be of short or long duration." His example is gunman Howard Unruh's 20-minute walking tour of Camden, New Jersey, which left thirteen dead and three wounded in September 1949. Serial murder, by contrast, involves three or more victims, each killed at a different place and time, with undefined "cooling-off" periods between the crimes.

At first glance, the FBI's classification seems tidy, but it harbors several built-in problems. For starters, "classic" mass murders committed by two or more killers — as in Chicago's notorious St. Valentine's Day massacre — have no place in the Bureau's taxonomy. In most cases, the only clear difference between "classic" mass murder and "spree" killing appears to lie in the slayer's mobility, suggesting an artificial distinction. What, we are tempted to ask, is the critical difference between a gunman who kills ten people in a restaurant and one who blasts ten motorists while cruising on the freeway? And how are we to label "family" killers if they visit several different sites to quench their thirst for blood?

The worst confusion, though, arises in comparison of "spree" and "serial" murders. The undefined "cooling-off" period is both critical and highly subjective, based on the analysis of Monday-morning quarterbacks who try to penetrate the killer's mind. Thus, Ted Bundy, with twenty-eight confessed murders in twenty months, is considered a serial killer; Christopher Wilder, slayer of six women in five weeks, is labeled a "spree" killer by the FBI. The Bureau's definition of serial murder excludes monsters like John Gacy, who kill all their victims at one location, and no category exists for specimens like William Sarmento, jailed in Rhode Island before he could find the mandatory third victim required for "serial" status.

So confusing is the FBI's "spree/serial" melee, in fact, that the National Institute of Justice has offered an alternate definition. Published in 1988, the NIJ's report defines serial murder as "a series of two or more murders, committed as separate events, usually, but not always, by one offender acting alone. The crimes may occur over a period of time ranging from hours to years. Quite often the motive is psychological, and the offender's behavior and the physical evidence observed at the crime scene will reflect sadistic, sexual overtones."

Professors Jack Levin and James Fox take a stab at simplifying matters in their book *Mass Murder: America's Growing Menace.* They accept the Bureau's four-kill minimum for openers, delete "spree" killings entirely, and lump the remaining categories together as "mass murder." (They also omit cases of murder by arson, without explanation and regardless of the body-count.) For Levin and Fox, "most" mass murders fall into one of three categories, including (a) family slayings, (b) murders "for profit or expediency," and (c) "killing for the sake of sex or sadism." The professors recognize exceptions, racist murders, for example, but dismiss them as unworthy of discussion.

No matter how we try to pigeonhole their crimes, some killers stubbornly defy classification. Richard Speck was linked to four serial murders before he went over the edge and slaughtered eight student nurses in July, 1966. James Pough had already served time for one killing, plea-bargained down to aggravated assault, when he killed eight persons and wounded eight more at a Florida shopping mall. Lillie Curtis murdered her husband and drew a sentence of probation three years before she decided that six of her children were "better off dead."

Short of creating a whole new vocabulary, I have tried to work within the limits of the FBI/NIJ definitions, as outlined above. The following pages include 183 cases of multiple murder committed by female offenders; sixteen other recognized cases were deliberately omitted on the basis of incomplete data at press time. A substantial majority — 129 cases, 70% of the total — fit the NIJ's definition of serial murder. Mass murders are second in frequency, with twenty-three cases (12%). Double slayings account for seventeen cases, or 9% of the total. Triple killings, with thirteen cases, constitute 7% of the field overall. Only two cases — Shirley Curry's Arkansas rampage of 1974 and the Kentucky case of Lafonda Foster and Tina Powell — appear to meet the official definition of "spree" killings. (Of the cases omitted, fourteen were apparently serial killings, with two double murders.)

Most female killers work alone, like their masculine counterparts, but thirty-nine of the cases reported here — some 21% — involve "team" slayers, operating with one or more accomplices. Of those, thirty joined forces with men to dispatch their chosen prey, while eight teamed with other women to commit their crimes. One case — that of the sinister Manson "family" — involved multiple killers of both sexes.

Suicide is not uncommon in the wake of murder, especially where family slayings are concerned, but female killers bear up fairly well. Of the 183 cases surveyed here, only twelve climaxed with the killer's suicide. Nine offenders killed themselves at the crime scene, while one committed suicide in jail and one allowed decades to pass before pulling the plug.

When it comes to choosing victims, 45% of our collected female multicides preyed on family members. The next largest group, 26% of the total, killed friends or acquaintances. Total strangers were preferred by 11% of our killers, while 10.5% murdered patients or other persons left in their care (including two cases of homicidal baby sitters). In 19.5% of the cases examined, criteria for victim selection varied from one crime to the next, impartially mixing up relatives, strangers, and friends.

Motives for multiple murder are as diverse as the killers themselves. Greed heads the list with female slayers; 35% of our cases involving a profit motive. Another 28% of the killings are motivated by apparent mental illness, including the elusive "Munchausen's syndrome by proxy" which drives its victims to harm their own children in a misguided quest for attention. Sadism, including so-called "thrill killings," account for 8% of the total. Five percent of female multicides are motivated, in the killer's words, by a twisted craving for romance. Criminal enterprise, as in organized drug-dealing, contributes another 3.2% to the list. Jealousy rears its ugly head in 2% of female multicides, while another 2% are described (by the slayers) as "mercy" killings. Three cases, or 1.6% of the total, involved religious human sacrifice. Killers in 11% of the cases varied the process of victim selection from crime to crime, and motives remain unknown in four of the cases examined.

Women are frequently described as "gentle" killers, shunning the bloodshed attendant in masculine crimes, but female multicides enjoy diversity. Thirty-three percent of those included here dispatched their victims by means of poison or drugs, in typical "female" style, but another 20% were hands-on killers, strangling or smothering their prey. A 12% minority used firearms in their murders, while 3.7% relied on poison gas, 3.2% used knives, and 3.2% bludgeoned their victims with hammers or axes. Three killers in this volume drowned their victims.

Three burned their victims to death, while two others starved their chosen prey. One lethal lady rammed her speeding car into a crowd of strangers; another disconnected terminal patients from their life-support equipment. One dropped her children from a lofty hotel balcony, while another hanged her offspring. As with motives and victim selection, choice of weapons varied from case to case in 17% of the crimes.

Some eighty years ago, arch-chauvinist Rudyard Kipling warned us that the female of the species is more deadly than the male. Statistically, he may have been mistaken, but the ladies have been catching up. Nurse Jane Toppan poisoned an estimated 100 patients around the turn of the century, three generations before Donald Harvey bagged eighty-seven in Ohio and Kentucky. The old boy's club of organized crime has yet to produce an Alice Capone, but the shift is probably inevitable, with the likes of Griselda Blanco — self-styled "Godmother" of Miami's cocaine trade — as a working example.

In crime, the sky's the limit.

If our modern feminists possess a single, overriding weakness, it is probably their bent toward viewing sexual equality with one eye closed. Aileen Wuornos isn't *really* a serial killer, we're told, simply a misunderstood rape victim forced to "defend" herself by flagging down male motorists and blowing their brains out before she rifled their pockets and stole their cars. Female gang members are products of a racist/sexist environment, while their male counterparts are simply... well... a bunch of macho little punks. A sadist like Charlene Gallego, who assists her man in raping, torturing, and killing teenage girls for sport *must* be a victim of abuse, since women are incapable of vicious crimes. Case closed.

Or, maybe not.

Before equality becomes reality, we must learn how to take the bitter with the sweet. On any given day in the United States, blacks *do* commit more violent crimes than whites, per capita. Female offenders *are* committing more crimes — and more *violent* crimes — than in years past. Perhaps, at last, equality means stepping back and learning to appreciate the brand-new crop of misfits, much as men have done throughout recorded history, from Robin Hood to Jesse James, John Dillinger to Richard Speck. Belle Gunness was a sister, after all, and sisterhood is powerful.

Sometimes, in fact, it's powerful enough to blow your head clean off.

ALDRETE VILLAREAL, SARAH MARIA

She was known to members of the ghoulish cult she served as *La Madrina* — "The Godmother" — or simply as *La Bruja*: "The Witch." She sits in jail today because of her participation in a string of grisly human sacrifices, executed in pursuit of cash and magic powers that would help her followers elude police. The cash was there, and plenty of it, but the magic failed when it came down to making members of the cult invisible and bullet-proof. That failure, in the end, would bring their gruesome side-show to a close.

Sarah Aldrete was born on September 6, 1964, the daughter of an electrician in the Tex-Mex border town of Matamoros. She crossed the border to attend Porter High School in Brownsville, Texas, where her teachers remember Sarah as "a real good kid." She maintained her star-pupil status in secretarial school, instructors urging her to attend a real college, but hormones intervened. On October 21, 1983, Sarah married Brownsville resident Miguel Zacharias, eleven years her senior. Two years later they were separated, moving inexorably toward divorce.

Late in 1985, Sarah applied for and received resident alien status in the United States. Her next step was enrollment at Texas Southmost College, a two-year school in Brownsville. Admitted on a "work-study" program that deferred part of her tuition, Sarah began classes in January 1986 as a physical education major, holding down two part-time jobs as an aerobics teacher and assistant secretary in the school's P.E. department.

By the end of her first semester at TSC, Sarah stood out physically and academically. She was tall for a Mexican woman, at six foot one, and her grades were excellent. She was one of thirty-three students chosen from TSC's 6,500-member student body for listings in the school's Who's Who directory for 1987-88. Aside from grades that placed her on the honor roll, Sarah also organized and led a Booster Club for TSC's soccer team, earning the school's Outstanding Physical Education Award in her spare time.

With the breakup of her marriage, Sarah had moved back home with her parents in Matamoros, constructing a special outside stairway to her second-floor room in the interest of privacy. She was home most weekends and during school vacations, looking forward to completion of her studies and the transfer to a four-year school that would bring her a P.E. teaching certificate. Attractive and popular with men, she was involved with 20-year-old Serafin Hernandez, Jr., a criminology student at TSC.

One scorching Sunday in July of 1987, Sarah was driving through downtown Matamoros when a shiny new Mercedes cut her off in traffic, narrowly avoiding a collision. The driver was apologetic, suave and handsome. He introduced himself as Adolfo Constanzo, a Cuban-American living in Mexico City. There was instant chemistry between them, but Constanzo did not "make a move" at first. It was enough for them to meet and talk, becoming the best of friends.

Adolfo de Jesus Constanzo was a native of Miami, born to Cuban immigrant parents on November 1, 1962. His father left the family within a year of Adolfo's birth, and his mother moved to Puerto Rico for a time, there acquiring the second of her three husbands. In Puerto Rico, Adolfo embraced the Catholic faith, becoming an altar boy, but it was only a phase. Back in Miami as an adolescent, he began to display "psychic powers" — at least to his mother's satisfaction — around age fourteen. She put him through rigorous training with several witch doctors in South Florida and the Caribbean, Adolfo picking up the fine points of voodoo, santeria, and the more sinister palo mayombe (which makes use of human remains to invoke demonic entities). A confirmed bisexual at age twenty-two, he moved to Mexico City, supporting himself as a fortune-teller who also performed *limpias* — "cleansing" rituals — for clients plagued by "curses" or bad luck. These rituals involved animal sacrifice, and Constanzo prepared a full menu, ranging from roosters and goats to zebras and African lions, depending on a client's ability to pay. Soon, his followers included Mexican celebrities and superstitious drug dealers, all anxious for support from the spirit world. Extreme cases called for human sacrifice, the souls of murdered victims viewed as captive messengers to the "other side," and Mexican police suspect Constanzo of at least six ritual murders in the year before he met Sarah Aldrete.

Even that meeting was not the simple accident it seemed to be. In fact, Constanzo had been watching Sarah's lover, well aware that Serafin Hernandez, Jr., was part of a major drug-dealing family. His meeting with Sarah was carefully stage-managed, as was their burgeoning friendship and Sarah's introduction into the occult. By summer's end, her TSC classmates found Sarah dramatically changed, an overnight expert in witchcraft and magic, eager to debate the relative powers of darkness and light.

Constanzo finally took Sarah to bed, but the sexual part of their relationship was short-lived. He plainly preferred men, and Sarah did not seem to mind. She offered no objection when he ordered her to dump Serafin Hernandez, Jr. and concentrate on older brother Emilio, designated trouble-shooter for the family's narco trade. It was Sarah who arranged the necessary introductions, putting Constanzo one step closer to his goal of controlling a personal smuggling network.

As it happened, the Hernandez family was ripe for a takeover, torn by internal dissension and threatened by outside competitors. Using every "magic" trick at his disposal, Constanzo persuaded Emilio, his brothers, and even patriarch Serafin Senior that palo mayombe could solve all their problems. Enemies could be disposed of in the course of magic rituals; those rituals, in turn, would keep the family and its employees safe from harm. If they were faithful to Constanzo, his disciples would become invisible to the authorities. In return, all he asked was 50% of the profits... and effective control of the family.

Incredibly, the street-wise dealers bought it, falling back on peasant superstition in their hour of need. Even Serafin Junior went along for the ride, abandoning his college studies and returning to the fold as a disciple of Constanzo, willing to accept the wizard's rule and murder on command.

Sarah Aldrete's role in transforming the Hernandez family from a gang of border smugglers to a homicidal cult remains a matter of debate. From prison, with a vested interest in proclaiming innocence, Aldrete claims she never witnessed or participated in a human sacrifice. Surviving members of the cult say otherwise, insisting that *La Bruja* joined Constanzo in the torture-slayings of at least twenty-five victims, inventing new refinements to prolong each captive's agony. She also picked a lurid horror movie based on santeria, *The Believers*, and required each member of the cult to watch it several times, as an example of the powers they would gain by following Adolfo's strategy.

Striking first at the competition, Constanzo and company orchestrated the massacre of the Calzada family in Mexico City. In early 1988, nine members of the drug-dealing clan were tortured, mutilated, and dumped in the Tula River, parts of their bodies retained as "sacred" relics for future rituals. (In June 1989, a member of Constanzo's cult who doubled as a Mexican police officer — one Vidal Garcia — was charged with participation in the Calzada murders.)

Other deaths followed, beginning in Mexico City's homosexual district, the "Zona Rosa," where Constanzo recruited his male lovers. One such victim, transvestite Ramon Paz-Esquivel, was found on July 2, 1988, his body cut into twenty-one pieces, consigned to four separate trash bags. Cult members have accused Constanzo of the murder; Sarah Aldrete was charged in 1989 with criminal association and obstruction of justice, for trying to conceal the crime.

When Mexico City began to heat up, Constanzo and Sarah shifted their base of operations to Rancho Santa Elena, twenty miles from the Hernandez family's home base in Matamoros. In the twelve months between May 1988 and April 1989, at least fifteen human victims would be sacrificed at the ranch, their cruel deaths mixing business, religion, and sadistic pleasure.

The first to die at Rancho Santa Elena were middle-aged locals Moise Castillo Vasquez and Hector de la Fuente Lozoya, reputedly killed for their marijuana stash. Another victim of greed was 30-year-old Ruben Vela-Garza, reported missing on February 14, 1989. Eleven days later, the cult kidnapped 14-year-old Jose Luis Garcia de Luna; the youth had been slaughtered before Elio Hernandez recognized his own teenage cousin. Cult member Jorge Valente del Fierro, an ex-policeman, was sacrificed for using cocaine in violation of Constanzo's standing order to abstain. Other past or present lawmen sacrificed at the ranch, some of them known to moonlight as pushers, included Saul Salceda Galvan, Gilberto Garza Susa, Joaquin Manzo-Rodriguez, and Robert Rodriguez (no relation). Matamoros farmer Esquivel Rodriguez Luna was abducted as a matter of convenience, while Ernesto Rivas-Diaz was killed for his stockpile of drugs. Three other male victims, unearthed by police in April 1989, remain unidentified today.

It was Constanzo's urge to sacrifice a "gringo" that finally led to the cult's undoing. Texas pre-med student Mark Kilroy was kidnapped in Matamoros on March 14, 1989, driven to the ranch and sacrificed. His disappearance in the middle of Spring Break prompted a search on both sides of the border, and the manhunt was still underway four weeks later, when the roof fell in on Constanzo's coven.

Serafin Hernandez, Jr., was driving out to Rancho Santa Elena on Sunday, April 9, when he passed a police roadblock without stopping. Hernandez thought himself invisible, a quirk that led him to ignore the squad cars following in hot pursuit. Arriving at the ranch, police arrested Serafin, his brother Elio, and three more members of the gang. The raiders confiscated several guns and found the shed where drugs were stashed beside a bloodstained altar. In a corner of the shed, aswarm with flies, a metal pot — the dreaded *nganga* of palo mayombe — contained a stew of human brains and animal ingredients required for personal communion with the spirit world.

In custody, the suspects named Constanzo and his female cohort as the leaders of the cult. By April 16, fifteen mutilated bodies had been unearthed at the ranch, including one identified as Mark Kilroy. Adolfo and his witch, meanwhile, had been spotted in Brownsville on April 11, cruising the streets in an $80,000 luxury sedan, but from there they disappeared without a trace.

The dominoes began falling in earnest on April 17, with Serafin Senior's arrest in Houston on outstanding drug warrants. The same day, police raided Constanzo's luxurious home in a suburb of Mexico City, finding an altar, occult paraphernalia, and stacks of homosexual pornography. They also found Sarah Aldrete's purse, passport, and airline tickets, prompting brief speculation that Constanzo may have killed her to eliminate a potential witness. On April 18, a federal grand jury in McAllen, Texas, indicted Constanzo on conspiracy charges; a week later, Adolfo, Sarah, and nine of their disciples were hit with new counts involving narcotics violations and the kidnapping of Gilberto Garza Sosa.

By early May, manhunters were seeking Constanzo and Sarah as far north as Chicago, where their reputed customers included members of the Windy City Mafia. In fact, the fugitives were still in Mexico City, as revealed on May 6, when a woman matching Sarah's description tried to pay her grocery tab with an American $100 bill. Police were summoned, and they found Adolfo's Chrysler parked outside a nearby apartment house. A stealthy approach was out of the question as someone saw them coming, smashed out an upstairs window and hosed the street with submachine gun fire.

The battle raged for forty-five minutes, Constanzo doing most of the shooting for his side, wounding one patrolman on the street below. At last, surrounded, *El Padrino* stepped into a closet with his lover, Martin Quintana, and ordered cultist Alvaro de Leon to kill them both. When de Leon hesitated, Sarah urged him on from the sidelines, shouting "Do it! Get it over with!"

In custody, Sarah insisted that she had been Constanzo's hostage in the shoot-out. She even claimed credit for bringing police to the scene, referring to an SOS note she allegedly dropped in the street, but detectives saw a different side of *La Madrina* when the television cameras took their leave. "She would talk to us like a witch," one officer said. "She never cried. She was cold. Cold."

For the record, Sarah described an all-night session of police torture, during which she was "almost raped." A self-described practitioner of "Christian santeria," she denied any participation in human sacrifice or other black magic rituals, blaming the various murders on Constanzo. Charged in a total of seventeen slayings, plus various narcotics charges, Sarah Aldrete was finally tried on two counts. She was acquitted of Constanzo's death, and found guilty on a charge of criminal association, for which she received the maximum six-year prison term. Charges in the fifteen murders at Rancho Santa Elena are still theoretically pending, with a maximum term of fifty years possible on conviction.

ALLEN, SHIRLEY GOUDE

Six times married, at least twice to the same man, blond Shirley Allen had a hard time keeping husbands. Some would leave and file divorce papers in the face of her unpredictable rages, while others simply died. In the latter cases, Shirley seemed to understand that life insurance was a girl's best friend.

And there was always antifreeze.

A native of St. Louis, born in 1941, Shirley Goude grew up poor in a neighborhood known as The Patch, compensating in later years with wild stories of an exotic childhood. She was really a foreigner, Shirley would say on occasion, smuggled into the United States by her grandmother, during infancy. She recalled a luxurious upbringing, in the care of a "highly educated" black maid, but none of her relatives shared Shirley's memories. In retrospect, the pathological lying may have suggested a deeper disturbance, but no one caught it at the time.

Shirley liked getting married, and while the records of her various unions are somewhat confused, it is clear that she especially liked marrying Joseph Sinclair. Officially, their first marriage occurred on October 30, 1968, though subsequent divorce proceedings suggest an earlier wedding, in 1963. (Likewise, Shirley's three children — including daughters born in 1965 and 1967 — all bear Sinclair's name.) A second wedding was performed for Joseph and Shirley on July 16, 1970, but it didn't take.

Twice, in the summer of 1969, Joe Sinclair suspected that Shirley was trying to kill him. On the first occasion, he drank a cup of coffee that "tasted like Listerine," collapsing moments later with a blinding headache. The second time around, after one of Shirley's home-cooked meals, Joseph was hospitalized with internal bleeding. He thought she was tampering with his food, but later told police "there was no way I could prove it." Daughter Patty claimed that Shirley had dosed her husband with rat poison, but no charges were ever filed.

From 1969 to 1971, Shirley worked sporadically as a nurse's aide at Alexian Brothers Hospital, in St. Louis. In years to come she would often describe herself as "an unemployed nurse," but she possessed no license or formal training, and most of her adult working hours were logged as a barmaid. In May 1975, while serving drinks in one establishment, she quarreled with a female patron and was shot, the bullet ripping through her right eye, leaving Shirley with a glass orb in its place.

In 1977, she married trucker John Gregg "on the spur of the moment." That September, Gregg altered his $17,000 teamsters life insurance policy, making Shirley the sole beneficiary, but he was having second thoughts a few weeks later. On Christmas Eve, Gregg told his brother Arthur that Shirley had filed for divorce; without her knowledge, John had changed his insurance again, making Arthur the beneficiary as trustee for Gregg's three children from a previous marriage. On February 17, 1978, John Gregg collapsed and died at home, physicians blaming the event on acute alcoholism and "arteriosclerotic heart disease." Shirley was furious when she found herself cut off from his insurance money, but a bitter court fight left her empty-handed.

In September 1981, she married affable Lloyd Allen and moved into his suburban home. Allen had buried his mother, a cancer victim, that May; he wanted someone to take care of, and vice versa. In Shirley's care, though, he began to fade, sickening and dropping weight, suffering dizzy spells and shortness of breath that left him unable to work by April 1982. A battery of doctors diagnosed Lloyd's condition as "general malaise," suggesting that he should be fit for work by June or July, but things only got worse. Shirley quit her latest job, at a St. Louis rest home, to nurse him full-time, but it did no good. On November 1, 1982, she returned from a shopping excursion to find him dead at home.

Authorities were curious about Lloyd's death, to say the least. For starters, Shirley had purchased a $25,000 life insurance policy on Lloyd around the time his health began to fail. Then, soon after his death, the sheriff and the coroner's office received a series of anonymous calls, asserting that Lloyd had been poisoned. Forensic toxicologists agreed, finding his tissues saturated with ethylene glycol — the main ingredient of antifreeze.

On November 5, Patty Sinclair dropped a bomb on her mother, describing eight occasions on which she had seen Shirley spiking Lloyd's drink with antifreeze or a gasoline additive. When Lloyd complained of the peculiar taste, Shirley told him the beverage was "an iron supplement" prescribed for his health. Patty Sinclair and sister Sandy had refrained from alerting police to the murder in progress "because a friend advised against it."

Shirley Allen was arrested on November 6; arraigned two days later on a charge of first-degree murder, she was held in lieu of $500,000 bond. Police exhumed John Gregg's body on November 16, for new toxicology tests, but there was insufficient evidence to support a second murder charge.

Legal maneuvers delayed Shirley's trial until April 1984. In the meantime, she accused a jailer of molesting her on three occasions between May and August of 1983, but no charges were filed. Allen's murder trial consumed four days, and jurors deliberated a mere three hours before convicting her on all counts. On July 6, 1984, Shirley was sentenced to life imprisonment with no parole for the first fifty years of her term.

ALMAREZ, STELLA DELORES

A resident of Norfolk, Nebraska, Stella Almarez was twenty-nine years old when her marriage failed, leaving her with four young daughters and no man around the house. The divorce left her despondent, Stella's mental state degenerating to an ugly flash point over several weeks. On June 18, 1980, she unleashed her pent-up anger on the children, slashing the throats of her two infant daughters, and shooting the other two girls, ages seven and ten. Arrested the following day and charged with four counts of murder, Stella was tried in November 1980. Jurors accepted the testimony of defense psychiatrists, voting Stella not guilty by reason of insanity, and she was committed to the Lincoln Regional Center for treatment.

The Norfolk verdict sparked a wave of outrage in Nebraska, with grass-roots demands for a change in the law governing insanity pleas. A new law, passed in 1981, shifted the burden of proof for a defendant's mental state from prosecutors to defense attorneys. It also changed the rules for handling defendants found to be insane. Enraged to hear that Stella Almarez was regularly sent to work outside the Lincoln Center, legislators called for annual reviews of mental fitness for a patient seeking work release. Finally, it was decreed that no "insane" defendant could be freed by state psychiatrists without a corresponding written order from a judge.

Ironically, despite the outcry prompted by her case, Stella Almarez was the first defendant to win release under the new statute. Psychiatrists at Lincoln Center pronounced her cured in 1985, and Madison County judge Merritt Warren agreed. Almarez was unconditionally released from custody on October 2 of that year.

AMBROSE, LYDA CATHERINE

A prolific American "black widow," linked to the deaths of at least five husbands and suitors,

Lyda Ambrose was born in 1891. Her early life is a virtual blank, and it was 1917 before she started leaving bodies in her wake. By that time, Lyda had decided that the surest way to fortune was through life insurance on the men who found her irresistible.

At twenty-six, she set her sights on young Ed Dooley, the son of a prosperous rancher in Keytesville, Missouri. They were engaged to be married in early 1917, but Ed would never make it to the altar. "Ulcers" were blamed when he died in agony, a few weeks short of marriage, and a new insurance policy paid his grieving fiancée $2,500.

Money was small consolation for Lyda, and she turned to Ed's older brother, Bob, for comfort. A whirlwind courtship followed, and Bob's wedding gift to his bride was another life insurance policy, in the amount of $2,500. Ed Dooley was barely three months in the grave when his brother collapsed and died, identical symptoms leading to a vague diagnosis of "stomach trouble."

With $5,000 in hand, Lyda moved on to Twin Falls, Idaho, finding work as a waitress at the Grille Cafe. It was love at first sight for owner Bill McHaffie, and Lyda tied the knot with her boss on June 10, 1918. Two weeks later, McHaffie sold his restaurant and packed his bride off to Hardin, Montana, where they purchased a small ranch. At Lyda's insistence, McHaffie applied for life insurance, but he failed to sign the necessary documents before his sudden death — from "stomach ulcers" — on October 22. Cheated out of her inheritance, Lyda recouped her loss by selling the ranch and moving on to husband number three.

Harlan Lewis had enjoyed a sexual affair with Lyda while McHaffie was alive, and he wasted no time in proposing once Bill was laid to rest. It was a typically brief relationship for Lyda, with Lewis surviving less than three months of married life. This time, though, she made sure that his $10,000 life insurance policy was duly signed and paid up in full.

Back in Twin Falls, Lyda made the acquaintance of cowman Ed Myer, saying "I do" for the fourth time in October 1920. Life on the ranch at Blue Lakes was a bit rustic for her taste, but Lyda didn't have to suffer long. Six weeks after the wedding, on November 20, Myer was admitted to Twin Falls General Hospital in critical condition, marked by violent stomach cramps. He died at two o'clock that afternoon, his death attributed to "typhoid," and his widow collected $12,000 from an insurance policy purchased on October 6.

In spite of everything, authorities were still oblivious to Lyda's run of rotten luck. Surviving members of the Dooley family suspected her of murder in Missouri, but they had no proof. Her web of lies began unraveling in mid-December 1920, when the Twin Falls sheriff first became aware of the insurance payment on Ed Myer. Earlier, the widow had informed him that she had no life insurance on her husband, and the lie set off alarm bells in his mind.

A search of Lyda's cottage at the Blue Lakes ranch revealed large quantities of old-fashioned, arsenic-based flypaper banned by state law. The sheriff also found an envelope addressed to one Frank Lovett, in Twin Falls. Lovett readily admitted having an affair with Lyda while she was married to Myer; they had planned to marry, but she broke it off and left for San Francisco after Frank refused to take out life insurance on himself. Forensic toxicology did the rest, with heavy doses of arsenic found in the remains of Ed Myer, Harlan Lewis, Bill McHaffie, and the Dooley brothers.

Police traced Lyda to Oakland, California, where she had recently married seaman Paul Southard. Fortunately for Southard, his ship had sailed for Hawaii the day after his wedding, thus sparing his life. In his absence, Lyda was indicted on five counts of first-degree murder, and returned to Idaho for trial in the most recent case.

Convicted of Ed Myer's murder in September 1921, she was sentenced to life. On May 4, 1931, Lyda escaped from the Idaho state prison, sawing through the bars of her cell, and scaling a 30-foot wall with a ladder provided by an accomplice. She remained at large until 1932, when she was finally captured in Kansas City.

parole was out of the question with an escape on her record, and Lyda Ambrose ultimately died in prison.

"ANGEL MAKERS OF NAGYREV"

Little is known of Julia Fazekas before 1911, when she suddenly appeared in the Hungarian village of Nagyrev, sixty miles southeast of Budapest on the River Tisza. She was pushing middle age, a widow by her own account, but no one seemed to know exactly what had happened to her husband. Between 1911 and 1921, midwife Fazekas was jailed ten times for performing illegal abortions, but sympathetic juries acquitted her in each case. Meanwhile, apparently unnoticed by police, she had inaugurated one of Europe's most bizarre and deadly murder sprees.

The rash of homicides is traceable to World War I, when able-bodied men from Nagyrev were drafted to fight for the Austro-Hungarian empire. At the same time, rural Nagyrev was deemed an ideal site for camps containing Allied prisoners of war — a circumstance that catered to the wildest fantasies of women suddenly deprived of men. It soon became a point of pride for lonely wives in Nagyrev to boast a foreign lover, sometimes three or four. An atmosphere of rampant promiscuity prevailed, and husbands straggling home from combat found their women strangely "liberated," frequently dissatisfied with one man in the marriage bed.

As wives began to voice complaints of boredom and abuse, midwife Fazekas offered them relief: supplies of arsenic obtained by boiling flypaper and skimming the lethal residue. Peter Hegedus was the first known victim, in 1914, and other husbands followed over time before the poisoning became a fad, the casualty list expanding to include parents, children, aunts, uncles, and neighbors.

By the mid-1920s, Nagyrev had earned its nickname as "the murder district," with an estimated fifty women using arsenic to trim their family trees. Julia Fazekas was the closest thing the village had to a physician, and her cousin was the clerk who filed all death certificates, thereby subverting homicide investigations in the embryonic stage. The final toll is still unknown, but most reports suggest 300 as a reasonable estimate for fifteen years of wholesale murder.

The "angel makers" saw their world unravel in July of 1929, when a choir master from neighboring Tiszakurt accused Mrs. Ladislaus Szabo of serving him poisoned wine. A stomach pump saved his life, and detectives were still pondering the charge when a second victim complained of being poisoned by his "nurse" — the same Mrs. Szabo. In custody, seeking leniency for herself, Szabo fingered a friend, Mrs. Bukenoveski as a fellow practitioner. Bukenoveski, in turn, was the first to name Julia Fazekas. In 1924, she said, Fazekas provided the arsenic used to kill Bukenoveski's 77-year-old mother, after which the old woman was dumped in the Tisza to simulate an accidental drowning.

Fazekas was hauled in for questioning and staunchly denied everything. Without solid evidence, police were forced to release her, but they mounted a roving surveillance, trailing Fazekas around Nagyrev as she cautioned her various clients, arresting each woman in turn. Thirty-eight were jailed on suspicion of murder, and police descended on the Fazekas home to seize the ringleader. They found her dead from a dose of her own medicine, surrounded by pots of flypaper soaking in water.

Twenty-six of the Nagyrev suspects were held for trial at Szolnok, where eight were sentenced to death, seven to life imprisonment, the rest to various prison terms. The condemned included Susannah Olah, a self-styled witch who boasted of training venomous snakes to attack her victims in bed, competing with Fazekas in sales of "Aunt Susi's inheritance powders;" Olah's sister Lydia, a septuagenarian whose flat denials of guilt failed to impress the jury; Maria Kardos, who murdered her husband, a lover, and her sickly 23-year-old son, persuading the young man to sing her a song on his deathbed; Rosalie Sebestyen and Rose Hoyba, condemned for the murder of "boring" husbands; Lydia Csery, convicted of killing her parents; Maria Varga, who confessed buying poison from Fazekas to kill her husband — a blind war hero — when he complained about her bringing lovers home; Juliane Lipke, whose seven victims included her stepmother, an aunt, a brother, a sister-in-law, and the husband she poisoned on Christmas Eve; and Maria Szendi, a true liberationist who told the court she killed her husband because "he always had his way. It's terrible the way men have all the power."

"ANGELS OF DEATH"

Built in 1839, Lainz General Hospital is the fourth largest medical facility in Vienna, Austria, with some 2,000 persons on staff. Pavilion 5 at Lainz is typically reserved for problem cases — patients in their seventies and older, many of them terminally ill. In such a setting, death is no surprise. If anything, it sometimes comes as a relief... but there are limits, even so. Beginning in the spring of 1983 and lasting through the early weeks of 1989, Death got a helping hand at Lainz. Officially, the body count would stand at forty-two, but educated guesses put the final tally closer to 300 victims for the hospital's hardworking "Angels of Death."

Waltraud Wagner, a nurse's aide on the graveyard shift at Pavilion 5, was twenty-four years old when she set the ball rolling in 1983. As later reconstructed for authorities, she got the notion of eliminating patients when a 77-year-old woman asked Wagner to "end her misery." Waltraud obliged the lady with a morphine overdose, discovering in the process that she enjoyed playing God, holding the power of life and death in her hands. It was too much fun to quit, too nice to keep from sharing with her special friends.

Over time, Wagner recruited three accomplices, all working the night shift in Pavilion 5. Maria Gruber, born in 1964, was a nursing school dropout and unwed mother. Irene Leidolf, two years older than Gruber, had a husband at home but preferred hanging out with the girls. Stephanija Mayer, a divorced grandmother twenty years Waltraud's senior, emigrated from Yugoslavia in 1987 and wound up at Lainz, soon joining ranks with her murderous cronies.

As described by prosecutors at her trial, Wagner was the sadistic Svengali of the group, instructing her disciples on the proper techniques of lethal injection, teaching them "the water cure" — wherein a patient's nose was pinched, the tongue depressed, and water was poured down the throat. The victim's death, while slow and agonizing, appeared "natural" on a ward where elderly patients frequently die with fluid in their lungs. In the police view, "Wagner awakened their sadistic instincts. Soon they were running a concentration camp, not a hospital ward. At the slightest sign of annoyance or complaint from a patient, they'd plan the patient's murder for the following night."

"Annoyances," in Waltraud's book, included snoring, soiling the sheets, refusing medication, or buzzing the nurse's station for help at inconvenient times. In such cases, Wagner would proclaim "This one gets a ticket to God," executing the murder herself or with help from one of her accomplices.

Even with four killers working the ward, it took some time for the deadly game to accelerate. Most of the homicides linked to Wagner and company occurred after early 1987, when Mayer rounded out the team, but Waltraud remained the prime mover and head executioner for what was soon nicknamed "the death pavilion." Rumors of a killer at large on Pavilion 5 were widespread by 1988, and Dr. Xavier Pesendorfer, in charge of the ward, was suspended in April 1989 for failure to launch a timely investigation.

Still, it would be negligence among the killers that led to their ultimate downfall. Waltraud and her cohorts liked to have a few drinks after work, reliving special cases that amused them, chuckling over this victim's dying expression or that one's convulsions. In February 1989 they were giggling over the death of elderly Julia Drapal — treated to the "water cure" for refusing medication and calling Wagner a "common slut" — when a doctor seated nearby picked up snatches of their conversation. Horrified, he went to the police, and a six-week investigation led to the arrest of all four suspects on April 7.

In custody, the "death angels" confessed to forty-nine specific murders, Wagner allegedly claiming thirty-nine on her own. "The ones who got on my nerves," she explained, "were dispatched directly to a free bed with the good Lord." It was not always simple, she allowed: "Of course the patients resisted, but we were stronger. We could decide whether these old fogies lived or died. Their ticket to God was long overdue in any case."

There was immediate speculation on a much higher body count, Wagner's accomplices pointing guilty fingers at their mentor in a bid to save themselves. Alois Stacher, head of Vienna's health department, quoted Irene Leidolf as being "convinced that 100 patients were killed by Wagner in each of the past two years." Stefanija Mayer admitted helping Wagner out on several homicides that Waltraud managed to forget.

Indeed, as the case progressed to trial, Wagner became increasingly reluctant to discuss her role in the murders. By late 1990, she had backed off her original boast of thirty-nine victims, claiming a maximum of ten patients killed "to ease their pain." Chancellor Franz Vranitzky was unimpressed with the turnabout, calling the Lainz murder spree "the most brutal and gruesome crime in Austria's history."

Nor were judge and jury sympathetic when the four defendants went to trial in March of 1991. Prosecutors failed to sell their case on forty-two counts of murder, but they proved enough to do the job. Waltraud Wagner was convicted of fifteen murders, seventeen attempted murders, and two counts of aggravated assault, drawing a sentence of life imprisonment. Irene Leidolf also got life, on conviction of five murders and two bungled attempts. Stephanija Mayer earned fifteen years for a manslaughter conviction and seven counts of attempted murder, while Maria Gruber received an identical term for two murder attempts.

ARCHER-GILLIGAN, AMY

Little is known about the early life of the woman who would later, in the words of her prosecutor, commit "the biggest crime that ever shocked New England." Born in 1873 and married to Joseph Archer in her early twenties, Amy Archer produced her only child — a daughter, Mary — in 1898. Three years later, billing herself as a nurse, without apparent qualifications, she opened a nursing home for the elderly in Newington, Connecticut. Despite "Sister Amy's" relative lack of experience, there were no complaints from her clients, and Newington was sad to see her go in 1907, when she moved to Windsor, ten miles north, and opened the Archer Home for the Elderly and Infirm.

For the first three years, it was business as usual in Windsor. Twelve of Amy's clients died between 1907 and 1910, a predictable mortality rate which brought her no unusual profit. The surprise casualty of 1910 was James Archer, his death ascribed to natural causes. Amy waited three years before she remarried, to Michael Gilligan, and her second husband lasted a mere twelve months. The family physician, Dr. Howard King, saw no reason for alarm... nor was he concerned by the deaths of forty-eight clients at Amy's rest home, lost between 1911 and 1916. The number might have seemed excessive for a home with only fourteen beds, but Dr. King accepted Sister Amy's diagnoses in the deaths, his negligence and senility combining to short-circuit suspicion.

In fact, Amy had devised what seemed to be the perfect get-rich scheme, inducing new clients to pay $1,000 in advance for "lifetime care," then cutting short their days with poison or a well-placed pillow, blaming each successive death on old age or disease. With Dr. King's obliging death certificates in hand, authorities were loathe to cast aspersions, but ugly rumors had begun to circulate around Windsor by 1914. Two years later, surviving relatives of elderly Maude Lynch took their suspicions to police, and an undercover officer was planted in the rest home, collecting evidence that led to Sister Amy's arrest in May 1916. Post-mortem examinations found traces of poison in Michael Gilligan and five deceased patients, leaving Amy charged with six counts of murder and suspected of numerous others. (Physicians calculated a "normal" resident death toll for 1911-16 at eight patients, compared to Amy's *forty*-eight.)

Dr. King came out swinging, his shaky reputation on the line, describing Sister Amy as a victim of foul persecution. Poison had been planted in several bodies, he maintained, by "ghouls to incriminate Mrs. Gilligan." Prosecutor Hugh Alcorn responded by calling the case "the worst poison plot this country has ever known." Objections from Amy's lawyer winnowed the charges to one murder count — in the May 1914 death of patient Frank Andrews — and she was convicted in July 1917. Amy's life sentence was successfully appealed on technical grounds, but a second jury returned the same verdict, leaving her caged in Weathersfield Prison. In 1923, a rash of "nervous fits" produced a diagnosis of insanity, and Amy was transferred to a state asylum where she died in 1962, at age eighty-nine.

ARRINGTON, MARIE DEAN

An habitual criminal, Marie Arrington boasted a record of arrests and convictions for assault and battery, robbery, grand larceny, issuing worthless checks, and escape from custody. In July 1964 she shot and killed her husband, receiving a 20-year sentence on conviction of manslaughter. While free on appeal, during April 1968, she committed a second brutal homicide. This time, the victim was Vivian Ritter, a legal secretary with the public defender's office in Lake County, Florida.

Arrington kidnapped her latest victim as part of a bizarre plan to free her two children from prison. Chips off the old block, Lloyd Arrington was serving life for armed robbery; Marie's daughter had been sentenced to two years on conviction of forgery. With Vivian Ritter in hand, Marie Arrington wrote to public defender Robert Pierce, threatening to return his secretary "piece by piece" unless her children were released at once. Of course, Pierce had no such authority, and nothing was accomplished by her threats. Ritter's body was later found in a citrus grove, shot in the back, afterward run over several times by a car in a ghoulish effort to "make sure" she was dead.

Convicted of first-degree murder this time, Marie Arrington was sentenced to die. On March 1, 1969, she escaped from the women's prison at Lowell, Florida, using a book of matches to burn through the mesh screen covering a window in her cell. Described by prosecutors as a "wild, cunning animal who will kill and laugh about it," she was charged with the federal offense of unlawful flight to avoid confinement on March 3. Shortly thereafter, the judge who sentenced her to die received a threatening letter from Arrington, accompanied by a voodoo doll with a pin through its chest. On May 29, 1969, Marie Arrington was added to the FBI's "Ten Most Wanted" list.

Her luck ran out on December 22, 1971, in New Orleans, where she was employed — as "Lola Nero" — at a local drugstore. When apprehended by the FBI, Arrington first claimed it was a case of mistaken identity, but she gave up the game when fingerprint comparisons checked out. Returned to Florida for execution, Arrington caught a break in 1972, when the U.S. Supreme Court issued its landmark ruling against capital punishment, thereby forcing commutation of her sentence to life imprisonment.

ATKINS, SUSAN DENISE: See MANSON "FAMILY"

"BABY FARMING"

Each historical era spawns its own peculiar types of crime, from piracy and slave trading to the modern age of "wilding" and computer "hackers." The occupation known as "baby farming" was a product of the Victorian era, when sex was equivalent to sin and illegitimate birth meant lifelong shame for mother and child alike. In that repressive atmosphere, the "baby farmer" — usually a woman — was prepared to help an unwed mother through her time of trial... but only for a price.

In most cases, the "farmer" provided room and board during a mother's confinement, allowing embarrassed families to tell the neighbors that their daughter had gone to "study abroad" or "stay with relatives." Facilities ranged from humble country cottages to the likes of Nova Scotia's spacious Ideal Maternity Home, where hundreds of infants were born between 1925 and 1947. Unwed mothers went home with their reputations and consciences intact, secure in the knowledge that their babies would be placed in good homes through black-market adoptions.

It was a no-lose proposition for the "baby farmer," paid by those who left a child and once again by those who came to pick one up. If certain laws were broken in the process, it was all the better reason for increasing the "adoption" fees. Most unwed mothers and adoptive parents doubtless viewed the "baby farmer's" occupation as a valuable public service, never mind prevailing law, but there were several headline cases where criminal negligence or deliberate murder were used as a short-cut to profit in the maternity game. Not even the United States has been exempt from lethal "baby farming," illustrated by a case reported in the *New York Times* while Europe was embroiled in World War I.

On September 29, 1915, Joseph Miller, night watchman at a pier on South 11th Street, in the Williamsburg section of New York City, noticed two dark objects floating in the Hudson River. Scrambling into a boat, Miller followed the current and fished out the pieces of flotsam, appalled to discover that two baby girls had been thrown in the river to drown. A coroner's report revealed the victims to be less than two days old. Worse yet, a scan of recent files told homicide detectives that a dozen other infants, three days old or less, had been recovered from the Hudson River in the past six weeks. Found floating anywhere from South 11th Street to Broadway, most of the tiny victims had been tossed naked into the water while still alive; a few were bundled up so tightly that they must have suffocated prior to entering the river, as no water was discovered in their lungs.

Without a single clue to work on, homicide investigators organized a special team to prowl the waterfront by night, but they were flying blind. An NYPD spokesman told the press that someone in the neighborhood was "systematically engaged in the slaying of new-born babies," but recognition of the problem offered no solution. With publicity, the grim parade of tiny corpses ceased, the "baby farmers" moving on or switching to a more efficient method of disposal, and the case remains unsolved today. [See also: Dean, Williamina; Dyer, Amelia; Sach, Amelia; Waters, Margaret; Young, Lila]

BACHER, JOHANNA

A Connecticut native, born in 1891, Johanna Healey married Henry Bacher, a divorced carpenter and occasional boxer, near the end of World War I. They settled in Greenwich and produced three children in as many years — Margaret in 1918, Johanna in 1919, and Henry Junior in 1920. Even so, the marriage fell on rocky times, and Henry left Johanna in late 1921, filing for divorce on charges of "intolerable cruelty."

Friends noted that Johanna seemed depressed by the impending divorce, and Greenwich police were alerted when she purchased rat poison in March 1922. Chief Andrew Talbot had Johanna and the children pulled in for some friendly conversation on March 23, and after brief denials she admitted buying the poison to kill her kids. Johanna was fearful of Henry's winning custody in court, complaining that her husband and his family had been harassing her non-stop since their separation. Chief Talbot offered to help if he could and secured Johanna's grudging promise not to harm the children. He promised to meet with Johanna once more in a few days time, and gave each Bacher child a box of candy as a parting gift.

On March 26, 1922, Johanna used a butcher knife to kill her three children, slitting the throat of each in turn, making sure they were dead. That done, she placed her bank book and insurance policies inside a paper bag, together with a brief suicide note, and addressed the bag to Chief Talbot before tossing it out a window of her home. Finally, Johanna turned the knife on herself, inflicting fatal wounds to her own throat. A neighbor found the bag around midnight and took it to the Greenwich police station, too late for all concerned.

BAILEY, SUSAN

In retrospect, it would appear that Susan Bailey had problems aplenty in the summer of her fifteenth year. The second of twelve children, she shared a ramshackle plywood-and-tarpaper home with her grandfather, parents, and eleven siblings in the Ohio River town of Parkersburg, West Virginia. She was also stuck in seventh grade at Franklin Junior High three years behind her peers, with no immediate hope of advancement.

And, then, there was love.

Susan's boyfriend was 18-year-old Johnny Baumgarner, a seventh-grade dropout who had his own car and picked Susan up every day after school. Their sex life was an open secret, and 41-year-old Charles Bailey had harsh words for his daughter, pointing out that Baumgarner was her first cousin. Susan fired back with a reminder that her parents were, in fact, second cousins, but Charles was unmoved. The next time Baumgarner came calling, her father declared, he would have the youth arrested for contributing to the delinquency of a minor.

The argument was still simmering on June 8, 1969, when a late-night fire broke out at the Bailey home. It was over in a flash, the tinderbox construction offering no resistance to hungry flames. When the smoke cleared, Charles Bailey lay dead in the rubble, along with his wife, 36-year-old Ruby, and ten of their children, ranging in age from eight months to seventeen years. Survivors included Susan, 13-year-old Roger, and their grandfather, 63-year-old Obie Bailey. Susan and Roger explained their survival by saying they spent the night in a smaller shack, some distance from the house.

Police were skeptical, grilling the teens at length, but when the confessions finally came, they were addressed to family members, rather than detectives. On June 10, Susan admitted recruiting her brother to siphon gasoline from the family pickup truck into a washtub, spilling it onto the floor in each of five rooms while the family slept, then striking a match.

Both children were held on murder charges, pending psychiatric tests, and were escorted by jailers to the family's mass funeral. It was reported that Susan and Roger burst into tears at the end of the service, before they were led back to jail and eventual disposition through West Virginia's juvenile justice system.

BARFIELD, MARGIE VELMA

Born October 23, 1932, in Cumberland County, North Carolina, Margie Bullard would look back on her childhood as a cruel period of "permissible slavery," made worse by the attentions of a father who began molesting her at age thirteen. The stories are refuted categorically by seven siblings, who deny all charges of abuse in any form, by either parent, and it must be granted that Margie's early development seemed normal for the given time and place. Dropping out of high school in her junior year, she eloped with Thomas Burke at seventeen, settling in Paxton, where she bore two children without incident.

The trouble started after fifteen years of marriage, when Burke's luck turned sour almost overnight. Discharged from his job and subsequently injured in a car crash, he began drinking heavily to drown his sorrows, the ever-present liquor an affront to Margie's fundamentalist religion. Marriage became a sort of guerrilla warfare, with Margie hiding her husband's whiskey, sometimes pouring it down the sink, finally committing him to Dorothea Dix Hospital, in Raleigh, as an alcoholic. Working at a local mill to support the family, she relied on prescription tranquilizers for peace of mind. Thomas came home from the hospital sober and sullen, bitter at his wife's "betrayal." In 1969, when he burned to death in bed, authorities dismissed the death as accidental, caused by careless smoking, but later, with the advantage of hindsight, there would be dark suspicions of foul play.

In 1971, Margie married Jennings Barfield. He lasted six months, his sudden death ascribed to "natural causes," but exhumation and autopsy in 1978 would reveal lethal doses of arsenic in his system.

By the time she murdered Barfield, Margie was already addicted to prescription drugs, carelessly mixing her pills, with the result that she was four times hospitalized for overdose symptoms. In contrast to her addiction, she maintained an active interest in religion, teaching Sunday school at the local Pentecostal church on a regular basis.

Short on cash, Margie was writing rubber checks to cover her "medical" expenses, and her several trips to court produced judicial wrist-slaps. In 1974, she forged her aged mother's name to a $1,000 loan application, panicking when she realized the bank might try to contact the real Lillie Bullard for verification. Margie eliminated the problem by feeding her mother a lethal dose of insecticide, and again the death was attributed to natural causes.

Two years later, Margie Barfield was employed by local matron Dollie Edwards as a live-in maid. A fringe benefit of the job was Dollie's nephew, Stuart Taylor, who began dating Margie on the side, but their romance did not stop Barfield from poisoning her employer in February 1977. Her motive remains unclear — there were no thefts involved — and physicians ascribed the death to "acute gastroenteritis."

Margie next moved in with 80-year-old John Lee and his wife Record, age 76. After forging a $50 check on Lee's account, she sought to "make him sick" and thereby gain some time to cover the shortage, but her plans obviously went awry. First poisoned in April 1977, John Lee lost 65 pounds before his eventual death, on June 4. After the funeral, Margie began feeding poison to Lee's widow, but she gave up her job in October 1977, leaving a frail survivor behind.

Moving on to work at a Lumberton rest home, Barfield was twice caught forging checks on Stuart Taylor's account. He forgave her each time, but they argued fiercely after her third offense, on January 31, 1978. That night, Margie spiked his beer with poison, keeping up the dosage until Taylor died on February 4. Relatives rejected the diagnosis of "acute gastroenteritis" and demanded a full autopsy, resulting in the discovery of arsenic.

Under interrogation, Margie confessed the murders of Taylor, her mother and second husband, Dollie Edwards and John Lee. Aside from the motiveless Edwards slaying, they were all "accidents," bungled attempts to cover up for forgery and theft. A jury deliberated for less than an hour before convicting Barfield of first-degree murder, and she was executed by lethal injection on November 2, 1984.

BATHORY, ERZSEBET

Born in 1560, Erzsebet (or Elizabeth) Bathory was the daughter of an aristocratic soldier and the sister of Poland's reigning king. Her family, in fact, was one of the oldest noble houses in Hungary, its family crest bearing the draconic symbol incorporated by King Sigismund into the Order of the Dragon. The Bathory clan included knights and judges, bishops, cardinals, and kings, but it had fallen into decadence by the mid-16th century, the royal bloodline marred by incest and epilepsy, with later family ranks including alcoholics, murderers and sadists, homosexuals and Satanists.

Though physically beautiful, Erzsebet was clearly the product of polluted genetics and twisted upbringing. Throughout her life, she was subject to blinding headaches and fainting seizures — probably epileptic in nature — which superstitious family members diagnosed as "demonic possession." Raised on the Bathory estate at the foot of the brooding Carpathian mountains, Erzsebet was introduced to devil-worship in adolescence, by one of her Satanist uncles. Her favorite aunt, one of Hungary's most notorious lesbians, taught Erzsebet the pleasures of flagellation and other perversions, but young Erzsebet always believed that where pain was concerned, it was better to give than receive.

When Erzsebet was barely eleven, her parents contracted a future marriage to Count Ferencz Nadasdy, an aristocratic warrior. Their wedding was postponed until Erzsebet turned fifteen, finally solemnized on May 5, 1575. The bride retained her maiden name as a sign that her family possessed greater status than Nadasdy's clan.

The newlyweds settled at Csejthe Castle, in northwestern Hungary, but Count Nadasdy also maintained other palatial homes around the country, each complete with a dungeon and torture chamber specially designed to meet Erzsebet's needs. Nadasdy was frequently absent for weeks or months at a time, leaving his bride alone and bored, to find her own diversions. Erzsebet dabbled in alchemy, indulged her sexual quirks with men and women alike, changing clothes and jewelry five or six times a day and admiring herself in full-length mirrors by the hour. Above all else, when she was angry, tense, or simply bored, the countess tortured servant girls for sport.

One major source of irritation in the early years of marriage was Erzsebet's mother-in-law. Eager for grandchildren, Nadasdy's mother nagged Erzsebet incessantly over her failure to conceive. Erzsebet would finally bear children, after a decade of marriage, but she felt no maternal urges in her late teens and early twenties. Young women on her household staff soon came to dread the visits of Nadasdy's mother, knowing that another round of brutal assaults would inevitably follow the old lady's departure.

Where torture was concerned, the bisexual countess possessed a ferocious imagination. Some of her tricks were learned in childhood, others picked up from Nadasdy's experience battling the Turks, but she contrived many techniques on her own. Pins and needles were favorite tools of the trade, piercing the lips and nipples of her victims, sometimes rammed beneath the fingernails. "The little slut!" she would sneer as her captive writhed in pain. "If it hurts, she's only got to take them out herself." Erzsebet also enjoyed biting her captives on the cheeks, breasts, and elsewhere, drawing blood with her teeth. Other victims were stripped, smeared with honey, and exposed to the attacks of ants and bees.

Count Nadasdy reportedly joined Erzsebet in some of the torture sessions, but over time he came to fear his wife, spending more and more time on the road or in the arms of his mistress. When he finally died in 1600 or 1604 (accounts vary), Erzsebet lost all restraint, devoting herself full-time to the torment and sexual degradation of younger women. In short order, she broadened her scope from the family staff to include nubile strangers. Trusted employees scoured the countryside for fresh meat, luring peasant girls with offers of employment, resorting to drugs or brute force as pervasive rumors thinned the ranks of willing recruits. None who entered Erzsebet's clutches ever escaped alive, but peasants had few legal rights in those days, and a noblewoman was not faulted by her peers if "discipline" around the house got out of hand.

By her early forties, Erzsebet Bathory presided over a miniature holocaust of her own design. Abetted by her aging nurse, Ilona Joo, and procuress Doratta Szentes — a.k.a. "Dorka" — Erzsebet ravaged the countryside, claiming peasant victims at will. She carried special silver pincers, designed for ripping flesh, but she was also comfortable with pins and needles, branding irons and red-hot pokers, whips and scissors... almost anything at all. Household accomplices would strip her victims, holding them down while Erzsebet tore their breasts to shreds or burned their vaginas with a candle flame, sometimes biting great chunks of flesh from their faces and bodies. One victim was forced to cook and eat a strip of her own flesh, while others were doused with cold water and left to freeze in the snow. Sometimes, Erzsebet would jerk a victim's mouth open with such force that the cheeks ripped apart. On other occasions, servants handled the dirty work, while Erzsebet paced the sidelines, shouting "More, more still, harder still!" before the countess slumped unconscious on the floor.

One special "toy" of Erzsebet's was a cylindrical cage, constructed with long spikes inside. A naked girl was forced into the cage, then hoisted several feet off the floor by means of a pulley. Erzsebet or one of her servants would circle the cage with a red-hot poker, jabbing at the girl and forcing her against the sharp spikes as she tried to escape. Whether she cast herself in the role of an observer or active participant, Erzsebet was always good for a running commentary of suggestions and sick "jokes," lapsing into crude obscenities and incoherent babble as the night wore on.

Disposal of her lifeless victims was a relatively simple matter in the Middle Ages. Some were buried, others left to rot around the castle, while a few were dumped outside to feed the local wolves and other predators. If a dismembered corpse was found from time to time, the countess had no fear of prosecution. In that place and time, royal blood was the ultimate insurance policy, a gold-plated pass to get out of jail free. It also helped that one of Erzsebet's cousins was the Hungarian prime minister, another serving as governor of the province where she lived.

Erzsebet finally overplayed her hand in 1609, shifting from hapless peasants to the daughters of lesser nobility, opening Csejthe Castle to offer twenty-five hand-picked ingenues "instruction in the social graces." This time, when none of her victims survived, complaints reached the ears of King Matthias, whose father had attended Erzsebet's wedding. The king, in turn, assigned Erzsebet's closest neighbor, Count Gyorgy Thurzo, to investigate the case. On December 26, 1610, Thurzo staged a late-night raid on Csejthe Castle and caught the countess red-handed, with an orgiastic torture session in progress.

A half-dozen of Erzsebet's accomplices were held for trial, the countess kept under house arrest while parliament cranked out a special statute to strip her of immunity from prosecution. The resultant trial opened in January 1611 and lasted through late February, with Chief Justice Theodosius Syrmiensis presiding over a panel of twenty lesser jurists. Eighty counts of murder were alleged in court, though most historical accounts place Erzsebet's final body-count somewhere between 300 and 650 victims. Erzsebet was excused from attending the trial, held in her apartment under heavy guard, but conviction on all counts was a foregone conclusion. The bloody countess had run out of time.

Erzsebet's servant-accomplices were executed, Dorka and Ilona Joo after public torture, but the countess was spared, sentenced to life imprisonment in a small suite of rooms at Csejthe Castle. The doors and windows of her apartment were bricked over, leaving only slits for ventilation and the passing of food trays. There, she lived in isolation for three and a half years, until she was found dead on August 21, 1614. The exact date of Erzsebet's death is unknown, since several meals had gone untouched before her corpse was found.

Bizarre as it is, the Bathory legend has grown in the telling, most recent accounts incorporating tales of vampirism and ritualistic blood baths supposed to help Erzsebet "stay young." Erzsebet's sanguinary fetish is usually linked to the spilling of some unnamed servant girl's blood, with the countess accidentally spattered, afterward impressed that her skin seemed more pale and translucent than usual — traits considered beautiful in those days before discovery of the "California tan." (A British horror film, *Countess Dracula*, added a supernatural twist to the legend in 1970.) In fact, extensive testimony at Erzsebet's trial made no reference to literal blood baths. Some victims *were* drained of blood, from savage wounds or by design, but deliberate exsanguination was linked to Erzsebet's practice of alchemy and black magic, rather than any desire for a warm bath. In any case, Erzsebet's murder spree began when she was in her teens or early twenties, long before the threat of aging ever crossed her mind.

BAZORE, ELINORE

A middle-aged resident of Fayetteville, Arkansas, Elinore Bazore had been separated from her husband for several months when a family reunion was announced for September 4, 1971. Their estrangement was marked by bitter recriminations, and Elinore was conspicuous by her omission from the list of invited guests.

Apparently, it was the final straw.

That Saturday afternoon she crashed the party, driving twenty miles from Fayetteville to surprise the family with a scowl on her face and a revolver in her hand. In a matter of seconds, she shot and killed her husband, his parents, and a brother-in-law. Elinore's 23-year-old son was also wounded, nonfatally, before she stuck the pistol in her mouth and killed herself with one last shot.

BEARCE, MRS. LEON

To a casual observer, nothing would have seemed unusual or out of place in the life of Mrs. Leon Bearce. Born in 1901 and married in her early twenties, she bore their first child in 1927, while helping Leon operate a small tourist camp near Glen Falls, New York. In 1930, soon after Mrs. Bearce gave birth to twins, a young waitress was found dead near the camp, hanging from a tree. A note suggested suicide, but Leon was convinced that bad publicity would doom the tourist camp. Rather than tough it out, he pulled up stakes and relocated at Lake George for the next year's season.

By that time, in early 1931, Leon's marriage had already soured, husband and wife spending several months apart. Mrs. Bearce had filed formal separation papers, with a court date scheduled for June 19, but Leon would only say that his wife had been "acting queerly" for several months. In early June, the hearing was postponed and Mrs. Bearce was reunited with her husband at the Lake George camp site. It appeared that she was looking forward to a reconciliation... but appearances can be deceiving.

Around 6:30 P.M. on June 20, Leon Bearce was working on the campgrounds when he heard his older daughter screaming, thrashing through the undergrowth to reach him. Four-year-old Dena was already losing strength as she reached her father, blood streaming from an open gash where her throat had been cut. "Mommy done it!" she blurted, before she collapsed.

Leon rushed Dena to the nearest hospital, where she died two hours later, despite the best efforts of emergency physicians. Back at the camp site with sheriff's deputies, Leon found his home deserted, searchers fanning out to check the surrounding woods. Within moments, an officer found the twins, ten-month-old Joyce and George, lying dead in a clump of bushes with their throats slashed. Mrs. Bearce stood nearby, still clutching a bloody knife, and she surrendered without a struggle.

"If that knife hadn't been so dull," she told arresting officers, "I'd have used it on myself and finished the job."

In custody, Mrs. Bearce explained the triple murder by citing her fears of divorce and separation from her children. Leon thought she was crazy, the prisoner maintained, and he had threatened to have her committed. Mrs. Bearce had opted to kill her three children, rather than lose them to Leon while she spent the rest of her days in a lunatic asylum.

The prisoner seemed to regain her composure in jail, sleeping soundly and cleaning her plate at each meal, seemingly unaware of her perilous legal situation. Ironically, her worst fears were realized in the end, as she was ruled insane and committed to a New York state hospital for the rest of her life.

BECK, MARTHA JULIE

In retrospect, it may be said that Martha Seabrook had three strikes against her from the day she was born in Milton, Florida, on May 6, 1920. Her father fled the family home for good when she was still a toddler, never bothering with child support. Plagued by a pituitary malfunction, Martha tipped the scales at 200 pounds in adolescence, facing constant ridicule from peers, but the weight did not prevent her brother from raping Martha at age thirteen. Against all odds, she managed to graduate from high school and moved on to nursing school, obtaining her Florida license in March 1942. No hospital would hire her, due to her appearance, and she wound up bathing corpses at a local funeral home.

LOG: 5/3/2002 HONEY-MOON KILLERS

Eight months in that position was enough for Martha, and she moved to California, where a wartime nurses' shortage helped her find a job at Victory Memorial Hospital. A brief fling with a bus driver left her pregnant, but the man preferred death to marriage, absconding as soon as he recovered from a bungled suicide attempt. Martha next surfaced in San Francisco, hospitalized for several days with apparent amnesia. On release, she drifted back to Florida, settling in Pensacola with a phony wedding ring and stories of a husband fighting Japanese in the Pacific. In time, she sent herself a telegram announcing "Joe Carmen's" death in combat. When her story hit the press, bus driver Alfred Beck proposed marriage, and they tied the knot on December 13, 1944. The newlyweds were quarreling by New Year's and filed for divorce in May, leaving Martha pregnant with her second child.

Somehow, the new misfortune seemed to make her stronger. In February 1946, she found a job at the Pensacola Crippled Children's Home, rising to the rank of superintendent within six months. On the side, Martha pored over pulp romance magazines and sought companionship through a "lonely-hearts" club. Ten days after joining the club, Martha received her first letter. It was postmarked from Brooklyn, New York, and signed by Raymond Fernandez.

Hawaiian born of Spanish parents in December 1914, Ray Fernandez was three years old when his family moved to Bridgeport, Connecticut. His father failed in business there, fell back on alcohol to cope with his frustration, and amused himself by slapping Ray around. At age fifteen, Raymond was jailed for stealing chickens, spending sixty days in custody when his father refused to bail him out. At liberty once more, he worked odd jobs to save up money for a trip to Spain, in search of his roots. At twenty, Raymond married into an affluent family and fathered a son, but paternity went against his grain. Fernandez quarreled with his wife and split for the United States, but soon returned to Spain on learning that his son was gravely ill. Enduring the Spanish Civil War, he struck off for Gibraltar in 1939, serving as an Allied spy against the Axis during World War II. In early 1945, he shipped out for Curacao as a merchant seaman, suffering a near-fatal accident when a hatch cover dropped on his head.

Hospitalized in Curacao with a skull fracture, Fernandez was released on March 15, scarred and missing most of his hair, plagued by blinding headaches. He found a berth on board a tanker bound for Mobile, Alabama, but the theft of U.S. government property sent him to the brig. Held for trial on the mainland, Raymond was convicted and sentenced to a year in federal prison, serving his time near Tallahassee, Florida. Upon release, he traveled north to Brooklyn and moved in with his sister, dabbling in voodoo between migraines, boasting of his ability to "hypnotize folks from a distance" and influence women by "thought concentration." The latter talent, he decided, could be useful in a brand-new scam, and to that end he started signing up with lonely-hearts clubs, answering the published prayers of widows desperate for a man.

Raymond's first target, in 1947, was Jane Thompson. She fell for Raymond's line of patter and the man behind it, covering expenses for a trip to Spain. They traveled as man and wife, seeming to enjoy each other's company at first, and Raymond's legal wife pitched in, allowing Fernandez to introduce her as "a friend." By autumn, though, the love affair had soured. Raymond quarreled with Jane and stormed out of their hotel suite on the night of November 7; the next morning, Thompson was dead from an overdose of digitalis. Police were anxious to question her companion, but Raymond had already booked passage back to the States. In New York, he finished looting Jane's estate of some $6,000 before he went shopping for another mark.

The note to Martha Beck was only one of dozens Raymond mailed that year, but it would be the most important of his life. They set a date to meet, and Raymond caught the bus to Pensacola, Martha waiting for him at the depot on a Friday night. Whatever his initial expectations, there was something in the hulking nurse that caught Fernandez with his guard down, and they spent the weekend in a cheap motel, indulging carnal appetites that Martha barely recognized within herself. Come Sunday, Raymond caught the northbound bus, prepared to write the weekend off as a peculiar one-time fling... but Martha was in love.

She might have stuck it out in Pensacola, even so, but the directors of the children's home found out about her steamy tryst and fired her. Martha took it as a sign and dropped her children off with relatives, never to see them again. Arriving in Brooklyn, she turned up on Raymond's doorstep unannounced. He blinked in surprise, invited her in, and their fates were sealed.

Martha Beck was apparently dominant in their new relationship from the start. Aside from her physical bulk, she was more ambitious and ruthless than Raymond, falling in line when he explained the lonely-hearts scam, refining the act with a supporting role for herself. What lonely woman could resist a Latin lover's charm, when Raymond's doting "sister" was prepared to act as chaperone for the affair?

It should not be inferred from this that Martha's feelings for her man were sisterly, by any means. Their sex life, based on testimony from the lethal lovers at their murder trial, was innovative to the point of rank perversity. Allowing for exaggeration on the witness stand, with Ray and Martha working overtime to sell a lame insanity defense, it still appears that Martha called the tune in bed, as she would do in every other aspect of their life together. Raymond, for his part, adapted swiftly to the new arrangement, giving it his all.

The couple's first known mark was Esther Henne, a 41-year-old teacher in Pennhurst, Pennsylvania. Raymond swept the lady off her feet in his inimitable style and married her in March of 1948. It seemed a bit peculiar when his "sister" joined them on their honeymoon — more so when Martha shared a room with Esther, leaving Ray to sleep alone — but there was worse in store. The ink was barely dry on Esther's marriage license when her groom began to tap the family bank account. By month's end she was destitute, and when the cash ran out, Fernandez and his "sister" followed suit.

Esther Henne had been lucky, at that. She came out of the marriage alive.

Beck and Fernandez plied their trade for the next two years, non-stop, but no reliable list of their victims exists. Typical reports allude to "scores" of women swindled, anywhere from twelve to twenty slain, but solid evidence has been produced for only four murders, committed between mid-August 1948 and March 1949. There may well have been more, but if so, Ray and Martha took the secret to their graves.

The first known victim was Myrtle Young, a middle-aged widow from Chicago who married Fernandez on August 14, 1948. That night, when she objected to sharing her bed with Ray's "sister," the swindlers forced a handful of barbiturates down her throat and placed her on a bus to Little Rock. Near-comatose when she arrived, Young was beyond help from emergency physicians who tried to save her life. Meanwhile, back in the Windy City, Martha and Raymond were busy ripping off her car and some $4,000 in cash and jewelry.

That December, Raymond set his sights on 66-year-old Janet Fay, a widow in Albany, New York. The couple moved into Fay's house on December 30, but Janet took pains to keep her new relationship a secret from family and friends. On January 3, she cleaned out her bank account and safe deposit box, packing most of her personal things in a trunk that she stored with the American Express Company. Nightfall found Janet in Valley Stream, New York, where Martha and Raymond had rented a small apartment for the duration. There, once the killers had Fay's cash in hand, Martha brained her with a hammer, finishing the job by strangulation with a scarf. That done, they took a break and made love on the floor, beside Fay's corpse.

Next morning, bright and early, Ray and Martha packed the body in a trunk and dropped it off with Raymond's sister. On the twelfth, they leased a house in Queens, retrieved the trunk, and planted it in the basement of their new residence, capping the grave with cement. Come January 16, with the concrete dry, they skipped out on the lease and went in search of other prey.

All might have been well, but the killers got greedy. Dissatisfied with the $6,000 in cash and jewelry they had already stolen from Fay, they decided to go for a clean sweep. Claiming her trunk in person was far too risky, but Martha had an alternate plan. She typed out a letter to one of Fay's friends, Mary Spencer, describing her whirlwind engagement to "Charles Martin," asking Spencer to visit American Express and have the trunk shipped to a Florida address.

In fact, Martha had outsmarted herself. Mary Spencer knew that her friend couldn't type — had never owned a typewriter, in fact — and she found the letter curious enough to warrant a police investigation. Officers tracked "Charles Martin" and his "sister" to the house in Queens, where excavation turned up iron-clad proof of murder in the basement. Further investigation identified the killers, but each new step took time. When Beck and Fernandez were finally traced, at the end of February, they already had another victim in their sights.

Delphine Downing was a 28-year-old widow, living near Grand Rapids, Michigan, with her two-year-old daughter, Rainelle. Easily the youngest of Raymond's victims, Downing allowed Fernandez and his "sister" to share her home for a month, stalling the nuptials in an effort to be sure of Ray's affection. She managed to mistake Fernandez for a younger man, but his cover was blown — literally — when she came home early on the evening of March 1 and caught Ray without his toupee. A screaming argument ensued, with Martha lending muscle, helping Raymond feed Delphine a handful of sleeping pills. Fernandez finished Downing with a bullet in the head, but there was still Rainelle. Martha drowned the girl in a washtub, and both victims were buried in the basement, covered with a layer of fresh cement.

The take was disappointing, overall. They cleared $500 on the deal, but Downing's bank account was permanently out of reach. The lovers went to catch a movie, planning to evacuate the house the next morning, but their time was running out. New York authorities had traced them to Michigan, and local officers were waiting when they got back from the theater. Ray tried to bluff it out, explaining his relationship to Downing, telling the police that Delphine and her daughter had embarked on a vacation trip. He challenged them to search the house... and thereby gave them ready access to the bodies in the cellar.

Jailed on double murder charges, Ray and Martha breathed a sigh of relief when they learned that Michigan had no death penalty. New York was a different story, however, and Michigan authorities were pleased to grant extradition, despite the objections of Beck and Fernandez. Back in the Empire State by March 16, they were scheduled for trial in June, falling back on insanity pleas when all else failed. Spectators were amused, some jurors revolted, by the graphic descriptions of wild, kinky sex, but it did no good in the end. Convicted of Janet Fay's murder, both defendants were sentenced to death on August 22, 1949. The U.S. Supreme Court rejected their final appeal on January 2, 1951, and the "Lonely-Hearts Killers" were executed at Sing Sing prison on March 8, twelve minutes apart. It was reported that guards had to carry Ray Fernandez to the electric chair, while Martha — fortified by a double helping of chicken, fried potatoes, and salad — walked in and sat down on her own.

BECKER, MARIE ALEXANDRINE

A native of Liege, Belgium, Marie Becker married late, at age thirty-four, and spent the next twenty years as a dutiful wife. Husband Charles was a cabinet maker, stolid and dependable, without a trace of romance in his soul. By 1932, Marie was starved for passion and excitement, anything at all to give her life some zest. She found it in a younger man, one Lambert Bayer, and embarked on a tempestuous affair.

Charles Becker was an obstacle, albeit one who kept his observations and opinions to himself. Marie removed the roadblock to her happiness that autumn, with a massive dose of digitalis, and physicians blamed her husband's death on cardiac arrest. She started spending all her time with Bayer, but romance paled in time, as Lambert failed to match her pace. Marie resorted to her trusty digitalis bottle in November 1934 and went in search of younger, more athletic playmates.

Bent on recapturing lost youth, she became a fixture in the local nightclubs, performing wild dances with men half her age, bribing a series of young lovers to share her bed. It all cost money she could ill afford, and Marie opened a small dress shop in Liege, supplementing her income by robbing and poisoning elderly patrons. Before her sideline was discovered, she dispatched at least nine women, stealing money, clothes, and jewelry from each.

The first to die was Julia Bossy, finished off with digitalis during March of 1935. Two months later, Marie went for a double-header, poisoning Jeanne Perot and Aline-Louise Damorette. A personal friend, Marie Castadot, fell ill in July 1935, and Marie nursed her faithfully until her death on July 23. Madame Lambert was the chosen victim for September, followed by Madame Crulle two months later. Marie outdid herself in September 1936, first poisoning Mathilde Bulte, following that murder with the execution of two elderly widows, Madame Lange and Madame Weiss.

A female friend was Becker's undoing, running to Marie with complaints about her husband, declaring that she wished the no-good scoundrel dead. Marie suggested digitalis, offering a sample from her own supply, and after several days of cooling off, her friend reported the discussion to police. Detectives scrutinized her recent past and started adding up the women who had died within the past twelve months, with Becker serving as their "nurse." She was arrested in October 1936, a vial of digitalis lifted from her handbag, while a search of her apartment turned up piles of women's clothes and jewelry. Examination of her victims indicated digitalis as the cause of death for each.

Charged with eleven counts of murder at her trial, Marie denied killing anyone, but still displayed a callous indifference to the suffering of her victims. One she described as resembling "an angel choked with sauerkraut," while another was recalled as "dying beautifully, lying flat on her back." Convicted on all counts, Marie was sentenced to death, her penalty later commuted to life imprisonment. She died in prison while her native land was occupied by German troops, in World War II.

BEETS, BETTY LOU

No one ever mistook Betty Beets for a lady. A hard-drinking Texas barmaid, born in 1937, she was fond of settling disagreements with her fists or firearms. Five times married, twice to the same unlucky man, she raised six children in her own image, contemptuous of law, society, and human life.

Husband number one was Robert Branson. Their union produced two children — daughter Shirley in 1959 and Robert II in 1964 — but offspring could not hold the marriage together. At that, Branson was lucky. He would survive to weep at Betty's murder trial, in 1985.

Love may be marvelous for some the second time around, but such was not the case for Betty Beets. She would divorce Jimmy Lane twice, in 1971 and '73, before she finally made it stick. Between splits, on January 17, 1972, she shot him twice during an argument at her apartment in Hutchins. Betty claimed self-defense in the shooting, though both slugs struck her once and future husband in the back. Prosecutors called it malicious assault with intent to kill, but Betty bargained down to misdemeanor assault and escaped with a $150 fine. Jimmy Lane was gratefully single again when a heart attack finished him off, in 1982.

By that time, Betty Lou had found and lost her third husband. Doyle Barker was forty-two years old when he disappeared from the family trailer on August 8, 1981. Betty told police that he "went out for cigarettes" and never came back. Detectives had no reason to doubt her at the time, and given Barker's home life, a desire to get away was understandable.

It wasn't only Betty, but her kids as well, who terrorized the neighborhood. They occupied a lakeside lot, and Betty's boys were fond of shooting turtles from the front yard, with a rifle. They also dabbled in burglary from time to time. Betty Lou, for her part, liked to show off for her friends and family, throwing knives and hatchets at a target in her yard. Between husbands, she entertained a series of men at the trailer, sometimes brawling with them in public. One neighbor described sharing space with Betty's brood as an experiment in "holy terror," sending her children to karate class as a means of self-defense.

Betty Lou married her fourth and last husband in October 1982. James Beets was a 45-year-old captain with the Dallas Fire Department, good at his job, but no great shakes when it came to taming Betty's wild bunch. Daughter Shirley was married and off on her own, but the rest of the tribe was on hand, Robert serving six years probation on a recent burglary conviction.

As usual for Betty, the magic wore off within months of her trip to the altar. Come August 6, 1983, she reported her husband missing on a fishing trip to Cedar Creek Lake. His boat was found the next day, drifting without its propeller, scattered tools and nitroglycerine tablets suggesting that Beets had suffered a heart attack and fallen overboard while working on the motor. There was "considerable speculation" that Beets may have been murdered, perhaps by his wife, but in the absence of proof, his disappearance was ascribed to accidental drowning. The body was still missing in late 1984, when Betty had him declared legally dead, thereby making herself eligible for $110,000 life insurance and a fire department pension of $1,200 per month.

Authorities in rural Henderson County reopened their investigation of Betty Beets in January 1985, when an informant told them Beets had killed her last two husbands, planting both within a few yards of her mobile home. Doyle Barker, they were told, was buried underneath a back-yard tool shed; Jimmy Beets, meanwhile, was fertilizing flowers in a decorative wishing well, out front. It took some time, but homicide investigators got their warrant for a search on June 8, 1985, unearthing skeletal remains of both dead men "within three or four inches" of where the informant had said they would be.

Betty Beets was jailed in Gun Barrel City that same afternoon, daughter Shirley Stegner arrested in Dallas the following day. Both were charged with capital murder, held in lieu of $1 million bond. Pathologists identified both corpses and determined that the men were shot to death. Betty Lou was formally indicted for both crimes on July 11; her daughter was charged in Barber's death only, released on $5,000 bail after testifying as a friendly witness before the grand jury.

Betty's trial for the murder of Jimmy Beets opened on October 7, with two of her children listed as prosecution witnesses. Son Robert led off for the state, describing how his mother sketched the plans for Beets's murder on the night of August 5, 1983. Robbie went out for a ride on his bike and returned to find the job done, his stepfather packed in an old sleeping bag. He never actually saw the corpse, but helped his mother lift the heavy bag outside and dump it in the phony wishing well. A bag of peat moss and some flower seeds concealed the evidence of murder. Robbie told the court it "bugged" him for awhile, but he kept quiet for the next two years because "I was protecting my mother."

Shirley Stegner was called on October 8 to discuss the Barker case, describing how her mother had grown tired of Doyle, announcing that she "didn't want him around any more." On August 7, 1981, Betty Lou had telephoned her daughter to discuss her husband's impending murder. Next morning, when Shirley dropped by, Doyle was already dead, shot twice in the head while he slept. Together, they zipped his body up inside a sleeping bag and buried it out back, where a shed was later erected to cover his grave.

Taking the stand on her own behalf, Betty denied killing anyone. It was Robbie, she said, who pulled the trigger on Jimmy Don Beets. She had helped him dispose of the body because he was still on probation, and she feared losing him to prison. Jurors dismissed the argument out of hand, deliberating six hours before they voted to convict on October 11. Three days later, it took them barely an hour to fix her sentence at death.

Betty Lou caught a break on November 12, 1987, when the Texas Court of Criminal Appeals voided her conviction and sentence, ruling that the prosecution had failed to prove its case of capital "murder for hire." Ten months later, on September 21, 1988, the same court reversed itself, deciding that "In essence, the appellant simply hired herself to kill the deceased, assured in her own mind that she would monetarily benefit from her own conduct." On June 26, 1989, the U.S. Supreme Court refused to consider her case.

BELL, MARY FLORA

Mary Bell was born in May of 1957, when her unwed, mentally unstable mother was, herself, a child of seventeen. Though Betty Bell would subsequently wed the baby's father, marriage did not guarantee a stable home. Mary's father was frequently out of work, occasionally in trouble with the law. Betty, for her part, often left her daughter with relatives or acquaintances, once "giving" the child to a woman she met on the street, outside an abortion clinic. The Bell home, in Newcastle, England, was filthy and sparsely furnished. At school, Mary became known as a chronic liar and disruptive pupil. On occasion, she voiced her desire to "hurt people."

The cruel urge surfaced on May 11, 1968, when Mary and Norma Bell (no relation) were playing with a three-year-old boy on top of a Newcastle air raid shelter. The boy fell and was severely injured, but the incident was written off as accidental. On May 12, the mothers of three young girls informed police that Mary had attacked and choked their children. She was interviewed and lectured by authorities, but no juvenile charges were filed.

On May 25, two boys playing in an old, abandoned house found the corpse of four-year-old Martin Brown lying in an upstairs room. Mary and Norma Bell had followed the boys inside, and had to be ordered out when police arrived. With no obvious cause of death, it was assumed that Martin Brown had swallowed pills from a discarded bottle, found nearby.

On May 26, Norma Bell's father caught Mary choking his 11-year-old daughter; he slapped her face and sent her home. Later that day, a local nursery school was vandalized. Police discovered notes that read "Fuck off, we murder, watch out, Fanny and Faggot," and "We did murder Martin Brown, fuck off you Bastard."

Four days later, Mary Bell appeared at the Brown residence, asking to see Martin. Reminded of the tragedy, she told his grieving mother, "Oh, I know he's dead. I wanted to see him in his coffin."

On May 31, a newly-installed burglar alarm at the vandalized nursery school brought patrolmen rushing to the scene, where they found Mary and Norma Bell loitering beside the building. Both girls fervently denied involvement in the previous break-in, and they were released to the custody of their parents.

Two months elapsed before the disappearance of three-year-old Brian Howe, in Newcastle. An immediate search was mounted, and Mary Bell told Brian's sister that he might be playing on a heap of concrete blocks that had been dumped on a nearby vacant lot. In fact, he was discovered there, among the tumbled slabs, but he was dead, a victim of manual strangulation, legs and stomach mutilated with a razor and a pair of scissors that police recovered at the scene. A medical examiner suggested that the killer could have been a child, since relatively little force was used.

Detectives started circulating questionnaires among the local children, asking suspects to account for their movements at the time of Brian's death. Answers from Mary and Norma Bell were inconsistent, and both girls were brought in for questioning. While Mary claimed that she had seen an older boy abusing Brian, Norma soon broke down and told of watching Mary kill the boy. At trial, in December 1968, Norma was acquitted of all charges, while Mary Bell was convicted on two counts of manslaughter.

Described by psychiatrists as "intelligent, manipulative, and dangerous," Mary proved herself a problem inmate. In 1970, she fabricated charges of indecent assault against one of her warders, but the man was acquitted in court. In September 1977, she escaped from Moor Court open prison with another inmate, but the runaways were captured three days later. In the meantime, they had met two boys with whom they spent the night, a circumstance that placed the egocentric Mary back in tabloid headlines, offering a blow-by-blow account of how she lost her virginity.

BENDER, KATE

Nothing is known of the Bender family's origins, beyond the fact that all four members spoke with varying degrees of a Germanic accent. Whether they were actually European immigrants is now impossible to learn, another aspect of the killer brood which shall, like so much else about their lives, remain forever wrapped in mystery.

The family enters recorded history in 1872, as new arrivals in the small community of Cherryvale, Kansas. William Bender was the patriarch, a bearded hulk whose age was estimated in the neighborhood of sixty years. No given name has been recorded for his wife, "Ma" Bender, some ten years her husband's junior. Their elder child was John, a brawny moron given to odd fits of giggling. The baby — and star — of the family was daughter Kate, an attractive blond in her early twenties who quickly emerged as the Bender family spokesperson... and, some said, the brains behind their infamous career in homicide.

Soon after their appearance on the scene, the Benders built a one-room cabin, sixteen feet by twenty, on the road between Cherryvale and Thayer. A sheet of canvas cut the room in half, with living quarters on one side, a public room on the other. Travelers could buy a homecooked meal or rent a cot, but some paid for the rest stop with their lives.

In practice, groups and hard-luck drifters had no problem with the Bender clan; a solitary traveler with cash or valuables in hand was something else again. The chosen mark was seated at a table, with the canvas curtain at his back. Kate Bender served his meal, distracting him with conversation or a bit of cleavage while her brother or the old man crept up on the victim's blind side and dispatched him with a crushing hammer blow. That done, the corpse was lowered through a trapdoor to the cellar, stripped and looted, finally buried on the grounds outside. Ma Bender did her part by planting flowers to conceal the graves.

When travelers were scarce, Kate Bender did her part to keep the family business going. On her own, she toured southeastern Kansas, billing herself as "Professor Miss Kate Bender," a medium with contacts in the spirit world. Her public seances earned money for the family, and young male members of the audience were sometimes more impressed with Kate's appearance than her ESP. A number of those would-be suitors made the trip to Cherryvale and wound up in Ma Bender's flowerbed.

The family's last victim was Dr. William York, from Fort Scott, Kansas. Passing through Cherryvale in March 1873, York asked about overnight lodging and was pointed toward the Bender spread. He never made it home, and it was May before his brother, Col. A.M. York, arrived in search of explanations. Questioning the Benders, York received denials. He declined their hospitality and cautioned them that he would soon return if he could not pick up his brother's trail.

Next morning, on the fifth of May, a passing neighbor saw the front door of the Bender cabin standing open, the family team and wagon missing. Stepping in, he found the place deserted. Fresh dirt in the cellar marked the grave of William York, and ten more bodies were unearthed around the cabin, all with shattered skulls. By then, the Benders had a two-day lead. Colonel York led a posse in pursuit, but they returned at length with word that no trace of their quarry could be found.

And there the matter rested... for awhile.

In 1884, an old man matching William Bender's description was arrested in Montana, for a homicide near Salmon, Idaho. The victim's skull had been crushed with a sledgehammer in that case, and a message was wired to Cherryvale, seeking a positive identification. That night, the suspect severed his own foot to escape from leg irons, and he was dead from loss of blood when his breakfast arrived in the morning. By the time a deputy arrived from Kansas, advanced decomposition had destroyed any hope of a positive I.D. (Even so, the "Bender skull" was publicly displayed in Salmon's Buckthorn Saloon until 1920, when Prohibition closed the tavern and the relic disappeared.)

Five years after the bizarre events in Idaho, Cherryvale resident Leroy Dick paid a visit to Michigan, where he fingered Mrs. Almira Griffith and her daughter, Mrs. Sarah Davis, as Ma and Kate Bender. The suspects were extradited to Kansas, where seven members of a 13-man panel agreed with Dick's identification. Then, on the eve of trial, a Michigan marriage license was found for one of the women, dated 1872, and all charges were dropped.

In 1909, George Downer, dying in Chicago, told his attorney that he had ridden with Col. York's posse in 1873. Far from coming up empty, he said, they had captured the "Hell Benders" and meted out brutal vigilante justice — saving Kate for last and burning her alive. The bodies were consigned to an abandoned well, and posse members swore among themselves that they would take the secret to their graves. A year later, before Downer's statement was widely aired, a similar deathbed confession emerged from New Mexico. The source, a man named Harker, admitted taking several thousand dollars from the dead before they went into the well. A search for the burial site was fruitless, the well — if it ever existed — long since vanished in a sea of cultivated corn, but the lynching tale resurfaced in 1940, published by the son of an alleged posse member named Stark.

Did vigilante justice overtake the Benders on a lonely stretch of Kansas prairie, some 120 years ago? Or did the lethal clan escape, perhaps to build another roadside lair and kill again? How many victims did they claim *before* they moved to Cherryvale? More than a century beyond their crimes, the only answer to these nagging questions is the silence of the grave.

BESNARD, MARIE

Around Loudon, in France, she is remembered as the "Queen of Poisoners," with thirteen victims charged against her name. She is a legend in the district — for her crimes, and for the way she managed, finally, to cheat the executioner.

The only child of frugal parents, born in 1896, Marie Davillaud was educated at a convent school where classmates would remember her as "vicious and immoral." She was "wild with boys," detractors said, adept at "snitching other people's things and lying to cover up." In 1920, already a spinster at the age of twenty-three, Marie was married to her cousin, one Auguste Antigny, who was known to suffer from tuberculosis. When he died in 1927, it was blamed on "pleurisy." The undertaker buried him with shoes on, an aesthetic oversight that would rebound against his grieving widow twenty-two years later.

During August 1929, Marie was married to Leon Besnard. The newlyweds were quick to realize that fortune lay beyond their grasp while certain of their relatives were still alive, but clearing out the family tree takes time. There were rewards in store when two of Leon's great-aunts died, in 1938 and 1940, but the bulk of the inheritance was claimed by Leon's parents, leading the Besnards to change their plans. In May, her wealthy father stricken down by a "cerebral hemorrhage," Marie insisted that her mother come to live with Leon and herself.

The stage was set for action. In November 1940, Leon's father died from eating "poison mushrooms." Three months later, Leon was orphaned when his mother fell prey to "pneumonia." Locals had begun to joke about the "Besnard jinx," but Leon and Marie were more concerned with their inheritance, a sum that was, unfortunately, split between themselves and Leon's sister Lucie. Counting on the jinx, they merely had to bide their time and wait. A "suicide" removed the final obstacle a few months later, bringing Lucie's share of the inheritance to Leon and Marie.

The family curse was turning out to be a gold mine. Next in line, a childless couple, the Rivets, were taken in by the Besnards, expressing their sincerest gratitude by altering their wills to make Marie their only heir. The ink was barely dry before Messr. Rivet was stricken by "pneumonia," dying in his bed. His widow's death, a short time later, marked by nausea and convulsions, was attributed by her physician to "the chest sickness."

Two elderly cousins, Pauline and Virginie Lallerone, were the next to go. Pauline, according to Marie, mistook a bowl of lye for her dessert one evening. Her excruciating death apparently made no impression on Virginie, who repeated the identical "mistake" a short week later. Careless as they may have been, the cousins had been clear about remembering Marie and Leon in their wills.

For all of its adventure, married life was paling for Marie. By 1947, she had fallen for a handsome German P.O.W. living in Loudon. In late October, Leon died at home, but not before confiding in a friend, Madame Pintou, that he was being poisoned by his wife. "She murdered me," he gasped as he lay dying, and the story swiftly made its way around Loudon.

Marie's decrepit mother died in January 1949, her last surviving relative to fall before the "jinx." By now, the local rumor mill was working overtime, but the authorities remained aloof. Marie attempted to intimidate her various accusers, sending garbled death threats through the mails. A burglar invaded Madame Pintou's home by night, selectively destroying every gift she had received from the Besnards. The Massip brothers, having passed the Pintou rumors on, were forced to leave Loudon when arsonists destroyed their home.

Enough was finally enough. Police were summoned, and on May 11, Leon was exhumed by order of the court. According to the coroner's report, his body had absorbed approximately twice the arsenic required to kill a man. A dozen other victims were exhumed, including the Rivets, Auguste Antigny, and assorted members of the Davillaud and Besnard families. Each, it seemed, had managed to ingest a fatal dose of arsenic before succumbing to the family "jinx." (In Auguste's case, the test was run on toenails, accidentally preserved for more than twenty years inside his shoes.)

From jail, Marie made last-ditch efforts to arrange her alibi. A friend was asked to spike the family's stock of wine with arsenic, thereby creating reasonable doubt of accidental death, but he refused. In desperation, the defendant tried to put a contract out on Madame Pintou and the Massip brothers, but her contacts ran to the police, in search of leniency in other cases. Shaken by her failures, the defendant told a visitor, "I am lost. I am guilty."

Brought to trial in February 1952, on thirteen counts of homicide, Marie Besnard displayed a different face in court. She had retained a battery of high-priced Paris lawyers, who demanded new examinations to confirm that all the victims had been slain with arsenic. A mistrial was declared, and bodies were unearthed a second time. As luck would have it, testable results of seven victims had been totally consumed in previous examinations, and the counts of murder were reduced to six for Besnard's second trial, in March of 1954. This time, the jury failed to reach a verdict, and Marie was freed on bond until a third trial could be scheduled. In the meantime, further exhumations, further tests, reduced the dwindling supply of evidence.

The case was finally disposed of in December 1961. Determined to proceed, the state reinstituted thirteen counts of homicide against Marie Besnard, but prosecutors failed to sell their case. Despite the evidence of arsenic in thirteen corpses, her confessions and attempts to murder witnesses, Marie Besnard was finally acquitted by a jury on December 12. The "Queen of Poisoners" had managed to commit the perfect crimes.

BESSARABO, MARIE-LOUISE VICTORINE

The daughter of a French silk trader, Marie-Louise Grones was born at Lyons on October 25, 1868. She spent her early life in convent school, returning home at age twenty to find her father's business in decline. Marie-Louise went to work for the family firm in an effort to help, and in 1892 she embarked on a business trip to Mexico, presumably intent on opening new markets for the trade.

In Mexico, it soon became apparent that her mind was not on business. Marie-Louise's love affairs were public knowledge, verging on a scandal, and they sometimes ended badly. One suitor reportedly killed himself when Marie-Louise rejected his advances, and those she accepted were no safer. Shortly after the suicide, police found Marie-Louise in the rural home of a prominent Mexican businessman, her host lying dead with a bullet in his heart. Marie-Louise blamed roving bandits, and the officers accepted her story, providing an armed escort back to Mexico City.

There, still enjoying the high life, Marie-Louise met Frenchman Paul Jacques, a silk merchant nearly twice her age. They were married and returned to France, where Marie-Louise bore a daughter, Paule, in 1904. Her role as wife and mother soon grew stale, and Marie-Louise began writing poetry, soon shifting to lurid romance novels published under the pen name of "Hera Myrtel." She enjoyed some success as an author over the next decade, building a modest nest egg, neglecting her husband and child to spend time with the series of young would-be writers who shared her bed. Paul Jacques, for his part, did not seem to mind until late 1913, when Marie-Louise announced her intention of returning to Mexico. Putting his foot down at last, Paul refused to let her leave France.

One night in January 1914, Marie-Louise summoned her maid to take Paul a bowl of soup, sprinkled with a curious white powder for "special seasoning." The maid remarked upon Madame's unusual culinary style, and Paul suspicious of the taste, hired a chemist to analyze the soup. Corrosive poison was found, but Jacques unaccountably forgave his wife and said no more of the incident.

On March 14, 1914, Marie-Louise called for her maid once again. This time, the servant found Paul Jacques sprawled dead upon the bedroom floor, blood seeping from a bullet wound in his temple. Ordered to fetch the concierge, she returned moments later to find Jacques propped up in a chair, a pistol on the floor beneath one dangling hand. Marie-Louise insisted that the maid should tell police *she* found the body, an apparent suicide, and the frightened young woman did as she was told.

Disposing of the marital estate, Marie-Louise set sail for Mexico with Paule, billing herself as a "mystical novelist." In Mexico City, she met Charles Bessarabo, a con man and fugitive from justice in his native Romania. Bessarabo courted Marie-Louise for her money, and they were married in 1916, promptly returning to Paris. Life for Marie-Louise in the City of Lights was much the same as before, an endless round of "literary" parties and private "counseling" sessions with her young, male "protégés." One acquaintance described Marie-Louise as the "high priestess of a feminist cult," but all her disciples appeared to be handsome young men.

Bessarabo, meanwhile, was content to spend his wife's money and try a few scams of his own on the side, leaving Marie-Louise to amuse herself. The game turned deadly one night in 1918, when Charles woke to find his wife strangling him, but he managed to thrust her aside, and she tearfully apologized for the inexplicable "seizure." Later, on July 8, 1920, Marie-Louise fired a pistol at Charles in the heat of an argument, but Bessarabo dismissed both incidents. Like Paul Jacques before him, he was making a fatal mistake.

Bessarabo vanished from home on July 31, 1920, Marie telling servants that he had gone on a business trip, his return scheduled for August 2. When Charles failed to return on that date, his chauffeur summoned the police. Marie-Louise admitted sending Bessarabo's trunk to Nancy, on orders from her husband, transmitted by an anonymous cab driver. Detectives took the bait and found the trunk — with Charles Bessarabo rotting inside, killed by a savage beating.

In custody, Paule Jacques broke down and admitted shipping the trunk herself, acting on Marie-Louise's instructions to send it "anywhere so that it won't be found for a long time." Charged as an accomplice to her stepfather's murder, Paule was acquitted at trial. Marie-Louise tried to save herself with testimony that Charles was living in America, and the dead man in the trunk was an unnamed "enemy." Convicted of murder, she was sentenced to life and subsequently died in prison.

BIRNIE, CATHERINE

An Australian native, born in 1951, Catherine Birnie was the product of a lonely, miserable childhood. Sent to live with her grandparents in

Perth, following her mother's death, Catherine would later watch her grandmother die in the throes of an epileptic seizure. Neighbors recall that the child "rarely laughed and had few pleasures. She never had a playmate and other children were not allowed in her grandparents' house." Finally, in her early teens, she met David Birnie and fell hopelessly in love.

The eldest of five children, Birnie had watched his family disintegrate when he was ten years old, siblings farmed out to foster homes and institutions. He showed an early taste for crime, and Catherine fell in line with anything he wanted. She was carrying his child at age sixteen, helping David burglarize a string of shops and factories in Perth. He was arrested and convicted, but escaped from custody, rejoining Catherine for another spree of theft before they both wound up in reform school.

On release, Catherine went to work as a domestic servant, marrying the son of her employers in 1968 and producing six children. David, meanwhile, was back on the street and regretting his own failed marriage, working as a jockey until he was fired for attempted rape. It was 1984 when his path crossed Catherine's again, and they made up for lost time by commencing a steamy affair. In early 1985, Catherine abandoned her husband and children, moving in with Birnie and soon becoming his wife.

By this time, Dave Birnie was lost in a world of bizarre sexual fantasy, stockpiling pornography, demanding intercourse six times a day, dreaming of compliant "sex slaves." It seemed to run in the family: brother James had also done time for sex offenses, and when David moved in with James, during a brief separation from Catherine, he sodomized his brother as a substitute for "pussy." Later, on James' twenty-first birthday, David provided Catherine as a sexual "gift" to his younger sibling.

Mary Neilson, a 22-year-old psychology student at the University of Western Australia, visited the Birnie home in Willagee on October 6, 1986, hoping to buy some tires that David had advertised for sale. On impulse, David pulled a knife and forced her into the bedroom, where she was chained to the bed and repeatedly raped. Catherine watched the attack without complaint, taking snapshots for posterity, going along for the ride when David drove his victim to the Glen Eagle National Park, thirty-four miles south of Perth. There, Neilson was raped again, finally strangled by David with a nylon cord. Catherine and David took turns slashing the corpse to prevent it from swelling in its shallow grave as it decomposed.

The first experiment with rape and murder had been a smashing success, leaving the Birnies anxious to try it again. On October 20, they found 15-year-old Susannah Candy hitchhiking near town, driving her back to their home on Moorhouse Street. Held and sexually abused for several days, the schoolgirl was forced to write two letters home, telling her parents that she was safe and well. The end came with another drive to Glen Eagle Park, where Catherine strangled Susannah and helped dig her grave.

The couple's third victim was an acquaintance, 31-year-old airline hostess Noelene Patterson. The Birnies had helped Noelene wallpaper her home, and she was glad to see them on the afternoon her car ran out of gas. Instead of helping her, however, David Birnie pulled his trusty knife and drove his latest hostage back to Willagee. Chained to the bed and raped over three days, Patterson was so alluring to David that Catherine became violently jealous, insisting that the woman must die. David finally relented, dosing Noelene with sleeping pills and strangling her to death as she lay unconscious. (Later, leading police to her grave in Glen Eagle Park, Catherine would spit on the ground where her "rival" was buried.)

Victim number four was Denise Brown, a 21-year-old computer operator, picked up while hitchhiking in Perth on November 4. After two days of rape and abuse, she was driven to a pine plantation near Wanneroo, forty miles north of the city. There, Brown was raped again, stabbed twice in the process while Catherine snapped photos. Still she lived, and Catherine handed Dave a bigger knife. When all else failed, his victim sitting upright in her grave, Birnie shattered her skull with an ax.

The killer couple's last victim, a teenage hitchhiker, was abducted and driven to Willagee on Sunday, November 9. Monday afternoon found the girl unchained and unguarded, giving her the chance to slip out through a bedroom window. Bruised and barely dressed, she staggered into a Freemantle shopping mall, crying for help. Police were summoned, and she led them back to Moorhouse Street, where the Birnies surrendered without a fight.

In custody, David and Catherine confessed everything, gloating over the details of their crimes and leading police to the sites where their victims were buried. Charged with four counts of murder and numerous other felonies, they were briefly suspected in the disappearance of three more women, but the free-flowing confessions persuaded detectives of their innocence in cases they denied. The couple's trial, on March 3, 1987, took a short half-hour to complete. They offered no defense and were promptly sentenced to life imprisonment, with a minimum of twenty years before parole. In David's case, at least, the judge expressed his hope that "you should not be let out of prison — ever."

"BLACK WIDOW MURDERS" CLEVELAND, OHIO

On May 1, 1922, police in Cleveland jailed a local woman on charges of poisoning her husband for the sum of $11,000 in life insurance. Announcing her arrest the next day, prosecutor Edward Stanton told reporters the suspect had been married five times, divorcing her first two husbands, after which the next three died in mysterious circumstances. Two children from her first marriage had also died years before, reportedly from "accidental" consumption of poison tablets kept around the house.

The suspect sat in jail, her name withheld from newsmen, while authorities exhumed the corpse of husband number five, deceased in May of 1921. Acquaintances recalled the woman saying of her mate, "I would like to get rid of him. I would like to give him poison." Several weeks before he died, she told a creditor "I've got $5,000 coming in a couple of weeks." It came as no surprise, therefore, when arsenic was found in the remains on May 5, 1922, and prosecutors spoke of digging up other possible victims, one of them interred at Pittsburgh.

There, incredibly, the story ends. Although the case had been reported in the *Cleveland Press* and in the *New York Times*, it disappeared without a trace beyond May 7, 1922, the suspect still unnamed. A search of Cleveland homicide records, conducted at the author's request in April 1988, revealed no documents relating to the prisoner, her victims, or the full-scale homicide investigation that made headlines at the time. At this remove, it is impossible to gather further information, and the case remains as it began, in mystery.

BLANCO de TRUJILLO, GRISELDA

A native of Medellin, Colombia, Griselda Blanco grew up in an atmosphere where violence and corruption were the norm. "La Violencia" claimed an estimated 300,000 Colombian lives between 1945 and 1962, a brief lull in the carnage long forgotten by the time cocaine emerged as the nation's chief export in the early 1970s. Today, near-anarchy prevails throughout the country, Medellin alone recording an average of ten drug-related murders each day.

It comes as no surprise, with such a background, that Griselda Blanco grew up idolizing gangsters, men of wealth and power who were generous to friends and merciless with enemies. She had ambition, courage of a sort, but it was still a man's world, both in terms of Latin culture and the raw mechanics of the cocaine trade. The road to power wound its way through countless bedrooms, but Griselda didn't mind... as long as she wound up with all the marbles in the end.

Beginning as a prostitute and pickpocket, Griselda "married up," selecting a smuggler with money enough to keep her in style. When her husband was killed by a rival, Griselda moved on — four marriages in all, each trip to the altar advancing her status in Medellin's netherworld of drugs and corruption. Some called her "the black widow," noting her bad luck with husbands, but violent death was an occupational hazard among *los narcotrafficantes*, an accepted business risk. It would be impolite to cast aspersions on the grieving widow, while her husbands had so many ruthless enemies at large.

By the time she buried husband number four, Griselda had a network of connections in the coke trade and a bankroll large enough for her relocate to the United States. She chose Miami as her base of operations, putting feelers out to several independent gangs, recruiting them as muscle, offering protection and a fair share of the profits in return for loyalty. Selecting young, attractive women as her "mules," Griselda opened pipelines of her own from Medellin to southern Florida, prepared to murder anyone who tampered with her trade.

As she grew stronger, wealthier, Griselda's fascination with the gangster mythos blossomed into an obsession. She had named her fourth son Michael Corleone, for Al Pacino's character in the *Godfather* movies, and now she began to call herself "La Madrina": The Godmother. When it came down to murder, though — especially the punishment of traitors — La Madrina could have taught the Corleones a thing or two.

An early disappointment for Griselda came in 1975, when trusted lieutenant Juan Guillermo stole $2 million from her in Miami, used it to recruit a private army in Colombia, and tried to seize her smuggling network for himself. A number of Guillermo's mercenaries died in the ensuing war, and three attempts were made on Juan himself; in one attack, Guillermo used his girlfriend as a human shield and managed to escape, while she took bullets meant for him. Guillermo was attempting to regroup in Medellin when time and luck ran out, a well-placed bullet serving as the payment for his treachery.

Another trusted ally, one German Panesso, rose in arms against Griselda's rule in 1978. Assassins raided the Miami home of Blanco's chief enforcer, killing three soldiers and gang-raping the target's wife when they found him absent. A leader of the raid was subsequently kidnapped, tortured, shot, his body drained of blood and buried in a packing crate. Panesso's housemaid was abducted in April 1979, stabbed and suffocated with duct tape, her body dumped in a rural field. Six days later, Panesso retaliated with the execution of Jaime Suescun, hog-tied and smothered with tape in identical style.

Panesso ran out of luck on July 11, 1979, while browsing at the Dadeland shopping mall. The mobster and a bodyguard were buying whiskey when a van bearing the logo "Happy Time Complete Party Supply" pulled up outside the liquor store, two passengers unloading, shopping bags in hand. Inside the booze shop, they drew submachine guns, blasting at Panesso and his sidekick from a range of several feet. Crown Liquor's manager attempted to escape, but other guns were waiting in the van, prepared to deal with runaways, and he was wounded in the feet while wriggling underneath a car. Examining the carnage with a scientific eye, Miami medical examiner Charles Diggs compared the bodies of Panesso and his gunman to Swiss cheese. (The van, specially customized with armor plate and one-way glass, was dumped 300 yards from where Panesso died; inside, police found a machine gun, two carbines, five pistols, and a shotgun — all of which had recently been fired.)

Removal of German Panesso from the scene did not eliminate Griselda's problem with competitors. Her handiwork is evident in files on "unsolved" homicides recorded by the Metro-Dade authorities into the early 1980s. "Cocaine cowboys" beaten, hog-tied, strangled, shot, dismembered. A young woman shot at point-blank range, her right ear severed. Bodies found in homes and in abandoned cars, discarded on the shoulder of a country road or floating in the Everglades. Sometimes, Griselda reached out for her enemies in Medellin. One such, a female rival, was assassinated in August 1982, while riding in a funeral procession. The victim's daughter, seated beside her when the guns went off, told newsmen that her mother "had it coming."

And so, in due time, did Griselda. Arrested with three of her sons at Irvine, California, in 1985, she was charged with multiple counts of trafficking in narcotics. At trial, her judge described Griselda's style of parenting as "the most incredible thing I have ever seen. If there was ever a case that truly has demonstrated what a mother's influence ought not to be, it's this one." On conviction, Griselda was sentenced to thirty-five years in federal prison, her sons drawing similar terms. In the event of her parole, Colombian authorities have open murder charges waiting for The Godmother of crime.

BOLIN, PATRICIA

From all appearances, 40-year-old Patricia Bolin had the perfect life. Her husband Ronald was a successful businessman, the founder of his own mechanical design company, and their marriage had been blessed with three children: Alicia in 1961, Tamela in 1964, and son Todd in 1967. Three years after Todd was born, the family moved to Upper Arlington, Ohio, a posh Columbus suburb, where Ronald had a spacious ranch-style home custom-built for his wife. Life seemed good, and if Patricia had recently graduated from "social" drinking to a more dedicated style of boozing, no one paid attention to the problem, much less to its causes.

In retrospect, police and newsmen would explain Patricia's actions of December 1976 by stating that she simply "went berserk," but her crime was carefully planned, despite its apparent lack of motive. On October 25, she purchased an inexpensive .22-caliber pistol and fifty rounds of ammunition, hiding them in her sewing box at home, unknown to her family. Ron Bolin's mother later told the press: "My son never liked guns. He never went hunting and never wanted a gun in the house." Police would count the cartridges and come up seven short, deciding those were used for target practice sometime prior to D-Day on December 8.

That afternoon, around 5:30, Pat and Ron were home alone, their children out with friends. The sequence of events remains uncertain, but police believe that Ron was running for his life when bullets struck him in the head, neck, and chest, dropping him just inside the front door of his home. A short time later, 12-year-old Tamela came home from school, entering through the garage. Patricia met her there and shot her dead, dragging the girl's body through a connecting door to the house, leaving a slick trail of blood behind her.

Next, Patricia called Todd in from playing outside. He entered the house, then quickly reemerged with a cry of "She's shooting everyone!" In spite of his alarm, the neighbors paid no heed, and Todd went back inside the house when Patricia called him a second time. He had blown his last chance to escape, and she killed him where he stood, before he could slip off his coat.

Daughter Alicia was the last to come home, around 6:00 P.M. Entering through the garage, she followed the blood trail to her sister's body, running from there to the back door, calling for her mother. Patricia met her in the kitchen, aiming a pistol and squeezing the trigger, but her gun was empty. Unperturbed, Pat ordered Alicia to wait in her room, but the girl fled to a neighbor's house and called police.

Officer Thomas French was first on the scene in response to the call. He found the front door of the Bolin home blocked by Ronald's body, so he circled the house, shining his flashlight through its darkened windows. In one room, Patricia stood dressed to go out, complete with her best winter coat, aiming her pistol at French, but she held her fire as he ducked out of sight. When French looked again, Patricia had the .22 pressed to her temple, preparing to fire. Officers were forcing the door when a last shot rang out, leaving four persons dead in the house.

Patricia Bolin had fired a total of eighteen shots in the course of her rampage, but for all her ferocity, police and relatives could never agree on a motive for the killings. Two empty bottles of vodka were found in the house, apparently drained on the day of the massacre, but whatever pain or fear Patricia felt in her last weeks of life, she took the secret with her to her grave.

BOMBEEK, CECILE

Early in 1977, nurses employed at the public hospital in picturesque Wetteren, Belgium, began comparing notes on curious events in the 38-bed geriatric ward. For openers, the death rate had increased dramatically in recent months, with twenty-one patients lost in the span of a year. Other cases revealed signs of sadistic treatment, including catheters ripped from the bladders of elderly patients by "persons unknown." In time, suspicion focused on 44-year-old Sister Godfrida, a Josephite nun assigned to the geriatric ward.

Born Cecile Bombeek, the product of a staunchly Catholic home, Sister Godfrida adopted her religious name after joining the Apostolic Order of St. Joseph. Her behavior appears to have been exemplary before 1976, when the aftermath of brain surgery left her addicted to morphine. Narcotics are available in Wetteren, despite stiff criminal penalties, but they are not inexpensive. Neither were Sister Godfrida's bisexual love affairs with a retired missionary and a local teacher; her lovers enjoyed expensive food, vintage wine, and Cecile was anxious to oblige.

Soon, police contended, she began to loot the savings and personal property of her aged patients, embezzling more than $30,000 in a year's time. On the side, she began to display sadistic tendencies, abusing her charges, killing at least three with insulin overdoses when they became "too difficult at night." In retrospect, it was impossible to estimate the lethal sister's body-count. Dr. Jean-Paul De Corte, spokesman for the hospital's governing board, declared: "It could just as well be thirty people as three."

In custody, Cecile's confession to three homicides was sufficient to bring an indictment. In March 1978, she was committed for psychiatric observation, finally ruled competent for trial and sentenced to a term of life imprisonment.

BONNY, ANNE

Born in 1700, Anne Brennan was the illegitimate daughter of a successful Irish attorney, William Cormac, and his housemaid, Peg Brennan. Initially, Cormac sought to avoid scandal by dressing the child as a boy, describing "him" as the son of friends left in Cormac's care, but the charade placed unbearable strain on his home life. Deserting his wife in due course, Cormac fled with his mistress and their child to Charleston, South Carolina, where he abandoned the practice of law and prospered as a merchant. The profits were invested in a great plantation, young Anne taking over household duties when her mother died.

By age fourteen, neighbors had noted Anne's "robust" body, along with her "fierce, courageous temper." Rumors spread that she had knifed a servant girl to death, but no investigation was pursued. One documented case involves a young man who attempted to molest her on the street; Anne broke his jaw and beat him so severely that he was hospitalized for three months.

At age sixteen, Anne married penniless seaman James Bonny. Neighbors suspected the groom was after her money, a risk William Cormac laid to rest by driving the newlyweds off his plantation. They drifted to the Bahamas, settling in New Providence, where Governor Woodes Rogers had lately declared open season on pirates. James Bonny signed on as an informer, paid to hang around taverns and brothels, but Anne found more in common with the pirates. Local buccaneers, for their part, liked her style, the more so after Anne produced a gun one afternoon and shot a man who tried to grab her on the street.

A general amnesty for pirates ruined the informer business, and Anne soon abandoned her husband in favor of Chidley Bayard, alias "Albert Backhouse," a fugitive from British justice operating as a fence for pirate loot. Bayard had a live-in mistress at the time, but Anne dispatched her with a well-placed rapier thrust and took the other woman's place almost before her corpse was cold.

In Bayard's company, Anne met such famous privateers as Henry Jennings, Benjamin Hornigold, and the inimitable "Blackbeard," Edward Teach. Before long, she grew tired of Bayard and shifted her affections to John ("Calico Jack") Rackham, quartermaster for pirate captain Pierre Bousquet. Overcoming brief resistance, she put to sea with Rackham as part of Bousquet's crew, already scheming to replace the captain with her lover.

In July 1718, Anne persuaded the crew to depose Bousquet and replace him with Calico Jack. Six months later, she gave birth to Rackham's daughter, but the child died in infancy. Stopping off in New Providence, Anne faced an adultery suit filed by James Bonny, but the governor let her off with a warning. Always one to get even, she torched Bonny's new home and shipyard before she set sail with the boys.

At sea, Bonny joined in looting scores of ships, proving herself as skilled as any man with a cutlass or pistol. One witness would later testify that Anne "cursed and swore with the best of males, and never cringed from murder." She dressed in shirt and trousers, like a man, but the disguise could not conceal her "breasts the size and strength of melons."

In October 1720, Governor Rogers commissioned an armed sloop under Captain Burnet, assigned to the sole task of caging Rackham's crew. Burnet overtook his prey while Rackham, Bonny and the rest were celebrating the capture of a merchant ship, debating the fate of a female hostage. The manhunters launched their assault, with Bonny, female pirate Mary Read, and one male member of the crew providing the only resistance. Calico Jack was locked in his cabin with a bottle of rum throughout the uneven battle, so infuriating Anne that she afterward spat in his face.

Six members of the pirate crew were sentenced to die, Bonny and Read postponing their dates with the hangman on grounds that both were pregnant. On the day of Rackham's execution, Anne dropped by his cell long enough to scold him for cowardice. "Had you fought like a man," she advised, "you need not have been hanged like a dog."

As for Anne, she would never stretch rope. Soon after the birth of her child, she vanished from the New Providence lockup, and rumor takes over from there. William Cormac was widely suspected of paving the way for his daughter's escape, while others blamed a new lover, Michael Radcliffe. Opinions are divided as to whether Anne settled in Charleston, under an alias, or married Radcliffe and migrated west.

BOTKIN, CORDELIA

A native of the Cornhusker State, Cordelia Brown was the pampered child of a banker for whom Brownsville, Nebraska, was named. She married Welcome Botkin in 1872 and produced a son, but the couple separated soon after young Beverly's birth. Living on alimony and an allowance from her family, Cordelia moved her child to San Francisco, adopting a footloose "Bohemian" life style on the Barbary Coast.

It was in San Francisco, during 1895, that Cordelia met John Presly Dunning on a stroll through Golden Gate Park. Dunning, San Francisco's bureau chief for the Associated Press, was unaccountably drawn to the short, overweight Botkin, and they began a steamy love affair. Before long, Dunning abandoned his wife and infant child, moving into an apartment with Botkin, her son, and Beverly's 40-year-old mistress, Louise Seeley.

Elizabeth Dunning gave up on her philandering husband in 1896, moving back to the home of her congressman father in Dover, Delaware. Botkin sought to make the rift permanent by dispatching a series of letters — signed "A Friend" — detailing John's amorous escapades in San Francisco.

For most of two years, life went smoothly, a non-stop round of drunken revels for the foursome at Botkin's apartment. Then, in 1898, Dunning's superiors at the Associated Press gave him his marching orders, packing him off to cover the Spanish-American War. His parting message to Cordelia was the word that he would not be coming back to San Francisco; rather, when the war was finished, Dunning planned to seek a reconciliation with his wife.

On September 9, 1898, a box of candy was delivered to Elizabeth Dunning in Dover, complete with a card that read: "With love to yourself and baby — Mrs. C." Overlooking the familiar penmanship, long since identified as Botkin's, Elizabeth mistook the sender for a family friend and shared the candy with some guests. Four persons tried the chocolates, and all grew ill immediately afterward; two would survive, but Mrs. Joshua Deane died in agony on September 11, followed by Elizabeth Dunning the next day.

Handwriting comparisons led police to Botkin's doorstep, and candy vendor George Haas confirmed her purchase of the chocolates. Convicted of murder on December 31, 1898, Cordelia was sentenced to life imprisonment. Confined at San Quentin, she found a guard willing to trade sexual favors for two days of freedom per week, but the scheme was exposed when Botkin met her trial judge on a San Francisco trolley. Stripped of her undeserved privileges, Botkin survived in prison until 1910. Her death was attributed to "softening of the brain due to melancholy."

BRAR, HARJIT KAUR

A Sikh native of the Punjab district, in northwestern India, Harjit Bhuller was born in 1947 and emigrated to Canada at age twenty. She settled first in Montreal, where she met and married Santokh Brar, a transplanted Indian businessman. They soon moved west to Calgary, Alberta, and Harjit bore a son, but the boy died of cancer at age five, after two years of suffering. Four more children followed, but they were all daughters: Ravinder in 1973; Savinder in 1975; Sukhjit in 1977; and Amrit in March 1979.

On the surface, Harjit's life seemed pleasant and well-ordered, with Santokh earning a good income from his fleet of six taxis and co-ownership of Calgary's Plaza Theatre. In private, though, the mother of four never stopped grieving for her lost son. As one friend later told the press, "She used to think about him a lot. She was always crying for him. She wanted a son very badly. Actually, she was expecting the fourth child to be a boy."

That final disappointment was the capper in a family whose cultural background placed a premium on male offspring. Sikh boys traditionally have the middle name Singh, meaning "lion," while girls — including Harjit and all four of her daughters — carry the middle name Kaur, roughly translated to "second in command." As a Sikh physician in Calgary later told the media: "Prejudice against girls is very, very common in our country. Sometimes women who produce only daughters are mistreated. There's beating, abusing, and even people committing suicide. This is common even among educated people. There is happiness when you have a boy, and misery when you have a girl."

No one can say with certainty if Harjit Brar had been mistreated in her home, but everything seemed normal on the afternoon of May 1, 1979. Harjit took her daughters swimming that day, but when Santokh went to bed at his usual nine o'clock, she stayed up, reporting that one of the children was ill and needed attention. Within a half hour, she telephoned a relative, suddenly emotional, spilling out a tale of depression. Police were told the call included "some indication she might commit suicide," but the relative was calm enough to wait an hour before calling back. No one answered at the Brar home, then, and an ambulance was called... but it arrived too late.

At 10:00 P.M., witnesses spotted Harjit and her children on a bridge spanning the Bow River, which flows through downtown Calgary. They watched, stunned, as she tossed her three older daughters into the river, then leaped in after them, holding two-month-old Amrit in her arms. It was noted that the children offered no resistance, and all five had drowned before help arrived, marking the worst murder-suicide in Calgary's history. Aside from speculation on Harjit's mental state and possible abuse at home, no motive was discovered for the crime.

BRINVILLIERS, MARIE MADELINE de

A child of French nobility, born July 22, 1630, Marie d'Aubray was the oldest of five children sired by a Councilor of State who also served as treasurer of France. Marie was an attractive and precocious girl who introduced her two younger brothers to sex while still in her teens. At twenty-one, she entered into a "suitable" marriage with the much older Marquis Antoine de Brinvilliers, Baron de Nourar.

It was a marriage of political convenience, more than anything, and the Marquis did not object when his wife took a lover, one Gaudin de Sainte-Croix, in 1658. Straight-laced Dreux d'Aubray held a different view of his daughter's affair, using his political connections to have Sainte-Croix locked up in the Bastille. Embittered by his circumstances, still madly in love with Marie, Sainte-Croix learned the fine points of poisoning from his cellmate, a professional killer named Exili. On release, Sainte-Croix found that Marie had spent most of her husband's personal fortune, and he had no difficulty persuading her that her father should be killed to expedite inheritance of his estate.

Marie was nothing if not meticulous. Before attempting to kill her father, she took a nursing job at the Hotel Dieu, a public hospital in Paris. There, by her own later estimate, she killed some fifty patients over a period of weeks, distributing poisoned fruit to experiment with recipes and dosage. Finally satisfied with a particular formula in 1866, Marie went home to visit her father, and the old man immediately fell sick. When he died in agony, three days later, autopsy surgeons found "his stomach all black, the liver gangrened and burnt," but his death was still attributed to natural causes.

A year after Dreux d'Aubray's death, Marie poisoned her two brothers and reaped a further inheritance from their estates. She longed to marry Sainte-Croix, but he had grown leery of her zeal for murdering loved ones. When Marie began dosing her husband's meals with poison, Sainte-Croix countered by slipping the old man an antidote. Sainte-Croix himself collapsed and died in 1673, from "natural causes" — some say exposure to his own lethal recipes — and his private papers were found to include letters naming Marie as a murderess.

Marie fled to Holland and found sanctuary in a convent, remaining there for three years before the lure of Paris proved irresistible. In the meantime, French authorities had jailed one of her servants, breaking him on the wheel, and thus obtained confessions verifying Sainte-Croix's parting shot. A three-month trial resulted in Marie's conviction and sentence of death. Following a period of torture, she was taken to Notre Dame Cathedral on July 17, 1776, there confessing her crimes to a huge crowd before she was beheaded, her body burned, its ashes scattered to the wind.

BROMLEY, DIANA MARION

A child of British aristocracy, born in 1918, Diana Pratt was the daughter of diplomat Sir John Pratt. An uncle on her father's side was actor Boris Karloff, star of *Frankenstein* and many other classic horror films. Diana's husband, Thomas Bromley, was another diplomat, attached to the Ministry of Defense. Their union produced two sons — Martin, born in 1945, and Stephen, born in 1948. The family lived in Haslemere, a stylish part of Surrey.

By the latter 1950s, Diana was plagued with recurring mental problems and "nervous disorders," treated by psychiatrists on three occasions prior to December 1958. The doctors considered her cured, or at least "stabilized," as the Christmas season approached.

They could not have been more wrong.

Diana's boys came home from boarding school on December 16, Stephen suffering from a cough that confined him to bed. On the seventeenth, unknown to her husband, Diana dosed both boys with barbiturates, repeating the dose on December 18. Thomas Bromley returned home from work around 9:45 that night, discovering his two sons dead in their pajamas, and his wife in what the media described as "a collapsed condition." Diana was rushed to a nearby hospital, where police stood watch at her bedside, waiting for answers. Initial press reports stated that Martin and Stephen had died from "deep cuts and stab wounds," including slashed throats.

On December 22, Diana was remanded into custody on a charge of murdering her older son; a statement from police revealed that Martin had been found in the garage. A coroner's inquest, convened the following day, reported that Martin was strangled to death, while his younger brother was drowned.

Diana's murder trial was scheduled to convene on January 14, 1959, but the proceedings were delayed by a January 7 suicide attempt that left the defendant hospitalized in serious condition. A month later, on February 18, Diana appeared in court to be charged with Stephen's murder. Prosecutors told the court that Diana had doped both boys with barbiturates and dressed them in pajamas before she fixed a makeshift bed in the garage, near the tailpipe of her car, and left the vehicle's engine running. Later, on discovering that both boys were alive, she strangled Martin with a belt, then carried

Stephen into the bathroom and drowned him in the tub. Finally, in an attempted suicide, Diana slashed her own throat and threw herself into a decorative lily pond, where Thomas found her still alive.

Diana's attorney stood fast on an insanity defense, refusing to let his client testify. On February 25, the court ruled that Diana's January suicide attempt had left her brain-damaged, finding her both insane and unfit to plead. Murder charges were dismissed, and Bromley was committed to a mental institution for treatment.

BROWN, DEBRA DENISE

The fifth of eleven children, born to an Illinois family in 1963, Debra Brown was engaged to be married at age twenty. As luck would have it, Debra never took her wedding vows. Instead, she met Alton Coleman, eight years her senior, and fell into a semblance of love. Breaking off her engagement, she became Coleman's live-in lover, sharing a small Waukegan apartment with his grandmother. Frequently beaten and abused by her man, she would stick by his side to the bitter end, finally becoming his confederate in crime.

Born Elton Coleman in November 1955, third of five children from a prostitute in the Waukegan ghetto, the future terror of the Midwest was raised by his maternal grandmother. Dubbed "Pissy" by his playmates, for a childhood tendency to wet his pants, Coleman grew up running with street gangs, cultivating an unsavory reputation. A black who preferred blacks as his victims, his numerous arrests were concentrated in the area of sex crimes, a propensity that led him on a lethal crime spree and, eventually, to the death house.

In January 1974, while Debra Brown was still in grade school, Coleman was arrested for the abduction, rape and robbery of an elderly woman in Waukegan. A bargained guilty plea to simple robbery earned him a sentence of two to six years in Joliet prison, where he was later accused of molesting male inmates. A prison psychiatrist dubbed Coleman a "pansexual, willing to have intercourse with any object, women, men, children, whatever." Free on parole, he was charged with rape again in 1976 and 1980, winning acquittal each time when a jury believed that his victims consented to sex. His record reveals a total of four rape charges, two counts of deviant sexual assault, five of unlawful restraint, and one count of indecent liberties with a child. The latter victim was a niece of Coleman's; an angry mother filed the charge, but later changed her mind in court. The judge, dismayed, branded her new story "completely implausible." "I think," he declared, "the woman as she stands here today is terrified by this man."

Briefly married, Coleman was abandoned by his teenaged wife, who sought police protection when she went to claim her various belongings from their home. She "just couldn't take it no more," and years later, in court, she would offer descriptions of Coleman's obsession with bondage, young girls, and perverse, violent sex.

In February 1980, still three years away from his meeting with Debra Brown, Coleman was accused of raping a Waukegan girl at knifepoint, and while never indicted, he was also suspected in the rape and strangling of Gina Frazier, age fifteen, in 1982. Reduction of his bail in the Waukegan case put Coleman on the street in time to launch a rampage that would place him on the FBI's "Most Wanted" list.

On May 29, 1984, nine-year-old Vernita Wheat convinced her mother to let her accompany "Robert Knight" and his girlfriend to Waukegan, fifteen miles from their home in Kenosha, Wisconsin. The purpose of the trip was to retrieve a stereo, described by Vernita and "Knight" as a belated Mother's Day present. When the three had not returned the next morning, police were notified. A photo lineup readily identified "Robert Knight" as Alton Coleman; his companion had been Debra Brown.

On May 30, as police were starting their search, Brown accompanied Coleman to court for another hearing on the Waukegan rape charge. Bail was continued, and Coleman dropped from sight that afternoon, before detectives made their I.D. Debra Brown was briefly questioned on June 1, vanishing the moment investigators turned their backs.

With Coleman's sinister record in mind, a federal grand jury indicted both suspects on kidnapping charges, and the FBI went to work. On June 18, Tamika Turks, age seven, was walking with her nine-year-old aunt near their home in Gary, Indiana, when Coleman and Brown pulled up to the curb, asking directions. Money was offered in exchange for help, and both girls climbed into the car. Confronted with a knife, they were driven to a wooded area twelve miles away, where Coleman raped and choked Tamika Turks, while Debra held her down. Tamika's aunt was also raped and beaten, but she managed to escape. Selection of familiar photographs by the survivor added further charges to the growing list, and still the fugitives remained at large.

The strangled body of Vernita Wheat was found on June 19, in an abandoned building in downtown Waukegan. That same afternoon, police in Gary received a missing-person report on Donna Williams, a 25-year-old beautician. She had last been seen en route to pick up a "nice young couple from Boston," who had agreed to visit her church. None of them showed for the service, but witnesses identified photos of Coleman and Brown as recent visitors to the salon where Williams worked. On June 27, the missing woman's car was found in Detroit, but Coleman and Brown had already surfaced in the Motor City, with a vengeance.

On June 24, the couple accosted a Detroit woman outside her home, brandishing knives and demanding that she drive them to Ohio. The intended victim saved herself by deliberately crashing into a parked truck, fleeing on foot while the killers took off in her damaged vehicle.

Four days later, Coleman and Brown invaded the home of Palmer and Maggie Jones, in Dearborn Heights, surprising the middle-aged couple at breakfast. The latest victims were beaten with a club, robbed of $86, and left bleeding on the floor while the fugitives fled in their car. On June 30, a pair of Detroit men offered the couple a ride. When Coleman drew a gun, the driver grappled with him briefly and escaped. His passenger, an invalid, was tossed out on the street, amazingly unharmed.

Verified sightings of Coleman and Brown were recorded every day between July 2 and 7. On July 2, a middle-aged Detroit couple was attacked in their home, beaten with a pipe and subjected to Coleman's incoherent harangue on how blacks were forcing him to murder other members of his own race. The victims' stolen car was dropped off in Toledo, where another couple was assaulted, handcuffed in their home, and relieved of transportation.

A Toledo bartender reportedly exchanged shots with Coleman, after the fugitives tried to abduct one of the bartender's patrons.

On July 7, Coleman and Brown spent the night with 30-year-old Virginia Temple and her 10-year-old daughter, Rochelle, in Toledo. Before they left the next morning, both were strangled, the girl raped, their bodies stuffed into a crawlspace beneath the looted home.

Four days later, on July 11, the remains of Donna Williams were discovered in Detroit. She had been strangled with a pair of pantyhose. That afternoon, the FBI announced that Coleman had been elevated to a most unusual eleventh place on its "Ten Most Wanted" list, an option used when vicious crimes in progress mark a suspect as particularly dangerous.

And the body-count kept rising. In Cincinnati, Toney Storey, age fifteen, had last been seen with individuals resembling Brown and Coleman; four days later, when her corpse was found, she had been stabbed repeatedly, with two shots in the head. On July 13, 44-year-old Marlene Walters became the first white victim of the crime spree, bludgeoned in her home at Norwood, Ohio, a Cincinnati suburb. Harry Walters, gravely injured, managed to describe the killers of his wife as two young blacks who had arrived on ten-speed bikes and talked their way inside the house, expressing interest in the purchase of a camper. When they fled, they had been driving Harry's car.

On July 16, Coleman and Brown abducted Oline Carmichal, a college professor from Lexington, Kentucky. Driving him back to Dayton, Ohio, they left Carmichal unharmed, locked in the trunk of his car. Rescued on July 17, he described the kidnappers as *two* black men and a woman. That mystery was solved with the arrest of Lexington native Thomas Harris, who explained that he was "kind of forced" to help the fugitives. Harris claimed that he had talked

Coleman and Brown out of killing their latest prisoner.

Thirty minutes after Carmichal was freed from his car, an elderly minister and his wife were found, battered but breathing, in their Dayton home. Investigation showed that Coleman and Brown, using pseudonyms, had met the couple a week earlier, spending two nights in their home and parting on amiable terms when the minister drove them to Cincinnati "for a prayer meeting." On July 17, the couple had returned, beating their former hosts severely and making off with the minister's station wagon.

The latest stolen vehicle was dumped the next day in Indianapolis, near a car wash where proprietor Eugene Scott, age seventy-seven, and *his* car were reported missing. Scott was found by searchers several hours later, in a ditch near Zionsville; he had been stabbed repeatedly, and shot four times in the head.

The long trail of death reached its end in Evanston, Illinois, on July 20, 1984. An anonymous tip from a "friend" of the fugitives alerted police to their presence in the neighborhood, and they were soon spotted at a local park. Five officers surrounded the couple, relieving Coleman of two bloody knives and lifting a .38 revolver from Brown's purse. That afternoon, Eugene Scott's missing car was found in Evanston, five blocks from where the suspects were arrested. Debra Brown had left her fingerprints inside.

In Chicago, a federal magistrate set Coleman's bond in the Wheat case at $25 million cash. "This nation has been under a siege," he declared. "This nation has been under a reign of terror not knowing when the next victim was going to be taken. I am going to make sure no other victim will be subject to this man." A bond of $20 million cash was set for Debra Brown.

The magistrate need not have worried. In May 1985, tried separately for the Cincinnati murder of Marlene Walters, Brown drew a life prison term, while Coleman was sentenced to die. With her own nonlethal sentence in the bag, Debra took the witness stand at Coleman's penalty hearing, telling jurors "I killed the bitch, and I don't give a damn. I had fun out of it." A month later, Cincinnati convictions in the death of Toney Storey condemned both defendants to die. On August 1, in Dayton, Coleman and Brown were sentenced to twenty years each for the kidnapping of Oline Carmichal. April 1986 brought separate trials in Gary, Indiana, with Coleman sentenced to death for killing Tamika Turks, plus 100 years for the rape and attempted murder of her aunt. Debra Brown was also convicted in that case, hoping for a lighter sentence when she slipped the judge a note that read: "I am a more kind and understanding and lovable person than people think I am." Unmoved, the judge sentenced her to death for murder, with consecutive 40-year terms for kidnapping and child-molesting. Illinois supplied the *coup de grace* in January 1987, sentencing Coleman to die for the kidnapping and murder of Vernita Wheat.

"I'm dead already," Coleman told the court before pronouncement of his sentence in Waukegan. "You are talking to a dead man." Satisfied that he was right, authorities declined to prosecute the couple in their four remaining homicides. To date, all appeals by Brown and Coleman have been rejected by higher courts.

BUENOANO, JUDIAS ANNA LOU

Born at Quanah, Texas, on April 4, 1943, Judias Welty was the daughter of an itinerant farm worker, named after her mother. In later years, Judi would describe her mother as a full-blooded member of the nonexistent "Mesquite Apache" tribe, but, in fact, they hardly knew each other. The elder Judias Welty died of tuberculosis when her daughter was barely two years old, and the family disintegrated. Judi and her infant brother Robert were sent to live with their grandparents, while two older siblings were placed for adoption.

It was all downhill from there, in terms of Judi's family life.

Reunited with her father in Roswell, New Mexico, after his next marriage, she found herself the target of abuse from both parents — beaten, starved, burned with cigarettes, forced to work slave hours around the house. At age fourteen, her anger finally exploded: Judi scalded two of her step-brothers with hot grease and lit into her parents with flying fists, feet, any object she could get her hands on. The episode cost her sixty days in jail, confined with adult prostitutes, but when the judge asked if she was ready to go home, Judi opted for reform school. She remained at Foothills High School — a girl's reformatory in Albuquerque — until her "graduation" in 1959, at age sixteen, and she would despise her family from that day on. Of brother Robert, she once said, "I wouldn't spit down his throat if his guts were on fire."

The year 1960 found Judi back in Roswell, working as a nurse's aide under the pseudonym of "Anna Schultz." She gave birth to an illegitimate son, christened Michael Schultz, on March 30, 1961, and ever after refused comment on rumors that his father was a pilot from the nearby air force base. On January 21, 1962, she married another air force officer, James Goodyear, and their first child — James, Jr. — was born four years later, on January 16, 1966, and Judi's husband celebrated by adopting Michael Schultz. Daughter Kimberly followed in 1967, after the family had moved to Orlando, Florida. A year later, Judias opened the Conway Acres Child Care Center in Orlando, listing her husband as co-owner despite his continuing service with the Air Force, which would soon include a tour of duty in Vietnam.

In fact, James Goodyear, Sr., had been home from Southeast Asia for barely three months when he was admitted to the U.S. Naval Hospital in Orlando, suffering with symptoms staff physicians never quite identified. He died on September 15, 1971, and Judi waited a discreet five days before cashing in his three life insurance policies. Before year's end, an "accidental" blaze at her Orlando home paid Judi another $90,000 in fire insurance. It was rotten luck all around... but at least it paid well.

Loneliness was not a problem for the recent widow. She moved her family to Pensacola in 1972, and was living with new lover Bobby Joe Morris the following year. Son Michael, meanwhile, had become a problem for his mother, raising hell in school, scoring in the "dull-normal" range on IQ tests. James Goodyear's death barred Mike from treatment at a residential facility reserved for military dependents, but Judi wangled an evaluation at the state hospital in 1974, farming her firstborn out to foster care with a provision for psychiatric treatment.

Bobby Morris moved to Trinidad, Colorado, in 1977, inviting Judi and her brood to join him. She hung around Pensacola long enough to collect fire insurance on a second house, then reclaimed Michael from foster care and moved west with her tribe, settling in Trinidad as "Judias Morris." Bobby Joe was admitted to San Rafael Hospital on January 4, 1978, but doctors could find no cause for his sudden illness, and he was released to Judi's care on January 21. Two days later, he collapsed at the dinner table and was rushed back to the hospital, where he died on January 28, his death officially ascribed to cardiac arrest and "metabolic acidosis." In early February, Judi cashed three life insurance policies on Morris, further fattening her bank account.

Bobby Joe's family suspected murder from the first, and Morris was not the only victim on their list. In 1974, Judi and Bobby Joe had been visiting Morris's hometown of Brewton, Alabama, when a male resident of Florida was found dead in a Brewton motel. An anonymous call, traced to a local pay phone, led police to the room where the victim was found, shot in the chest with a .22-caliber weapon, his throat slashed for good measure.

After the news broke, Bobby Joe's mother overheard Judi telling Bobby Joe, "The son of a bitch shouldn't have come up here in the first place. He knew if he came up he was gonna die." Later, raving in delirium on his deathbed, Morris blurted out, "Judi, we should never have done that terrible thing." Police in Brewton, meanwhile, report that they could find no fingerprints inside the room, no bullet was recovered from the corpse, and they have no firm suspects in the case.

On May 3, 1978, Judias legally changed her own last name and that of her children to "Buenoano," the Spanish equivalent of "Goodyear," in an apparent tribute to her late husband and mythical Apache mother. A month later, the family was back in Pensacola, settling into a home on Whisper Pine Drive, in suburban Gulf Breeze.

Michael Buenoano had continued his pattern of academic failure by dropping out of high school in his sophomore year, and he joined the army in June 1979, drawing an assignment to Ft. Benning, Georgia, after basic training. En route to his new post, he stopped off to visit his mother in Florida, and that was the beginning of the end. When he reached Ft. Benning on November 6, he was already showing symptoms of base metal poisoning. Army physicians found seven times the normal level of arsenic in Michael's body, and there was little they could do to reverse its destructive action. After six weeks of care, the muscles of his arms and lower legs had atrophied to the point where Michael could neither walk nor use his hands. He finally left the hospital wearing leg braces and a prosthetic device on one arm, the gear weighing a total of sixty pounds.

On May 13, 1980, Michael was canoeing with his mother and younger brother on the East River, near Milton, Florida, when their boat overturned. James and Judi — described in press reports of the accident as "Dr. Judias Buenoano," a "clinical physician" in Ft. Walton — made it safely to shore, but Michael sank like a stone and drowned. Local authorities accepted "Dr." Judi's description of the "accident" and closed their files, but army investigators were more persistent, launching their own search for evidence on May 27. Michael's military life insurance finally paid off in mid-September, to the tune of $20,000, and sheriff's officers began taking a new look at the case when they discovered two civilian policies on Michael's life. Handwriting experts suggested that Michael's signature on the insurance applications may have been forged.

Judi, meanwhile, went on as best she could without her eldest son, opening a beauty parlor in Gulf Breeze, dating Pensacola businessman John Gentry II. For Gentry's benefit, she fabricated a stint at nursing school, with Ph.D.s in biochemistry and psychology from the University of Alabama, plus a recent tour of duty as the head of nursing at West Florida Hospital. It was all nonsense, but Gentry swallowed the bait, indulging Judi's taste for expensive gifts, Caribbean cruises, and imported champagne.

In October 1982, John and Judi purchased life insurance policies on one another, Judi later boosting the coverage from $50,000 to $500,000 without Gentry's knowledge, paying the premiums out of her own pocket. By December, she was feeding Gentry "vitamin" capsules that produced dizziness and vomiting. Hospitalized for twelve days beginning December 16, Gentry noted that his symptoms disappeared when he stopped taking the "vitamins."

Even so, he was not suspicious enough to break off his relationship with Judi in the interest of survival.

On June 25, 1983, Gentry left a dinner party early, planning to pick up some French champagne for a private session with Judi. They had much to celebrate, it seemed, for Judi had told him she was carrying his child. John never made it to the liquor store, however, as a bomb exploded in his car when he turned the ignition key. Near death, he was rushed to the hospital where trauma surgeons managed to save his life.

Police got their first crack at questioning Gentry on June 29, learning for the first time of the victim's curious insurance scheme. A background check revealed the gaping holes in "Dr. Buenoano's" new biography, and Gentry was stunned to discover that her pregnancy was also a lie, Judi having been surgically sterilized in 1975. Detectives further learned that Judi had been telling friends about Gentry's "terminal illness" since November 1982, lately booking tickets for a world cruise including herself and her children... without Gentry.

It was enough for John, and he provided police with several of the "vitamin" capsules Judi had prescribed in 1982. Analysis revealed that they contained parformaldehyde, a poison with no known medical uses, but Florida's state attorney declined to file charges of attempted murder, citing "insufficient evidence" to prosecute.

On July 27, county officers and federal agents searched Judi's home in Gulf Breeze, retrieving wire and tape from her bedroom that seemed to match the Gentry car bomb. In James's room, they also found marijuana and a sawed-off shotgun, jailing him for possession of drugs and an illegal weapon. Judi, meanwhile, was arrested at her beauty shop on charges of attempted murder. By mid-August, authorities had traced the source of the dynamite used in the bomb, linking the Alabama buyer to Judi via phone records showing a dozen long-distance calls from her home.

Judi made bail on the attempted murder charge, but there was worse in store. On January 11, 1984, she was indicted for first-degree murder in the death of her son, with an additional count of grand theft for the insurance scam. Arrested that evening, she staged a fit of convulsions and wound up in Santa Rosa Hospital under guard.

The wheels of justice were sluggish, but there was no stopping them once they started to roll. Bobby Joe Morris was exhumed on February 11, with arsenic found in his remains. Identical results were obtained with the exhumation of James Goodyear, on March 14, 1984. Judi's trial in the first murder case — Michael's — began on March 22, and she was convicted on all counts nine days later. On June 6, she was sentenced to life imprisonment without parole for the first twenty-five years.

July found Florida authorities exhuming the body of late boyfriend Gerald Dossett, deceased since 1980, in another search for arsenic, but no charges were filed in that case. On August 10, James Buenoano was acquitted of trying to kill James Gentry, but his mother would be less fortunate. Judi's trial in that case opened October 15 and lasted three days; jurors deliberated a mere two hours before voting to convict, and Judi's 12-year sentence was made consecutive with her life term for Michael's slaying.

A year later, on October 22, 1985, Judi went to trial for the murder of husband James Goodyear. The trial consumed a week, with Judi denying any criminal activity, but jurors weren't buying her act. Convicted on her second charge of first-degree murder, she was formally sentenced to death on November 16. Her latest stay of execution was granted by a federal court in June 1990, and the case remains under appeal. In the unlikely event of Judi's release from Florida, Colorado authorities stand ready to prosecute capital charges in the death of Bobby Joe Morris.

BUNDY, CAROL

At age thirty-six, in January 1979, Carol Bundy seemed to have three strikes against her. An obese diabetic, nearly blinded by cataracts, she had left an abusive husband, moving her five- and eight-year-old sons into a small Los Angeles apartment. Carol was licensed as a vocational nurse, but failing eyesight left her unemployable, forced to walk with a white cane. Time and cash were running out, when suddenly her luck began to change.

The source of Carol's brand-new optimism was apartment manager John Murray, a 45-year-old Australian immigrant who sang part-time at Little Nashville, a country-western bar in North Hollywood. Murray befriended Carol, driving her to a Social Security office where she was deemed legally blind, thus entitled to payments of $620 per month. Next, Murray took her to an optometrist and had her fitted with contact lenses, enabling her to discard her cane and find work. Enraptured, Carol began inventing excuses to spend time with Murray, deliberately clogging her toilet and sinks, anything to bring the manager around. Soon they were lovers, but Murray was married, refusing to give up his family. In October, Carol approached his wife, offering $1,500 if the woman would disappear, but the effort backfired, with Murray berating her, coldly suggesting that she find other lodgings.

Three months later, in January 1980, Carol was pining away at Little Nashville when she met Douglas Clark, five years her junior, and the young man swept her off her feet. The son of a retired navy admiral turned international engineer, Clark had lived in thirty-seven countries by the time he settled in Southern California. He liked to call himself "the king of the one-night stands," supplementing his machinist's income through affairs with frowsy matrons, reserving his leisure time for kinky liaisons with underage girls. In private moments, Clark cherished dark fantasies of rape and murder, mutilation and necrophilia, yearning for the moment when his dreams could graduate to sick reality.

Clark moved in with Bundy the same night they met, working by day in the boiler room of a Burbank soap factory, devoting his nights to a crash course in ecstasy that made Carol his virtual slave. She swallowed her pride when he brought younger women home for sex, dutifully snapping photographs on command. One of Clark's conquests was an 11-year-old, picked up while roller skating in a nearby park, but Carol made no complaint as kinky sex gave way to pedophilia, increasingly spiced with discussions of death and mutilation.

On June 11, 1980, half-sisters Gina Narano, fifteen, and Cynthia Chandler, sixteen, vanished from Huntington Beach, en route to a meeting with friends. They were found the next morning, beside the Ventura Freeway near Griffith Park, in Los Angeles; each had been shot in the head with a small-caliber pistol. At home, Clark gleefully confessed the murders to Carol, regaling her with details of how he had forced the girls to fellate him, shooting each in the head as she brought him to climax. On June 15 and 22, a friend of Chandler's received telephone calls from a man who introduced himself as "Detective Clark," gloating over details of the double rape-slaying and telling the young woman, "Now I want to do the same to you." The caller made it clear, in no uncertain terms, that he was masturbating as he spoke.

In the predawn hours of June 24, Karen Jones, a 24-year-old hooker, was found behind a Burbank steakhouse, murdered by a single gunshot to the head. Later that morning, police were summoned to Studio City, where another female victim — this one headless — had been found by horrified pedestrians. Despite the missing head, she was identified as Exxie Wilson, age twenty, another veteran streetwalker.

That afternoon, while Bundy's sons were visiting relatives, Clark surprised her by plucking a woman's head from the refrigerator, placing it on the kitchen counter. He ordered Carol to make up the twisted face with cosmetics, and she later recalled "We had a lot of fun with her. I was making her up like a Barbie with makeup." Tiring of the game, Clark took his trophy to the bathroom, for a shower and a bout of necrophilic oral sex.

Newspaper headlines were already touting the crimes of a new "Sunset Slayer" by June 27, when Exxie Wilson's head was found in a Hollywood alley, stuffed inside an ornate wooden box. Authorities noted that the head had been thoroughly scrubbed before it was discarded by the killer. Three days later, a group of snake hunters near Sylmar, in the San Fernando Valley, stumbled on a woman's mummified corpse, identified as Sacramento runaway Marnette Comer. Last seen alive on June 1, the 17-year-old prostitute had been dead at least three weeks when she was found. Like other victims in the series, she was known to work the Sunset Strip.

And the murders continued. On July 25, a young "Jane Doe" was found on Sunset Boulevard, killed by a shot to the head. Two weeks later, hikers in the Fernwood area, near Malibu, turned up another unidentified corpse, dismembered by predators, a small-caliber bullet hole visible in the skull.

Despite her hot romance with Clark, Carol Bundy had continued visiting John Murray at the country-western bar where he performed by night. She did not hold her liquor well, and after dropping several hints about her newest lover's criminal activities, she was appalled by Murray's comment that he might report Doug Clark to the police. On August 5, she kept a midnight rendezvous with Murray in his van, parked two blocks from the bar, and she killed him there. Found four days later, the singer had been stabbed nine times and slashed across the buttocks, his head severed and missing from the murder scene.

It had become too much for Carol Bundy. On August 11, she broke down on the job, sobbing out to a fellow nurse, "I can't take it anymore. I'm supposed to save lives, not take them." Her friend tipped police, and they called on Bundy at home, confiscating three pairs of panties removed from victims as trophies, along with snapshots of Clark and his 11-year-old playmate. Arrested on the job in Burbank, Clark was still in jail four days later, when police retrieved a pistol from the boiler room. Ballistics tests would link the gun with bullets recovered from five of the known "Sunset" victims.

At his trial, serving as his own attorney, Clark blamed Carol Bundy and John Murray for the slayings, contending that they had patterned their crimes after the case of serial killer Ted Bundy (no relation). Jurors saw through the flimsy ruse, and on January 28, 1983, they convicted Clark across the board, including six counts of first-degree murder with "special circumstances," plus one count each of attempted murder (in the case of a surviving prostitute), mayhem, and mutilating human remains. Strutting before the jury in the penalty phase of his trial, Clark declared, "We have to vote for the death penalty in this case. The evidence cries out for it." The panel agreed with his logic, and he was sentenced to death on February 15.

Three months later, at her own trial for murdering Murray and one of the unidentified women, Carol Bundy first pled insanity, then reversed herself and admitted the slayings. According to her statement, John Murray was shot in the head, then decapitated to remove ballistic evidence. She had also handed Clark the gun with which he shot an unnamed prostitute, found dead along the Sunset Strip in July 1980. Convicted on the basis of her own confession, Bundy received consecutive terms of twenty-seven years to life on one count, and twenty-five years to life on the other.

CALBECK, LORENE

In retrospect, there seemed to be no warning of the violence that erupted from the mind of 34-year-old Lorene Calbeck. She was a "neat freak," true enough, but that spoke well of a housewife with three young daughters. Looking back, neighbors in her Polk County, Florida, trailer park had no explanation for the grisly events of May 24, 1956.

That afternoon, with her husband Mark off on a business trip to Michigan, Lorene packed her three children into the car for a drive. It is doubtful that the girls — five-year-old Shirley, three-year-old Pamela, and 18-month-old Jane — had any clue where they were going. Certainly, they could not have expected their mother to park on the roadside, draw a pistol from her bag, and shoot each of her daughters four times in the chest.

Driving back to her trailer, Lorene carried the small corpses inside, wrapped each one in cellophane, then telephoned the family doctor, asking him to drop by in half an hour. Finishing her ritual, she wrote out a suicide note, complete with instructions for her husband on how to water their small flower garden. That done, she sat down and fired two bullets into her own chest.

This time, her aim was faulty, and emergency physicians saved her life. A county grand jury refused to indict her for murder, remanding Lorene to the state hospital at Chattahoochee. Subsequently "cured" and released to her husband's care, Calbeck resumed a semblance of normal life, but three decades could not erase the haunting echoes of her mad rampage.

On January 3, 1989, despondent over husband Mark's recent death, Lorene carried a lawn chair and a .32-caliber pistol to the nearby Lake Wales Cemetery. Seated at the family plot, she pumped a slug into the left side of her chest. Still breathing, she staggered back to her car and drove home to her trailer off U.S. Highway 57. Paramedics responded to her emergency call, but this time they arrived too late, and Calbeck died on the ambulance ride to the hospital. A search of her trailer turned up another compulsive suicide note, including advice on the proper maintenance of her car and household appliances. Authorities honored Calbeck's request that she be laid to rest with her husband and daughters.

CAMPBELL, INEZ ETHEL

A native of Plentywood, Montana, born April 17, 1921, Inez Kapphann bore her first child out of wedlock at age seventeen. Little Johnny Kapphann never knew his father; he was barely one year old when Inez married Andrew Campbell, an employee of the Montana-Dakota Utilities Company, and they settled in rural Glasgow, Montana. Five more children followed in rapid succession: Janet in 1940; Jerry in 1941; Bud in 1942; Larry in 1944; and little Howard, the baby, in February 1945. If there was trouble brewing in the marriage, neighbors missed it by a mile.

And yet...

On May 25, 1945, with Andrew at work and three-year-old Bud off visiting relatives, Inez took the rest of her brood for a walk. Ostensibly, she was on her way to meet a neighbor named Clarence, who had offered to let the Campbells plant a small vegetable garden on his land. In fact, her trek ended at the midpoint of a bridge spanning the Milk River, where she produced a hammer and began to bludgeon her children in order of descending age.

Johnny was first, clubbed on the head and tossed into the river, where he somehow remained conscious, witnessing the slaughter of his siblings. Five-year-old Janet was next, followed in turn by Jerry, Larry, and three-month-old Howard. When she had run out of children to batter, Inez took the leap on her own and went down like a rock. All were drowned except Johnny, who struggled ashore and walked to the home of an aunt, at which time the police were called to the scene.

Back at the Campbell house, investigators found a handwritten note from Inez, addressed to "Dear brother," and signed "From your crazy sister." Department spokesmen said the note was incoherent, except for one line: "I know I was going crazy over it and cannot stand it any longer." Few would argue with the dead woman's self-diagnosis, but to this day no one knows what the "it" was that drove her to madness and murder.

CANNON, LUCRETIA PATRICIA

Lucretia Hanly, known as "Patty" for most of her life, was born near Montreal, Canada, in 1783. Her father was the son of a wealthy British nobleman, but he had blown his fortune and his reputation on "intemperance," hoping to start fresh in a new land. Sadly, for his wife and five children — of whom Patty was the youngest — Hanly's "fresh start" amounted to a career in smuggling and petty crime, climaxed by a trip to the gallows on conviction of murder. His widow opened a boarding house to support her brood, and it was there that Patty met her future husband.

Alonzo Cannon was a Delaware wheelwright, traveling on business. He only planned a brief stay with the Cannons, but illness stalled his departure and 16-year-old Patty was drafted to serve as his nurse, Mother Hanly plotting her strategy with a consummate matchmaker's skill. At the time, Patty was described by friends as "an uncommonly agreeable person and by no means bad looking, although rather large. She was extravagantly fond of music and dancing, a great talker, very witty and fascinating in her conversation." In fact, she seemed ideal to Cannon, his gratitude rapidly turning to love. They were married in 1799, and Patty returned with her husband to southern Delaware, settling near the town of Reliance, close to the Maryland border.

Despite its auspicious beginning, Patty's marriage was a brief one, marred by tragedy. Her only child died of apparent illness, three days after birth, and Alonzo followed in 1802, his death ascribed to "natural causes." (A quarter-century later, Patty would confess the murders of both husband and child.) Without family to lean on, Patty took a sudden turn for the worse, becoming "one of the most abandoned and notorious of women, giving loose to every species of licentiousness and extravagance." In short order, she moved a few miles down the road and opened a "low tavern," hand-picking a team of male accomplices who joined in trading slaves and killing well-heeled travelers for profit.

Guests at Patty's tavern rarely had to pay in cash for bed and board. Her hospitality was legendary, but it also had a down-side. Strangers with some extra money in their pockets would be welcomed to the fold like long-lost friends, seated at the best table in the house... with their backs to a convenient window. When the coast was clear, one of Patty's pet thugs would step up to the window and shoot the pigeon where he sat. Once the body had been stripped of cash and other valuables, it was consigned to a special basement cemetery, safe from prying eyes.

It was a rough and unforgiving life, but Patty held her own among the killers who surrounded her. In fact, she was tougher than most, renowned for her violent temper, able to hoist 300-pound grain sacks with ease. A servant or associate who crossed her faced the prospect of a one-way ticket to the cellar, and few were rash enough to rile their mistress twice.

In those days before secession and civil war, Patty's patrons included numerous slave traders, working the border between North and South. Inspired by the bankrolls they carried, Patty decided to enter the slave trade herself, dispatching her henchmen to Philadelphia in a search for likely prospects. There, her goon squad prowled the bars, luring free blacks aboard Patty's own slave ship for sale to the highest bidder. Once at sea, those too old or decrepit for sale were thrown overboard to drown, while Patty used a custom-designed club to brain any noisy or troublesome children. The "lucky" survivors were transferred to other slave ships, Dixie-bound, while Patty pocketed the cash.

Black children, in fact, were a special target of Patty's sadistic outbursts. One, age five, so angered Patty by some trivial offense that she ripped his clothes off, beat him senseless, and shoved his head into the fireplace, holding him there until he burned to death. Another black, her 15-year-old servant, threatened to run away and tattle to police after he witnessed a particularly gruesome murder. Patty responded by grabbing a shovel, beating the youth half to death, and locking him in the cellar with several fresh corpses to reconsider his threat. After two days with no food or water, Patty returned to the boy and asked if he still planned to squeal. When he defiantly replied in the affirmative, she grabbed a heavy stone and bludgeoned him to death.

Rival slave traders also fell prey to Patty's gang from time to time. One who stopped at the tavern, with two of his captives in tow, was beaten to death in his sleep, the hapless slaves held in Patty's clutches for another week, before they were sold to a dealer heading south.

Patty's neighbors, meanwhile, grew increasingly suspicious of the many guests who came but never seemed to leave her premises. In early 1829, a makeshift posse came to check things out, one member of the group pretending that he planned to build a house like Patty's, asking her permission for a look around the place. She welcomed them inside, but they were barred from visiting the cellar where she did her dirty work. At that, two members of the deputation met a female servant in the tavern, huddling briefly while her mistress was distracted in another room. The girl was clearly frightened, once alluding to "something terrible" in the cellar, clamming up with the advice that Patty would kill her if she said more.

Next morning, the county sheriff turned up on Patty's doorstep with a search warrant and twelve stout men to enforce it. Patty and several of her thugs were arrested, one of the hoodlums buckling under pressure and spilling everything he knew. Twenty-one blacks were released from the tavern, set at liberty, and basement excavation soon revealed Patty's personal boneyard. At her trial on murder charges, Patty and two male accomplices were sentenced to hang; three other cohorts escaped with seven-year sentences, pleading relative innocence through recent admission to the gang.

In April 1829, a few days before her scheduled execution, Patty swallowed a dose of poison in her cell and lapsed into raving hysterics, shredding her clothes, ripping handfuls of hair from her scalp, and snapping at jailers with her teeth. Finally subdued an hour before she died, Patty called for a priest to hear her confession. With deputies listening in, she admitted to poisoning her husband and killing her own newborn child, along with eleven more victims slain by her own hand. She further admitted participation, with her male cronies, in another dozen murders, but it was unclear whether she counted black victims as human beings, and the final tally may have been much higher.

An unnamed phrenologist received Patty's skull, anxious to test it for signs of "inherited criminal tendencies," but the results of his study were never published. As late as 1841, the skull was kept as a souvenir by Mr. O.C. Fowler, in Philadelphia.

CARSON, SUSAN

The bright, pampered daughter of a wealthy newspaper executive, born September 14, 1941, Susan Barnes appeared to have every advantage in life. In fact, severe dyslexia left her functionally illiterate when she dropped out of high school at age sixteen. It hardly mattered, with her family's money, and she soon married well, to Arizona businessman Leland Hamilton, bearing the first of two children at age seventeen. With motherhood behind her at an early age, Susan settled into a comfy routine of tennis, jogging, and country-club parties... but something dark and deadly simmered just below the surface, waiting to erupt.

Leland and Susan separated in 1970, the children remaining with Susan in Scottsdale for a time, until they wearied of her new life style and went to live with their father. In fact, Susan had begun to act "crazy," spelling her name with a "z" and dabbling in the occult, smoking weed and dropping acid, indulging in "artistic" vandalism, sampling an estimated 150 lovers — by her own count — between the breakup of her marriage and November 1977. By that time, she had settled on Islam as her religion of choice, but "Suzan" was unable to read the Koran or anything else, absorbing prescribed doctrine through lectures, making up bits and pieces to suit herself as she went along.

On Thanksgiving Day, 1977, Susan met James Clifford Carson, nine years her junior and recently divorced from his wife in Phoenix. They were on a double date, Susan paired with one of Carson's former classmates from the University of Iowa, but weed and acid blurred the guidelines of propriety, and they wound up in bed together. Next morning, Carson moved into Susan's unfurnished Scottsdale townhouse. It was love at first sight, Susan quickly informing Carson that his "true name" was Michael, "the name of an angel in the Bible."

It might have seemed an odd choice for a Moslem, but Carson didn't mind. They were "Michael and Suzan" from that moment on, blending their mutual love of drugs and loony-tune politics into new and dangerous configurations. Carson's father was a ranking oil company executive, tapped as an energy advisor to President Nixon in the early 1970s, but "Michael" was the family's black sheep. Weakened by a childhood illness that turned his bones brittle, Carson had become a bookworm, leaning toward Marxist tracts and founding a tiny SDS chapter in his Tulsa, Oklahoma, high school. Later, he drifted into the Twilight Zone of San Francisco's Haight-Ashbury district, somehow winding up at the University of Iowa, where he immersed himself in left-wing campus politics.

Now, he had "Suzan." Carson was absolutely smitten by her intelligence and sexual know-how, her gift of gab and wide experience in the occult. Susan was also obsessed with nudity, and they spent most of their days at the townhouse stark naked, dressing reluctantly when they were forced to go out for fresh supplies of food or drugs. In the summer of 1978, they sold their meager belongings and flew to Europe, stopping in London long enough to be "married" — sans license, in a free-form hippie ceremony — on June 21.

Back in Scottsdale as summer waned, Susan ran afoul of the law with her penchant for exhibitionism. Neighbors reported a nude woman cavorting on the lawn, and a flying squad of police rolled out to catch the show. Invading the townhouse without a warrant, officers found marijuana on the premises and slapped the cuffs on Susan. They refused to let her dress before the trip downtown, requiring her naked body as "evidence" of indecent exposure. In court, after months of legal wrangling, the felony drug counts were dismissed and Susan pled guilty to the exposure charge, receiving a sentence of six months probation. She emerged from the experience profoundly changed, embittered toward the government and laws in general, devoted to the prospect of a Moslem "holy war." As far as Carson was concerned, whatever Susan said was tantamount to gospel; if she said a revolution was required to cleanse the land with blood, so be it. He would tag along.

Early 1981 found the couple in Haight-Ashbury, soaking up chemicals, sponging room and board from various acquaintances. Their last known benefactor in The Haight was Karen Barnes (no relation to Susan), a 23-year-old doper, failed actress, and topless dancer who made room for "Suzan and Michael" in her basement flat on Shrader Street. None of them had been seen for several days when Karen's landlord dropped by on March 7 and found her dead, her skull crushed with a blunt instrument, stabbed thirteen times in the face and throat. As an afterthought, the killer had draped Karen's body with a quilt, slipping a pillow under her head. The name "Suzan" was scrawled across Karen's refrigerator in crayon, and neighbors recalled her live-in guests, but self-styled Moslems "Suzan and Michael" were nowhere to be found in San Francisco.

By mid-March, the Carsons were well into Oregon, hiking the Cascades and staking out an abandoned shack on a peak Susan dubbed "Allah's Mountain." In early May, she "felt the call of Los Angeles" and sent James off on an aimless two-week pilgrimage, thumbing rides around the Golden State while Susan kept the home fires burning in Oregon. Carson returned on May 24 to find her half-starved and hysterical, raving about the harassment she had suffered in his absence, from "witches" living nearby. James nursed her back to a semblance of health, plotting revenge on the neighbors, but he never got the chance to act. In August, before his plans were finalized, a ranger from the Bureau of Land Management arrived to evict them from their shack.

They hit the road with a vengeance, drifting through New Mexico, Arizona, Colorado, Montana, circling back to California. At Garberville, in Humboldt County, they found work on a marijuana farm, harvesting and curing the black-market crop. It was a fairly profitable occupation, and they earned enough to winter in Portland, Oregon, shunning regular work while Carson cranked out a rambling manuscript titled *Cry For War*. In essence, it was a mock-Islamic blueprint for revolution, complete with a hit list including such diverse targets as President Ronald Reagan, California Governor Jerry Brown, British Prime Minister Margaret Thatcher, the Ayatollah Khomeini, and cult killer Charles Manson. With spring's arrival, the self-ordained *hashashin* — Islamic assassins — drifted south once more, in search of prey.

March 1982 found them at Big Sur, California, where they rented a tree house from a local construction worker. Everything was cool at first, until they quarreled with their landlord and he sent a pistol-packing thug to kick them out. "Michael" took a beating in the process, but Susan was unwilling to let the matter drop. At her insistence, Carson brewed himself a batch of Molotov cocktails and went looking for revenge, torching the tree house, his landlord's cabin, and a tent occupied by his recent assailant. Holed up at an abandoned cabin in the wake of their blitz, Carson found a rusty .38 revolver and a box of ammo. Susan took it as "a sign."

Back in Humboldt County by April, they helped plant and irrigate the new marijuana crop, Carson standing guard with a rifle to keep narcs and poachers at bay. Trouble arrived in the form of Clark Stephens, a hard-core San Diego junkie who went out of his way to insult James and Susan. The tension reached its peak on Clark's third day at the ranch, following an altercation in which he hurled sexual insults at Susan. Three rounds from the rusty .38 shut him up for good, and Susan helped drag his corpse into the woods, where it was burned with kerosene and buried in a shallow grave.

The Carsons kept on drifting. On Tuesday, May 11, they were trudging through the Trinity National Forest, when they met a sheriff's posse on a search-and-rescue mission. Fearing arrest, they struck off through the trees at top speed, leaving the bewildered deputies to search their cast-off packs. Inside, they found a stolen driver's license, "Michael's" box of ammunition, and a manuscript of *Cry For War*.

The hunt began.

Eight days later and far to the south, James was arrested in Monterey Park on suspicion of rape, booked with an alias lifted from the stolen driver's license lost in Trinity County. Police were looking for a long-haired, bearded rapist, but the latest victim took one look at Carson and pronounced him innocent. He was long gone, reunited with Susan, when careless officers found his loaded .38, stashed behind the back seat of their patrol car, and new warrants were issued. A pattern was forming, but police still didn't know who they were looking for, or where the fugitives might be found.

Another piece of the puzzle was added on May 17, when the skeletal remains of Clark Stephens were found in Humboldt County. "Michael and Suzan" were down on the list as prime suspects, but where had they gone? Police in Northern California were desperate for leads, coordinating efforts with their brothers to the south, finally catching a break through Carson's sheer stupidity. Asked for a reference in Monterey Park, James had given his jailers the name of Susan's ex-husband, in Scottsdale. Phone calls and a visit brought the game full-circle, Leland Hamilton more than happy to fill in the blanks for his visitors in uniform.

The lawmen knew their suspects now, but finding them would still take time.

Thumbing rides near Bakersfield on January 11, 1983, the Carsons were picked up by motorist John Hellyer, and driven to Santa Rosa, seventy-five miles north of San Francisco. Along the way, Hellyer offended Susan by patting her knee and rubbing his leg against hers, dropping comments which she interpreted as satanic witch-speak. She had decided to kill Hellyer by the time they reached Santa Rosa, spending the night with a friend of Hellyer's before continuing the drive north. "Michael," she told Carson in bed, "either you kill that demon or I will."

Next morning, as Hellyer prepared to drop the couple at their chosen off-ramp, James drew a pistol and demanded money. They fought for the gun, tumbling from the pickup, and Susan lent a hand, stabbing Hellyer with her trusty boot knife. James finished their victim off with two shots in the head, but a passing motorist had seen it all, racing to alert police. The Carsons fled in Hellyer's pickup, the authorities in hot pursuit, finally ditching the truck in a vineyard and lighting out on foot. They were captured separately, trying to ford the Napa river at different points.

James told the Napa County booking officer his name was "Michael Bear," but he was running out of time and luck. Arraigned for Hellyer's murder on January 28, the Carsons were held over for trial without bond. Six weeks later, the news hit San Francisco after "Michael" wrote a peevish letter to the *Chronicle*, demanding publicity for himself "in the important press." One of the subscribers was a San Francisco homicide detective working on the case of Karen Barnes, still searching for "Suzan and Michael." Interviews were arranged on May 4... and the Carsons confessed everything.

Karen Barnes, according to the transient killers, had been marked for execution as a "witch" who dabbled in black magic and tried to steal Susan's "Moslem warrior" for some extramarital sex. In defense of their action, the Carsons cited matching texts from the Koran and Holy Bible, proclaiming: "Thou shalt not suffer a witch to live." John Hellyer was another witch, in Susan's estimation, and both male victims had sealed their own fates by "sexually abusing" Susan — Stephens through his insults, Hellyer by patting and "rubbing against" her leg.

Defense attorneys for the Carsons requested a psychiatric evaluation on October 23, 1983, but both defendants were judged sane and competent for trial. Eight months later, in June 1984, both were convicted of killing Karen Barnes, drawing terms of twenty-five years to life on July 2, 1984. Identical sentences were later pronounced in the cases of Stephens and Hellyer, providing a virtual guarantee that neither witch-hunter will ever make parole.

"CHAMBRE ARDENTE AFFAIR"

In the latter part of the 17th century, with the Inquisition already fading, France experienced a sudden rash of cases linking Satanism to the upper crust of affluent society. Between 1673 and 1680, at least fifty French priests were executed for performing Black Masses, with many additional clerics imprisoned, but none of those cases matched the scandal that eventually touched the very court of "Sun King" Louis XIV himself.

Exposure of the labyrinthine plot began one night in Paris, near the end of 1678. A wealthy socialite named Madame Vigoureux was hosting a banquet for friends, when one of her guests, Marie Bosse, began regaling the guests with her exploits as a well-paid fortuneteller for the cream of high society. Along the way, she let slip a curious comment: "Only three more poisonings, and I shall be able to retire with a fine fortune!" All the diners were amused, except for a young lawyer named Perrin, who filed the remark away and soon carried his tale to a friend on the Parisian police force.

Detectives in Paris were no strangers to murder by poison. Two years earlier, the infamous Marie de Brinvilliers had been executed for a series of aristocratic poisonings, and rumor had it that she was not the only practitioner in town. A quiet investigation was mounted, with the wife of a detective sent to purchase poison from the talkative Madame Bosse. In custody, Bosse began singing to save herself, painting her operation as strictly small-time, compared with the business conducted by one Catherine Deshayes, a.k.a. "La Voisin" — "The Widow."

Little is known of Deshayes' early life; the first public record of her existence dates from her marriage to Antoine Monvoisin, a Parisian street peddler of cheap costume jewelry. Catherine encouraged Antoine to open a small shop on the Pont-Marie, but the business failed and she began telling fortunes to make ends meet. "It was chiromancy and face-reading," she later told police, "that I learned at the age of nine." By the mid-1660s, Catherine's rituals had paid off well enough to finance a mansion in the St. Denis quarter of Paris, keeping herself and her husband in style.

La Voisin's home soon became the hub of Parisian occult activity, with affluent clients paying for animal sacrifices and "readings" of entrails. "Some women asked if they would soon become widows," Deshayes told police, "because they wished to marry someone else. Almost all asked this and came for no other reason. When those who come to have their hands read ask for anything else, they nevertheless always come to the point in time and ask to be ridded of someone, and when I gave those who came to me for that purpose my usual answer — that those they wished to be rid of would die when it pleased God — they told me that I was not very clever."

Deshayes got the point, and she soon began furnishing poisons in addition to her famous "love potions." Within a year, some of the wealthiest nobles in France were beating a path to her door, boosting Catherine's annual income above 400,000 francs — the modern equivalent of $50,000. Her first acknowledged victim was Judge Leferon, whose 50-year-old wife found him "insufficient" in bed. Deshayes supplied the poison that killed him on September 8, 1669, and word of mouth did the rest. Over time, her killing clients included such luminaries as the Duchesse de Bouillon, the Duchesse de Lusignan, the Duchesse de Vivonne, the Comtesse de Rouse, Madame de Dreux, Madame de Bauce, Madame d'Argenton... the list went on and on. Abortions were another specialty of La Voisin, expunging the evidence of indiscreet liaisons. Male clients, meanwhile, were less inclined toward murder than communication with the spirit world, pursuing social advancement by means of black magic. One such, the Duc de Luxembourg, paid Deshayes handsomely for arranging a personal meeting with Satan.

With friends in high places, Deshayes grew reckless. She was drunk much of the time, disporting herself with numerous lovers. One of her paramours was Andre Guillaume, the chief executioner of Paris, who furnished the severed limbs of murderers for refinement into black ritual candles. Deshayes also displayed a taste for sadomasochism, encouraging one young lover to slap her around in public, while another was ordered to beat Catherine's husband each morning, for La Voisin's amusement. Her home became a virtual freak show, populated by the likes of Romani (an Italian torture specialist), La Trianon (a hermaphrodite and alchemist), and various crones who took part in the ongoing black magic rites.

Finally arrested on March 12, 1679, Deshayes boasted of her crimes and social contacts, naming names for the police. Aside from husbands murdered by their wives with poison she supplied, La Voisin freely confessed to the ritual murders of some 2,500 babies, most of them buried in her garden or cremated in a furnace at her home. No final body count for poison victims was established, but excavation of several thousand bones bore out her story where the children were concerned, and La Voisin was burned alive on February 22, 1680. Her last recorded words sum up La Voisin's life: "I am loaded with so many crimes that I could not wish God to work a miracle and snatch me from the flames, because I cannot suffer too much for the sins I have committed." A witness to the execution reports that "She surrendered her soul to the devil very prettily."

At that, Deshayes was dead and buried before police uncovered the most bizarre aspect of her crimes. Returning for a final search of her home in the spring of 1680, detectives found a hidden ritual chamber, done all in black, with candles and a black drape covering a mattress on the altar. By July, Marguerite Deshayes was describing her mother's participation in satanic rituals, alternately led by a trio of Catholic priests identified as Abbe Guibourg, Abbe Lesage, and Abbe Mariette. Black Masses were performed at the Deshayes mansion on a regular basis, invoking this or that demon on behalf of paying clients.

First among La Voisin's customers, in fact, had been Francois-Athenais de Rochechouart de Mortemart, the Marquise de Montespan, chief mistress of King Louis XIV. Her specialty was the perverse "Amatory Mass," initially designed to win the king's love, and later — after she had borne him seven children — aimed at holding his affections when they went astray. Montespan herself had served as the nude "altar" for ritual sacrifice of infants, provided by Deshayes, with Abbe Guibourg invoking Astaroth and Asmodeus, the demons of love and lust. On more than one occasion, Montespan had smuggled renegade priests into the Royal Palace at Versailles, where they performed dark rituals. King Louis had been the unsuspecting recipient of "unholy wafers," concocted out of flour and the blood of murdered babies, but his wandering eye defied common magic. At last, a jealous Montespan planned to kill the king, but La Voisin's first attempt to poison Louis failed. A second attempt, scheduled for March 13, 1679, was forestalled by the witch's arrest.

With the exposure of a royal connection, King Louis established a special investigative commission. The group met in a black-draped room, lit with candles — hence its nickname as the *chambre ardente*, or "burning chamber." Some 442 persons were called to testify, with 218 imprisoned, thirty-six condemned (none of them aristocrats), and twenty-six banished (all nobles). Madame de Dreux, with two cousins on the panel, escaped with a reprimand for murdering her husband. King Louis ultimately quashed the probe to spare himself from scandal, and Madame Montespan went free, remaining with the royal court for another decade. Abbe Guibourg, then sixty-seven, was sentenced to prison, where he survived for three years chained to the wall of his gloomy cell. [See also: Brinvilliers, Marie de]

CHOATE, PEARL

Texas born in 1907, Pearl Choate was a veritable Amazon, standing well over six feet tall, tipping the scales at some 250 pounds in her prime. She earned her living as a private nurse, habitually serving elderly men with fat bank accounts. By the early 1950s, she had buried six husbands, all retired millionaires in their nineties who died soon after their weddings to Pearl. Death is hardly unusual at such advanced ages, but Choate had trouble with husband number six. It took four bullets to finish him off, and jurors discounted her plea of self-defense. Convicted of murder, she served twelve years before she was paroled for good behavior.

Back in Houston, good behavior was in short supply. Arrested for grand larceny, Pearl served another stretch in jail. In 1965, she met and married 95-year-old A.O. Birch, a millionaire living at Grand Prairie. Authorities suspected Pearl of homicide when Birch expired, in March 1966, but nothing could be proved against her. Angrily, she told the press: "They keep bringing up my other six husbands. What's that got to do with today's love? They were all about Mr. Birch's age when I married them. So what? I done the decent thing. You never heard of Pearl Choate not marrying a man. Pearl Choate don't shack up!"

CHRISTOFI, STYLLOU

A native of Cyprus, born in 1900, Styllou Christofi was tried in 1925 on a charge of murdering her mother-in-law by ramming a lighted torch down the old woman's throat. She persuaded a jury of her innocence and was released, but her problems with in-laws were not at an end.

In 1953, Christofi went to live with her son and his German wife in Hampstead, England. The women failed to hit it off, and things became so tense around the house that Hella Christofi announced her intention of taking the children to Germany for a holiday in July 1954. She let her husband understand that she did not expect to find his mother in the house when she returned.

On the night of July 28, Styllou ambushed her daughter-in-law in the bathroom, knocking her unconscious with an ash plate lifted from the stove. Dragging Hella into the kitchen, she strangled the younger woman with a scarf and tried to hide the evidence by pouring paraffin over the body, setting it on fire. In moments, the flames leaped out of control, threatening to consume the house and her grandchildren, sleeping upstairs.

At 1 A.M., a married couple parked near Hampstead station was approached by Christofi, babbling in broken English about a fire at her home. Returning with her to the scene, they doused the flames and found a woman's body, charred in places, with the livid mark of strangulation still visible on her throat. Police were summoned, and a neighbor came forward to describe Christofi stirring the flames around a prostrate "tailor's dummy."

Prison doctors found Styllou Christofi insane, but she refused to permit an insanity defense at her trial. Convicted and sentenced to death in October 1954, her subsequent appeals were dismissed and she was executed after three doctors pronounced her sane. Stavros Christofi did not attend his mother's hanging.

CHURCH, ELLEN

As the wife of a prominent doctor and mother of four, Ellen Church appeared to have the perfect life. Her husband, Dr. Brookes Church, was a microbiologist of national renown, and their union had produced four loving children — Elizabeth in 1944, Stephen in 1949, Katherine in 1956, and baby Kenneth in 1958. The family occupied a stylish home in Denville, New Jersey, and their neighbors had no inkling of the problems festering behind a calm facade.

On March 25, 1959, police were summoned to the Church residence on an emergency distress call. They found two-year-old Katherine Church beaten to death, her six-month-old brother Kenneth strangled; Elizabeth and Stephen had been dosed with sleeping tablets, but physicians saved their lives and both recovered without lasting physical damage.

In custody, Ellen Church admitted killing her two youngest children and trying to make a clean sweep with the pills. Her motive was a personal belief that she and all her offspring were insane. Psychiatrists agreed in Ellen's case, pronouncing her schizophrenic and unfit for trial. She was committed to a state institution for treatment.

COFFMAN, CYNTHIA LYNN

Born in 1962, Cynthia Coffman was the privileged daughter of a St. Louis businessman, raised by her parents as a devout Catholic. Abortion was unthinkable when she got pregnant at age seventeen, and she was forced into a loveless marriage, enduring five years of domestic captivity before she left home and fled west, traveling with little more than her car and the clothes on her back. She wound up in Page, Arizona, waiting tables in a diner, moving in with a local man after several weeks. In the fall of 1985, they were evicted from their small apartment after numerous complaints from neighbors of their drunken, all-night parties.

On May 8, 1986, Cynthia and her boyfriend were stopped for running a stop sign in Barstow, California. Police found a loaded derringer and a quantity of methamphetamine in her purse, but she was released on her own recognizance, the charges subsequently dropped. Her lover wound up serving six weeks in the county jail, and it was during one of Cynthia's visits that she first met his cellmate, the man who would irrevocably change her life.

James Gregory Marlow was doing time for the theft of his sixth wife's car when Cynthia walked into his wasted life. Born in 1957, he had been a dedicated thief from age ten, committed to Folsom Prison in 1980 for a series of home invasions and knifepoint robberies. Marlow served three years on that conviction, earning himself a reputation as "The Folsom Wolf," proudly wearing tattoos of the neo-Nazi Aryan Brotherhood.

It was love at first sight for Cynthia and James, her boyfriend instantly forgotten when Marlow hit the street and they left California together in June. Marlow had relatives in the Border South, and the couple began working their way through his family tree, sponging room and board where they could, ripping off any obvious valuables when they were finally asked to leave. In time, it reached the point where Marlow's relatives could see them coming, turning them away with angry words or pocket change, depending on the latest pigeon's mood. At last, they were reduced to sleeping in the woods, where Cynthia contracted head lice and James was forced to bathe in kerosene to rid himself of biting chiggers.

On July 26, 1986, Coffman and Marlow were linked to the burglary of a home in Whitley County, Kentucky, making off with cash, some jewelry, and a shotgun. Days later, in Tennessee, they were married. Cynthia celebrated the occasion by having her buttocks tattooed with the legend: "I belong to the Folsom Wolf." That done, they drifted west again, in search of easy prey.

On the evening of October 11, 1986, 32-year-old Sandra Neary left her home in Costa Mesa, California, to obtain some cash from the automatic teller machine at her bank. She never returned, though her car was found by police in a local parking lot. Two weeks later, on October 24, her strangled, decomposing corpse was found by hikers near Corona, in Riverside County.

Pamela Simmons, age thirty-five, was the next to die, reported missing in Bullhead City, Arizona, on October 28. Her car was found abandoned near police headquarters, detectives theorizing that she had been snatched while drawing money from a curbside ATM. Ten days later, on November 7, 20-year-old Corinna Novis vanished on a similar errand in Redlands, California. The latest victim had been kidnapped from an urban shopping mall in broad daylight.

Lynel Murray's boyfriend was worried on November 12, when the 19-year-old psychology student failed to keep a date after work. He found her car outside the dry cleaning shop where she worked, in Orange County, California, but another day would pass before her naked, strangled body was discovered in a Huntington Beach motel room. In addition to kidnapping and murder, there was also evidence of sexual assault.

Police were praying for a break, and when it came, the case unraveled swiftly. First, Corinna Novis's checkbook was found in a Laguna Niguel trash dumpster, tucked inside a fast-food takeout bag with papers bearing the names of Cynthia Coffman and James Morris. Around the same time, Coffman and Morris were linked to a San Bernadino motel room, where the manager found stationery bearing "practice" signatures of Lynel Murray's name. A glance at Morris's criminal record did the rest, and a statewide alert was issued for both fugitives.

On November 14, 1986, police were summoned to a mountain lodge at Big Bear City, California, where the proprietor identified his latest guests as Morris and Coffman. A 100-man posse found the lodge empty, fanning out through the woods for a sweep that paid off around 3:00 P.M., when the suspects were found hiking along a mountain road. Coffman and Morris surrendered without a fight, both wearing outfits stolen from the dry cleaning shop where Lynel Murray worked. Within hours, Cynthia led officers to a vineyard near Fontana, where they found Corinna Novis, sodomized and strangled, lying in a shallow grave.

Coffman and Morris were formally charged with that murder on November 17, held over for trial without bond. If any further proof of guilt were needed, homicide investigators told the press that fingerprints from both defendants had been found inside Corinna's car, and Coffman had been linked to a Fontana pawn shop where the victim's typewriter was pawned.

Another thirty-two months would pass before the killer couple went to trial, and in the meantime they experienced a falling-out, each blaming the other for their plight. On one jailhouse visit, Cynthia's lawyer asked if there was anything she needed from the outside world. "Yeah," she told him, pointing to her backside. "You can find someone to help me lose this damn tattoo!"

The couple's murder trial finally opened in San Bernardino County on July 18, 1989. Both defendants were convicted across the board, and both were sentenced to death on August 30. Cynthia Coffman thus became the first woman sentenced to die in California since that state restored capital punishment under a new statute in 1977. It seems unlikely that a woman will actually be put to death in "liberal" California, but the 1992 execution of Robert Alton Harris cancels all bets, making anything possible.

COLLINS, OPAL JUANITA

A Kentucky native, born in 1931, Opal Collins married for the first time at age fourteen. That stormy, short-lived union produced one child, and another was born of her second marriage, but neither child was living with Opal when she met Ben Collins, Jr., in 1953. A 26-year-old veteran of World War II, Collins had been paralyzed from the chest down in a 1947 auto crash. He retained the use of his arms and was able to operate a wheel-chair, hoisting himself in and out of bed with chains and pulleys.

Opal's relationship with Ben was strained from the start, her behavior erratic and unpredictable, soon degenerating into violence. In mid-1955, she locked Ben in a car after lighting his wheelchair cushion on fire and tossing it into the vehicle with him. Collins managed to break a window and open the door, dragging himself from the car, after which Opal extinguished the flames. Ben stayed away from Opal for a few months after that, but she continued to harass his family, driving by their home in Louisa, Kentucky, and honking her horn to attract attention.

In December 1955, the Collins family pulled up stakes and moved to Hammond, Indiana, settling in a new three-bedroom house. Living with Ben were his parents, Ben Senior and Julia, and his three younger siblings: 14-year-old Martha Ann, 11-year-old Mary Sue, and six-year-old Bobby. Everything was fine until mid-April 1956, when Opal turned up on their doorstep, asking to speak with Ben Junior. She was on her way to Columbus, Ohio, in search of work, Opal claimed, and she wanted to visit briefly before moving on.

In fact, she never made it to Ohio. Opal was invited to stay, and she eloped with Ben Junior on May 1, tying the marital knot in Crown Point. She found a job in Hammond, at a textile factory, but quit after one week, unable to get along with her co-workers.

At home, matters were even worse. Ben Collins, Sr., remarked that Opal "acted nice for three or four days after the marriage," then began "pouting and fussing" with her young sisters-in-law. Julia Collins horned in on the arguments, threatening Opal with a wrench and a beer bottle at different times, taunting Opal with the remark that she had used Opal's marriage license for toilet paper.

Still, the worst quarrels arose between Opal and Ben Junior, with money a frequent bone of contention. Opal resented the fact that she was not the beneficiary of Ben's $10,000 life insurance policy, and she nagged him to have her name placed on the title deed to their home. The arguments got physical, with Opal trying to strangle Ben in mid-May. On May 23, she blacked his eye, pulled his hair, and raked his face with her fingernails, leaving the crippled man's shirt stained with blood.

For Ben Junior, that assault was the final straw. He wanted Opal out and offered her $350 for the trip back to Kentucky, but she spurned the money, telling him, "It won't be that easy now." On May 25, Ben filed for divorce, citing Opal's heavy drinking and violence as grounds. That night, he advised his family to sleep elsewhere, fearing Opal's reaction to the divorce proceedings, but they had reassembled for dinner on Saturday, May 26.

As Opal later reconstructed events for police, she was talking to her husband around 4:30 P.M., in their bedroom, while Julia Collins huddled with her daughters in another room. "I heard Mrs. Collins say that she had asked me to leave," Opal said, "and if I didn't leave they would haul me out. I looked up and saw Mrs. Collins and the girls coming in the door of the bedroom. I remember going for the gun, but which one I shot first or how many times I don't know. The next thing I remember is shooting my husband."

According to investigators, Opal chased her three female victims into the living room, armed with Ben Junior's .22-caliber rifle, and killed all three of them there, pumping nine slugs into one body. Back in the bedroom, Ben Junior begged her not to shoot, but Opal responded, "If I can't have you nobody can." Bobby Collins, meanwhile, had run next door, sobbing for help and police were summoned to the scene. Opal was arrested at another neighbor's home, telling officers, "I'm the one that did it. I'm ready to go with you. I just shot up the whole damn family."

Later, in a written statement, Opal changed her description of the killings. "I got that rifle out," she wrote, "and walked into the kitchen and fired a shot at my mother-in-law, Julia. She ran to the living room, as did Martha Ann and Mary Sue. There I shot Julia. I don't know how many times. Then I shot the two girls. But I don't know which I shot first or how many times. Then I went into my husband's bedroom and he was in his wheelchair... Then I shot him one time."

Tried on one count of murder, in the death of Mary Sue Collins, Opal filed a plea of innocent by reason of insanity. Jurors disagreed, finding her both sane and guilty. On October 26, 1956, Opal Collins was sentenced to die in Indiana's electric chair.

COLUMBO, PATRICIA ANN

Born June 21, 1956, Patricia Columbo enjoyed an idyllic childhood in suburban Elk Grove Village before her brother Michael came along, in April 1963. Overnight, she found herself relegated to second place in her parents' affection, father Frank Columbo doting on his infant son and heir, mother Mary assigning Patricia to "look out for" her younger sibling. Bitter jealousy was the result, marked by ghoulish nightmares at age twelve, vicious arguments flaring with the onset of adolescence.

In junior high school, Patricia quickly learned that her blossoming body would bring the attention she craved. She began to experiment with hair dyes and provocative clothing, her parents responding with curfews and a ban on dating before age sixteen — at which time, they decreed, brother Mike would be tagging along as her chaperone. Predictably, the new restrictions only heightened Patricia's resentment, and in 1972 her rebellion found its focus in the person of Frank de Luca.

At age thirty-four, Frank de Luca was married with five children, a pharmacist who met Patricia Columbo while she was working part-time in a coffee shop, next door to his drug store. They hit it off at once, Frank "coming on" to Patricia with all his dubious charm, soon hiring her to sell cosmetics in his shop. Frank Columbo was concerned by his daughter's obvious infatuation with a much older man, but when he approached de Luca, warning that Patricia was "developing a crush," de Luca merely stared across the counter at him, refusing to speak. More worried than ever, Patricia's parents took her to a priest for counseling, unnerved by the clergyman's description of their daughter as "a bad seed."

Before long, Patricia and de Luca were having sex on a regular basis, Patty's obsession consuming her life. At school, she displayed snapshots of herself having sex with Frank's dog. Fierce arguments at home intensified when she dropped out of high school, four months short of graduation, to work with de Luca full-time. Soon after her seventeenth birthday, Patricia was arrested for charging expensive items to a stolen credit card. When Frank Columbo came to bail her out, she raged at him, "You motherfucker! Don't talk to me. This is all your fault." She told psychologists the spending spree had been designed "to get back at my parents," a rationale that juvenile authorities called an "adjustment reaction to adolescence."

In April 1974, Patricia left home, moving in with Frank de Luca and his family. At work, de Luca boasted of his dream come true, servicing his wife and teenage mistress simultaneously, but Marilyn de Luca seemed ignorant of the torrid affair going on beneath her own roof. When Mary Columbo phoned a warning to de Luca's wife, Marilyn responded, "You don't understand. We're trying to straighten your daughter out."

The Columbos caught a glimpse of hope soon after Patricia's eighteenth birthday. Patty was leaving de Luca, she said, and looking for another job. Her parents fronted the money for an apartment in suburban Lombard, crushed when they learned Frank de Luca had left his family, moving in with Patricia while they paid the rent. Frank Columbo confronted de Luca at work, armed with a shotgun, beating him up in the drugstore's parking lot and threatening his life. Patricia signed the assault complaint that landed her father in jail overnight.

Enough was enough. The Columbos changed their wills without Patricia's knowledge, leaving all but a flat $5,000 legacy to brother Michael in the event of their deaths. Despite her new status as persona non grata in the family home, Patricia kept turning up to provoke fresh arguments, targeting Mike in particular. More than once, the Columbos came home to discover that someone had tampered with windows and doors.

The Lombard apartment, meanwhile, had become a sexual fantasy world for Patty and de Luca. Together, they indulged Frank's every twisted whim, Patricia having sex with strangers while he watched and photographed their coupling, masturbating with wine bottles, letting Frank's dog lick maple syrup from her vagina. The reels of film and snapshots — some blown up to poster size — were Patty's record of their love for one another.

Life was not a bed of roses, even so. De Luca lived in fear of Patty's father, more than half convinced that Frank Columbo had obtained a "contract" on his life through Mafia connections in Chicago. Patty fed the fantasy with convoluted tales of mob connections, already plotting to wipe out her family for the presumed inheritance she would receive. She made no secret of the murder plan with friends, though Frank de Luca was apparently omitted from the early plotting stages.

In September 1975, a girlfriend introduced Patricia to one Lanyon Mitchell, a fast-talking car dealer who liked to boast of his nonexistent mob connections. Patty spelled her problem out, and Mitchell put her in touch with Roman Sobczynski, a Cook County employee who posed as a Mafia hit man. Sobczynski suggested the "hits" could be purchased for $10,000 a head, but Patricia was painfully short of cash. Sobczynski saw his opening and suggested an alternate method of payment. "What do you want me to do," Patty asked him, "put my cunt on the table?" The bogus gunman readily agreed, and Patricia promised to "fuck his eyeballs out" in return for the execution of her parents and brother.

Over the next few months, Patricia met Sobczynski and Mitchell frequently for sex, their orgies designated as "payment up front." For a time, Patricia limited her services to anal intercourse, insisting that "the rest is only for de Luca." By January 1976 she had dropped all restrictions, submitting to sex with several of Sobczynski's friends as partial payment for the promised triple murder. When not so engaged, she provided Mitchell with a full dossier on her family, including photographs of each and floor plans to the house in Elk Grove Village. By late February, with no hit in sight, her frustration was showing. Patricia pulled a gun one night, after bedding both men, and threatened to do the job herself if they kept stalling.

It was finally too much for Mitchell and Sobczynski. They stopped returning Patty's calls, and she turned to de Luca for help. With her parents dead, she informed him, the "contract" on his life would be canceled. She was also counting on her father's life insurance, a $100,000 policy, and proceeds from the house, which she would sell as soon as possible.

On the night of May 4, 1976, an armed prowler invaded the Columbo home in Elk Grove Village. Frank died in the living room, shot four times in the head with a .32-caliber pistol, bludgeoned with a crystal lamp. Upstairs, the gunman caught Mary Columbo emerging from the bathroom, panties still around her knees; one shot between the eyes knocked Mary sprawling, and her throat was slashed for emphasis. The worst violence was reserved for Mike Columbo, killed in his bedroom with a shot between the eyes, bludgeoned with a bowling trophy, stabbed ninety-seven times in the face, neck, and chest with a pair of barber's scissors.

No one had discovered the bodies by May 7, when police found Frank Columbo's car abandoned in a black Chicago neighborhood, one window smashed and the ignition stripped, its hubcaps and radio missing. Ownership was quickly traced, but Frank Columbo's telephone was off the hook. Elk Grove patrolmen paid a courtesy call and found the front door open, a scene of carnage waiting inside.

Patricia seemed unusually calm that evening, in her first interview with homicide detectives. Her parents had no enemies she said, suggesting that the killers were "kids high on drugs." Frank de Luca showed up with Patty for her second interview, on May 9, and while both appeared anxious to help, they left detectives with a distinct impression that they were "bullshitting."

By that time, homicide investigators had recovered a unique handprint from the trunk of Frank Columbo's car. Specifically, it was a left hand, with the second finger missing, but its owner was not listed in Chicago P.D.'s files. Detectives ruled out robbery as a compelling motive in the massacre, with quantities of cash and valuable jewelry untouched inside the house. Considering the wills, in fact, there seemed to be no motive for the crime at all.

The case began unraveling when Frank Columbo's employer offered a $5,000 reward for information in the case. Almost at once, police were approached by a friend of Patricia's, reporting that she had been plotting to murder her parents for months. An interview led them to Mitchell, and then to Sobczynski, revealing Patty's murder dossier. Patricia and de Luca were arrested on May 15, a search of their squalid apartment turning up Frank's library of homemade porno films and snapshots. De Luca's arrest also solved the mystery of the four-fingered suspect; as explained by Frank, his missing digit had been lost in a freak skydiving accident.

On May 17, Patricia reported having "a vision" of the triple murder in her cell. "I felt that I was there," she told police. "I'm confused. I see someone there with me. I believe I was there and did it." She later recanted the statement, too late to escape indictment on three counts of first-degree murder. Identical charges were filed against Frank two months later, and both defendants were held in lieu of $250,000 bond.

With de Luca safely in jail, his employees felt free to approach the police. Bert Green and Joy Heysek recalled de Luca boasting of the murders on May 5, describing one shot to Frank Columbo's mouth as payback for his own dental injuries, sustained in the parking lot beating. Green had found de Luca burning clothes in the drugstore's basement. "He said that the Columbo house was a mess," Green recalled. "He said he was a mess and said that he was covered from head to toe with blood." After spilling his guts to the help, de Luca tried to silence them with threats. According to Joy Heysek, "He said he would have my son run over on his bike, my daughter raped, and have me beat up so badly that no one would ever recognize me."

De Luca struck back at his enemies in February 1977, instructing his wife to post bail for a cellmate, Clifford Childs. Another inmate told police that Childs was working for de Luca, acting on instructions to eliminate two prosecution witnesses. Picked up for questioning, Childs readily admitted that de Luca had boasted of "the perfect murder," offering $10,000 each for the deaths of Bert Green and Joy Heysek. Childs had gone along with the charade, he said, "just to get out of jail." Overnight, he joined Lyman Mitchell and Roman Sobczynski on the list of prosecution witnesses who agreed to testify in return for immunity.

The Columbo murder trial opened in May 1977 and lasted six weeks, attorneys for each defendant trying to help their clients by casting doubt on the other. Chicago jurors saw through the ruse, deliberating barely two hours on July 1, before they convicted both suspects on all counts. A month later, on August 8, Patricia and de Luca received identical sentences of 203 years for murder and fifty years for solicitation of murder.

Controversy continued to haunt Patricia behind bars. In September 1979, she was accused of helping organize sex orgies at the women's prison in Dwight, Illinois, where she served as secretary for the director of internal investigations. Half a dozen female inmates reported they were forced to perform "deviate sexual acts" which they described as "totally humiliating." Patricia was named as the procuress for two high-ranking guards, with kinky sex exchanged for favorable work assignments. Both guards were fired when the inmates passed polygraph tests; Patty's boss, the warden, and his chief of security were forced to resign.

Eligible for parole since 1988, Patricia remains in touch with the press through her lawyer, lately blaming her father for childhood sexual abuse; on more than one occasion, she maintains, Frank brought friends home to rape her while he watched. Detectives on her case reject the story, insisting that their broad investigation found no evidence of child abuse. Off the record, speaking to one detective in private, Patricia sang a different tune. "If you hadn't stopped me," she told him, "I would have killed more."

COOPER, GLENDA

A New York native, born in 1943, Glenda Benson was still a teenager when she married welder James Cooper in Schenectady. Their marriage was blessed with three children — James in 1961, Joann in 1964, and Jeffrey in 1966 — but things began to go sour when they moved thirty miles to the small country town of Watsonville, in early 1967. Glenda disliked rural living, expressing an almost paranoid fear of prowlers. Her meticulous housekeeping soon took a turn for the worse, and she began neglecting the children.

In March 1968, Glenda was admitted to the hospital on James's complaint that she was "acting strange." (In fact, he feared that Glenda was following in the footsteps of her mother, committed to a state asylum in the late 1950s.) Transferred to a mental hospital for observation, she spent time in a closed ward before she was shifted to the general population. Glenda told her psychiatrist, a Dr. Funk, that she disliked sex and motherhood intensely. She claimed to have fallen in love only once, at age fifteen, but the relationship had not worked out. Her release was approved despite the fact that Glenda refused to initiate conversations, evaded straight answers to questions, and repeatedly expressed a wish to join her mother. Dr. Funk did not consider her violence-prone, but he suggested that Glenda separate from her husband. Sadly, no one heeded his advice.

On February 23, 1969, while James was working the night shift, Glenda picked up a hatchet and killed her three children in bed. Next, she set fire to the house and slashed her own wrists, lying down in bed to die, but the encroaching heat changed her mind, and she fled to a neighbor's home. Firefighters found her children — and the murder weapon — in the smoking ruins of her home.

Jailed on murder charges, Glenda told Dr. Funk, "It was a terrible thing I did, but better I did it to them than someone else." She admitted threatening her husband's life on one occasion, and expressed the hope that she would be convicted. "She knows she did it," Dr. Funk explained, "but she was afraid her husband would commit her to a mental hospital."

In another statement to police, Glenda seemed more concerned over the possibility that her husband would win custody of the children should they separate. District Attorney Robert Ecker emerged from a jailhouse interview to report that Glenda committed the crime "because she hated her husband." Convicted on three counts of murder in February 1970, despite a failed insanity plea, Glenda drew the minimum sentence of fifteen years to life on each count, her sentences scheduled to run concurrently.

COTTON, MARY ANN

The product of a teenage marriage, Mary Robson was born in October 1832, in the English mining town of Low Moorsly, in County Durham. She was an attractive, outgoing child, noted for her regular church attendance by age fourteen, hired out as a domestic servant in

South Hetton two years later. In July 1852, she married miner William Mowbray, six years her senior, and they spent the next five years traveling widely in search of work. When the Mowbrays returned to Durham in 1857, they brought a one-year-old daughter named Mary Ann. Mother Mary Ann told friends that she had lost four other children in the intervening years, all dying soon after birth.

And more babies followed. In the very year of her return to Durham, Mary Ann bore a child that died days later. Daughter Isabella came along in September 1858, Margaret June in October 1861, and son John Robert in November 1863. In the meantime, on June 24, 1860, four-year-old Mary Ann died of "gastric fever," prompting William Mowbray to purchase life insurance on himself and the surviving children.

It was a dangerous move.

John Robert was the next to die, in September 1864, the cause listed as "diarrhea." Four months later — on January 18, 1865 — William Mowbray was laid off work with an injured foot when diarrhea struck again, so violently that he died the same day. Margaret June was stricken with "gastric fever" in March, dying after a two-day illness. By April 1865, Mary Ann Mowbray was a widow with one surviving child — daughter Isabella — whom she left with her maternal grandmother, Mrs. Stott. Life insurance on William and two of the children paid her a total of thirty pounds sterling.

Mary Ann used her windfall to move from Durham to Seaview Harbor. There, she met and fell in love with 28-year-old Joseph Nattrass, but he was married and refused to leave his wife. Mary Ann found work as a nurse in the Sunderland infirmary, marrying ex-patient George Ward in August 1865. Ward lasted fourteen months before he died of "fever," leaving everything to his 24-year-old wife.

Next in line was widower John Robinson, a shipyard foreman with five children. Mary Ann moved in as his housekeeper in December 1866, and Robinson's youngest child — a 10-month-old infant — died of "gastric fever" a week later. In March 1867, when Mrs. Stott took ill, Mary Ann dropped by long enough to loot the house, collect nine-year-old Isabella, and see her grandmother buried at age fifty-four. By late April, Isabella was dead, along with eight-year-old Eliza Robinson and six-year-old James Robinson, Jr. "Gastric fever" was officially listed as the cause in all three deaths.

James Robinson saw nothing peculiar in the series of deaths, and he tied the knot with Mary Ann in August 1867. She bore him a daughter three months later, but the infant died of "gastric fever" in February 1868. Another child was born in 1869, but Mary Ann was already growing weary of marriage. Husband James refused her pleas to purchase life insurance on himself and the children, but he otherwise trusted Mary Ann to handle the family's financial affairs. She promptly set about draining his bank account, but the thefts were discovered before she could finish the job. James demanded repayment, but Mary Ann preferred to skip town, leaving her baby with friends.

At loose ends, Mary Ann drifted through a series of odd jobs. She served briefly as a prison matron in Sunderland, then went to work as a ship captain's housekeeper, selling his goods and absconding with the cash while he was at sea. In Spennymoor, she worked in a doctor's office until the physician caught her rifling his cashbox. From there, she moved on to the Northumberland mining town of Walbottle, where she befriended Margaret Cotton and was soon introduced to Margaret's brother Frederick, a widower with two sons. Margaret Cotton died a short time later, suffering from "gastric fever," and Mary Ann was pregnant with Frederick's child when they married in September 1870.

It was a bigamous union for Mary Ann, marred by the fact that she had never divorced John Robinson, but ignorance was bliss for her new husband. Mary Ann bore him a son, and life seemed idyllic until neighboring farmers complained that their hogs were dying in unusual numbers. Suspicion fell on the Cotton tribe, and local hostility grew to the point that Frederick soon moved his brood to West Auckland. Coincidentally or otherwise, they took a house on the same street where Mary

Ann's old lover, Joe Nattrass — now widowed — resided on his own.

Fred Cotton's luck ran out on September 19, 1871, when a virulent bout of "gastric fever" claimed his life. Three months later, Nattrass moved in with Mary Ann and her latest batch of children as a "lodger." Ten-year-old Frederick Junior was the next to die, on March 10, 1872, followed closely by infant Robert Cotton, fourteen months of age. Joe Nattrass, for his part, made the mistake of taking out a life insurance policy before he fell to "gastric fever" on April Fool's Day, 1872.

The last obstacle to Mary Ann's freedom was seven-year-old Charles Cotton. She first offered the boy to a neighborhood workhouse, but he was rejected. Taking the setback in stride, Mary Ann told supervisor Thomas Riley, "I could have married again but for the child. Well, he won't live long and will go the way of all the Cotton family." When Charles died of "gastric fever" on July 12, 1872, Riley remembered the comment and passed it along to police. An autopsy found traces of arsenic, with identical results for other members of the family as each one was exhumed.

Tried for murder in March 1873, Mary Ann insisted that the unlucky Cottons died from exposure to wallpaper colored with an arsenic-based dye. Prosecutors dismissed the claim as absurd, pointing to earlier victims who never set foot in the "arsenic room," and Mary Ann was convicted on all counts. She fainted when her death sentence was pronounced, but Mary Ann had regained her composure in time to mount the scaffold at Durham County jail, on March 24, 1873. Her status as one of Britain's most prolific serial killers had already been immortalized in a children's rhyme:

Mary Ann Cotton
She's dead and she's rotten
She lies in her bed
With her eyes wide oppen [sic].
Sing, sing, oh what can I sing?
Mary Ann Cotton is tied up wi' string.
Where, where? Up in the air.
Sellin' black puddens a penny a pair.

CREIGHTON, MARY FRANCES

On the surface, there was nothing remarkable about the marriage of Mary Frances Avery and John Creighton. They lived in New Jersey and produced two children there: daughter Ruth, born in 1910, and son Jackie, born in 1913. The trouble came about when they ran short of money and decided it was easier to kill than find a better-paying job.

In 1923, John and Mary were tried for poisoning Mary's brother, Raymond Avery, in hopes of reaping an insurance windfall. Prosecutors found circumstantial evidence that Mary had dosed Raymond with arsenic before his death, but in the absence of an eyewitness, jurors preferred to see no evil. Both defendants were acquitted and released.

A decade later, when the same fate overtook John's mother, authorities were instantly suspicious. This time, only Mary was charged with murder, but forensic experts disagreed as to whether the corpse contained a lethal amount of arsenic. Mary won her second acquittal, but enough was enough, and the Creighton family soon left New Jersey in disgrace.

They settled on Long Island, there befriending Earl and Ada Appelgate. Earl was a 36-year-old investigator for the Nassau County Veteran's Unemployment Bureau, but his salary was insufficient for him to purchase a house in those dark years of the Great Depression. Earl, Ada, and their two children were sharing quarters with Ada's mother, a situation that maximized tension for all concerned, until 1934, when the Appelgates moved in with the Creightons.

It was a change of scene, but hardly an improvement. The small two-bedroom quarters made for some curious sleeping arrangements, the most bizarre of which involved Earl and Ada inviting 14-year-old Ruth Creighton to share their bed. Ada raised no objection when Earl began having sex with the child, and John Creighton seemed oblivious when Mary joined Earl's list of conquests. Mary, for her part, would later claim she was blackmailed into bed,

Earl threatening to spread the story of her murder trials if she refused him.

Be that as it may, she offered no resistance in September 1935, when Earl brought home a bag of arsenic and briefed her on his plan to do away with Ada. On September 25, Mary spiked Ada's eggnog with the poison, and her dear friend's death was listed as a "heart attack." Reporters on Long Island smelled a story, though, and in a few days' time they went to press with stories summarizing Mary Creighton's early trials. The Nassau County prosecutor asked some questions, charging Appelgate with rape when Ruth admitted bedding "Uncle Earl." It was the final straw, and Mary soon confessed her role in Ada's death.

The defendants were tried together in January 1936, Mary's lawyer trying to create a sympathetic portrait of his client as a woman used, abused, and dominated by an evil man. It didn't work, and both were convicted of first-degree murder on January 30, sentenced to die for their crime. On July 19 of that year, Earl Appelgate walked to Sing Sing's electric chair under his own power. Mary Creighton, stricken with a sudden fainting spell, was wheeled unconscious to her death.

CRIMMINS, ALICE

An attractive New York divorcée with a free-swinging life style, later described as "amoral" by her own defense attorney, Alice Crimmins was twenty-six years old when her two small children disappeared from home on July 14, 1965. Four-year-old Alice, known as "Missy," was found hours later, clad in pajamas and strangled to death, her body still warm to the touch. Another week passed before five-year-old Eddie was discovered, a mile from home, advanced decomposition leaving the specific cause of death unclear.

When questioned by police, Alice Crimmins offered a precise description of her children's last night alive. She had fed them a meal of manicotti and string beans at 7:30 P.M., after which they both went to bed. Alice checked their room and found them sleeping peacefully at midnight, remaining awake herself until 4:00 A.M. on July 14. As the children's door was latched from the outside — to prevent their "raiding the refrigerator" — Alice concluded that a prowler had entered through the bedroom window, stealing both children away in the predawn hours.

Police thought otherwise, collecting evidence of the young mother's numerous sexual affairs and apparent neglect of her children, concluding that she viewed the kids as a disposable intrusion on her private life. Esteemed pathologist Milton Helpern performed the autopsy on Missy Crimmins, and his expert testimony ultimately doomed the suspect's precise timetable of events for July 13. Missy's last meal had indeed been manicotti and beans, Helpern found, but no appreciable digestion had occurred before she died. In Dr. Helpern's view, the 7:30 feeding was "impossible — just impossible."

Prosecutors believed that Crimmins killed her daughter in a fit of rage, then coldly planned the murder of her son to eliminate the only witness. Even so, the evidence on Eddie's death was vague, and Crimmins only faced charges on Missy's death at her first trial, in May 1968. The proceedings were enlivened by lurid testimony on Alice's sex life, and her fate was sealed when a witness recalled seeing Crimmins with an unidentified man on the night of the murders. Alice had been holding one child's hand, the witness said, and carrying an ominous bundle beneath her arm.

Convicted of first-degree manslaughter in Missy's death, Crimmins drew a prison term of five to twenty years. The verdict was overturned on appeal, when it was learned that several jurors had visited the murder site on their own time, playing amateur detective. A new trial was scheduled for March 1971, with prosecutors filing new counts of murder for both Crimmins children.

By this time, Alice Crimmins had become a *cause célèbre* for feminists who claimed that she was being persecuted for her "liberated" life style, rather than prosecuted for homicide. Her supporters were willing to ignore the scientific evidence in Missy's case, accepting Alice's tale at face value, casting blame on some anonymous male prowler — or the defendant's estranged husband — rather than blame an "innocent woman."

The second trial, lasting five weeks, was largely a replay of the first. One new twist was provided by a former boyfriend, testifying that Alice had confessed Missy's murder to him, back in 1965. This time, the implication was that Crimmins chose to kill her children rather than surrender them in the event she lost a pending custody battle to her ex-husband. Jurors bought the argument, convicting Alice of manslaughter in Missy's death and first-degree murder in Eddie's. Crimmins received concurrent sentences of life on the murder count and five years to life for manslaughter. The murder conviction was later thrown out on appeal, due to insufficient evidence, but the higher court cited "overwhelming proof" of the defendant's guilt in Missy's death.

Consigned to prison in May 1971, Alice Crimmins next made headlines in 1976, when New York journalists discovered her admission to a work-release program in Queens. Aside from routine office chores, she found the time to marry Anthony Grace, a wealthy contractor who admitted having an affair with Crimmins at the time her children died. Alice had been spending weekends on her lover/husband's yacht, a breach of protocol which did not interfere with her parole in September 1977. At this writing, the murder of her son remains technically "unsolved."

CSERY, LYDIA: See "ANGEL MAKERS OF NAGYREV"

CUNNINGHAM, ANNA

A native of Gary, Indiana, born in 1878, Anna Cunningham was married young to her husband David, eleven years her senior. They settled on a farm at Valparaiso, and Anna bore six children between 1897 and 1910. Life seemed normal in all respects until the spring of 1918, when 15-year-old Charles Cunningham accidentally shot and killed a neighbor's son. No charges were filed, but the whole family was traumatized, with Anna taking the shock worst of all. From the time of the shooting, her behavior grew unbalanced, sometimes violent, noted for her threats to murder those around her. A physician recommended that she be consigned to an asylum, but the family rejected his advice.

In July 1918, 51-year-old David Cunningham fell suddenly ill, dying after two weeks of agonizing stomach cramps. His life insurance paid Anna $1,000, and sale of the farm brought another $4,000 when she moved the family back to Gary. Anna's erratic behavior continued, her last doctor refusing to examine her again unless the family agreed to commit her. Instead, Anna's children found a new physician who pronounced her sound in body and mind.

In December 1920, 18-year-old Isabelle Cunningham died after two weeks of illness, complete with partial paralysis and agonizing cramps. Son Harry was the next to die, in October 1921, at age twenty-four. Charles Cunningham was nineteen when the family curse claimed his life in September 1922. Thirteen-year-old Walter went next, in September 1923. In each case, Anna's children lingered between ten days and two weeks from the onset of their mysterious ailments.

The family curse took a break in 1924, but 24-year-old David Cunningham was stricken the following year. Familiar symptoms set in one day after David ate a lunch prepared by his mother, and he lingered near death for two weeks before he recovered enough to resume working. Two days later, after yet another home-cooked meal, David was hospitalized in Gary, stricken with paralysis. He continued to fade, losing forty pounds over the next six weeks, before physicians managed to arrest his slide.

Through it all, the dwindling family remained oblivious, except for nephew George Arnold and his mother. Arnold later said of Anna Cunningham, "Whenever a member of her family was sick, she would write a letter to my mother, telling of the illness and predicting that the patient would die." When Anna wrote about David, the Arnolds urged her to have him hospitalized in nearby Chicago. At first, Anna resisted — "What's the use worrying about him?" she asked. "He'll soon die anyway." — but she finally relented and packed him off to a hospital where doctors diagnosed his condition as arsenic poisoning.

Police were summoned, and a search of Anna's home revealed large quantities of arsenic. "I've always kept arsenic in my house," Anna told detectives. "Lots of it. Why, only a short time ago I got a half-gallon of arsenic from a Gary drug store." It was Anna's habit, she said, "to spray my plants with it every spring." Seventeen-year-old Mae Cunningham also admitted buying poison "to kill rats," but she later changed her story to deny it.

Held for observation in a Gary hospital, Anna tried to strangle herself with a strip of cloth torn from a sheet. When a jailer foiled the suicide attempt, she blurted out, "Oh, I'm sick and I wanted to end it all." Psychiatrists diagnosed her as suffering from "epileptic psychosis, a dangerous mental condition." She was transferred to jail, but a sanity hearing was delayed while Anna lay rigid in bed, seemingly comatose. Physicians disagreed as to whether the condition was real or feigned, but similar "seizures" continued sporadically throughout Anna's trial.

On April 25, 1925, Anna confessed to poisoning Isabelle, Charles, and Walter with arsenic. She denied killing her husband or Harry, despite the fact that arsenic was found in Harry's remains, and no mention of David's condition was made, either way. Anna's explanation of the murders was peculiar: she not only killed her children out of love, but so that she would have more company in Heaven when she killed herself.

According to Anna's statement, she was so depressed by her husband's death that she sought to join him, but it grieved her to think of the children being left alone. Thus, each time she dosed herself with arsenic, hoping to die, Anna also poisoned her favorite living child. "Something seemed to draw in my head," she explained, "and told me I had to get rid of them. I thought I was going to die and wanted to take them with me. I only poisoned the ones I liked best in turn because I wanted them with me." (Daughter Mae survived because Anna liked her least, complaining that she spent too much time carousing in dance halls.) Oddly, Anna's suicide plan had a flaw. "There was something the matter with me," she told police. "I took as much as they, but I couldn't die."

No solid evidence of bungled suicide attempts was ever found, and Gary's sheriff remained steadfast in his opinion that "The woman is either an arch fiend or a maniac." Ruled sane and competent for trial, Anna Cunningham was convicted of Walter's murder in July 1925, and sentenced to a term of life imprisonment.

CURRY, SHIRLEY MARIE

An Arkansas native and mother of three, 30-year-old Shirley Curry was involved in a bitter divorce from her husband in 1967. The arrangement left Shirley with custody of the children, but there was a catch: each child was free to leave and join her husband at age fourteen. Daughter Sabrina was the first to exercise that option, and Shirley viewed the defection as a personal betrayal. According to family reports, she refused to see or speak with her daughter for the next seven years.

On Friday, July 19, 1974, Shirley was back in court, watching another child slip from her grasp. Richard Curry had expressed a wish to join his dad and sister some months earlier, and Shirley had replied with threats. The day her husband came to pick up Richard's things, she said, "I'll blow his guts out." Now, at age fourteen, her son received permission from the court to make his move. He would be leaving Shirley's home in Lowell on Saturday.

That Friday night, Shirley began her rampage at home, pumping bullets into Richard and 11-year-old Jessie, killing both. From there, she drove to her husband's home in Fayetteville, gunning him down when he answered the door, proceeding to Sabrina's bedroom and shooting her daughter twice in the head. Her next stop was Springdale and the home of her ex-husband's half-sister, 27-year-old Jo Ann Brophy, shot and killed by Curry in her own living room.

Finally, in nearby Farmington, Shirley ambushed her own sister's ex-husband, James Dodson, leaving him wounded with two close-range shots. Arrested the same evening, she asked police, "I missed the sixth one, didn't I?"

Authorities filed murder charges Monday, July 22, but Shirley was already slated for psychiatric examination, after telling a jailhouse matron she had never been happier, knowing her kids were in heaven. Deemed incompetent for trial, Curry spent the next four years in a state hospital before she was judged competent to participate in her own defense. Even then, four doctors testified that she was legally insane at the time of the shootings, but jurors disagreed, convicting her on two counts of murder and fixing her sentence at life without parole. (Separate charges were never pursued in the deaths of her two sons and Jo Ann Brophy.)

Curry's appeal wound its way through the courts over the next three years, asserting that jurors had erred in finding her sane. On February 16, 1981, the Arkansas Supreme Court ratified that verdict by a vote of five to two, the majority ruling that Curry's behavior throughout the shooting spree gave jurors ample grounds to question psychiatric testimony. One dissenting justice found the evidence of insanity "overwhelming," but his view did not prevail, and Curry's life sentence remains in effect.

CURTIS, LILLIE MAE

Texas born in 1900, Lillie Curtis spent her first thirty-eight years in Center, a farming community 200 miles north of Houston and twenty miles from the Louisiana border. Married as a teen, she bore nine children between 1919 and 1933, presenting the image of a perfect rural wife and mother. Whether she was truly satisfied or simply in a rut, she would not leave her small hometown until the Texas Rangers took her off to Huntsville, sentenced to 500 years in prison for multiple murder.

The first crack in Lillie's facade of domestic bliss appeared in June 1935, when she took up a pistol and killed husband Robert Curtis in his sleep. She never denied the shooting, but reports of her stated motive vary. In one version, she accused Robert of bootlegging and decided he had to go for the good of her children; an alternate story tags Robert with adultery and spousal abuse. Convicted of murder, Lillie got off with a five-year suspended sentence and the judge's stern advice to exercise more self-control in dealing with the trials of life. At the time, there was speculation that the lenient sentence may have hinged on doubts regarding Lillie's mental state.

On March 15, 1938, Lillie dropped by the local hardware store and purchased a .22-caliber pistol for $9.50. She told a clerk she needed it to chase thieves from her cornfield, but in fact she had another plan in mind. On March 16, with seven of her kids at home, she made her move.

"About two or three days ago is the first time I began thinking about killing my children," she told police the next day. "I was studying about trouble and how I was going to take care of the children and was in bad health and was unable to do nothing. About nine o'clock last night they, the children, all went to bed about the same time. Then I went to bed and stayed there about an hour and was just studying trouble, the fact that I was unable to take care of them; that is that I was not physically able and not able in way of money. I had not undressed when I went to bed and I was thinking kinda about killing them when I went to bed. The gun was under the bed and I got it and went to T.O. and he was laying on his left side and I put the gun to his breast and it was in front and I pulled the trigger. He just hollered — he did not get up, but hollered. That did not wake up the others."

Lillie proceeded to kill six of her seven children in the same manner. Sixteen-year-old Travis was spared because she thought "he could take care of himself." The dead included 13-year-old T.O., 11-year-old Gloria Jean, 10-year-old Billie Burke, nine-year-old Robert, seven-year-old Margie Ree, and five-year-old Marcie Jack. Each was shot in the left side, as Lillie did her best to kill them instantly with bullets to the heart.

"After I had shot them all," Lillie's statement went on, "I went back to see if they were dead. They all died pretty fast. None of them said anything at all. I could see most of them struggling. I did not say anything to them. I just kissed them all before I shot any of them, and then after I had shot all of them, I felt of them to see if they were dead and after they had all quit breathing I kissed them again."

Travis fled the house while this was going on and reached a neighbor's home, where the police were called. Authorities found Lillie in the woods, 400 yards from her home, and she pointed out the steps where she had concealed the murder weapon. Inside the charnel house, officers found a note from Lillie, reading: "I couldn't stand to see them starve to death and I didn't know what else to do with them." In custody, Lillie said, "I knew it was wrong to kill these children. I killed the father of these children about three years ago. I am sorry now that I killed them, and if I had it back I would not do it now."

At her trial, in April 1938, evidence suggested that Lillie's fears of poverty and starvation were all in her mind. A sister testified that the family had ample food on hand, together with a modest but adequate bank account. A panel of four psychiatrists agreed that Lillie was paranoid, informing the court that "there is no recovery for a paranoiac." Lillie herself testified: "The court ought not to try me for killing my six children. My children had not done anything to me to make me want to kill them. I guess my children would not have wanted me to kill them. I don't think the courts ought to do anything with me or try me, for I think my mind is bad. I don't feel right all the time. Over there, when I was being tried for killing my husband, they said my mind was not right, and I don't think it is right."

In lieu of pressing an insanity defense, Lillie's lawyer struck a bargain with the state. Prosecutors waived the death penalty in return for Lillie's guilty plea on five murder counts, with a sixth count held in abeyance. Under terms of the agreement, Lillie was sentenced to ninety-nine years on each murder count, plus the original five years for her husband's slaying, the sentences to run consecutively for a total of 500 years.

DAVID, RACHAL

Mystery surrounds the early life of Utah's worst mass murderess. Margit Brigitta Ericsson was born in Sweden on November 4, 1939, but little else is known about her life before she surfaced in Provo, Utah, during the early 1960s. She lived near the campus of Brigham Young University but was not enrolled for classes when she met and fell in love with student Charles Bruce Longo.

The son of a prominent New York physician, born in November 1938, Longo was raised without religious training but emerged from a four-year stint in the U.S. Marine Corps devoted to Mormonism. Baptized in 1958, he left for Uruguay as a Mormon missionary in March 1960. Over the next eleven months, church officials in Uruguay remarked on Longo's curious behavior, and he was back in the States by February 1961, dodging official recommendations that he seek psychiatric treatment. Enrolled at BYU that fall, Charles was known around campus as "an extremely devout man," but doubts were raised, in the words of Longo's faculty advisor, "when he blessed his first son to be a prophet."

It would take some time for that son to appear, but Charles and Margit were well on their way by 1963, with the birth of daughter Eva. Another daughter, Elizabeth, followed in 1964, and the growing family moved to Salt Lake City after Charles graduated the following year. Frank Longo was born in 1965, Deborah in 1966, Joseph in 1969, Bruce in 1970, and Rebecca in 1972. Long before then, however, Charles had run afoul of the church that seemed to dominate his life.

By 1965, Longo regarded himself as God's prophet on earth, destined to lead the Mormon church in a worldwide revival. Ranking elders disagreed, and when Charles persisted with claims of divine inspiration, he was formally excommunicated on June 18, 1969. Somehow, he managed to persuade a group of followers to join him when his family moved to Manti, settling there from 1969 to 1971. The cult was tiny but devoted, twelve adults and thirty-one children packed into a one-bedroom house, worshipping Longo as their messiah. On the side, Charles practiced throwing knives and honing his karate skills. He wore a three-foot sword and sometimes threatened those who angered him, including Judge Forest Washburn. Longo's sermons to the faithful included a promise to "lop off thousands of heads" if necessary, to promote the word of God.

In 1970, that Word decreed that Charles should change his name to one that sounded more religious. Henceforth, he would be "Immanuel David," while Margit became "Rachal David," the name-change ratified in court. Some of the children's names were also changed, with Eva switched to "Rachal," Frank to "Joshua," and Bruce to "David." The others, apparently, were considered pious enough as they were.

In 1971, the Davids moved to Duchesne, Utah, sharing a two-bedroom house with three other families, promoting Immanuel's curious view of the scripture. Neighbors in Duchesne were told that he expected a shipment of gold that would leave his commune "in clover." He was also corresponding with residents of Washington state, so he said, on plans to "take over the universe." Despite high hopes, the cult scraped by on food stamps and unrepayable loans, with debts piling up by the day. When David felt the heat at last, his family skipped to Salt Lake City, living in a series of hotels.

And overnight, their luck appeared to change. They suddenly had cash to burn, dining at expensive restaurants and settling the tab with hundred-dollar bills, shelling out an estimated $75,000 in rent alone over two years' time. In July 1978, Immanuel placed an order for two $47,000 pianos, seemingly confident of his ability to pay on delivery.

It was a strange life, even so. None of the children attended school, and they rarely left their hotel suite more than once a week. In public, they were forbidden to speak a word without their father's permission. Immanuel himself had ballooned to some 300 pounds, billing himself to the faithful as a one-man merger of Jehovah, Jesus, and the Holy Ghost.

Police, meanwhile, suspected that the prophet's business dealings were far from holy. By late 1976, several of his associates were in jail or facing indictment on various charges, and the FBI was tracking Immanuel on suspicion of wire fraud. That December, shots were fired into the family's hotel suite by persons unknown, and their car was set afire in the parking lot.

On August 1, 1978, Immanuel borrowed a van and drove to a point outside town, where he connected a hose to the exhaust pipe and gassed himself to death with carbon monoxide. His body was found the next day and Rachal, informed of his death, voiced concern that her family would soon be evicted from the Dunes Hotel for lack of funds.

At 7:20 A.M. on August 3, Rachal led her seven children onto the balcony of their eleventh-story suite, 250 feet above the street. A crowd of fifty horrified pedestrians stood watching as Rachal tossed six-year-old Rebecca over the side, the other children following one by one. "There was no emotion in the thing," one witness told the press. "They didn't scream and they didn't seem to fight." Observers disagreed on whether Rachal's older children jumped or were pushed to their fate, but the end result was the same. Six bodies tumbled to the street below, and only one — 15-year-old Eva/Rachal — survived, spending a year in the hospital before she was released to a foster home in July 1979.

With the children gone, spectators began to howl at Rachal, some calling for her to jump, others shouting at her to wait for help. She joined her children in the silent plunge a moment later, hurtling to her death. Officially, police in Salt Lake City described the incident as six homicides, one attempted homicide, and one suicide. No status report is available on the remainder of the David cult.

DCYZHESKI, NELLIE

The Great Depression brought financial ruin to thousands of families in the United States, but few suffered as tragically as the Dcyzheskis, of Saxonville, Massachusetts. In 1931, Paul and Nellie Dcyzheski lived with their four children in a two-bedroom tenement, owned by the Roxbury Carpet Company and reserved for employees. On December 31 of that year, Paul was stabbed in a neighborhood brawl, losing his job as a result. Eighteen months later, he was still out of work, 34-year-old Nellie taking up the slack at Roxbury Carpet as a part-time rug-loom operator.

Nellie's supervisor was so impressed with her work that he offered her full-time employment, managing a three-loom unit, but she was tired of the work and rejected the job. With no family members left on the company payroll, the Dcyzheskis received an eviction notice on May 23, 1933. Faced with the prospect of destitution and homelessness, Nellie decided the time had come "to get rid of the kids."

On May 24, Nellie sent eight-year-old Paul Junior to buy three gallons of kerosene she needed "for fuel." Husband Paul spent the night with his in-laws, after inviting Nellie's mother to visit that weekend. Unable to sleep for her financial worries, Nellie rose from bed near 11 P.M. and took a hammer to the bedroom where her children slept. There, in swift succession, she bludgeoned 11-year-old Irene, seven-year-old Chester, and five-year-old Eugene. Paul Junior woke in time to save himself and scurried to the basement, while his mother doused the flat with kerosene and struck a match. Firefighters found the boy in time to rescue him, and he was hospitalized in critical condition.

Autopsy surgeons confirmed that the other three children were beaten to death, and Nellie Dcyzheski was charged with three counts of murder. District Attorney Warren Bishop interviewed Nellie in jail, describing her as "a woman of culture and refinement. She asks for no sympathy or mercy, but rather begs for immediate punishment. In the most pitiful way she begged me to send her to the electric chair as soon as possible. She said, 'Why all this trouble? Why all this fuss? Why all this procedure? There is no problem here. There is no difficulty. I must be guilty, and I want to be punished. I don't know why I did it. I loved my children.'"

Instead of the chair, Nellie was committed to a psychiatric hospital for observation, claiming a total memory loss for the hours between 9 P.M. on May 24 and 8 A.M. on May 25. Deemed incompetent for trial, she was committed to a mental institution where she spent the rest of her life.

DEAN, WILLIAMINA ("MINNIE")

A native of Edinburgh, Scotland, born in 1847, Williamina emigrated to New Zealand in 1865 and soon married Charles Dean. They occupied a modest — some said squalid — home in East Winton, near Invercargill, and Minnie's flower garden soon became the talk of the neighborhood, renowned for its dahlias and chrysanthemums. Despite the pretentions that led them to call their home "The Larches," times were hard for Charles and Minnie Dean. By 1890, to supplement her husband's meager income, Minnie had begun to dabble in "baby farming." Two infants died in her care over the next year, and while both deaths were ascribed to "natural causes," official censure for unsanitary conditions at home led Minnie Dean to advertise her services under a variety of pseudonyms.

In April 1895, using the alias of "Cameron," Minnie ran a new ad for her service in the *Timaru Herald.* A Mrs. Hornsby responded, paying Dean four pounds to care for her one-month-old child, but the infant soon vanished without a trace. Witnesses recalled seeing Minnie with a baby in her arms at a local railway station, but she denied everything... until the missing infant's clothes were found at her home. Both Deans were arrested, and a search of "The Larches" revealed three babies buried in the famous flower garden. One of them was the Hornsby infant, and post-mortem tests blamed its death on a morphine overdose. Murder charges were inevitable after homicide detectives found a quantity of morphine in the house.

Further inquiry revealed that Charles Dean had been strictly forbidden to work in his wife's garden, barred even from plucking stray weeds, and he was ultimately freed without charges in the case. Williamina's trial before the Invercargill Supreme Court opened on June 18, 1895, and she was swiftly convicted of murder. On August 12, she entered history as the only woman ever hanged in New Zealand. Despite the nature of her crimes, some journalists appeared to be infatuated with the homicidal baby farmer, one article in *The Times* of London noting that she went to the gallows "without a flinch or falter; she died a brave, a wonderful woman." [See also: "Baby Farming"; Dyer, Amelia; Sach, Amelia; Waters, Margaret; Young, Lila]

DE MELKER, DAISY LOUISA

South Africa's most infamous "black widow" was born Daisy Hancorn-Smith, on June 1, 1886. She qualified as a nurse in 1907 and was engaged to marry Bert Fuller in March of the following year, but Fuller took ill before the wedding, dying in Daisy's care (and leaving her 236 pounds in his will). On March 3, 1909, she married William Cowle, a 36-year-old plumber, and their union produced five children. Four of those died in infancy with identical convulsive symptoms; only Rhodes Cowle, born in June 1911, would survive to adulthood.

By the early 1920s, Daisy de Melker had discovered the wonders of life insurance. In September 1922, she purchased a term life policy on Rhodes, scheduled to mature at his death or on his twenty-first birthday, whichever came first. Marriage had lost its appeal by this time, and she poisoned husband William on January 11, 1923, collecting the sum of 1,700 pounds from his life insurance policy. Daisy spent the next three years working at the Johannesburg Children's Hospital, before she met Robert Sproat and married him on January 1, 1926. It was a star-crossed union, and Sproat died suddenly on November 6, 1927... shortly after he agreed to change his will, leaving 4,000 pounds to Daisy, rather than to his mother.

Just over three years later, on January 21, 1931, Daisy married rugby player Sydney de Melker. Her one surviving child, now twenty-one years old, moved in with the family, hounding Daisy for a share of the inheritance from his father's death, hinting darkly that police might be interested in her long string of familial misfortunes.

Rhodes Cowle died suddenly on March 5, 1932, and while physicians in Johannesburg initially blamed malaria, Daisy's former brother-in-law, Alfred Sproat, felt differently. Suspicious of his brother's death, Sproat had been looking into Daisy's past and counting tombstones. The authorities were curious, to say the least. An autopsy revealed arsenic in Rhodes Cowle's remains; exhumation of his father and Robert Sproat showed that both men had been poisoned with strychnine. In Rhodesia, similar results were found for three of Daisy's late, lamented children.

Arrested in April 1932, Daisy stood for trial that October. In court, a pharmacist recalled selling her rat poison six days before Rhodes Cowle died. With the medical evidence in hand, it was more than enough to convict her on three counts of murder. Rhodesian officers were standing by in court to arrest her, in the event of an acquittal, but they were wasting their time. Sentenced to die for her crimes, Daisy de Melker was hanged at Pretoria Central Prison on December 30, 1932.

DESHAYES, CATHERINE: See "CHAMBRE ARDENTE AFFAIR"

DOSS, NANNY HAZEL

A daughter of Dixie, born in 1905, Nanny Doss had been molested by a string of local men before she reached her middle teens. At age sixteen, she married Charles Braggs, bearing him four children in rapid succession. Braggs was mystified when two of them died suddenly, a few months apart, but Nanny could offer no explanation. Each child had seemed healthy when Charles left for work, but they cried at his leaving and died in convulsions not long after breakfast.

Small insurance payments eased the pain a bit, but Braggs became increasingly suspicious of his wife. One afternoon, he took their oldest living child and struck off for parts unknown, leaving Nanny behind with their daughter, Florine. Packing up their meager belongings, Nanny moved to Cedar Town, Georgia, where she met and subsequently married Frank Harrelson. Florine was barely two years old when Harrelson and Nanny hit the road, leaving the child alone in their abandoned house. Neighbors managed to find Charles Braggs and he came to retrieve the child. Nanny would not see her daughter again for nine years.

Their reunion evidently smoothed things over, and by 1945 Florine — now married — felt secure enough to leave her infant son at Nanny's home in Jacksonville, Alabama, while Florine took off to see her father. Baby Lee survived three days in Nanny's care, his death producing anguished speculation that he accidentally "got hold of some rat poison." Three months later, Frank Harrelson fell suddenly ill and died within the week. Nanny used the insurance money to buy ten acres of land and build a small house for herself outside Jacksonville.

The early 1950s were a lethal time for Nanny's relatives. Her third husband, Arlie Lanning, died at Lexington, North Carolina, in 1952. A few months later, in January 1953, her mother died while Nanny nursed the older woman for a broken hip. Two of her sisters died the same year, in different towns; each collapsed while Nanny was visiting, each with the same mysterious symptoms of stomach cramps and convulsions. In 1953, it was husband number four — Richard Morton — laid to rest at Emporia, Kansas.

Nanny married her fifth and last husband, Samuel Doss, in Tulsa, Oklahoma, during July 1954. He died a month later, and the obligatory autopsy revealed enough arsenic to kill twenty men. Confronted with the evidence of guilt, Nanny Doss issued confessions spanning three decades and at least ten murders, drawing a term of life imprisonment for the Tulsa case in 1955. She served ten years before succumbing to leukemia in 1965.

Throughout her various confessions and the years in jail, Nanny insisted that money played no significant role in her crimes. Despite various insurance payments, her murders were actually motivated, she said, by marital boredom, a dream of discovering the ideal husband, as described in her favorite "true romance" magazines. "That's about it," Nanny told her interrogators. "I was searching for the perfect mate, the real romance of life."

DYER, AMELIA ELIZABETH

An Englishwoman, born in 1839, Amelia Dyer was an officer in the Salvation Army who resigned her godly commission and entered the sinister realm of "baby farming" after her husband left her in 1880. At first, she set up shop in Bristol, serving as the paid "foster mother" for an unknown number of infants and earning six weeks in jail from the illegal operation. In November 1891, she was admitted to Gloucester Asylum following a bungled suicide attempt. Two years later, in December 1893, she spent a month in Wells Asylum after trying to drown herself. In December 1894, she was returned to Gloucester Asylum, four "adopted" children retrieved from her home and packed off to the workhouse. Doctors described her as violent and prone to delusions, including hallucinations of birds speaking to her with human voices.

Feeling better after two months at Gloucester, Amelia was transferred to a workhouse where she stayed until June 1895. Upon release, she pulled up stakes and moved to Reading, anxious to resume her murderous adoption racket. It was there, through simple negligence, that homicide investigators finally exposed her lethal methods to the light of day.

The first discovery came about by accident. A barge was navigating up the Thames on March 30, 1896, when the pilot spotted a brown paper package floating in the water. He retrieved it with his punt-hook, startled to behold an infant's leg protruding from the soggy parcel where the wrapping had been torn. Police were summoned, and the package opened at a local mortuary to reveal a baby girl, her death attributed to strangulation with a piece of tape wound tight around her neck. Between the layers of wrapping paper, wet but legible, detectives found another scrap of paper with an address: "Mrs. Harding, 20 Wiggots Road, Caversham."

There was no Wiggots Road in Caversham, but officers discovered that a Mrs. Harding had resided until recently on *Piggot's* Road, departing to live with her daughter and son-in-law, Mary and Arthur Palmer, in Reading. By the time they reached her new address, the Palmers had moved on to London, but neighbors recalled Mrs. Harding leaving the house with a carpetbag one morning after the baby was found in the Thames. Inspector Anderson, in charge of the case, learned that Mrs. Harding was in the habit of "adopting" infants, and he waited for the woman to return, arranging for a female friend to call and inquire about placing an infant for adoption.

The undercover spy was greeted by a crone who introduced herself as "Granny Smith," informed that Mrs. Harding would be interested in the adoption, and a meeting was arranged in two days' time. Mrs. Harding kept the appointment on schedule and agreed to accept the child with no questions asked, in return for a payment of 100 pounds. The exchange was set for the following night, but Inspector Anderson showed up instead, with a uniformed sergeant to back him up. Confronted by police, "Mrs. Harding" admitted her real name was Amelia Dyer. "In a cupboard under the stairs," Anderson wrote, "we found a quantity of baby clothing and noticed a most unpleasant odor, as if some decomposing substance had been kept there. Doubtless, as subsequent events showed, the body of a little child had been concealed in this cupboard for some days before being taken out and disposed of."

Amelia Dyer was charged with murder on April 2, 1896, twice failing in jailhouse suicide attempts (with a pair of scissors and her own bootlace). By that time, the Thames was being dragged for evidence and yielding more remains. The decomposing body of a baby boy was found on April 8, a carpetbag containing two more tiny corpses on the tenth. A 10-month-old infant was next, with another boy rounding off the count at six a week later. All had been throttled, the strangling tape left around their necks like a signature by their killer. In custody, Dyer admitted "adopting" and killing children over a period of fifteen years, charging endless maintenance payments on some of her long-dead victims. Her memory was poor when it came to numbers, but she told police, "You'll know mine by the tape around their necks."

At trial, in May 1896, Amelia's lawyer advanced an insanity defense. Dr. Logan, of the Gloucester Asylum, recalled her violent outbursts and delusions of talkative birds. Dr. Forbes Winslow agreed that she was a victim of delusional insanity, complicated by depression and melancholia, but a Dr. Scott, the medical officer at Holloway Prison, denounced her delusions as feigned. Jurors were inclined to agree, deliberating a mere five minutes before they pronounced Dyer guilty and sane. She was hanged at Newgate Gaol on June 10, 1896. Two years later, the Palmers were tried as accomplices to Dyer's crime and both were convicted, sentenced to terms of two years at hard labor. In 1900, excavation at another of Amelia's homes unearthed remains of four more children, but police did not pursue the case. [See also: "Baby Farming"; Dean, Williamina; Sach, Amelia; Waters, Margaret; Young, Lila]

EDWARDS, LILLIAN

California born in 1906, Lillian Ralston was the daughter of a clergyman in San Jose. She grew up there and graduated from San Jose State College, teaching for three years in the Monterey County school district before she met and married Kenneth Edwards. The newlyweds settled in nearby San Francisco, where daughter Veryl Ann was born in 1931. Two years later, they moved to Fresno, California, and two more children followed — Donald in 1934 and Susan in January 1940.

With the birth of her third child, Lillian's mental state suffered a sudden and rapid decline. Soon after Susan's birth, she was admitted to a private San Francisco hospital for treatment of an unspecified "nervous disorder." Lillian spent several months there, before her September 1940 transfer to the Stockton State Hospital for the Insane. Staff doctors at Stockton diagnosed her condition as manic-depressive psychosis, noting a serious depression that gradually improved over the next two months. Lillian repeatedly asked to go home and care for her children, a wish that was granted on December 5, with her trial release for a one-month period. Dr. Margaret Smyth would later note that Lillian "always talked quite rationally. There was never any indication of any violent element in her nature."

In Lillian's absence, Kenneth Edwards had retained housekeeper Faye Reuter to care for the children, having her stay overnight when his job as a salesman took him away from home. On December 11, Edwards left Fresno on another business trip, remarking that "My wife seemed to be in pretty good shape. I felt more cheerful about her condition than I had in a long time." Fay Reuter also left the house around 7 P.M., reporting that Lillian Edwards seemed "perfectly rational at that time."

Soon after the housekeeper left, Lillian bathed her children, put them to bed... and then strangled each of them to death with strips of cloth torn from a bedsheet. Reuter arrived for work next morning to find Lillian dressed in a blood-spattered slip, bleeding from superficial cuts on her neck and both wrists, brandishing a knife. The housekeeper fled to a neighbor's home and telephoned police, who discovered the three children's bodies and took the dazed mother into custody.

In jail, Lillian appeared to have no recollection of the murders. She remembered putting her children to bed, but things got weird after that. "Then they came," she told authorities, "the man and woman in white, and unlocked the front door. They had lots of keys and a big black car. I don't care about myself, but I love my babies and they took them away to operate on them just like they did to me. Why wasn't Kenny there? He loved us and didn't want us to go away forever."

Recriminations followed in the wake of tragedy. Dr. Smyth, with an eye on bad publicity for Stockton Hospital, told reporters that Ken Edwards had promised Lillian would never be left alone with the children. Edwards, for his part, could remember no such promise, but he did blame Fay Reuter for leaving the house in his absence. Reuter, in turn, denied that Edwards had ever required her to stay in the house overnight.

It mattered little to the victims or their killer, either way. A panel of psychiatrists confirmed Lillian's amnesia as genuine, perhaps permanent, and she was judged incompetent for trial, swiftly returned to Stockton State Hospital for life.

ENRIQUETA, MARTI

A self-styled witch, who made her living through the sale of charms and potions, Enriqueta was arrested by police in Barcelona, Spain, in March 1912, jailed on charges of abducting and murdering local children. Her most recent victim, a young girl named Angelita, was rescued alive from the witch's lair, appalling police with a tale of butchery and cannibalism. According to the girl, she had been forced by Enriqueta to partake of human flesh. Her "meal" had been the pitiful remains of yet another child, abducted by the murderess a short time earlier.

As ultimately pieced together by authorities, the local crimes of Marti Enriqueta had already claimed at least six victims. After murdering the children, she would boil their bodies down for use as prime ingredients in her expensive "love potions." Convicted on the basis of her own confession, Enriqueta was condemned to death and executed for her crimes.

ETHERIDGE, ELLEN

A solid family background and religious training did not spare the second wife of Texas rancher J.D. Etheridge from pangs of jealousy. When they were married in the spring of 1912, she thought the wealthy widower admired her for herself. It soon became apparent, though, that he was more interested in finding someone who would cook his meals and clean his large Bosque County home, northwest of Waco. Ellen warmed his lonely bed and tended house, but she began to feel neglected as her husband showered his affection on the children — eight in all — who were the living images of her lamented predecessor.

Over time, the jealousy gave way to envy, then to hatred. During June of 1913, Ellen launched her plan to thin the herd, employing poison to eliminate a pair of the offensive children. On October 2, two more died, but the coincidence was too extreme. Authorities were curious, and poison was discovered by post-mortem tests. In custody, the second Mrs. Etheridge confessed her crimes and drew a term of life imprisonment.

FALLING, CHRISTINE LAVERNE SLAUGHTER

Christine Falling was born at Perry, Florida, on March 12, 1963, the second child of a 65-year-old father and his 16-year-old wife. Reared in poverty, obese and dull-witted, she required regular doses of medication to control her epileptic seizures. As a child, she showed her "love" for cats by strangling them and dropping them from lethal heights in order to "test their nine lives." At age nine, Christine and her sister were removed for a year to a children's refuge in Orlando, following domestic battles that resulted in police being summoned to their home.

In September 1977, at age fourteen, Christine was married to a man in his twenties. Their chaotic relationship lasted six weeks and was punctuated by violence, Christine once hurling a 25-pound stereo at her husband in the heat of battle. With the collapse of her marriage, Falling lapsed into a bizarre hypochondriac phase, logging fifty trips to the hospital in the space of two years. She complained of ailments ranging from "red spots" to vaginal bleeding and "snakebite," but physicians rarely found any treatable symptoms.

Rendered virtually unemployable by her appearance and mentality, Christine picked up spending money by baby-sitting for neighbors and relatives. On February 25, 1980 one of her charges — two-year-old Cassidy Johnson — was rushed to a doctor's office in Blountstown, tentatively diagnosed as suffering from encephalitis. The girl died on February 28, an autopsy listing cause of death as blunt trauma to the skull. Christine described the baby "passing out" and toppling from her crib, but she was unconvincing. One physician wrote a note to the police, advising them to check the baby sitter out, but it was "lost" in transit and the case was closed.

Christine moved on to Lakeland, and two months after her arrival, four-year-old Jeffrey Davis "stopped breathing" in her care. An autopsy revealed symptoms of myocarditis, a heart inflammation rarely fatal in itself. Three days later, while the family attended Jeffrey's funeral, Falling was retained to sit with two-year-old Joseph Spring, a cousin of the dead boy. Joseph died in his crib that afternoon, while "napping," and physicians noted evidence of a viral infection, suggesting it might have killed Jeffrey, as well.

Christine was back in Perry — and in business — by July of 1981. She had received a clean bill of health from the doctors in Lakeland, but her bad luck was holding. She tried her hand at housekeeping, but 77-year-old William Swindle died in his kitchen her first day on the job. A short time later, Falling accompanied her stepsister to the doctor's office, where an eight-month-old niece, Jennifer Daniels, received some standard childhood vaccinations. Stopping by the market on her way home, the stepsister left Christine in the car with her child, returning to find that the baby had simply "stopped breathing."

Thus far, physicians had sympathized with Christine as an unfortunate "victim of circumstance," but their view changed on July 2, 1982, when ten-week-old Travis Coleman died in Falling's care. This time, an autopsy revealed internal ruptures, caused by suffocation, and Christine was hauled in for questioning. In custody, she confessed to killing three of the children by means of "smotheration," pressing a blanket over their faces in response to disembodied voices chanting "Kill the baby."

"The way I done it, I seen it done on TV shows," Christine explained. "I had my own way, though. Simple and easy. No one would hear them scream." Convicted on the basis of her own confession, she was sentenced to a term of life imprisonment, with no parole for the first twenty-five years.

FAVATO, CARINO

An Italian faith healer known as "the Witch" in her Philadelphia neighborhood, Carino Favato cultivated an unsavory reputation in the late 1920s and early 1930s. Three of her spouses died under mysterious circumstances before she went into business full-time as a "marriage consultant," poisoning unwanted husbands for a fee. She might have gone on indefinitely, toiling for women's liberation on a local scale, if she had not encountered Dr. Morris Bolber in the early part of 1934.

A Philadelphia physician, Bolber had conceived a profitable murder scheme in 1932, collaborating with his good friend Paul Petrillo. After one of Bolber's female patients aired complaints about her husband's infidelity, the doctor and Petrillo planned for Paul to woo the lonely lady, gaining her cooperation in a plan to kill her wayward spouse and split $10,000 in insurance benefits. The victim, Anthony Giscobbe, was a heavy drinker, and it proved a simple matter for his wife to strip him as he lay unconscious, leaving him beside an open window in the dead of winter while he caught his death of cold. The grieving widow split her cash with Bolber and Petrillo, whereupon her "lover" promptly went in search of other restless, greedy wives.

It soon became apparent that Italian husbands, caught up in the middle of the Great Depression, carried little life insurance of their own. Petrillo called upon his cousin Herman, an accomplished actor, to impersonate potential victims and apply for heavy policies. Once several payments had been made, the husbands were eliminated swiftly and efficiently through "accidents" or "natural causes." Dr. Bolber's favorite methods included poison and blows to the head with a sandbag, producing cerebral hemorrhage, but methods were varied according to circumstance. One target, a roofer named Lorenzo, was hurled to his death from an eight-story building, the Petrillo cousins first handing him some French postcards to explain his careless distraction.

The trio had dispatched an estimated dozen victims when they heard about The Witch's deadly game in Little Italy. Impressed by Dr. Bolber's explanation of the life insurance scam, Favato came on board and brought the gang a list of her prospective clients, wives in search of some relief at any price. By 1937, Bolber's ring had polished off an estimated fifty victims, at least thirty of which were fairly well documented by subsequent investigations. With Bolber's signature on the death certificates, there were no questions asked.

The roof fell in when an ex-convict approached Herman Petrillo, pushing a new get-rich scheme. Unimpressed, Petrillo countered with a pitch for his acquaintance to secure potential murder victims, and the felon panicked, running to police. As members of the gang were rounded up, they "squealed" on one another in the hope of finding leniency, their clients chiming in as ripples spread throughout a stunned community. While several wives were sent to prison, most escaped by testifying for the state. The two Petrillos were condemned and put to death in the electric chair, while Bolber and Favato each drew terms of life imprisonment.

FAZEKAS, JULIA:

See "ANGEL MAKERS OF NAGYREV"

FIEDERER, ELIZABETH

A housewife and mother of three in Passaic, New Jersey, Elizabeth Fiederer seemed normal in all respects until the autumn of 1935. From early October through January 1936, she turned up almost daily at Passaic General Hospital, insisting that she suffered from terminal cancer, voicing fears that the disease would soon spread to the rest of her family. Doctors found no symptoms of cancer or any other malady, but Elizabeth rejected their diagnoses, her insistence growing strident over time.

At 7:30 A.M. on January 21, 1936, three early drinkers turned up at the tavern owned by Elizabeth's husband, Hans. They were surprised and disappointed to discover it was closed, and in their quest for beer they trooped upstairs to roust Hans Fiederer from his second-floor apartment. No one answered to their knock, and they were bold enough to force the door, recoiling from a cloud of noxious gas.

Inside the small apartment, Hans was dead, along with his three children: 13-year-old Tessie, 11-year-old John, and four-year-old Elsie. Elizabeth, though close to death, would be revived by doctors at Passaic General. Investigators found that someone had plugged the apartment's keyholes with wads of paper, then opened all the gas jets on the stove.

It was February 1 before Elizabeth recovered enough to be told that her husband and children were dead. "If they died," she sobbed, "why did you let me live?" She readily confessed the slayings to police, explaining that she had decided to spare her loved ones from cancer by killing them all while they slept.

Indicted on four counts of murder, Elizabeth appeared in court on February 14, 1936. Her lawyer declared, "The prisoner is unable to coherently comprehend her position and stands mute." The judge directed jurors to determine "whether the prisoner stands mute through obstinacy or by providence or an act of God." The panel deliberated for seven minutes before pronouncing Elizabeth insane, and she was instantly committed to a state asylum.

FORD, PRISCILLA JOYCE

One of eleven children, born in 1929, Priscilla Lawrence was the pride of her family in Berrien Springs, Michigan. Her hard-working parents were devout Seventh-Day Adventists, but few black families had a chance to see their daughters through college in those days. Priscilla went further, adding a teacher's certificate to her diploma. Popular with colleagues and students alike, Priscilla failed in her race for a seat on the local school board, but the final vote tally confirmed her solid margin of respect in the community.

Priscilla's one great failing was her choice of husbands. In all, she would marry four times, two sons born from the first union, a daughter from the second. That marriage, to William Scott, was a turbulent match that also yielded Priscilla's first arrest, for shooting her husband and turning the gun on herself. Both survived, but the scandal cost Priscilla her teaching job, and she left Michigan in 1968, taking her six-year-old daughter along for the ride.

Two more husbands would follow, one of them white, but Priscilla's main focus in life had already shifted to religion. Drifting across country, working a series of menial jobs, she became obsessed with the notion of her own divinity. Wynter Scott was nine years old when her mother began giving the girl marijuana as a "religious sacrament." Priscilla also considered subjecting her daughter to artificial insemination. As she explained to Wynter, "The child you shall have will be Jesus Christ, even as I am Jesus Christ."

The virgin birth was ultimately canceled, but Priscilla's other quirks kept her in touch with the authorities. While lodging with her son in Illinois, though drunk most of the time, she somehow convinced him that she had been invited to the 1972 Republican National Convention in Miami, to speak on the topic of religion. GOP ushers disagreed, and Priscilla's entourage was forcibly ejected from the convention hall.

Moving on to Reno, Nevada, in 1973, Priscilla was three times arrested on misdemeanor charges. Each time she went to jail, juvenile authorities took charge of Wynter; on the third occasion, they delayed the child's return until Priscilla found a job and place to stay. Instead, she took off for Chicago, breaking contact with her daughter's keepers for over a year. Her next — and last — contact with Reno authorities was a 1974 call to caseworker Susan Nelson, warning that she would "take the law into my own hands and dispose of you" if Wynter was not instantly released. (Finally discharged from foster care as a legal adult, Wynter Scott moved to Los Angeles, angrily rejecting further contact from the mother who abandoned her in Reno.)

By 1978, Priscilla was settled in Boise, Idaho, where she filed a $500,000 federal lawsuit against the Mormon Church, Seventh-Day Adventists, and Joseph Califano (Secretary of Health, Education and Welfare) for damages stemming from a conspiracy to make her suffer "the keenest anguish and a sense of God's displeasure and discrimination." The suit was dismissed, and Priscilla moved on to Buffalo, New York in 1979, logging eight arrests for drug possession, theft of services, and writing bad checks. Held for psychiatric examination, she told counselors of a persistent fantasy, in which she drove her car through a large crowd, killing many victims.

From New York, Priscilla moved on to Jackman, Maine. A telephone call to U.S. Attorney Thomas Delanty, in Portland, demanded federal action in the 1973 "kidnapping" of her daughter. Delanty recalls: "She said if I wasn't going to help her, she would get in her car and drive from Jackman to Portland and kill everybody she saw along the way."

In fact, she drove her black Lincoln Continental back to Reno, arriving in early November 1980. Employed as a gift wrapper at Macy's department store, Priscilla drank and brooded over the injustices of life for weeks before she finally put her fantasy in action.

Officer Pam Engle was rousting a drunk from the bus stop at Second and North Virginia Streets, on Thanksgiving day, when screams and screeching tires alerted her to a disaster in the making. Stunned, she watched a black Lincoln race along the crowded sidewalk of Casino Row, scattering bodies like so many bowling pins. At the next intersection, 64-year-old Tom Jaffe witnessed the massacre and swerved his own car in front of the Lincoln, forcing it to a halt in the middle of the block. Patrolman Steve Baring confronted the driver, noting a strong smell of liquor, and demanded her name.

"Priscilla Joyce Ford," the woman answered. "Sometimes I'm called Jesus Christ."

Transported to Washoe Medical Center for blood alcohol tests, Ford described herself as "a New York teacher, tired of life. I'm sick of trouble." Questioned by police, she added that "I deliberately planned to get as many as possible. A Lincoln Continental can do a lot of damage, can't it?"

Indeed. Along Casino Row, paramedics were busy transporting the bodies of five dead and twenty-four wounded pedestrians. A sixth victim would die before the day was out, leaving Priscilla to face six murder counts and twenty-three counts of attempted murder. Unable to raise the prescribed $500,000 bond, she remained in custody.

From jail, Priscilla said that she drank wine before the "accident" to make herself seem less malicious, and hospital records confirmed a blood-alcohol content of .162 — in a state where .10 is considered legally drunk. At the same time, Ford blamed the commands of disembodied voices for her rampage. The voices had been taunting her since June, she said, one urging her to plow through a Boston theater crowd, while another insisted "She's too much of a lady to do that." By November, Priscilla had identified the dominant voice in her head as belonging to Joan Kennedy, then married to Massachusetts Senator Edward M. Kennedy.

At Priscilla's December arraignment, defense attorney Lew Carnahan asked for a full-scale psychiatric examination of his client, and D.A. Cal Dunlap agreed. Two psychiatrists found her incompetent for trial, but Carnahan opposed institutionalizing Priscilla without a formal ruling of insanity... which would have rendered her immune to murder charges. Specifically, Carnahan objected to the use of psychotropic drugs which might leave his client *sane*, thereby scuttling a planned insanity defense. It took a Reno judge three months to settle the question, ordering treatment for Ford, and she was finally ruled competent for trial in July 1981.

Priscilla's murder trial convened in October 1981, dragging on for five months. The high point was Priscilla's own testimony, lasting for over three days. Beginning with a firm denial of her own insanity, she rambled on to cover a wide range of extraneous subjects. Newswoman Barbara Walters rated mention as "a wild, fierce beast." Priscilla had collected books on Nazism because "I've always had a soft spot in my heart for Hitler." She despised Mormons because "Joseph Smith did not see Jesus. I was Jesus." In closing, she told the jury: "I am human and I am divine. I don't like it any more than anyone else does. I don't want to be divine."

Jurors deliberated for thirteen hours before convicting Ford on all counts. The penalty phase of her trial consumed an unprecedented five days, climaxed with a sentence of death by lethal injection. Ford's subsequent appeals have been denied by higher courts.

FOSTER, LAFONDA FAY and POWELL, TINA MARIE

A native of Anderson, Indiana, born in 1963, Lafonda Foster was the daughter of an unwed teenage mother. She spent much of her youth shuttling between foster homes and the custody of various relatives. At one such stop, she was molested by a great-uncle who tortured the child, holding her feet against a hot furnace, when she complained of the sexual abuse. Lafonda started using drugs around age nine, and by her early teens she was a full-fledged alcoholic, falling back on various drugs and household solvents for a high when liquor failed to do the job. Frequently truant, she quit school after the ninth grade and experienced her first brush with the law, for shoplifting, at age thirteen. Between 1979 and 1982, Lafonda spent time in at least five different juvenile homes. By age eighteen she was hooking to support her drug habit, and the same year saw her sentenced to ten years in prison on conviction of second-degree robbery. (In fact, she served only one month before her release on five years probation.) Lafonda tried suicide at least three times, at ages twelve, fourteen, and nineteen, but she never seemed to get it right.

She would prove more efficient when it came to killing others.

Arrested for parole violation in 1983, Lafonda was released again when 65-year-old Oaklie May promised to find her an apartment and give her a job at his Lexington, Kentucky, supermarket. Acquaintances regarded Lafonda as May's lover, and the young woman never refuted that claim. Before May killed himself, later that same year, Lafonda met another hard-luck lady, Tina Powell.

Born Tina Hickey in 1958, a native of Youngstown, Ohio, Powell spent most of her undistinguished life in Lexington. Her alcoholic father left the family when she was four years old, and Tina dropped out of high school before graduation, producing an uncertain number of children over the next few years. In 1979, she briefly married a man named Powell, their union described by friends as "a destructive relationship." Tina's long string of arrests for public drunkenness began the following year; additional charges included endangering the welfare of a minor, carrying a deadly weapon, and obtaining a controlled substance by fraud. Tina was arrested when she failed to appear for trial on the latter charge, escaping with probation even after jailers found a quantity of Valium and marijuana in her cell.

Tina's parole officer, Rod Planck, recalls a typical incident: "I arrested her in my office one day for being real high on drugs. She came in that way, which is a violation of parole. She was hostile. She had terribly vulgar language. She had a very low self-esteem and was on a very self-destructive thing. Everything she did was for herself. She was out to have a good time and what she thought was a good time was getting high on alcohol and drugs. She was very promiscuous and would go with any guy who supported her with drugs and alcohol."

Together, Powell and Foster became regular fixtures on the Lexington saloon circuit. They were also lovers of a sort, more bisexual than lesbian, with Lafonda clearly the dominant partner. She took a fling at wedded bliss in 1985, the relationship ending when her husband tore their marriage license up and threw it in her face.

Aside from Tina Powell, Lafonda's most enduring connection in Lexington was Carlos Kearns, introduced to her by Oaklie May before May killed himself in 1983. An elderly man whose generosity often outweighed his good judgment, Kearns was fond of opening his home to human strays. Neighbor Charles Cowan remarked that "Carlos took in about everything that came along," but the old man also had a dark side. He had been convicted of assault in 1974, public intoxication in 1981, and twice for carrying a concealed weapon, in 1979 and 1983. (In response to the latter charges, Kearns took to wearing a pistol openly, strapped to his hip.) Kearns's wife Virginia, twenty-eight years his junior, also boasted convictions for theft in 1981, plus public drunkenness in 1981, '82, and '85. Apartment manager Mary Martin frankly described Virginia Kearns as "crazier than hell."

Lafonda lived with Kearns and his wife for a time, sharing their flat with live-in alcoholic Trudy Harrell, but her presence was constantly disruptive. She stole from Carlos when she felt the need, sometimes assaulting him when she was caught and he objected. Once, while bathing Kearns, she poured shampoo in his eyes and fled the apartment with $450 in cash.

In February 1986, Lafonda was arrested on drug charges and sentenced to sixty days in jail. She hit the street again on April 14, and reportedly spent the next nine days with Tina Powell in a chemical blur, brooding over real or imagined insults suffered from Kearns and his neighbors at the Skid Row apartment complex. Somewhere along the way, the wasted lovers started dwelling on revenge.

Foster and Powell turned up at the complex around 2 P.M. on April 23. Tenants saw them knocking at the Kearns apartment and that of a neighbor, 47-year-old Roger Keene, but Carlos wasn't answering and Keene — another drunk — was still locked up from his latest arrest for public intoxication. The women left, thumbing a ride with a man who drove them to the nearest liquor store, where they purchased a bottle of whiskey. He later drove them back to the apartment building and dropped them there, declining their offer of sex for money.

Tina and Lafonda were admitted to the Kearns apartment on their second try. Neighbors heard angry shouting through the flimsy walls, and Virginia telephoned police at four o'clock, complaining that two drunken women were in her apartment, refusing to leave. Patrolmen were dispatched to check it out and found Virginia "very intoxicated," raving furiously at Foster and Powell. The younger women, by contrast, seemed calm and collected, explaining that they had stopped by to give 73-year-old Carlos a bath. Both agreed to leave without argument, the officers reporting that "We considered Ms. Powell and Ms. Foster to be sincere in their concern for Mr. Kearns."

Tempers had cooled a bit by early evening, when neighbors watched seven passengers wedge themselves into Carlos' car. Along with Kearns and his wife, Lafonda and Tina, the group included Roger Keene (released from jail at 4 P.M.), 59-year-old Trudy Harrell, and 52-year-old Theodore Sweet, a friend of the others and a frequent visitor to the complex. Stopping at a drugstore, Lafonda was seen to grab Virginia Kearns and shake her violently. Around 7 P.M., they stopped at another store, where Carlos cashed a check for $25. The killing began soon after, and while details remain hazy, the night would end with five persons dead.

At 8:30 P.M., Lafonda entered a liquor store and asked manager John Haggard if he could give her some bullets. She expressed a desire to "shoot some rats," and Haggard handed over four spare cartridges. He also noted bloodstains on the passenger door of Lafonda's car and advised her to get it washed. She returned a short time later, with a clean vehicle and a request for more ammunition, but Haggard was fresh out of lead.

At nine o'clock, police found Trudy Harrell in the parking lot of a Lexington shopping mall. She had been shot in the back of the head, stabbed five times, then run over and dragged 100 feet by a car. Ninety minutes later, 45-year-old Virginia Kearns was found dead, shot in the back of the head, stabbed numerous times — with sixteen wounds in her neck alone — and flattened by a car.

Soon after midnight, officers were summoned to investigate a burning car, abandoned on a narrow service road, and they discovered three more victims. Theodore Sweet lay near the flaming vehicle, shot once in each ear, stabbed numerous times in the face, chest, and back. Beneath the car lay Richard Keene, shot twice, five stab wounds in his chest and twelve in his back, run over by a vehicle, his body partly burned. Carlos Kearns was found inside the vehicle, shot twice in the head and twice more in the neck, stabbed in the throat, run over by a car and seriously burned. Incredibly, Kearns was still alive when police reached the scene, but he died a short time later.

While police were still dousing the flames, Foster and Powell walked into a nearby hospital, asking the duty nurse to phone for a taxi. Their belligerent demeanor, blood-soaked clothes, and obvious intoxication prompted members of the staff to summon help from the authorities, and both women were jailed on charges of public intoxication, soon upgraded to five counts of first-degree murder.

In custody, the lovers had a sudden falling out. Lafonda told a cellmate, Ethel Kissic, that she planned to murder Tina with the other five, but she was stymied when her last few bullets would not fit her gun. The two defendants blamed each other for Lexington's worst mass murder, each denouncing her partner as the instigator and chief triggerwoman. Powell's attorney went further, comparing his client to a battered spouse who lived in terror of Lafonda Foster, fearing to oppose even the most bizarre plans.

At trial, in February 1987, neither woman denied the charges, falling back instead on the defense that they were both too high on booze and drugs to be responsible for their behavior. Jurors disagreed, convicting both defendants on all counts. Before sentence was passed, Lafonda told the court, "I don't know why Tina and I killed those people. I don't understand it. I know it wasn't for money or any logical reason." Powell drew a sentence of life imprisonment with no parole for the first twenty-five years, while Foster was sentenced to die.

Two days after their sentencing, Tina Powell signed an affidavit reversing her previous plea of innocence, naming herself as the brains behind the massacre. Prosecutors were skeptical, but the move earned Lafonda a new penalty hearing in July 1988. There, Powell pulled another switch, claiming her Fifth Amendment privilege in refusing to testify on Foster's behalf. With no new evidence before the court, Lafonda's death sentence remains in effect, still under appeal.

FREEMAN, JEANNACE and JACKSON, GERTRUDE

In recent years, "gay" activists have taken pains to defend homosexuality as a natural lifestyle, coded into the genes of specific individuals from the moment of conception, just as the majority of human beings are born "straight." The argument attempts to scuttle moralistic claims that homosexuals are somehow "warped" in childhood, either through sexual molestation or by exposure to some other "sinful" influence. It is an argument that rages long and loud on tabloid talk shows, probably incapable of a definitive solution.

One who disagrees emphatically with the revisionist approach is Jeannace Freeman, an active lesbian who attributes her "butch" outlook to rape by a male baby sitter when she was four years old. In later life, she often told acquaintances, "I'd vomit if a man touched me." Her brooding rage, in fact, extended beyond adult men to encompass males of any age... and it would ultimately lead to brutal homicide.

Born in 1941, Freeman was twenty years old when she met Gertrude Jackson, a divorced mother of two, twelve years Freeman's senior. They moved in together as lovers, sharing an apartment in Eugene, Oregon, with Freeman asserting her dominance from the start. She demanded that Jackson be nude at all times, except when her children were present, and even that concession to modesty chafed at Freeman's nerves. In time, she came to see the children — and especially Jackson's son — as an enduring obstacle to the affair.

On May 10, 1961, Freeman and Jackson drove the children to Oregon's Peter Skene Ogden Park. Once there, Jeannace took the kids for a walk, sending Gertrude away to kill time in the woods while she dealt with the boy she despised. With Jackson out of sight, Freeman quickly strangled the six-year-old boy, stripped his corpse, and slashed his tiny genitals with a knife before tossing him over a cliff, into Crooked River Canyon. Jackson returned in time to help strangle her four-year-old daughter, strip and mutilate the corpse, and drop it to the rocks below.

Picnickers found the bodies on May 12 and called police. When the discovery was publicized, a neighbor of Jackson's became suspicious, noting that she had not seen the kids around for several days. The neighbor told police of seeing Jackson, Freeman, and the children leave home on the tenth of May, but there had been no sign of either child since then. Detectives paid a call next door, and Freeman happily admitted her affair with Jackson. "I'm the butch," she told investigators, pleased to voice her general disgust toward men.

In custody, Gertrude Jackson soon confessed her role in the murders of her children. Both defendants were convicted of first-degree murder and sentenced to die in 1964, their sentences commuted to life imprisonment eight years later, when the U.S. Supreme Court voided existing statutes on capital punishment.

FREYDIS

North America's first mass-slayer of European descent was Freydis, the sister-in-law of Viking explorer Leif Ericson. Records are sparse from the era of Norse exploration, but we know that Leif colonized Greenland and Iceland around 1000 A.D., moving on from there to explore "Vinland," in the neighborhood of modern Nova Scotia and New England. Aboriginal natives, dubbed "skrellings," were the first to be attacked and slain, but over time the Norsemen turned on one another with a vengeance... and in one dramatic case, a spiteful woman was to blame.

As the wife of Leif's brother Thorwald, Freydis accompanied her husband's war party to Vinland, a few years after the Greenland colony was established. Harsh weather and resistance by the stubborn "skrellings" caused dissatisfaction early on, and Freydis stirred the pot by quarreling incessantly with two brothers, Helgi and Finnbogi, who claimed a substantial following of their own. By wintertime, dissent had split the Viking band in two, with Thorwald's clique residing in one camp, followers of Helgi and Finnbogi in another. The two groups barely spoke, but they had managed to avoid overt hostilities so far.

One morning in the early spring, Freydis rose before her husband, walking barefoot to the long house where the brothers lived. She woke Finnbogi, offering to swap his ship for Thorwald's, and Finnbogi readily agreed. Returning to her husband's bed, the scheming Freydis pressed her cold, wet feet against Thorwald's back, rousing him from sleep. He asked where she had been, and Freydis spun a tale that sealed the fate of her opponents in the other camp.

"I went to see the brothers," she explained, "to try to buy their ship, for I wished to have a larger vessel. They received my overture so ill that they struck me and handled me very roughly."

Enraged by the mythical assault on Freydis, Thorwald called his men to arms and marched against his adversaries, catching Helgi and Finnbogi asleep, disarming their group and binding the men before they could defend themselves. One by one, the captives were led from their cabin, hacked to death on orders from Freydis, but Thorwald drew the line at murdering five women in the party.

"Hand me an ax!" commanded Freydis, and she set upon the women by herself, killing all five before her rage was exhausted. Finally, smeared with blood from head to foot, she turned to Thorwald and his warriors, persuading them to keep the massacre a secret from their countrymen in Greenland. Sailing home in the long ship stolen from Finnbogi's party, Freydis and company informed Leif Ericson that the brothers and their followers had decided to stay on in Vinland. At the time, Leif accepted the lie with no questions asked.

FULLER, EDNA

No one ever promised Edna Fuller that her married life would be a bed of roses, but it would have been impossible for her to predict the thorny path that lay ahead when she tied the knot with husband Otto, four years her senior. A California native, born in 1890, Edna produced five children between 1915 and 1924, striving to raise them on the salary Otto earned as a night watchman in San Francisco.

The 1920s are remembered as an era of runaway prosperity, but the Fullers missed out, somehow. Evicted from an Oakland dwelling in February 1926, for failure to pay the rent, they had barely settled in a San Francisco apartment when more trouble arose. Landlord C.J. Mauer described Edna Fuller as "demented," complaining that she neglected her children and let them run wild, annoying the neighbors. "The mother acted queerly," Mauer said. "She would lock her three oldest children out of the house and they tore up shrubbery and kicked at doors. I don't think her two youngest ones ever saw the outdoors. The children whooped and yelled all day, and even past midnight at times."

Police investigated the complaints and found the family destitute, barely scraping by on Otto's salary of $140 a month. In mid-August, San Francisco's Society for the Prevention of Cruelty to Children cited Edna as an unfit mother, with her court hearing scheduled for early September.

Another eviction was pending when Otto Fuller left for work on the night of August 30, 1926. The family had twenty-four hours to leave their apartment and nowhere to go. As Otto left that evening, Edna told him, "I have found a place for the children and me." Surprised at her initiative, he went to work believing she had found another home for them to occupy.

In fact, the sad, "demented" mother had a rather different solution in mind.

It was shortly after 7 A.M. on August 31 when Otto returned to his two-bedroom basement flat. Inside, he found the gas jets open, spewing noxious fumes, his wife and children dead. Edna lay in one bedroom with her daughters, aged ten and two; in the second bedroom, Otto found his sons, aged eleven, nine, and four. The deaths were officially listed as a mass murder and suicide.

GALLEGO, CHARLENE ADELLE

The pampered only child of a supermarket executive in Stockton, California, Charlene Williams was born October 10, 1956. A certified genius, her IQ tested at 160 in high school, she also possessed a photographic memory and played classical violin well enough to rate an invitation from San Francisco's Conservatory of Music. Despite that early promise, though, she drifted into drug abuse at twelve, lost her virginity a year later, and qualified as a borderline alcoholic by age fourteen. A year later, she was boasting to classmates of her ongoing affair with a black college student — one of the few indiscretions she managed to hide from her doting parents.

Genius IQ notwithstanding, Charlene's extracurricular activities played havoc with her studies at Rio Americano High School, in Sacramento. She squeaked through graduation, but washed out of junior college in her first semester. Bent on becoming "a businesswoman," Charlene persuaded her parents to invest $15,000 in a Folsom gift shop, aptly christened "The Dingaling Shop." When that venture went belly-up, she tried her hand at marriage, with equally disastrous results.

Charlene's first husband, an impotent junkie, was discarded for failing to please her in bed. In retrospect, he thought the relationship might have gone better if he had played along with Charlene's plan to hire a prostitute for kinky threesomes, but he preferred to spend his money on heroin. Husband number two shunned drugs; he also shunned his bride, dumping Charlene after several weeks of marriage to live with another woman. On September 10, 1977, Charlene was shopping for drugs at a Sacramento poker club when she met the great love of her life.

Gerald Armand Gallego could have been a poster child for mandatory birth control. His father was the first man to die in Mississippi's gas chamber, condemned for killing two police officers, and Gerald had followed in the old man's footsteps, logging dozens of arrests from age thirteen. His adult record listed twenty-seven felony arrests and seven convictions, with outstanding warrants for incest, rape, and sodomy. By age thirty-two, he had also been married seven times — twice to the same woman — with several bigamous unions along the way. The incest charge related to his daughter, Mary Ellen, whom he had repeatedly molested from the age of six.

Despite the overwhelming down side, Gallego could turn on the charm when he chose, and Charlene piqued his interest at once. He laid siege to the petite blond divorcée with flowers and phone calls, sweeping Charlene off her admittedly shaky feet. A week after their first meeting, the love birds moved in together, renting a small house on Sacramento's Bluebird Lane.

Variety was the spice of life for Gerald Gallego, and monogamy ran against the grain. Charlene was willing to accommodate his taste for strangers, if it kept him home at night, and she made no complaint when he moved a teenage runaway into their love nest. Gallego enjoyed having sex with two women at once, but it was a different story when he came home early one afternoon to find the teenager sharing a dildo with Charlene. Enraged, he threw the youngster out an open window and gave Charlene the first of many beatings that would soon become a staple of their turbulent relationship.

The revelation of Charlene's bisexuality turned Gallego's world upside-down. The self-styled "macho man" was suddenly unable to perform in bed, except on those occasions when Charlene was subjected to forcible sodomy. Violence bred of frustration became a daily event in their home, Charlene sometimes giving as good as she got. In one free-for-all, Gallego broke a finger while punching Charlene in the face; she responded by splitting his scalp with a club, and Gerald was holding her at gunpoint when Charlene's mother interrupted the fracas.

In July 1978, Charlene dreamed up a surprise for Gerald's thirty-third birthday, inviting daughter Mary Ellen and one of her adolescent girlfriends to spend the night on Bluebird Lane. It quickly turned into an orgy, all three females serving Gerald, and his impotence seemed to be cured... for the moment.

Mary Ellen's departure brought a swift relapse, however, and Charlene conceived the idea of using "disposable sex slaves" to keep her man happy. They spent two months refining the plan, in which Charlene — dressed up to make herself look like a teen — would lure the chosen prey into her "Daddy's" waiting hands.

On September 11, 1978, 17-year-old Rhonda Scheffler and a friend, 16-year-old Kippi Vaught, disappeared from Sacramento, on a short walk to a local shopping center. Two days passed before their ravaged, battered bodies were recovered outside Baxter, fifteen miles away. Each girl had been sodomized by Gallego, forced to perform oral sex on Charlene, after which Charlene gnawed on their buttocks and breasts. After the rapes, both victims were bound and beaten with a tire iron, a single bullet fired into each skull at close range.

The experiment was a grand success, and the homicidal lovers celebrated by driving to Reno on September 30, where they were married with Charlene's parents as witnesses. Back in Sacramento, Charles Williams found his daughter a job in a meat packing plant, thereby satisfying Gerald's demand that she pay her own way.

On June 24, 1979, 14-year-old Brenda Judd and 13-year-old Sandra Colley vanished from the Washoe County fairgrounds, in Reno. Wheeling the murder van along a desert highway, Charlene grew so furious at Gerald's starting the rape without her that she swerved off the road and grabbed a gun, intent on killing him. Shots were exchanged, a bullet grazing Gerald's arm before the macho man called for a cease-fire, complaining that the van's abrupt halt had bruised his genitals. Temporarily out of action, Gallego watched Charlene molest both girls before he finished them off with point-blank gunfire.

Judd and Colley were still missing in 1982, when Charlene's jailhouse confession solved the mystery of their disappearance. In the meantime, she suggested they find two black girls for their next outing, but Gerald refused to "contaminate" himself with interracial sex. Finding herself pregnant three weeks after the second double murder, Charlene told her husband the good news. Gallego angrily insisted that she go for an abortion — at her own expense, of course.

On April 24, 1980, teenagers Karen Chipman and Stacey Redican disappeared from a Reno shopping mall, their remains discovered near Lovelock, Nevada, on July 27. Both victims had been sexually abused by the Gallegos, separately and in tandem, before they were beaten to death with a blunt instrument.

Five weeks later, on June 1, Charlene's parents joined the killer couple on another drive to Reno, where Gerald and Charlene repeated their marriage vows. This time around, Gallego used the name of "Steven Robert Feil," a false identity he had secured by stealing a policeman's I.D. card, using the vital information to request a "duplicate" birth certificate and driver's license for himself. If Charlene's parents questioned the curious move, they kept all doubts to themselves. Charlene was eight weeks pregnant on her wedding day, but this time Gerald took the news well, deciding the baby was "a keeper."

The "newlyweds" celebrated their second wedding with a fishing trip to Oregon. Linda Aguilar, age twenty-one, was four months pregnant when she disappeared from Port Orford on June 8, 1980. Relatives reported her missing on June 20, and her body was found two days later, planted in a shallow grave south of Gold Beach. Sexually abused by both Gallegos, the victim's skull was shattered, her wrists and ankles bound with nylon cord, but an autopsy revealed sand in her nose, mouth, and throat, indicating that she was buried alive.

Somehow, the latest murder failed to satisfy Charlene and Gerald, perhaps because they only had one victim to abuse. Tension mounted around the Gallego homestead, with neighbors calling police to break up screaming fights on July 12 and 14. Both times, Charlene convinced patrolmen that the sounds of combat emanated from their TV set, denying any conflict with her spouse.

On July 17, 1980, 34-year-old Virginia Mochel was abducted from the parking lot of a West Sacramento tavern, where she worked as a barmaid. For the first time, Gerald and Charlene drove their victim back to Bluebird Lane, smuggling her into the house under cover of darkness. Three times sodomized by Gerald while simultaneously performing cunnilingus on Charlene, the barmaid was also flogged with a rope and otherwise abused before Gerald dragged her back to the van and strangled her there. Mochel's skeletal remains, still bound with nylon fishing line, were found outside of Clarksburg, California, on October 30.

Three days later, around 1:30 A.M., 22-year-old Craig Miller left a Sacramento fraternity dance with his date, 21-year-old Beth Sowers. Moments later, friends observed the couple seated in a car outside, a rough-looking stranger sitting up front, on the passenger's side. One of Craig's friends was sliding behind the wheel, to make small talk, when Charlene Gallego appeared, slapping his face as she ordered him out of the car and sped away. Miller's frat brothers memorized the license plate, telling their story to police when Craig was found dead the next day, at Bass Lake. Beth Sowers would not be found until November 22, shot three times and dumped in a Placer County ditch.

Officers traced the vehicle to Charlene's parents, recording a flat denial from "Mrs. Steven Feil." The Gallegos promptly skipped town, but Charlene phoned her parents for money a few days later. Police were ready when the next call came, from Omaha, and FBI agents dropped the net on November 17, when Gerald and Charlene called for their money at a Western Union office.

The killer team of man and wife hung tough for eight months, but July 1981 found Charlene shopping for a way to save herself. On July 27, she offered a confession linking Gerald to the Miller-Sowers homicides, if only she could be released on bail. Prosecutors ignored her, and Charlene tried again on March 2, 1982, announcing her desire to clear *ten* murder cases in exchange for leniency. Police were skeptical until they heard the details, some resisting the plea-bargain even then, but the deal was struck by late summer. In return for testimony against her husband, Charlene would receive a maximum sentence of sixteen years and eight months in prison.

Gerald Gallego's first trial, in the Miller-Sowers case, opened on November 15, 1982, in Martinez, California. Jury selection took more than a month, with Gallego serving as his own attorney, and the trial dragged on through May. Charlene's self-serving testimony did the trick, and her husband was sentenced to death on June 22, 1983.

Transferred to Nevada for trial in the Chipman-Redican murders, Gerald became the target of an unprecedented public subscription campaign, with California residents donating $23,000 to help defray prosecution expenses. Gallego's second trial opened on May 23, 1984, with Charlene taking the stand on May 24. On June 7, jurors convicted Gallego on two counts of murder and two counts of kidnapping, recommending execution. Gerald received his second death sentence two weeks later, and his subsequent appeals have been denied.

Charlene, for her part, is also jailed in Nevada, for reasons of personal security. Exempt from further punishment, she will be eligible for parole in August 1997, at age forty-one.

GARCIA, GUINEVERE FALAKASSA

A Chicago native, born in 1959, Guinevere Garcia had three strikes against her by the time she entered elementary school. Her father fled the family home when Guinevere was born, and her alcoholic mother died fourteen months later, plunging through a second-story window in a drunken stupor. Raised by her maternal grandparents, Guinevere would later claim that an uncle sexually abused her from age six through her early teens. An unwed mother at age seventeen, she was convicted of prostitution and placed on probation the following year.

On August 8, 1977, paramedics were summoned to Guinevere's tiny apartment, arriving too late to save her daughter's life. Eleven-month-old Sara Swan had crawled into a plastic clothing bag, said Guinevere, and the child had stopped breathing before she was found. Attempts to revive her were fruitless, and police initially accepted Guinevere's description of an accidental death.

Detectives had a change of heart in 1981, when Guinevere was arrested on four counts of arson, charged with setting fires in three North Side apartment buildings. Two blazes broke out in Guinevere's building by mid-September 1977; the others were recorded in buildings she occupied on the third and fourth anniversaries of Sara's death. Further investigation revealed that Sara had been suffocated following an argument between Guinevere and her boyfriend, prompting interrogation that produced a murder confession. In 1982, Guinevere pled guilty to her daughter's slaying and was sentenced to twenty years in prison. Paroled in March 1991, she was on the street barely four months when she killed a second time.

Little is known about Guinevere's marriage to 60-year-old George Garcia. Acquaintances would later describe George as "crazy" about his young bride, but the feeling wasn't mutual, and they were separated by the end of June 1991. On July 23, a passer-by found George Garcia slumped in the driver's seat of his pickup truck, parked outside his condominium in Bensenville, blood streaming from a bullet hole in his chest. Guinevere initially denied any knowledge of the shooting, but she called back that evening, reporting that her boyfriend, 28-year-old John Gonzalez, had confessed the murder over drinks at a Chicago tavern.

Officers went to the bar, where they found Garcia and Gonzalez killing time. A pistol was recovered from the boyfriend's car, linked to George's murder through ballistics tests. Under questioning, the suspects told divergent stories. Gonzalez admitted plotting to rob George Garcia, driving Guinevere to the scene and watching from his car as she grappled with George for the gun. Guinevere, for her part, spun a tale of self-defense, with George as the aggressor in a physical assault. Both suspects were charged with murder, Gonzalez turning state's evidence against his lover in return for a lenient seven-year sentence.

Guinevere's trial opened on August 4, 1992, Garcia pleading self-defense, the prosecution pointing to George's $15,000 life insurance policy as a possible motive for murder. A psychiatrist employed by the defense called Guinevere a victim of chronic depression, testifying that she suffered from "borderline personality" disorder, but the diagnosis fell short of legal insanity. The jury found her sane and guilty as charged on August 10.

In Illinois, a second murder conviction may only be punished by death or life imprisonment without parole. Guinevere's attorney argued for life, citing his client's poor mental state, but Assistant State's Attorney Kathryn Creswell posed a telling question to the court. "Is there a shred of humanity left in Guinevere Garcia?" she asked. "Is there a shred of humanity in a person who kills a child, her own child, and then kills her husband?" Du Page County jurors answered that question in the negative, and Guinevere was sentenced to death on October 9, 1992.

GATES, ANNE

When sheriff's officers in Rushville, Indiana talked about the death of David Plue, they came up empty in their search for motives. The proverbial man without enemies, Plue had been shot in the head, execution-style, his body discarded alongside a rural highway in 1978. No one suspected his widow of playing a role in the crime, although in retrospect, Sheriff David Clevenger recalled that the 29-year-old woman "told us a lot of lies."

Nine years later, in Arabi, Louisiana, 65-year-old Raymond Gates was found dead in his home, his skull crushed by a dozen blows from something resembling a poker. Raymond's estranged wife, 38-year-old Anne Gates, "discovered" the body and phoned for police. A former nurse, residing at her mother's home in Mississippi since the break-up of her May-December marriage, Anne seemed stricken by her husband's death, but homicide detectives weren't convinced.

For openers, police had found a cigarette — Anne's brand — still smoldering in Raymond's living room when they arrived, and they were told the victim did not smoke. A set of fireplace tools was missing from the murder scene, and officers believed they'd found their motive in the form of an insurance policy, scheduled to pay Anne Gates $82,000 in the event of her aging husband's death. Forensics experts noted that the suspect, five full inches taller than the victim, could have easily inflicted wounds which cracked his skull.

A conversation with authorities in Indiana led to Anne's arrest on December 9, 1987, two months after the murder. Released on $40,000 bond, she also faced the prospect of another charge in Indiana, where Rush County authorities had reopened their investigation of her first husband's slaying. A grand jury in St. Bernard Parish indicted Gates for first-degree murder on May 18, 1988, but legal maneuvers postponed disposition of her case for another year. In 1989, Gates pled "no contest" to a reduced charge of manslaughter and was sentenced to ten years in prison.

Louisiana statutes provide for nullification of wills where the prime beneficiary is convicted of murder, but Anne's lawyer insisted on pressing her claim to Raymond's estate, reminding the courts that a "no contest" plea is not technically equivalent to an admission of guilt. In 1992, a bizarre settlement was reached, allowing Anne Gates to inherit $25,000 from Raymond's estate, while the remainder was divided among surviving members of his family.

GIBBS, JANIE LOU

A Georgia native, born in 1932, Janie Lou Gibbs was married at the tender age of fifteen, a grandmother at thirty-three. Soft-spoken and bespectacled, she was renowned for her religious fervor in rural Cordele, where she taught

Sunday school, served on numerous church committees, and worked incessantly to be "a witness for the Lord." When not engaged in church work, Janie ran a day-care center for working mothers, but her special joy was cooking for her family.

Unfortunately, some of Janie's dishes did not set well with her husband or their offspring. Charles Gibbs was the first to go, in January 1966, his death blamed on a "heart attack." Thirteen-year-old Marvin went next, diagnosed as a victim of "hepatitis" when he died on August 29, 1966. Melvin, age sixteen, was hospitalized with "a rare muscular disease" in January 1967, dying under doctor's care on January 23. The oldest Gibbs boy, Roger, was married but still living at home when he made Janie a grandmother in August 1967. Infant Ronnie Edward Gibbs died two months later, on October 7, from an alleged "heart infection." Roger himself was the last to die, exactly three weeks later. In all, the decimation of her family had enriched Janie Gibbs to the tune of $31,000 from life insurance policies, and she dutifully tithed ten percent of the income to her church.

Insurance adjusters were openly suspicious of Janie Lou's "bad luck," but it took the combination of her family physician and grieving daughter-in-law to put the wheels of justice in motion. Tissue samples from Roger Gibbs were sent to the Georgia state crime lab for testing, two months of detailed analysis revealing lethal doses of arsenic. Other members of the family were then exhumed, and while forensic reports were never published, Cordele authorities confirmed that all had been poisoned.

Arrested in December 1967, Janie confessed to poisoning her family and was charged with five counts of first-degree murder. Psychiatric reports pronounced the defendant schizophrenic, convinced the world was such an evil place that her loved ones were "better off dead." Judged incompetent for trial on February 7, 1968, Janie was confined to a state asylum until June 1974, when she was found sufficiently improved to participate in her own defense. Finally tried in 1976, she was convicted on all counts and sentenced to five consecutive terms of life imprisonment.

GIRIAT, MADAME

A professional "lady's companion" in France, Giriat tired of working for her money near the turn of the century, shifting to murder for profit. On September 21, 1902, police were summoned to investigate reports of a break-in at the Aix-les-Bains home of Eugenie Fourgere. They found Giriat bound and gagged, but otherwise unharmed, while her employer and a maid lay strangled in another room. A quantity of jewelry had been stolen from the house.

Detectives could not understand why Madame Giriat alone was left alive, and they began to follow her around in search of clues. The next time she was questioned, Giriat broke down, confessing that she helped to plan the burglary. Most of the blame, she said, lay with her lover, Henri Bassot, and a thug named Cesar Ladermann, from Lyons. Bassot, an ex-con who had turned to managing a nightclub, was arrested for interrogation; Ladermann, for his part, shot himself as officers broke down his door.

As Madame Giriat described the crime, she left a window open at the Fourgere home for Ladermann, who crept in after dark. He was supposed to tie the other women up and loot the house of jewelry — later found in Giriat's possession — but he lost his grip and strangled them instead.

Or, so she asked detectives to believe.

When she was taken to the murder scene, to reenact her crime, Giriat alternated between "the most disgusting levity" and dubious hysterics. Standing over Fourgere's bed, she kicked one leg and wailed, "To think that poor Eugenie was strangled on these pillows!" Overall, detectives agreed that Giriat knew too much for a non-witness bound and stranded in a different room. At trial, she was convicted on all charges with Bassot, both defendants sentenced to life imprisonment.

GONZALES, DELFINA and MARIA de JESUS

For at least a decade, beginning in the early 1950s, the Gonzales sisters operated one of Mexico's most profitable and most ruthless white slave operations, luring young girls into prostitution with false offers of legitimate employment, afterward holding them captive in an underground empire complete with armed guards, systematic torture, and compulsory drug addiction. Those who tried to run away, defied authority, or simply lost their looks, were murdered and replaced with younger, more compliant slaves.

Throughout 1963, police in the western coastal city of Guadalajara noted a sharp rise in the number of missing-person reports involving young girls. Most had vanished after being offered jobs as maids, and while authorities suspected white slavers at work, they had no hard evidence to support criminal charges. That changed a few days after Christmas, when 16-year-old Maria Hernandez disappeared from her Guadalajara home.

Maria was a good girl, seeking work to help her family through a time when illness left her father unemployed. She met an older woman in the park and was offered a job as her personal maid at a starting salary of 250 pesos — about $16 — per week. Nothing more had been heard from Maria since she packed her bag and caught the bus for San Juan de los Lagos, to join her new employer. Maria's parents did not know the older woman's name, but she was memorable for a large mole on her cheek, thus matching the description of suspected procuress Josefina Guttierez.

Police began their investigation with a visit to the town brothel in San Juan de los Lagos. No one on the staff could remember meeting Maria Hernandez or Josefina Guttierez, but neighbors instantly recalled the older woman making frequent visits to the whorehouse. Officers staked out the place and nabbed Guttierez when she turned up, several days later. Under questioning, she admitted selling Maria to the brothelkeeper for 1,000 pesos, but Maria was no longer there. With a promise of police protection, Josefina blew the whistle on her employers, the Gonzales sisters, and fingered their headquarters at Rancho El Angel — "Angel Ranch" — near San Francisco del Rincon, in the state of Guanajuato.

On arrival at the ranch, police found it surrounded by a tall fence, with an armed guard at the gate. Outnumbered and outgunned, the guard admitted them and spilled his guts. The sisters had been tipped off to a federal drive against white slavers; they had recently departed for Purisma de Bustos, where they planned to sell their ranch and flee to the United States with cash in hand. The woman left in charge, 28-year-old Lucila, had forgotten her own last name in the eleven years since she was kidnapped and sold into slavery, but a flair for managing the business saved her life when beauty faded. Police found thirteen other girls locked up in separate rooms, some riddled with venereal disease, most of them addicted to cocaine or heroin. Maria Hernandez was one of the few fit to travel, along with a 14-year-old abducted from Leon in November 1963.

Before she left the Angel Ranch, Maria told police a story that her fellow captives would describe as typical. Confined to the brothel in San Juan de los Lagos, on her first night away from home, she had been "broken in" by means of beating and gang rape, with liquor forced down her throat. Too sick to work the next morning, she was beaten again, finally turned out for paying customers on her third night of captivity. Later, she was driven to another Gonzales-owned brothel at San Francisco del Rincon, and from there to the ranch where she was found.

Long-term prisoners elaborated on Maria's tale of terror, describing a daily pattern of sadistic abuse. Women who defied their captors at the ranch were forced to kneel against a wall, a brick in each hand and one balanced on their heads, while they were whipped. Unwanted pregnancies were "cured" by hanging a girl by her wrists, and beating her stomach until she aborted the fetus. Survivors were put back to work; those who died found a place in the rancho's private cemetery. Captives were also murdered for defiance, attempting escape, and "getting old." In one case, when a popular girl named Ernestina tried to run away, the sisters feared a mass revolt if they killed her themselves. Instead, they provoked a fight between Ernestina and her own sister, drug-addicted Adela, in which Adela brained Ernestina with a hammer.

The stories were bizarre, but excavation at the Angel Ranch soon proved them accurate. Police uncovered eighty female corpses on the property, plus an unspecified "large number" of infant remains. Eleven men were also buried at the ranch, described by witnesses as migrant workers who had stopped off at the rancho for a party on their way back from the States, their pockets filled with cash. They never made it home, and most of them would never be identified.

Manhunters scoured Purisma de Bustos for the Gonzales sisters, but Delfina and Maria were able to hide for several days before they were finally captured. They kept silent in custody, but officers knew that a network of such scope could not operate for ten years without some official protection. One of their neighbors in Guanajuato was Capt. Hermenegildo Zuniga, a retired soldier and wealthy rancher, whose friends in high places had seen fit to warn the sisters of impending trouble... for a price.

At their trial in November 1964, the sisters were convicted of multiple murder and other charges, sentenced to the maximum allowable term of forty years each. Investigation of their contacts went on for another two years, with several accomplices drawing long prison terms for bribery and other charges. The Gonzales fortune was distributed among surviving victims and the families of the dead as partial compensation for their pain.

GOTTFRIED, GESSINA MARGARETHA

Pretty, blonde Gessina Gottfried was born in Bremen, Germany, in 1798, spoiled as a child despite her family's limited means. At twenty, flying in the face of parental objections, she married a notorious drunkard named Miltenburg. The union produced two children, but Miltenburg's boozing soon interfered with romance, and Gessina complained of his failures in bed. She took a lover named Gottfried, to keep herself satisfied, plotting Miltenburg's death when neighbors learned of her affair and started gossiping.

Gessina induced her mother to purchase some arsenic, for the extermination of "mice," and promptly spiked her husband's beer. His death was no surprise, officially attributed to alcohol, and no questions were asked. Gessina had anticipated swift remarriage, but Gottfried balked at acquiring a ready-made family. Never one to let human life stand in her way, Gessina promptly poisoned her two children, their deaths blamed on a "sudden illness." When Gessina's parents objected to her premature engagement, they were invited to lunch and poisoned. Physicians ascribed their passing to old age and "inflammation of the bowels."

By this time, Gottfried was even more resistant to the notion of marriage, perhaps fearing Gessina's quick hand with the arsenic bottle. Trying a new tack, Gessina began to feed him small doses of poison, leaving Gottfried bedridden while she attentively "nursed" him. At last, delirious, Gottfried agreed to marry Gessina, and a minister was summoned. The ceremony was performed, Gottfried signed over all his worldly goods to Gessina... and he died in agony, hours later.

Widowed for the second time, Gessina could not break the killing habit. Next up was her brother, an alcoholic ex-soldier who moved in with Gessina, poisoned after signing over all his savings. (Doctors blamed his death on "venereal disease"!) A wealthy suitor soon went the way of all flesh, first willing his estate to Gessina. When an old friend asked her to repay a debt, Gessina visited his Hamburg home and polished him off with a "special" recipe.

In 1825, the bank foreclosed on Gessina's mortgage in Bremen, selling the house to a wheelwright named Rumf. The new owner kept Gessina on as a housekeeper for his family, and Mrs. Rumf died two days after bearing a new son, her death blamed on "complications of childbirth." Next, the children started dying, until only Gessina and Mr. Rumf were left by

1828. Rumf was ill after each meal Gessina prepared, finally coming to suspect the white powder she sprinkled over every dish. Gessina was arrested on March 5, 1828, accused of murdering six members of the Rumf family. In custody, she boldly confessed to poisoning thirty victims, sixteen of whom had died.

At her trial on murder charges, Gessina appeared as "almost a skeleton," stripped of the dentures, cosmetics, and thirteen corsets she wore to maintain a youthful air. She repeated her confession in court, admitting sensations of near-ecstasy as she watched her victims suffer and die. Conviction carried a mandatory death sentence, and Gessina Gottfried was beheaded for her crimes in 1828. In a parting statement, she told authorities, "I was born without a conscience, which allowed me to live without fear."

GRAHAM, GWENDOLYN GAIL and WOOD, CATHERINE MAY

The deaths at Alpine Manor started as a game. At first, the killers planned to choose their victims alphabetically, with their initials spelling "MURDER" as a private joke on the police. As luck would have it, though, the aging women first selected still had too much fight left in them, and the plotters had to shift their strategy.

No matter. In the end, they still found easy prey to satisfy their taste for death.

Born in 1963, Gwen Graham was a California native who grew up in Tyler, Texas. She was "quiet and respectful" to her teachers, but she "always had a sad look on her face." In later years, she claimed the sadness was occasioned by her father's sexual attentions, but the charge — which he denies — was never proved in court. Moving to Michigan in 1986, Graham found work as a nurse's aide at the Alpine Manor Nursing Home in Walker, a Grand Rapids suburb.

Graham's immediate superior at Alpine Manor was 24-year-old Cathy Wood. Wed as a teenager, Wood had ballooned to 450 pounds when her seven-year marriage broke up, leaving her alone and friendless in Grand Rapids. Hired at Alpine Manor in July 1985, she was soon promoted to supervisor of nurse's aides, but her social life remained in a vacuum until she met Gwen Graham on the job. Their friendship swiftly crossed the line into a lesbian affair, Wood dieting the pounds away and relishing the social whirl of gay bars, parties, and casual sex. Her chief devotion was to Graham, though, and by late 1986 the two women had pledged undying love for one another, come what may.

Gwen broached the subject of premeditated murder that October, but her lover "thought we were just playing." During sex, Gwen got a kick from tying Cathy down and choking her or covering her face with a pillow until she trembled on the verge of blacking out. If Cathy had complaints about the game, she kept them to herself. By slow degrees, she learned that pain and pleasure may be flip-sides of the same exciting coin.

The homicides at Alpine Manor spanned a three-month period, from January to the early part of April 1987. Gwen's first plan, the "MURDER" game, fell through when her selected targets put up such a fight that she was forced to let them live. Despite her bungled efforts, there were no complaints on file. Both Wood and Graham earned exemplary reports from their superiors and were "well liked by patients" on the ward.

In the future, Gwen decided, she would only pick on women who were too far gone for self-defense. Her lover was the lookout, standing by where she could watch the murder and the nurse's station all at once, diverting any member of the staff who strayed too close while Graham snuffed her chosen victim with a washcloth pressed across the nose and mouth. Sometimes the sheer excitement of a killing was too much, and they retired immediately to an empty room for sex while memories were fresh. In several cases, Gwen kept souvenirs — an anklet or a handkerchief, a broach, a set of dentures.

Murder is a risky business, but the lethal lovers seemed to thrive on danger, boasting of their body-count to colleagues who dismissed the comments as "sick jokes." At least three nurse's aides saw the shelf of souvenirs in the house

Wood shared with Graham, but none took the gloating tales of murder seriously... yet.

By April 1987, the honeymoon was over for Wood and Graham. Cathy balked at personally killing anyone to "prove her love," and she was shortly rescued by her transfer to a different shift. By that time, Gwen was spending time with Heather Barager, another lesbian, who ultimately joined her on a trip back home to Texas, leaving Cathy in the lurch. Come August, Cathy spilled the story to her former husband, but Ken Wood stalled another fourteen months before he called police. Gwen Graham, meanwhile, had gone to work at Mother Frances Hospital in Tyler, keeping in touch with Cathy on the telephone.

Grand Rapids police were skeptical of Ken Wood's story at first. Some forty patients had died at Alpine Manor in the first quarter of 1987, all listed as natural deaths, but on reflection eight cases seemed to stand out. Three of those were finally eliminated by detectives, leaving a victim list that included 60-year-old Marguerite Chambers, 89-year-old Edith Cole, 95-year-old Myrtle Luce, 79-year-old Mae Mason, and 74-year-old Belle Burkhard. In no case was there any scientific evidence of murder, but Ken Wood's statement and the second thoughts of staffers at the home were strong enough to make a case.

Both women were arrested in December 1988, Wood held without bond in Grand Rapids on charges of killing victims Cook and Chambers. In Texas, where rumors of the Michigan investigation had already cost Gwen her job, a $1 million bond was sufficient to keep her in jail. A brief extradition fight grew tedious, and Graham soon waived the legalities, returning to face charges on her own volition.

The Alpine Manor staff was "overwhelmed" by the arrests, though some remembered Gwen as "unpredictable," remarking casually on Graham's quick temper. Former nurse's aides like Deborah Kidder, Nancy Harris, Lisa Lynch, Dawn Male and Russell Thatcher reevaluated the "sick jokes" and souvenirs they had managed to ignore while lives were on the line. At trial, all four would testify against Gwen Graham for the prosecution, with Cathy Wood emerging as the state's star witness overnight.

A September 1989 guilty plea to charges of second-degree murder spared Wood from life imprisonment, earning her a sentence of twenty to forty years. In return for that relative leniency, she took the stand against Gwen three months later, thereby sealing her ex-lover's fate.

Aside from the five victims murdered, said Cathy, Gwen had tried to suffocate at least five others who survived. Wood's ultimate confession to her husband had been prompted less by guilt than fear that Graham would continue killing in her new position at the Texas hospital, this time with infants as her chosen prey.

"When she was killing people at Alpine and I didn't do anything," Wood told the court, "that was bad enough. But when she would call me and say how she wanted to smash a baby, I had to stop her somehow. I knew she was working in a hospital there. She said she wanted to take one of the babies and smash it up against a window. I had to do something. I didn't care about myself anymore."

Graham's attorney tried to portray Wood as a jealous, vindictive liar, setting his client up as "a sacrificial lamb," but jurors disagreed. They deliberated for seven hours before convicting Gwen on five counts of first-degree murder and one count of conspiracy to commit first-degree murder. On November 2, 1989, Graham was sentenced to six life terms without possibility of parole.

GRANT, ROSALIE

The daughter of a Dixie prostitute, Rosalie Grant was still a toddler on the night she watched her mother stab a man to death, leaving Rosalie spattered with blood. Resettled in Youngstown, Ohio, Rosalie conceived her first child — daughter Sheylene — in her teens, without benefit of marriage. In fact, she never married, though she later bore two sons by boyfriend Joseph Clinkscale. The first boy, Joseph Junior, was born in 1981. A year later, with their relationship on the rocks and Clinkscale in the wind, Rosalie reverted to her maiden name, calling her youngest child Donovan Grant.

Rosalie was known for her explosive temper, several times dragging her sons to the hospital for treatment after furious beatings. Sheylene, meanwhile, was generally exempt from punishment, suggesting that the boys had become surrogate targets for her hatred of Joe Clinkscale, Sr. It was odd, therefore, when Rosalie took out life insurance on the boys — $5,000 each — but neglected to buy a policy on her daughter.

Two weeks after that transaction, on April 1, 1983, firefighters were summoned to a blaze on Orrin Avenue, in Youngstown. A woman had placed the call, shouting, "My kids are burning up! My babies are on fire! Please help me!"

Help arrived too late, and Rosalie's sons were found in the bedroom they shared, burned beyond recognition. (Sheylene, "coincidentally," had spent the night with her grandparents.) A strong smell of chemicals brought arson investigators to the scene, where they discovered fires deliberately set in three areas of the small home's basement — one beneath each of the main rooms upstairs. Forensic evidence revealed that lighter fluid had been spilled throughout the house, including quantities splashed on the children themselves as they slept.

Detectives found Rosalie Grant at St. Elizabeth's Hospital, where her sons had been taken for autopsy. The grieving mother told police she had fallen asleep on the couch, watching TV, and woke to the smell of smoke. Trying to rescue her children, she was driven from their bedroom by a wall of flame and ran in search of help. Investigators noted for the record that she had no burns, nor did her clothing smell of smoke. Meanwhile, an empty can of lighter fluid was discovered in a tool shed, near the burned-out home... complete with fingerprints identified as Rosalie's.

Renewed interrogation brought a change of tune from the accused. Now, Grant remembered a series of threatening calls that preceded the fire, but police had no record of her alleged complaints. Witnesses on Orrin Avenue recalled Grant calmly watching the fire from a neighbor's porch until press photographers arrived, whereupon she rushed toward the barricades, screaming in mock anguish.

Indicted on two counts of murder, Grant stood for trial in October 1983. Her lawyer hammered at the state's "weak" evidence and lack of witnesses, but jurors voted to convict across the board. Testifying for the first time in the trial's penalty phase, Rosalie produced a third version of the fire, this time inventing a one-armed stranger, armed with a lead pipe, who forcibly kept her from saving her children. The rambling diatribe went on until her father rose at the back of the courtroom, saying "That's enough, Rosalie. Get down."

Prosecutor Jim Coyle called it "probably the strangest thing I've ever seen in a court of law," but jurors were unimpressed with Grant's new alibi. They recommended capital punishment, and a formal sentence of death was passed on October 22. Police, meanwhile, suspect that Grant was not alone in plotting the murder of her sons. "I have a candidate," Detective Mike Landers told newsmen, "but I don't have a case. If I did, I'd snag the bastard and he'd be up there with her."

GRILLS, CAROLINE

A resident of Sydney, Australia, Caroline Grills — neé Mickelson — was known among her neighbors as "a kindly old lady to whom people looked in time of trouble." It is characteristic of serial killers and their persuasive "mask of sanity" that such opinions were still being offered as Grills, aged sixty-three, was facing trial on four counts of murder and two counts of attempted murder.

Caroline's first documented victim was her stepmother, Christina Mickelson, with whom Grills had quarreled nonstop since her widowed father remarried in 1908. At that, it took four decades for Caroline to resolve her problem with poison, and no one was unduly suspicious when Christina Mickelson died in 1947, at the ripe old age of eighty-seven. Another octogenarian, family friend Angelina Thomas, was the next to go — and once again, her age prevented any speculation of foul play.

John Lundberg, a relative of Caroline's, was sixty years old when he fell prey to a strange illness, inexplicably losing all his hair before he finally died in October 1948. Mary Ann Mickelson soon displayed identical symptoms, and doctors were admittedly perplexed when she followed her late relatives to the grave. In short order, John Lundberg's widow and daughter began reporting hair loss, accompanied by numbness in their limbs, and Caroline volunteered to nurse them through their illness, back to health.

By this time, family members and police were sharing their suspicions of the strange "disease." Investigators analyzed a pot of Caroline's special tea, reporting that the brew contained a hefty does of the metallic poison thallium. Eveline Lundberg had already lost her sight from the poison, but doctors were able to save her life, along with that of her daughter.

Initially charged with murder, Caroline Grills was finally prosecuted only for attempted murder in the case of Eveline Lundberg. At trial, her primary motive was described as greed — the desire to hasten a family inheritance — but prosecutors also alluded to her lust for power over life and death. Convicted by a jury of her peers, Grills was sentenced to life in prison, where she was nicknamed "Aunt Thally" by fellow inmates.

GRUBER, MARIA:

See "ANGELS OF DEATH"

GUNNESS, BELLE PAULSDATTER

America's first "black widow" of the 20th century was born Brynhild Paulsdatter Storset on November 11, 1859, in the fishing hamlet of Selbu, on Norway's west coast. The daughter of an unsuccessful merchant, Brynhild immigrated to the United States in 1881; three years later, she settled in Chicago, Americanizing her given name to "Belle" or "Bella." In 1884, at age twenty-five, she married a Norwegian immigrant, Mads Sorenson.

The couple opened a confectioner's shop in 1896, but the business was wiped out by fire the following year. Belle told her insurance agents that a kerosene lamp had exploded, and the company paid off on her policy, although no lamp was found in the wreckage. The Sorensons used their found money to purchase a home, but fire leveled the house in 1898, bringing further insurance payments. Bad luck dogged the couple, and a second house burned down before they found a home on Alma Street that met their needs.

As everything Belle touched was soon reduced to ashes, her family began to dwindle in the latter 1890s. Daughter Caroline, her oldest child, went first, in 1896. Two years later, Axel, her first son, was laid to rest. In each case, the children were diagnosed as victims of "acute colitis," demonstrating symptoms which — in hindsight — may have indicated they were poisoned.

On July 30, 1900, Mads Sorenson died at home, exhibiting the classic symptoms of strychnine poisoning. Belle admitted giving her husband "a powder," in an effort to "help his cold," but the family physician did not request an autopsy. With Mads under treatment for an enlarged heart, the death was automatically ascribed to natural causes.

The widow Sorenson collected her insurance money and departed from Chicago, settling outside La Porte, Indiana, with three children under her wing. Two were her natural daughters: Myrtle, born in 1897, and Lucy, in 1899. The new addition, Jennie Olsen, was a foster daughter, passed along to Belle by parents who, apparently, were tired of dealing with their child.

In April 1902, Belle married a Norwegian farmer named Peter Gunness. Less durable than Sorenson before him, Gunness lasted only eight months. On December 16, 1902, he was killed when a heavy sausage grinder "fell" from its place on a shelf, fracturing his skull. A son, named Phillip, was born of the brief union in 1903, and Jennie Olsen vanished from the farm three years later. When neighbors inquired, Belle explained that her foster child had been sent "to a finishing school in California."

Widowed for a second time, with only children to assist her on the farm, Belle started hiring drifters who would work awhile and then, apparently, move on. She also started placing "lonely-hearts" ads in Norwegian-language newspapers throughout the Midwest, entertaining a series of prospective husbands at her farm.

Somehow, none of them measured up to Belle's standards... and none of them were ever seen again.

On April 28, 1908, the Gunness homestead was destroyed by fire. Searchers digging through the rubble found a quartet of incinerated bodies in the basement; three were clearly children, while the fourth — a woman's headless corpse, without a skull in evidence — was taken for the last remains of Mrs. Gunness. The local sheriff arrested handyman Ray Lamphere, employed by Belle from 1906 until his dismissal in February 1908, on charges of arson and murder.

The case became more complicated on May 5, when searchers started finding other bodies on the Gunness farm. Dismembered, wrapped in gunny sacks and doused with lye, a few reduced to skeletons, the corpses told a graphic tale of wholesale slaughter spanning years. The final body-count had been a subject of enduring controversy. Without citing its source, the *Guinness Book of World Records* credits Belle with sixteen known victims and another twelve "possibles." The local coroner's report was more modest, listing — in addition to the basement bodies — ten male victims, two females, and an unspecified quantity of human bone fragments. Belle's suitors were buried together in the muck of a hog pen, while her female victims had been planted in a nearby garden patch.

Only six of the dead were positively identified. Jennie Olsen was there, far removed from the mythical finishing school. Farm hands Eric Gurhold and Olaf Lindblom had ended their days in the hog pen, beside farmers John Moo (of Elbow Lake, Minnesota) and Ole Budsberg (of Iola, Wisconsin). Both of the latter had answered Belle's newspaper ads — and so, presumably, had their six anonymous companions in death. The "Jane Doe" corpse buried beside Jennie Olsen is an anomaly, unexplained to this day.

A coroner's inquest was launched on April 29, and witness depositions taken through May 1 reflect a standard heading: "Over the dead body of Belle Gunness..." After May 5, with the discovery of new corpses, official documents began describing the headless woman as "an unidentified adult female," assuming that Belle might have faked her own death to escape from the scene. A futile search for the missing skull was launched on May 19, resulting in discovery of Belle's dental bridge, complete with anchor teeth attached. Ignoring various unanswered questions, the coroner issued his final report on May 20, declaring that Belle Gunness had died "at the hands of persons unknown."

Ray Lamphere, from his cell, was adamant in claiming that Belle was still alive. On April 28, he said, once Belle had set the house on fire, he drove her to the railway station at Stillwell, Indiana. Police initially took his story at face value, mistakenly arresting Flora Heerin, an innocent widow en route from Chicago to visit relatives in New York City. Hauled off the train at Syracuse and briefly detained as Belle Gunness, Mrs. Heerin retaliated with a civil lawsuit for false arrest.

Charged with four counts of murder and one count of arson, Ray Lamphere's case went to the jury in November 1908. On November 26, he was convicted on the arson charge alone, suggesting that jurors felt Belle's death had not been proved "beyond a reasonable doubt." Surviving for two years in prison, Lamphere talked endlessly about the case, crediting Belle with forty-nine murders, netting more than $100,000 from her victims between 1903 and 1908. The woman in the basement, he contended, had been found in a saloon and hired for the evening, murdered to serve as a stand-in. Belle had promised she would get in touch with Lamphere after she was settled elsewhere, but it seemed that she had changed her plans.

The first reported sighting of a resurrected Belle was logged on April 29, six days before new bodies were uncovered at the farm. Conductor Jesse Hurst was certain Mrs. Gunness went aboard his train at the Decatur, Indiana station. She was bundled on a stretcher, Hurst recalled, and seemed quite ill.

Perhaps, but what are we to make of the reported sighting at La Porte, on April 30? While visiting Belle's closest friend, Almetta Hay, a local farmer claimed he saw the missing woman sitting down to coffee. When Almetta died, in 1916, neighbors picking through the litter in her crowded shack retrieved a woman's skull, wedged in between two mattresses. In spite of speculation that it might belong to the decapitated basement victim, the intriguing lead was not pursued.

More "sightings" were recorded through the years. In 1917, a childhood neighbor recognized Belle Gunness on admission, as a patient, to the South Bend hospital where he was working as a student nurse. He called police, but Belle had slipped away before detectives reached the scene. In 1931, a Los Angeles prosecutor wrote to La Porte's sheriff, claiming that murder defendant Esther Carlson — charged with poisoning 81-year-old August Lindstrom for his money — might be Mrs. Gunness. Carlson carried photographs of three children resembling Belle's, but La Porte could not afford to send its sheriff west in those Depression days, and the suspect died of tuberculosis before her trial, leaving the question forever open.

As late as 1935, subscribers to a magazine allegedly recognized Belle's photograph as the likeness of a whorehouse madam in Ohio. Confronting the old woman and addressing her as "Belle," one amateur detective was impressed by the vehemence of her reaction. Pursuing the matter through friends, he was urgently warned to let the matter rest... and so it has.

If Gunness did, in fact, survive her "death," she stands in that elite society of killers who, although identified with ample evidence to win convictions, manage to evade arrest and so live out their lives in anonymity. Her legacy is rumor, and a snatch of tawdry rhyme that reads, in part:

There's red upon the Hoosier moon
For Belle was strong and full of doom;
And think of all those Norska men
Who'll never see St. Paul again.

HAHN, ANNA MARIE

The first woman to die in Ohio's electric chair, Anna Hahn was a German native, born in 1906, who immigrated to Cincinnati at age twenty-one. There, in 1929, she married a young telephone operator, briefly managing a bakery in Cincinnati's German district before she tired of the hours and set her sights on easy money. Life insurance seemed to be the answer, and she twice tried to insure her husband for $25,000, meeting resistance each time. Soon after rejecting her second demand, Philip Hahn fell suddenly ill, and was rushed to the hospital by his mother over Anna's objections. Physicians saved his life, but there was nothing they could do to save his marriage.

Despite a total lack of training or experience, Anna began to offer her services as a live-in "nurse" to elderly men in the German community. Her first client, septuagenarian Ernest Koch, seemed healthy in spite of his years, but that soon changed under Hahn's tender care. Koch died on May 6, 1932, leaving Anna a house in his will. Its ground floor was occupied by a doctor's office, and Hahn visited her new tenant frequently, stealing prescription blanks to keep herself supplied with "medicine" for her new "nursing" business.

Her next client, retired railroad man Albert Parker, died swiftly under Anna's ministrations. This time, she avoided the embarrassment of a convenient will by "borrowing" Parker's money before he died, signing an I.O.U. that predictably vanished soon after the old man expired. Jacob Wagner was next, willing a lump sum of $17,000 to his beloved "niece" Anna, and Hahn soon picked up another $15,000 for tending George Gsellman in the months before his death.

George Heiss was a rare survivor, growing suspicious one day after Anna served him a mug of beer. A couple of house flies had sampled the brew, dropping dead on the spot, and when Anna refused to share the drink herself, Heiss sent her packing. He did not inform police of his suspicions, though, and so the lethal nurse was free to go in search of other "patients."

George Obendoerfer was the last to die, in 1937, lured to Colorado on a supposed visit to Hahn's nonexistent ranch. Obendoerfer died in his hotel room, soon after arriving in Denver, and Anna took the opportunity to loot his bank account, pocketing $5,000 for her efforts. Police became suspicious when she balked at picking up the tab for George's funeral, demanding an autopsy after they turned up evidence of the unorthodox bank transfer. Arsenic was found in Obendoerfer's body, and detectives were waiting for Hahn when she reached Cincinnati, armed with arrest warrants and court orders demanding exhumation of her previous clients. Each had been slain with a different potion, and a search of Hahn's lodgings reportedly turned up "enough poison to kill half of Cincinnati."

Convicted of multiple murder and sentenced to die, Hahn kept her nerve, maintaining her pose as an "angel of mercy." On June 20, 1938, she hosted a small party for local newsmen in her cell, lapsing into hysterics as she began her last walk to the death chamber. It took a prison chaplain to restore her calm, holding Anna's hand as she was buckled into the electric chair. Before the customary hood was lowered into place, she warned the priest to step back, with the advice that "You might be killed too, Father."

HILLEY, AUDREY MARIE

A native of Anniston, Alabama, Audrey Frazier was born in 1933 and seemed to enjoy a normal childhood. Married to Frank Hilley at eighteen, she was having marital problems nine years later when her second daughter, Carol, was born. Psychiatrists, applying hindsight, feel the birth may have somehow triggered a radical shift in Hilley's personality, finally surfacing in a series of lethal attacks upon family members.

When Audrey's husband passed away in 1975, cancer was blamed for his death. The same diagnosis was made two years later, in the death of Hilley's mother, Lucille Frazier. By 1979, victims had begun to pile up, with daughter Carol lingering on the brink of death for several weeks before doctors managed to pull her back. They were too late for mother-in-law Carrie Hilley, who died in November after a prolonged illness.

By that time, authorities were already closing the ring around Audrey. Doctors had discovered abnormal levels of arsenic in Carol's blood, and on a hunch they started checking other family members recently deceased. On October 25, 1979, Hilley was indicted for attempted murder of her daughter, plus an unrelated count of check fraud. Three weeks later, free on $14,000 bond, she vanished from a Birmingham motel where she had been awaiting trial. Indictments were handed down in the murder of her husband on January 11, 1980, but they meant little without a suspect in custody.

In flight, Hilley adopted the identity of "Robbi Hannon," attaching herself to bachelor John Homan in Marlow, New Hampshire. They lived together for several months before they were married, in May 1981, and "Robbi" was talking divorce a month later, lighting out for Texas in a search for "space." She spent the summer in the Lone Star State, occasionally telephoning Homan as herself, or in the guise of her own alleged twin, "Teri Martin." A brief reconciliation with Homan was followed by yet another separation in September 1982, and "Robbi" moved on to Florida, where she contrived to fake her own death. Incredibly, she then returned to New Hampshire — as "Teri Martin" — and spent time consoling her "brother-in-law" before she moved on to Vermont. There, her suspicious behavior finally alerted authorities, and Hilley was arrested in January 1983.

Her trial opened in Anniston four months later, and Audrey was convicted on two counts, receiving a life term for the murder of Frank Hilley, plus twenty years for the attempted murder of her daughter. On February 19, 1987, Hilley was granted a three-day furlough from the women's prison at Wetumpka, Alabama, and she never returned. Discovered on the porch of an Anniston home on February 26, in the midst of a winter rainstorm, Hilley was soaked to the skin and spattered with mud, suffering from severe hypothermia. Fading in and out of consciousness, she gave her name as "Sellers," but authorities identified her from the wanted posters issued after her escape. Stricken by a heart attack en route to the local hospital, Hilley was beyond the help of medical science, and doctors pronounced her dead that afternoon.

In retrospect, there seems to be no rational motive for Hilley's various crimes. She maintained her innocence to the end, while admitting to "blackouts" and memory lapses, but she remains a suspect in several other cases. In the late 1970s, Hilley repeatedly complained to police about prowlers and threatening phone calls, always greeting patrolmen with fresh pots of coffee when they arrived at her home. At least two of those officers suffered severe stomach cramps and nausea after drinking the coffee, and Hilley was also linked to the chronic, unexplained illness of various neighborhood children who played with her daughter around Hilley's home. One such playmate, 11-year-old Sonya Gibson, died of unknown causes in 1975, but a 1983 autopsy revealed only "normal" levels of arsenic in her remains. The final count of Marie Hilley's victims — like her motive itself — remains unknown.

HINDLEY, MYRA

Born July 23, 1942, in Manchester, England, Myra Hindley was sent to live with her maternal grandmother, a few doors from her mother's home, when a younger sister was born in August 1946. Poor attendance at school was climaxed when she quit entirely, at age fifteen, and the pattern of absenteeism continued into her first job, as a clerk for an electrical engineering firm. Myra converted to Catholicism at sixteen, and took her first communion in November 1958. Homely and shy, she was still a virgin in January 1961, when she met Ian Stewart at her new job, working as a typist for a chemical supply company in Manchester.

Four years Myra's senior, Ian was the illegitimate son of a Scottish waitress. He never met his father, and despite sporadic visits from his mother he was raised by foster parents in Gorbals, Glasgow's toughest slum. In childhood, he earned a reputation as a budding sadist, torturing other children and maiming animals "for fun." He also tried his hand at petty crime, earning several terms of probation on charges that included housebreaking and theft. In 1954, the courts sent him to Manchester, to live with his mother and her new husband, Patrick Brady. Ian would use his stepfather's surname in the future, continuing his criminal activities as he blossomed into a full-fledged teenage alcoholic. A week after his eighteenth birthday, Ian was sentenced to two years on conviction for theft. His last arrest, before indictment on murder charges, was settled by payment of a fine for drunk and disorderly conduct, in 1958. Along the way, he had acquired new interests, building up a library of books on Nazi Germany, sadism, and sexual perversion.

Myra was soon fascinated, then infatuated, with this "intellectual" invoice clerk who read *Mein Kampf* in the original German and debated "master race" theories as if they made sense. She penned lavish professions of love in her diary but feared to approach him directly, exulting when he finally asked her out. They took in a movie — about the Nuremburg War Crimes Tribunal — and then returned to her grandmother's house, where Brady introduced her to sex.

Soon, they were inseparable, Myra bleaching her hair to please Ian, dressing in Nazi-style boots and leather to mimic Nazi Irma Grese, with Brady dubbing her "Myra Hess." They used Ian's automatic camera to pose for obscene photos — complete with hoods, whips, and a dog — but Ian was unsuccessful in his efforts to crack the local pornography market. Next, he toyed with the idea of armed robbery, but Brady's nerve failed in the crunch, leaving Myra to take shooting lessons, purchase two pistols, and pass a driver's test in expectation of wheeling the getaway car. Finally, unable to go through with the plan, they turned their attention to kidnapping, child molestation, and murder.

Police did not connect the crimes, at first. Pauline Reade, sixteen, was the first to vanish, missing from her Gorton home — two doors from the residence of Myra's brother-in-law — on July 12, 1963. Four months later, on November 23, 12-year-old John Kilbride disappeared from Ashton-under-Lyne. Keith Bennett, also twelve, was reported missing from Manchester on June 16, 1964, last seen near the home occupied by Brady's mother. Another Manchester victim, 10-year-old Leslie Ann Downey, disappeared without a trace on December 26, 1964.

Authorities were baffled by the "unrelated" cases, left without a single piece of solid evidence. The twisted lovers, meanwhile, were intent on a campaign to corrupt Myra's brother-in-law, David Smith, and recruit him into their circle. A petty criminal with several arrests of his own, Smith was amused when the conversation turned to murder, and he questioned Brady's ability to follow through. On October 6, 1965, Brady offered a practical demonstration with Edward Evans, a 17-year-old homosexual, striking him fourteen times with a hatchet before finishing the job by means of strangulation.

Horrified, Smith phoned police the next morning, directing them to Brady's address. The raiders caught Ian and Myra at home, retrieving a fresh corpse from the bedroom, along with the bloody hatchet and Brady's library of volumes on perversion and sadism. A 12-year-old neighbor recalled several trips she had made with the couple to Saddleworth Moor, northeast of Manchester, near the Penine Way, and authorities launched a search that uncovered the body of Leslie Ann Downey on October 16.

Four days later, another search of Brady's flat turned up two left-luggage tickets for Manchester Central Station, leading police to a pair of hidden suitcases. Inside, they found nude photographs of Leslie Ann, along with tape recordings of her final tortured moments, pleading for her life as she was brutally abused. A series of seemingly innocent snapshots depicted portions of Saddleworth Moor, and detectives paid another visit to the desolate region on October 21, unearthing the body of John Kilbride.

In custody, Brady seemed proud of his crimes, boasting of "three or four" victims planted on the moors. Myra, meanwhile, was amused by their media designation as the "Moors Murderers;" playfully, she wrote to Ian, "I didn't kill any moors, did you?" Police announced that they were reopening their files on eight missing persons, lost over the past four years, but no new charges had been added by the time Ian and Myra went to trial. Jurors were stunned by the Downey tape, and by Brady's bland description of the recording as "unusual." On May 6, both defendants were convicted of killing Edward Evans and Leslie Ann Downey; Brady was also convicted of murdering John Kilbride, while Myra was convicted as an accessory after the fact in that crime. Brady was sentenced to concurrent life terms on each count, while Hindley received two life terms, plus seven years in the Kilbride case.

In Holloway women's prison, Myra initially required special guards to protect her, following an assault by fellow inmates. In time, passions cooled toward the child-killer, and she fell in with a clique of prison lesbians, enjoying affairs with various partners. One of her lovers, scandalized when the news finally broke, was Pat Cairn, a former nun turned prison guard at Holloway, who fell in love with Myra and disgraced herself in the pursuit of their relationship.

In November 1985, Ian Brady was transferred from prison to a maximum-security mental hospital, there confessing the Reade-Bennett murders in an interview with tabloid reporters. Another year passed before searchers returned to the moors, with Myra Hindley joining them for an abortive outing on December 15, 1986. The effort was fruitless, but Pauline Reade's skeleton was finally recovered on June 30, 1987, nearly a quarter-century after her disappearance. It took pathologists a month to decide that the girl had been sexually assaulted, her throat slashed from behind.

In August 1987, Brady mailed a letter to the BBC, containing sketchy information on five "new" murders. In the letter, Ian claimed another victim buried on the moor, a man murdered in Manchester, a woman dumped in a canal, and two victims gunned down in Scotland, at Glasgow and Loch Long. None of the victims were identified, but police announced that they were reopening the files on two ancient murders, including the 1963 beating death of 55-year-old Veronica Bondi in Manchester, and the 1965 strangulation of Edith Gleave, a 38-year-old prostitute, in Stockport. No further information is forthcoming in those cases, but it was announced — on January 14, 1988 — that no prosecution is anticipated in the cases of Pauline Reade and Keith Bennett.

HULTBERG, VIOLET

A native of Long Lake, Minnesota, born in 1909, Violet Hultberg was nineteen years old when she met Herbert Moreau, a father of five who was fourteen years her senior. Moreau had separated from his wife in 1927, winning custody of his four older sons, while the youngest remained with his wife. Violet and Walter soon became lovers, and she followed him to Minneapolis in September 1928, looking forward to marriage when his divorce became final a month later. Her own parents, meanwhile, were staunchly opposed to the match, and Herbert passed Violet off to the world at large as his children's nurse.

On Monday, November 5, 1928, Herbert left for work at his usual time of 6:30 A.M. He was not due home until 6 P.M., leaving Violet ample time to seal the doors and windows, turn on all the gas jets of her stove, and lie down in the bedroom with Moreau's four sons: eight-year-old George, seven-year-old Herbert, five-year-old Edward, and four-year-old Robert. All had been dead for hours when Moreau returned and forced the door. On the bedroom dresser, police found a note addressed to Herbert. It read:

> Dear Hub — Please don't hate me or feel angry for what I am doing, but you needn't worry. I think God will forgive us. Hub, please forgive me and pray for me. The clock just struck 10. I wish I could have seen the folks, but I cannot wait a week. You have been so good to me; no one can blame you for what I am doing. Don't do any harm to yourself.

No motive was suggested for the murder-suicide. Moreau told police that Violet seemed normal when he left for work, and neighbors thought nothing of the silent house, since Moreau's home had lately been quarantined for scarlet fever. Police speculated, perhaps incorrectly, that Violet "felt sorry" for Moreau and sought to remove the "burden" imposed by his sons.

JACKSON, GERTRUDE: See FREEMAN, JEANNACE

JACKSON, MARY JANE

A native of New Orleans, born in 1836 and nicknamed "Bricktop" for her mane of fiery red hair, Mary Jackson became a working prostitute at age thirteen. After a year on the street, she became the live-in mistress of a Poydras Street saloon owner, but Mary's violent temper was already well known in the French Quarter. Sick of her unpredictable rages by 1854, Mary's lover tossed her out, sparking a brawl that cost him one ear and most of his nose.

Over the next two years, Bricktop worked her way through a series of New Orleans brothels, losing each new job in the wake of some screaming outburst, finally settling at Archie Murphy's Dance Hall, where no behavior was too outrageous. In 1856, Mary Jane committed her first murder, clubbing a stranger to death after he "insulted" her by calling her a whore.

Her second victim, in 1857, was a skeletal, seven-foot character called Long Charley. It seems that Charley and Bricktop were arguing over which way he would fall if she stabbed him to death, and Mary Jane settled the quarrel with a thrust of her custom-made, twin-bladed knife. (He fell forward.)

Beating customers was one thing; killing them was something else. Mary's landlord showed her the door, and she soon established her own seedy crib, recruiting like-minded hellions in the persons of Ellen Collins, six-foot America Williams, and Delia Swift — a.k.a. "Bridget Fury." Delia lived up to her nickname in 1858, axing a man to death in front of several dozen witnesses, and she was jailed for life. It should have been an object lesson to Mary Jane, and yet...

On November 7, 1859, Jackson and her two remaining partners were swilling booze in a neighborhood bar, when patron Laurent Fleury remarked on their crude behavior. An argument ensued, exploding into violence when Fleury slapped Bricktop's face and all three hookers waded into him as one. Mary was swinging her knife when bartender Joe Seidensahl tried to intervene, and she turned the double blades on him. It took a dozen coppers to subdue Bricktop and Williams, while Collins escaped in the confusion. Seidensahl would survive his wounds, but Fleury was dead at the scene, prompting a murder charge. Mary was rescued by a combination of bribery and a vague coroner's report, allowing her lawyer to blame Fleury's death on "heart trouble."

Meanwhile, Mary had fallen in love with one of her jailers, 29-year-old John Miller. A one-armed convicted killer who wore a deadly ball and chain attached to his stump, Miller had purchased the turnkey's job after serving his own time in jail. With Mary acquitted, he promptly resigned and they moved in together, launching a stormy two-year relationship noted for its screaming brawls and bouts of public fornication.

In October 1861, Mary stabbed Miller in the heat of battle and fled New Orleans, fearing a new murder charge if he died. Upon recovery, the one-armed bandit begged her to return, plotting revenge behind a bland mask of forgiveness. As Mary stepped through the door on December 5, Miller attacked her with a bullwhip, but she quickly disarmed him, afterward ripping the ball and chain from his stub of an arm when he tried to brain her. Leaping to the attack, Mary stabbed him five times, and Miller was dead when he hit the floor.

Convicted of second-degree murder at her trial, Jackson was sentenced to ten years in prison. She served nine months before Louisiana fell to Union troops, and military governor George Shipley issued a blanket reprieve to convicted felons as one of his first acts in office. The move was conceived as a gesture of contempt for Dixie, but Mary Jane was less concerned with patriotism than self-preservation. Knowing she would soon be re-arrested when the Yankees left, Bricktop departed from New Orleans and was never seen again.

JACKSON, PATRICIA ANN

The first of three daughters in a poor, black family, Patricia Thomas was born at Praco, Alabama, on December 3, 1949. Her father died when Patricia was only six, stabbed in an otherwise trivial argument, and poverty forced the family from their rural home three years later. They settled in Tuscaloosa, where Patricia finished eighth grade before giving up on school for good.

By that time, she was getting all her education from the streets. Self-described as "fast," Patricia found herself pregnant the summer before she was scheduled to enter high school. In those days, Alabama law prescribed that pregnant teens could not return to class for a full year after giving birth, and Patricia took advantage of the free vacation, leaving her mother to care for the baby while she embarked on a spree of self-indulgence. Slashed by a girlfriend in the heat of argument, she took to carrying a blade for self-defense. Her mother threw the first one out, but knives are easily replaced, and Patricia would seldom leave the house unarmed.

In 1966, she quarreled with boyfriend Andrew Hughes and settled their dispute with a straight razor. Hughes was dead on arrival at emergency receiving, and authorities charged Patricia with first-degree murder. A plea bargain reduced the count to second-degree, and

Patricia was sentenced to twelve years in prison, paroled after serving four.

In 1972, she married a man named Jackson, from Bibb County, but the union dissolved after three months, Patricia's husband absconding with another woman. Her mother's death, a short time later, was the final straw, and Patricia sought relief in alcohol. She moved in with a boyfriend to defray expenses, meanwhile picking up a reputation as a mean, unruly drunk. A spate of arrests included charges of hit and run, malicious destruction of property, resisting arrest, assaulting a police officer, and seven counts of disorderly conduct.

On February 28, 1981, Jackson quarreled with Bonnie May Walker, the 50-year-old proprietor of a Tuscaloosa "shot house" — an unlicensed ghetto saloon — who refused to serve her any booze. Patricia drew a knife and plunged it into Walker's chest, while witnesses looked on. The wound was fatal, Alabama law mandating capital punishment for a second murder conviction within twenty years.

The new case was open-and-shut, no rational defense possible against the charge, and Jackson was convicted of first-degree murder on December 28, 1981. Attorney Joel Sogol tried an end run, seeking to avoid the death penalty by attacking her *first* conviction on appeal. The grounds: a belated plea of self-defense. The original trial judge and court reporter were dead, the transcript missing, but Patricia did her part on the witness stand, insisting that Andy Hughes was the first to pull a knife back in 1966. Attorney Tom Wood appeared for the prosecution, recalling that Jackson had never once raised the self-defense issue at her first trial. The appeal was denied, and the death sentence stands.

JEANNERET, MARIE

The daughter of a respectable Swiss family, born in 1836, Marie Jeanneret was orphaned as a child and raised by an uncle to age eighteen. A mysterious fever is said to have retarded her development, and the Jeanneret family tree was riddled with mental defectives. Marie's great-grandmother became "deranged" during pregnancy; she was later described as generally bad-tempered and malicious. Marie's mother was "nervous." Her great-aunt was a hypochondriac who killed herself, and the woman's daughter displayed identical symptoms, living under a constant suicide watch. Yet another close relative was also diagnosed as suffering from extreme hypochondria.

With that background, it is no surprise that Marie displayed similar traits, habitually complaining of imaginary ailments from the onset of her menstrual cycle. A lifelong virgin, she rejected her only prospective suitor in the paranoid belief that he meant to rob her blind. Meanwhile, she kept herself busy with various doctors, demanding treatment for non-existent symptoms. In the process, she convinced herself that she was medically proficient, destined to care for the sick.

In 1866, at age thirty, Marie enrolled at a nursing school in Lausanne. She lasted a bare two months in the classroom, checking out with the excuse that she was going blind. Physicians could find nothing wrong with her eyes, but one — a Dr. Dor, at Veney — suspected Marie of dosing herself with atropine, a belladonna derivative, to simulate eye trouble.

Marie's early departure from school did not stop her from billing herself as a qualified nurse. Her first patient, elderly Madame Chabloz of Lausanne, declined rapidly under Jeanneret's care. She suffered from delirium, dilated pupils, and fits of violent nausea — symptoms common to all Marie's later victims. Madame Chabloz attributed her symptoms to the "medicine" Marie made her drink, but Jeanneret denied having her patient drink anything. While visiting with Madame Eichenberg, the patient's daughter, Marie dropped off a gift of "special" bonbons that left the family weak from vomiting.

A few weeks later, Marie found employment at a new private hospital, operated by one Madame Jouvet. She agreed to work for room and board, with no salary, and at least three patients died suddenly in her first few days on the job. One, a Mademoiselle Junod, entered the hospital in September 1866; a month later, Marie informed the patient's family that she "would probably have a congestion of the brain." The prophecy fulfilled itself a few days later, and Mademoiselle Junod died after two days of delirium and vomiting.

Marie kept up a brave front, meanwhile, acting respectful and solicitous of her patients' welfare in the presence of physicians, calling the doctors "damn fools" behind their backs. Friends knew the truth, that Marie didn't "care a hang" for the survival of her charges. She described one patient as "a piece of carrion, a poison."

Nor was her hostility limited to patients. Marie also took a strong dislike to Julie Jouvet, her employer's young daughter. One evening, the girl's parents responded to cries from her bedroom and found Marie beating the child. Jeanneret escaped punishment with a show of repentance, setting out to poison the whole family with spiked bonbons and cocoa. Julie Jovet died on December 27, 1866, and her mother followed a month later. Household servants reported that Jeanneret predicted Madame Jouvet's illness "three or four days beforehand," when the woman was still in apparent good health. Subsequent tests revealed traces of copper and atropine in Madame Jouvet's body, along with large amounts of morphine.

The death of her employer closed the hospital, and Marie was unemployed for several weeks before she found work as a live-in nurse with one Mademoiselle Lenoir. Her patient died three weeks later, and Marie moved on to Mademoiselle Boucart, residing near Geneva. She brought along a basket filled with medicines and offered explanations of their purpose. "If Madame has need of drugs," she told one servant, "I have some here, in my basket." Another maid was told Marie planned to take the drugs herself, "for treatment of my eyes and of my spine." Mademoiselle Boucart fell violently ill within three days of Marie's arrival, but she managed to survive and Jeanneret was dismissed. Suspicion was starting to spread, and a doctor who treated the Jouvet family warned another prospective client against hiring Marie. "Don't have anything to do with her," he said. "All her patients die."

Before and after her stay with Mademoiselle Boucart, Marie rented quarters in a rooming house owned by Monsieur Gros. As soon as she returned, another tenant — Madame Bouvier — became suddenly ill, dying on May 22, 1867. Two weeks later, landlord Gros came down with the same symptoms, one day after Marie told his family, "I am sure he is going to have the same attack as Madame Bouvier." Sure enough, Gros was dead within days. Both bodies were found to contain atropine and morphine, with additional traces of antimony found in Bouvier's remains. During this same period, a casual visitor to the Gros residence also fell ill with identical symptoms. She survived, and her physician correctly diagnosed her ailment as belladonna poisoning.

Marie Jeanneret was running out of time.

In June of 1867, she moved into a new rooming house, spiking the meals of three tenants, but all three survived. This time, police were summoned, and Marie was taken into custody. Detectives estimated that she poisoned at least thirty persons, including seven or eight who died, but most of the survivors declined to testify in court.

Marie was finally charged with six counts of murder and eleven non-fatal poisonings. A panel of physicians found her sane and responsible, with nothing to support her endless shopping list of ailments. They viewed her early near-engagement as a pivotal event in Marie's life, piling malicious hostility on top of her "already far from sympathetic feelings" toward mankind at large. In her own words, Marie was unable "to endure the sight of happy people." She had even come to hate her own relatives, the panel found, and "took pleasure in placing obstacles, wherever it was possible, in the way of peace and happiness to her associates."

At her trial, Dr. Dor called Marie "unbalanced, ill and hysterical, untruthful, perverse, and malicious." He noted her insistence on painful treatments for imaginary illness and suggested that Marie had been dosing herself with atropine for the past three years. "We can recognize as a symptom of intoxication," Dor testified, "a retention of urine which occurred during that time — a fact sufficient to have kept the accused in a state of over excitement similar to that of eaters of opium and hashish."

In her own bland testimony, Marie admitted giving atropine to nine persons, including six who had died, but she denied any criminal intent. Rather, she said she was trying to help her patients rest after various doctors gave them medicine that left them agitated, unable to sleep. The judge asked Marie why she continued with her "treatments" after witnessing the first grim failures; she replied that she "had always believed the remedies that she gave ought to do good, to calm the patient." Marie had only reconsidered the matter in jail, finally telling the court, "I was in the wrong. I forgot myself. I tried to give remedies that were not in the doctor's prescription, and that's my fault."

The judge found her mental state defective, but her "low moral standards and capacities" left her criminally responsible. Convicted on six counts of murder, Marie Jeanneret was sentenced to twenty years in prison. She died behind bars in 1884.

JEGADO, HELENE

Born in Brittany around 1803 and orphaned at age seven, Helene Jegado grew up in a French orphanage where educational facilities were nonexistent. Still illiterate in adolescence, when she left the "home" to enter domestic service, Jegado nursed a brooding grudge against society at large, with special hatred for affluent families. It took some time for rage to translate into action, but she finally adopted poison as her weapon of revenge in the late 1820s.

In choosing victims, Helene played no favorites. Her first experiment in homicide, spanning three months, wiped out all seven members of the household where she was employed. Helene's display of grief was so convincing that police dismissed her as a suspect after cursory interrogation.

Once she got a taste of sudden death, Helene found out that she enjoyed it. No sooner did she find a new position than the family members and her fellow servants started dying off. Mobility and a facade of wounded innocence protected her. "Wherever I go," she complained tearfully, "people die."

Helene's reputation for "fatal influence" was spreading by 1831, when Mademoiselle Keraly of Hennebont hired her against the advice of friends. Before Helene moved on, Mademoiselle Keraly's father and another household servant were dead. In the village of Guern, she murdered a party of seven, including her own sister; afterward, she took her sister's job and poisoned three more members of the household. Drifting through a dozen towns in Brittany, she killed repeatedly, poisoning men, women, and children without regard to age or social status.

At length, tiring of the game or fearing arrest, Jegado entered a convent and took her vows as Sister Helene. A penchant for petty theft soon got her expelled, but there were always other convents. Helene's next transgression, in 1833, was more serious — she poisoned some of the other nuns — but her order declined to prosecute, fearing bad publicity.

Returning to her first profession as a maid, Helene picked up where she had left off prior to her "religious" period... and the body-count continued to grow. In 1848, Jegado was working for a Monsieur Rabot, at Rennes, when she was caught stealing trinkets and ordered to leave the house. Next morning, after breakfast, the entire family was stricken with nausea and stomach pains, but no fatalities resulted.

Jegado enjoyed her last fling at the home of Professor Theodore Bidard, also at Rennes, where she poisoned a servant named Rosalie Sarrazin on July 1, 1851. This time, an autopsy found traces of arsenic in the corpse, and police were summoned to investigate. Still without suspects, detectives focused on Jegado when she entered the interrogation room and blurted out "I'm innocent!"

"Of what?" they asked.

The rest is history. Jegado crumbled, rattling off the list of victims she was able to remember. Authorities linked Jegado to twenty-three murders, five nonfatal poisonings, and eleven thefts in the period between 1833 and 1841. There were doubtless other homicides, before and after that period, but a ten-year statute of limitations reduced the number of potential charges. At her trial, in 1851, Helene was charged with three counts of murder, three attempted murders, and eleven thefts. Conviction carried a mandatory death sentence, and Jegado was guillotined before year's end.

JOHNSON, MARTHA ANN

Monday-morning quarterbacks in Georgia had a field day with the case of Martha Johnson, trying to explain how the murders of four children "fell through the cracks" of the criminal justice system. Homicide investigators blamed their failure on the suspect's change of address, noting ruefully that different jurisdictions often fail to keep in touch. Physicians dropped the ball repeatedly, misdiagnosing the cause of death in Martha's first three murders. On the fourth, detectives and a medical examiner suggested prosecution, but the Clayton County D.A. never followed through. Even Martha's husband, after noting a distinctive pattern in the deaths, could not persuade authorities to act.

However the responsibility is portioned out, the bungling cost four lives.

A Georgia native, born in 1955, Martha Johnson was working on her third marriage at age twenty-two. The first had produced a daughter, Jennyann Wright, born in 1971. James William Taylor, the product of Martha's second marriage, followed in 1975. Husband number three, Earl Bowen, got along well with Martha's children and fathered two of his own — Earl Wayne in 1979 and Tibitha Janeel in 1980 — but he did not get along so well with Martha.

In fact, the couple argued bitterly, and Earl repeatedly walked out to let his temper cool. They always patched things up, or so it seemed, but Martha had begun to feel the strain. Perhaps she saw the children as a stumbling block to happiness, or simply pawns to be manipulated in a deadly private game. In either case, the end result was lethal.

Two-year-old James Taylor was the first to go, already dead when Martha brought him to a Clayton County hospital on September 25, 1977. He had failed to wake up that morning, she said, and doctors were unable to revive him. Despite his relatively advanced age, they blamed the boy's death on Sudden Infant Death Syndrome (SIDS) and closed the file. Earl Bowen shared his wife's apparent grief and came back home.

In 1980, the couple separated again, and Martha made another emergency trip to the hospital. This time, the victim was three-month-old Tibitha, and the diagnosed cause of death was identical. Earl Bowen was openly suspicious, and experts consider two SIDS deaths in the same family improbable, but Clayton County physicians and detectives accepted Martha's plea of "bad luck."

Yet another quarrel and separation preceded the death of two-year-old Earl Wayne Bowen, on February 15, 1981. This time, physicians gave SIDS a break and blamed the child's death on "seizure disorder of unknown etiology." Following Earl's funeral, 10-year-old Jennyann told her father and a Fulton County social worker that she was afraid to stay home with her mother. Welfare workers interviewed the family but found no legal grounds for removing Jennyann to a foster home. Detectives and the county medical examiner agreed there was no evidence of homicide to build a case in court.

A year and six days after little Earl's death, Martha summoned police to her new home in Jonesboro, declaring that her daughter had "stopped breathing." Patrolmen found the child lying face-down in her bed, beyond help by the time paramedics arrived. An autopsy blamed her death on "probable asphyxia" of "undetermined cause," and the medical examiner called it "suspicious," noting that "this 11-year-old Caucasian female is the fourth child in the family to die following domestic arguments between the parents." Even so, the coroner declined to hold an inquest, and the district attorney's office ignored a recommendation that Martha be prosecuted.

It was finally too much for Bowen, and the couple split for good. Martha was remarried to Charles Johnson, living in Locust Grove, when the Atlanta *Journal-Constitution* launched a new investigation of her case in December 1988. A month later, Dr. William Anderson declared that his 1977 diagnosis of SIDS for James Taylor was probably wrong. With twenty-twenty hindsight, the doctor told newsmen, "I wouldn't hesitate to say there's a 90% chance that this is homicide."

This time, police were listening. Martha was arrested on July 3, 1989, held without bail on a charge of murdering Jennyann. In a videotaped confession, made the same day, she admitted smothering Jennyann and James Taylor by rolling her 250-pound bulk on top of the children as they slept. In each case, Martha said, her motive was to bring Earl Bowen home. The deaths of Tibitha and little Earl, she told police, were not her fault. Clayton County prosecutors disagreed, charging Johnson with two more counts of murder in the week following her arrest. (No charge has been filed to date for the death of James Taylor, in Fulton County.)

Martha changed her mind and recanted the confession before her murder trial began, on April 30, 1990, but the tape was still admitted into evidence. Charles Johnson did his best for the defense, tearfully describing Martha as a good wife and mother who "could never do anything like they're saying." Jurors disagreed, convicting her of first-degree murder on May 5, and she was sentenced to death. Georgia's Supreme Court rejected Martha's appeal in March 1991. [See also: Lumbrera, Diana; Tinning, Marybeth; Tuggle, Debra; Turner, Lise; Woods, Martha]

JONES, ANNIE

A native Canadian, born at Woodstock, New Brunswick, in 1904, Annie Jones migrated with her husband Erwin to the small town of Madison, Maine. Their union produced five children: Charles in 1922; Shirley in 1924; twins Robert and Edward in 1932; and Norman in 1934. Erwin Jones supported his brood from the proceeds of an auto repair shop, planted across the road from their home.

There is no record of discord in the family, but Annie spent the last two years of her life under a physician's care for various real or imagined ailments. Friends and relatives described her as despondent, sometimes threatening to kill her children and herself, but they were quick to note that she had made no actual attempt to carry out her threats. In mid-June 1936, Annie bought a box of ammunition for the family rifle; 14-year-old Charles found out about the purchase, and she threatened to kill him if he told his father.

Early on the morning of June 21, Annie packed a bag of cookies, telling her three youngest children they were going on a picnic. Also in the bag, unseen, were lengths of rope and several shredded rags. She took her three boys back into the woods behind their house, well out of sight from the road, to a point where she had stashed her rifle in advance. There, she bound the twins together hand and foot, blindfolding each with a rag. Two-year-old Norman was tied to his brothers with a rope around his waist, sans blindfold.

Next, she picked the rifle up and shot each boy in the head at close range, killing them instantly. She laid them out together on a blanket, face-up toward the sky, before she turned the rifle on herself and sent a bullet ripping from beneath her chin, into her brain.

Daughter Shirley grew concerned when her mother and brothers failed to return on time, fetching her father from his shop across the road. It was Erwin Jones who found the bodies of his wife and sons, reporting the discovery to police. In the absence of a suicide note or positive statements from Annie before her death, no clear-cut motive was determined for the crime.

JONES, GENENE: See TURK, GENENE

JONES, ROXANNE

A California native, born in 1958, Roxanne Jones married her first husband, Joachim Fernandez, when she was barely sixteen. Their first child, daughter Brandy, was born that same year, and a second daughter — Leticia — followed in 1976. Three years later, their relationship on the rocks, Joachim and Roxanne were divorced. In 1980, Roxanne married housepainter Jeff Jones and bore him a son, Jeremiah. This marriage endured for nine years, and their separation in 1989 seemed amiable. Jeff moved out of the family home in Reseda, California, describing their problems as "nothing major." The estranged couple kept in touch on a regular basis, with Roxanne holding custody of the children.

Neighbors in Reseda viewed Roxanne as "unusual," a woman who dressed in 1960s style and talked like an overaged hippy, raising goats and chickens in her yard, allowing her daughters to roam the streets at all hours of the night. As one neighbor remarked, "They were just kind of strange people, and we kept away from them."

Without Jeff's paycheck, money was a persistent problem for Roxanne and her kids. She baby-sat and worked odd jobs from time to time, while Brandy donated her wages from a part-time pizzeria job. Media reports differ on whether or not the family received welfare payments, and the welfare department cited rules of privacy in refusing to comment. It is known that Roxanne sometimes asked her neighbors for small loans, and rumor has it that she sold her blood from time to time, to make ends meet.

By March 1990, Roxanne was speaking frequently of suicide, but friends and neighbors ignored the warning signs. When Jeremiah told his first-grade teacher that his mother was taking him to "a good place where God is and there are no worries," the teacher assumed he was referring to a religious retreat. When Roxanne told her neighbors she wanted to "get out of here," they understood her to mean she was moving away.

Jeff Jones saw Roxanne for the last time on March 19, 1990. She told him she was leaving California with the children "for a couple of months" and gave him a parting hug on the doorstep. That evening, Brandy and Letitia went bowling, returning home at 4 A.M. on Tuesday. Sometime later, Roxanne took a .22-caliber rifle and killed her three children as they slept, shooting each victim once in the head and once in the chest. That done, she turned the rifle on herself and fired a single bullet through her brain.

A teenage friend of Brandy and Letitia stopped by the house on Wednesday, March 21, concerned about the fact that her telephone calls went unanswered. She entered the house through a dog door and found the four bodies, then hastily retreated to summon police.

Inside the house, patrolmen found a message scrawled across one wall with a black marker. It read: "God please forgive me. My loved ones please forget me." A note on the desk said, "If we are not dead, then don't call an ambulance." In the bedroom, a longer suicide note outlined Roxanne's problems, asked God's forgiveness, and proclaimed that love for her children made it unbearable for her to see them trapped in a world full of strife. News of the slaughter brought scores of morbid gawkers to the normally quiet street, overflowing sidewalks and lawns. At the height of the circus, three cars collided in front of the house, leaving two persons injured.

JUDD, WINNIE RUTH

America's so-called "Tiger Woman" was an Illinois native, born in 1909. She contracted tuberculosis in her youth and was sent to recuperate at an Arizona sanitarium, where she met and fell in love with a physician, Dr. William Judd, whom she married. She found work at a Phoenix medical clinic, there befriending co-worker Agnes LeRoi, sometimes sleeping overnight at the apartment LeRoi shared with roommate Hedvig Samuelson.

On the night of October 16, 1931, neighbors heard screams from the apartment, but the noise subsided before they grew concerned enough to call police. Next morning, Winnie Judd was late for work at the clinic, while Agnes LeRoi never showed up at all. That evening, Winnie called a moving van to fetch a pair of heavy trunks, and she caught a train for Los Angeles with her ponderous luggage on October 18.

Arriving at L.A.'s Union Pacific station, Winnie asked a porter to help put the trunks in her car. The porter noted a dark liquid seeping from one of the trunks, and pointed it out to Mrs. Judd. Her car was just outside, she said; if the porter would wait where he was, she would fetch her keys, unlock the trunk, and find out what was leaking. Suspicious by now, the porter followed her outside and memorized the license number of her vehicle as Winnie sped away.

Back inside the station, her trunks were forced open, revealing Agnes LeRoi's body in the larger one, Hedvig Samuelson dismembered to fit in the smaller. Police were summoned, quickly tracing the car to Winnie Ruth's brother, but their suspect had vanished from sight. A letter to her husband, never mailed but found by the authorities, described all manner of sexual hi-jinx at the Phoenix apartment, including "straight," bisexual and homosexual couplings by various parties. Dr. Judd broadcast a public appeal for his wife's surrender on October 23, and she met police that afternoon at a Los Angeles funeral home.

In custody, and later at her Phoenix murder trial, Winnie Judd described the double slaying as a matter of self-defense. She had been arguing with Hedvig Samuelson, she said, when "Sammy" pulled a gun and threatened her. They grappled for the weapon, one shot drilling Winnie's hand before she turned the gun on Samuelson and killed her. Agnes LeRoi had allegedly joined the battle at that point, forcing Judd to shoot her as well. With two corpses on her hands, Winnie had summoned a friend, Phoenix businessman Carl Harris, to help her hide the remains. It was Harris, she said, who dismembered Samuelson's body, and while Harris was initially charged as an accomplice, the charges were soon dismissed.

At trial, prosecutors hammered away at Winnie's self-defense alibi, suggesting a vague jealousy motive, noting that no one had seen a wound on her hand when she showed up for work at the clinic on October 17. It was a self-inflicted wound, they said, intended to confuse the court, and jurors agreed, convicting Mrs. Judd on two counts of first-degree murder. Condemned to hang, she behaved so erratically in prison that Arizona's governor granted a special sanity hearing, seventy-two hours before her scheduled execution.

The hearing was an instant media sideshow, with Winnie Judd clapping, laughing, and shouting at the jury, sometimes tearing at her hair, once trying to remove her clothes in court. Her mother testified that Winnie had been "more or less insane all her life," and her father traced the family's taint of madness back 125 years, to its root in their native Scotland. When all was said and done, Winnie's death sentence was commuted to a life prison term, the defendant committed to Arizona's state hospital for the criminally insane.

At the asylum, Winnie showed a sudden and remarkable improvement. There were no more screaming fits or tantrums as she settled into the routine, quiet and calculating, biding her time. Before long, she staged her first escape, leaving a crude dummy in her bed to fool the guards while she slipped away. Recaptured days later, she was placed under close watch, but it seemed to make no difference. In all, she would escape seven times, prompting journalists to remark on slow news days, "Well, maybe Winnie Ruth Judd will escape again." One sensational crime magazine opened an article on Judd's case with this warning to subscribers: "When you read this story, the country's cleverest maniac may be at large again, perhaps walking down your street, or sitting next to you!" Returned to custody after a typical escape in 1952, Winnie was called to testify before a grand jury probing state hospital conditions. A search, preliminary to her trip, revealed a key hidden in her hair and a razor blade concealed beneath her tongue.

Winnie staged her last and most successful break-out in 1962, moving in with a California couple who sheltered her until she was identified and recaptured in 1969. Attorney Melvin Belli fought extradition to Arizona, but Governor Ronald Reagan had enough criminals on his hands as it was, and he ordered Winnie's return. Back in Phoenix, she was finally judged sane and ordered to spend the remainder of her time in prison, but her stay behind bars was short-lived. Paroled on December 22, 1971, Judd moved back to California and a life of comfortable obscurity.

JUENEMANN, CHARLOTTE

German housewife Charlotte Juenemann was the very model of propriety until 1934, when her husband was committed to a lunatic asylum. Then, overnight, the 34-year-old mother of three seemed to change. For openers, she pulled her children out of school and locked them in a tiny basement room where they would spend the remainder of their short lives huddled in dank quarters, slowly starving to death. Charlotte received a government pension, earmarked for child support, but she preferred to spend the money on herself, promoting a frenetic nightlife.

Inevitably, disappearing children sparked official questions — first from teachers, then from the police, when Charlotte's answers failed to satisfy. Investigators came too late to save the children, but they did the next best thing, arresting Charlotte on a triple murder charge. By that time, Juenemann was reportedly pregnant, the result of an impassioned one-night stand, but Nazi courts had little sympathy for "undesirables." Convicted of murder despite her condition, Charlotte was sentenced to death by decapitation on March 30, 1935. No appeals were allowed, and she was beheaded at Plotzenee Prison five months later, on August 27.

KANTARIAN, NANCY LEE

Born in 1959, Nancy Heselden was the daughter of media magnate John Heselden, deputy chairman of the same Gannett Corporation that publishes *USA Today* and various other newspapers. By age twenty-five she was married to Harry Kantarian, living in Great Falls, Virginia, with her attorney husband and their two children. On the surface, it appeared to be a perfect life, complete with money and prestige, a suburban home valued at $400,000, and frequent excursions into nearby Washington, D.C. Still, there was something... On the night of May 23, 1984, with Harry in Denver on business, Nancy Kantarian inexplicably killed her two children and set their house on fire. Police found her at a neighbor's home, hysterical and incoherent. Fire-fighters retrieved six-year-old Talia and five-year-old Jamie Lee from the blazing house, but it was already too late. Flames and smoke inhalation had finished the younger girl, while Talia had been stabbed a total of thirty-two times. With no other suspects in sight, Nancy Kantarian was held for questioning on suspicion of murder and arson.

In custody, she first tried to blame the fire on her children, but Talia's numerous stab wounds posed a problem. Finally, Kantarian admitted to police that she "got mad" and lost control when Jamie "wouldn't sleep." It was a lame excuse for double murder, and a panel of psychiatrists agreed that Nancy was irrational.

On October 2, 1984, Kantarian pled guilty on two counts of voluntary manslaughter. Judge Bernard Jennings told the court, "There is no question that the killings are the result of some form of mental or emotional illness." Prosecutor Robert Horan supported the defense recommendation for psychiatric treatment in lieu of jail time, and Judge Jennings agreed on October 6. Nancy was sentenced to ten years in prison, the sentence suspended on condition that she enter a private mental institution at her own expense. "There is no need to incarcerate you as a deterrent to others," the judge declared, "and I don't think we really need to protect society from you."

KARDOS, MARIA: See "ANGEL MAKERS OF NAGYREV"

KELLIHER, MARY

Between 1905 and 1908, six close relatives of Boston resident Mary Kelliher died under mysterious circumstances, all displaying similar symptoms of stomach cramps, vomiting, and diarrhea. The dead included Mary's husband, three of her children, her sister, and a sister-in-law. In July 1908, autopsy surgeons found lethal amounts of arsenic in Mary's daughter, and similar results were obtained when other family members were exhumed. Authorities suspected Mary, but police were short of evidence until they searched her home, discovering a mattress soaked in arsenic. All six victims, it appeared, had slept in the polluted bed before they died, presumably absorbing poison through their skin. At her trial on murder charges, Mary denied any knowledge of the poisoned mattress, and she had no explanation for her own miraculous survival in the midst of so much death. The prosecution's case ran aground on unanswered questions, and Mary was finally acquitted, but no other suspect has ever been named in the killings. Kelliher's case is sometimes compared to that of French poisoner Marie Besnard, who likewise escaped punishment for the "perfect crime."

KIMURA, FUMIKO

A Japanese immigrant to Southern California, Fumiko Kimura viewed her life as a series of depressing failures. Her parents divorced when Fumiko was an infant, and her father died before she ever had a chance to know him. Her mother remarried, but Fumiko's stepfather was cold and unfeeling, fond of introducing her to strangers as "a relative's daughter." Pregnant as a teenager, she opted for abortion but later regretted her choice. She married for the first time in 1976, but the relationship disintegrated after less than three years. Her second marriage, to a 40-year-old man, was no more successful. Finally, in 1981, Fumiko seemed to get it right with Itsuroku Kimura.

The newlyweds moved to California, where Fumiko gave birth to a son, Kazutaka. She became a compulsive housewife and mother, fretting over domestic details in an effort to forestall further disappointment. At one point, following the birth of daughter Yuri in late 1984, Fumiko became so obsessed with her children's safety that she removed all furniture from the living room, afraid that one of them would stub a toe or have some other kind of accident. She also brooded over Yuri "losing weight," despite the chubby girl's apparent health, Fumiko convincing herself that her breast milk was somehow inadequate to feed the child.

In mid-January 1985, a Japanese-American woman appeared on Fumiko's doorstep, introducing herself as Itsuroku's mistress. The affair had been going on for three years, she explained, including an aborted pregnancy and one attempted suicide. The stranger seemed grief-stricken, offering to kill herself as a form of atonement, but Fumiko put her off. She also refused to confront Itsuroku about the affair, maintaining her pose as a perfect mate, bathing her husband's feet each night when he returned from work, regardless of the hour. Proceeding from her basic insecurity, Fumiko convinced herself the affair was her fault, the inevitable product of her own "incompetence."

On January 25, Fumiko telephoned her sister in Japan to discuss Itsuroku's affair. She "sounded strange" on the phone, but claimed that she was doing well. A second call that evening closed with Fumiko's promise to "make it all right." Her brother called back the next morning and spoke to Itsuroku, who acknowledged that his wife was "acting strange" these days. A doctor was consulted and prescribed mild tranquilizers for "a slight case of neurosis." Plans were made to send Fumiko's mother from Japan, to check things out and see her daughter through the rocky days ahead.

On January 29, before her mother caught a trans-Pacific flight, Fumiko took her children on a bus ride to the beach at Santa Monica. With one child underneath each arm, she waded out to sea, proceeding stolidly until the water closed above her head. It took another moment for the nearest bystanders to realize that they were witnessing a murder-suicide, and neither child was breathing by the time rescuers dragged them back ashore. Yuri and Kazutaka were dead on arrival at a local hospital, but doctors managed to revive Fumiko, holding her for psychiatric observation pending criminal charges.

News of the incident produced an outpouring of public sympathy, with hundreds of letters received from Japan. Torn between Japanese culture and American law, prosecutors charged Fumiko with two counts of first-degree murder, citing "special circumstances" that would make her eligible for capital punishment. The defense got a boost when psychiatrist Robert Markman diagnosed Fumiko as suffering from severe postpartum depression, exacerbated by her recent marital turmoil. The D.A. finally accepted her guilty plea to charges of involuntary manslaughter, and Fumiko was released on probation. At last report, she had reconciled with Itsuroku and was hoping for another child.

KING, KATHLEEN

California born in 1922, Kathleen King had received extensive psychiatric counseling before she met and wed her husband Charles. The newlyweds settled in Dayton, Ohio, where Charles was employed as a postman, but wedded bliss did not improve Kathleen's mental state. In 1945, while visiting California, she was accidentally struck on the head by an auto trunk lid, producing disorientation and "strange" behavior. Back in Dayton, her doctor tried electroshock therapy to cure the problem, with limited results. Further outbursts of mental instability followed the birth of each child, in 1953, '54, and '56. In 1954, Kathleen was hospitalized following an apparent suicide attempt with sleeping pills. Twice, she tried to leap from the upstairs window of her hospital room, and physicians responded with a dozen more shock treatments. This time, Kathleen went home convinced that she was doing better.

As it turned out, she was wrong.

In November 1956, the Kings purchased a small home in nearby Xenia, Ohio, but the move put a serious strain on their family budget. By April 1958, they had put the house up for sale, planning a return to Dayton. On Tuesday, April 8, Kathleen received a prescription of thirty tranquilizers from her doctor, swallowing half the pills in a fit of depression the following day. Charles had trouble rousing Kathleen when he got home from work that night, and he stayed home from work to watch her on Thursday, hiding the pills from his wife. On Friday, before he left for work, Charles gave Kathleen two pills to get her through the day.

On Saturday, April 12, Charles left for work around 6 A.M. Kathleen was up and pleading with him to stay home, threatening to kill the children and herself, but Charles had heard such threats before and shrugged them off. He left Kathleen two tranquilizers, and she took them both at once, returning to bed when he left. Still brooding over the family debts, she lay awake, rising again at 8:30 to fix breakfast for her children. Somewhere, in the midst of dishing out bacon and eggs, Kathleen decided that the best solution for her family's financial problems was to kill the kids.

After breakfast, Kathleen returned two-year-old Brian to his crib. Charleen, age five, stretched out beside her brother on the bedroom floor, while three-year-old Donald occupied the living room sofa. Armed with a hammer, Kathleen slugged Donald first, proceeding to the bedroom where she told her daughter, "I'm going to send you to heaven, and I'm going to hell." Charleen, imagining her mother had a game in mind, sat up and said, "Okay." Kathleen administered two crushing blows to Charleen's skull, then turned and bludgeoned Brian in his crib.

Returning to the living room, she found her older son alive. In fact, Donald had staggered into the kitchen, leaving a trail of blood behind. Kathleen pursued him, struck him down, and finished the job by plunging an eight-inch butcher knife into the back of his head. Satisfied, she carried Donald back to the couch and lay down with the corpse in her arms, to watch television. Asked later if Donald had spoken, she replied, "No. He probably didn't like the program and he had his eyes closed."

As the day wore on, Kathleen rose and tried to kill herself by removing a fuse from the kitchen fuse box, and inserting her finger in the socket. Failing there, she slashed her wrists and forearms with a knife and razor blade, but she inflicted only superficial wounds. Around 7:30 P.M., Kathleen contemplated cooking dinner for Charles, but he failed to appear, so she drank oven cleaner instead. Finally, in frustration, she tried to choke herself by wrapping a cloth belt around her neck and tying the opposite end to a bedpost.

It was past midnight when Charles returned from work, having spent the past nine hours dining on pizza and drinking with friends at a lodge. (Later, he would tell police that Kathleen's constant nagging made him bitterly reluctant to come home.) The children were all dead, but Kathleen was rushed to a hospital, where burns to her tongue and throat prevented her from speaking for the next three days.

On April 15, Kathleen turned violent and nearly escaped from her hospital room. She regained her voice the same day, admitting that she killed her children because "I thought they would be better off dead." Family debt was the motive, although she described her husband as "a good provider." She expressed a desire for more electroshock treatments to help clear her mind.

Charged with three counts of murder on April 16, Kathleen pled not guilty by reason of insanity. She was transferred to Lima State Hospital for thirty days of psychiatric observation, and doctors there diagnosed her as schizophrenic, incompetent for trial. A Dayton judge agreed, and Kathleen was returned to Lima for an indefinite period of treatment.

In October 1960, state psychiatrists judged Kathleen competent for trial, and the proceedings began that December. A panel of judges found her not guilty by reason of insanity, and she was returned to Lima for an indefinite term. Seven years later, Kathleen petitioned for release under a new state law governing mental patients. Found sane at a subsequent court hearing, she was unconditionally released in December 1967.

KINNE, SHARON

When James and Sharon Kinne were married in October 1956, it was a matter of necessity. At sixteen, she was pregnant, and while neither loved the other, marriage was "the thing to do" for teenage parents-to-be in Independence, Missouri. A miscarriage eventually solved the problem, but it came too late. By March of 1960, the Kinnes had a mortgage and two children to support, but Sharon was restless, yearning for a life with someone other than a hometown boy who still included "shucks" in his vocabulary.

On March 19, police were summoned to the Kinne residence, where they found James lying on the bed, a bullet in his brain. Sharon told detectives that her two-year-old daughter had been playing with a loaded pistol when the weapon discharged, striking James in the head. Police remarked upon the youngster's seeming familiarity with the weapon, including manipulation of its safety lever, but the death was ultimately ruled an accident.

Suddenly flush with insurance money, Sharon bought herself a new car, becoming "friendly" with the salesman, Walter Jones. On May 27, 1960, she placed another call to the police, reporting her discovery of a woman's lifeless body on a lonely, wooded lane in rural Jackson County. Shot four times, the victim proved to be Patricia Jones, Walter's wife. Sharon explained that she was helping Walter look for his missing spouse, whom he suspected of meeting another man in the secluded lover's lane. Instead of catching Patricia in *flagrante delicto*, they found her dead and called for the authorities.

Patricia Jones had been shot with a .22-caliber pistol, and investigators learned that Sharon had recently acquired such a weapon. She had asked a male co-worker to buy the gun for her, specifically requesting that it not be registered in her name. Indicted for murder in September 1960, Sharon was subsequently acquitted when ballistics tests indicated that the gun in her possession was not the murder weapon.

Upon release, Sharon was immediately re-arrested for the murder of her husband, homicide detectives having chucked the "accident" theory in favor of darker suspicions. A two-year-old child, experts testified at Sharon's trial in January 1962, could not have pulled the trigger on the gun that killed James Kinne. Convicted of murder and sentenced to life, Sharon fought the verdict through a series of appeals. The jury deadlocked in her third trial, unable to reach a decision. A fourth trial was scheduled for October 1964, but Sharon Kinne had other plans.

On September 14, Sharon and her new boyfriend, Frank Puglise, checked into the Hotel Gin, in Mexico City. Quarreling with her lover four days later, she went out alone and picked up a local radio announcer, Francisco Ordonez, returning with him to his motel room. A short time later, the proprietor heard shots and rushed to Ordonez's room, surprised to find Ordonez sprawled on the floor, two bullets in his heart.

Sharon stood over the corpse, gun in hand, and as the manager retreated she shot him in the shoulder. They were grappling for the gun when officers arrived, responding to reports of gunfire.

A Mexican court was unimpressed with Sharon's tale of self-defense, and she was sentenced to ten years in prison; an unsuccessful appeal resulted in three more years being added to her term. In the meantime, Kansas authorities had a chance to examine the gun that killed Ordonez, discovering that it had also killed Patricia Jones. New murder charges would be waiting stateside, if and when the prisoner discharged her sentence in a foreign jail.

KLIMEK, TILLIE

Born in 1865, in Chicago's "Little Poland," Tillie Gbrurek went to work in a sweatshop as a child. She grew up beefy, muscular and unattractive, but she was a wizard in the kitchen, and her specialty was hearty stew. In 1885, a marriage broker paired her off with one John Mitkiewitz, a shiftless lay-about whom she supported, fed, and pampered for a quarter of a century before the tables finally turned.

One afternoon in 1911, Tillie was working her usual job in the sweatshop when she observed her employer bullying a child. Fed up at last, she crossed the room and decked the foreman with a single punch. From there, with the applause still ringing in her ears, she turned for home and gave her worthless spouse a thrashing which induced him to evacuate the house and find a steady job.

Around the time of Tillie's sudden turnaround, she also started having "visions" which allowed her to "predict the future" with amazing accuracy. Staring at a mongrel dog one afternoon, she solemnly predicted it would die within a set amount of time. The mutt fell dead on cue, and others followed. Tillie Mitkiewitz was building up a reputation as a "seer."

In 1914, Tillie's "ancient powers" led her to announce that husband John had only three more weeks to live. Her prophecy was accurate, and with a thousand dollars from his life insurance in her purse, she paid another visit to the marriage broker. Soon, she was the blushing bride of John Rukowski, but again the "powers" brought bad news. Three months after the wedding, Tillie began dropping hints that her husband would die in two weeks. Again, her reputation as a visionary was upheld — and more insurance money came her way.

Creeping up on fifty now, the portly widow had no time to spare for mourning. John was barely in the ground before she married Joe Guszkowski, but her luck was running true to form. The "powers" spoke. Joe died. His life insurance paid.

In 1916, Tillie married husband number four, Frank Kupczyk. She seemed happier with Frank — he managed to survive four anniversaries — but in the meantime, Tillie's extrasensory perception found another target. Neighbor Rose Chudzinsky made no secret of the fact that she regarded Tillie's miserable luck — and her predictions of disaster — with extreme suspicion. Tillie huddled with the spirits, and they told her Chudzinsky's days were numbered. Neighbors waited patiently for yet another funeral, and no one seemed surprised when Rose collapsed on schedule.

Shortly after the removal of her neighbor, Tillie visited a fabric store and purchased black material to make a dress in preparation for her husband's funeral. The clerk was sympathetic. When had Mr. Kupczyk died? "Ten days from now," came the reply.

Frank kept his schedule, to the day, and Tillie married Anton Klimek, husband number five, in 1921. By now, Chicago's finest had become suspicious of the high mortality in Tillie's household. When detectives paid a visit, on October 27, they discovered Anton Klimek sick in bed, his wife beside him, feeding him his stew. A stomach pump saved Anton's life, and lab analysis discovered arsenic in Tillie's winning recipe. She grappled with police and sent a couple of patrolmen to emergency receiving as they dragged her to a cell, but Tillie's run was over. On conviction, she was sentenced to a term of life imprisonment, with the express condition that she never be allowed to cook for other inmates.

KNAPP, LORRAINE

A Montana miner's daughter, born in 1928, mass-killer Lorraine Knapp betrayed no signs of violence or mental disturbance until the last weeks of her life. At age twenty-one, she had left home to work as a mechanic's secretary in Dillon, Montana, but she lost the job and returned home to Butte in mid-November 1949. Unemployed for the moment, Lorraine was described by a brother as "brooding and acting strangely," but no one anticipated the explosive violence that consumed her family on New Year's Eve 1949.

That night, armed with a .22-caliber rifle, Lorraine killed four members of her household before turning the gun on herself. Victims included Lorraine's mother Hazel, her seven-year-old sister Winifred, and two brothers: 12-year-old Fay and three-year-old Ernest. Surviving brothers Jack and George Knapp returned home from a party to find Lorraine dead on the living room couch, her other victims scattered throughout the house. Fay and Ernest had been killed outright; Lorraine, Hazel, and Winifred died a short time later, at St. James Hospital.

No concrete motive was suggested for the massacre. The morning after, Deputy County Attorney J. Frank Sullivan could only tell the press "there was some doubt that Lorraine was in her right mind."

KRENWINKEL, PATRICIA:

See MANSON "FAMILY"

KSZEPKA, JENNIFER

A rebellious "army brat," born in 1975, Jennifer Kszepka lived with her parents and older sister in Gloucester, Virginia. Sgt. Jerome Kszepka was a strict disciplinarian, and his wife Linda shared Jerome's negative opinion of Jennifer's 16-year-old boyfriend, Dominic Hendrix. Family arguments raged back and forth until the first week of June 1992. At last, reluctantly, Jerome and Linda decided to write their younger daughter off as hopeless and kick her out of the house.

Sunday, June 7, should have been a joyous occasion for the Kszepka family. Daughter Ranae, age twenty-one, had just become engaged to fiancée Billy D'Amico, but the glad tidings were overshadowed by Jennifer's impending exile. That night, when Ranae and Billy stopped by to announce their engagement, Jerome asked them to leave the house. They complied with his request, but Jerome's behavior was so unusual that Ranae later went back on her own to see what was wrong with her dad. In retrospect, Billy D'Amico would suspect that Jerome's killers were already inside the house.

Linda Kszepka came home around 11 P.M. Sunday night and walked in on a murder in progress. Confronted by Jennifer, Dominic Hendrix, and another youth, she was clubbed to the floor, her assailants fleeing in the family car. When she regained her senses and surveyed the scene, Linda found her husband and Ranae knifed to death in the midst of a bloody charnel house.

Police broadcast a nationwide alert for Jennifer, her boyfriend, and the stolen car. On June 11, Nevada highway patrolmen stopped the vehicle for speeding on U.S. Highway 50, twenty miles north of Eureka. The Virginia license plates were on file, and bloody clothing was found in the car. Arrested with Jennifer and Dominic was their accomplice, 17-year-old Michael Gauman. The three waived extradition and were returned to Gloucester on June 11, under guard.

Detectives announced that one of the boys had confessed his role in the murders, but no further details were aired. Jennifer Kszepka was described as the "brains" behind the double murder, prosecutors noting that she had written a letter to Dominic days earlier, threatening to kill her parents for their opposition to the teenage romance. On February 1, 1993, Jennifer pled guilty to the murders, calling them "a terrible mistake." The judge agreed and sentenced her to life imprisonment.

LALAURIE, DELPHINE

Louisiana was still a French colony when Delphine McCarty was born in 1790, the daughter of a powerful New Orleans family. Beautiful and arrogant, she married three times, the last to a mousy physician, Dr. Louis Lalaurie, who permitted her to dominate his life. Their mansion on Royal Street was staffed by dozens of African slaves, and while a mulatto butler served as the family overseer, Delphine took a personal hand in the punishments meted out for real or imagined infractions.

In fact, by her mid-thirties, Delphine Lalaurie was a hard-core sadist who derived perverse satisfaction from torturing helpless blacks. Rumors of her vicious temperament were rife on Royal Street and throughout New Orleans, but her wealth and social standing placed Delphine above public criticism. Lafayette himself had dined at her home in 1825, and mistreatment of slaves in 19th-century Louisiana was hardly a rare circumstance. The blacks her husband purchased *were* Lalaurie's chattel, after all, and neighbors shied away from telling one another how to deal with children, animals, or other private property.

Delphine Lalaurie crossed the line from "bad manners" to blatant lunacy one night in 1833. A Royal Street neighbor was attracted to the sound of screams from Delphine's home, and she arrived in time to see a young black girl burst from the house, Delphine in hot pursuit, brandishing a whip. Lalaurie flogged the child around the courtyard, drawing blood, and chased her back inside the mansion. Moments later, they were spotted scrambling on the roof, the child hysterical with pain and fear, Delphine beside herself with the excitement of the chase. It ended when the girl plunged screaming from the roof and landed in a crumpled, lifeless heap.

At last police were summoned, and they found the broken corpse where it had been concealed, inside a well. No murder charge was filed, as blacks were not considered human beings in the strictest sense; instead Delphine was forced to pay a fine, and her other servants confiscated for sale to more merciful masters.

In fact, as the Lalaurie slaves soon learned, there would be no escape. Delphine arranged for relatives to buy her scrawny, battered servants, smuggling them back to the Royal Street mansion under cover of night. Her neighbors never knew the difference, since they only saw her butler now, but punishment of her "ungrateful" slaves had passed beyond the level of a hobby with Delphine, plumbing the depths of morbid obsession.

On April 10, 1834, a fire broke out at the Lalaurie mansion. Neighbors and volunteer firemen turned out to battle the flames, Delphine coolly directing them as to which items of furniture were most valuable. By chance, one of her neighbors entered the kitchen, where he found Delphine's cook — a 70-year-old black woman — lying unconscious from smoke inhalation, trapped in the room by a shackle and 20-foot chain. The chain was broken, the old woman dragged outside, where she revived. When she regained her breath, the cook confessed that she had set the fire, preferring death to further torment from her mistress.

Searchers followed her directions to a padlocked attic chamber, where they found another seven blacks in irons and cruel spiked collars, scarred and battered, starved almost to death. The captives told a grisly tale of torture for the hell of it, Delphine inflicting savage beatings on a whim, trembling with excitement as she jabbed and gouged her captives with sharp instruments. When she grew tired, the butler would take over while his mistress watched, cheeks flushed, a satisfied expression on her face.

A crowd of some 2,000 angry citizens was forming up on Royal Street when Lalaurie's carriage hurtled through the ranks, Delphine inside, her butler in the driver's seat. They fled to St. John Bayou, where her husband had a schooner waiting, the Lalauries sailing off to their estate on Lake Pontchartrain. The butler, unaccountably, returned to Royal Street, where the mob immediately lynched him, trashing Delphine's fancy carriage as an afterthought.

No charges were filed against Delphine Lalaurie in New Orleans, nor was any final tally of her slaves available to show how many may have died or disappeared. Delphine and her husband moved to New York, and on from there to Paris, but her vile reputation preceded her. Once, arriving at the Paris opera, she was booed so vehemently by the audience that she took fright and fled. In 1836, while horseback riding near the town of Pau, Lalaurie toppled from her mount and broke her neck.

LEHMAN, CHRISTA

Born in 1922 at Worms, Germany, young Christa Ambros lost her mother to an asylum while still in her teens. Neglected by her alcoholic father, she grew up wild and undisciplined, serving a term of probation on conviction for petty theft. In 1944, she married a drunkard named Karl Lehman, responding to his inattention with several affairs that became open secrets in her hometown.

On September 17, 1952, Karl Lehman died at his home, in convulsions, a doctor listing the cause of death as a ruptured stomach ulcer. Thirteen months later, on October 14, 1953, Christa's father-in-law collapsed on the street and died in convulsions, twenty minutes after leaving her house. Ignoring the strange coincidence, authorities accepted another verdict of death by natural causes, and the case was closed.

On February 12, 1954, Christa handed out chocolate truffles to some of her neighbors, with startling results. One recipient, Annie Hamann, bit into a piece and pronounced it bitter, lapsing into convulsions and death a short time later. A dog that ate the truffles also died, and tests revealed traces of a new phosphorous-based pesticide, known as E-605.

Arrested on February 23, Lehman confessed to spiking the truffles with poison in an effort to kill elderly Eva Ruh, a neighbor who lived with Annie Hamann, but the murder scheme backfired, landing her in court on multiple homicide charges. Lehman was convicted on September 20 and sentenced to life, reports of her trial ironically prompting dozens of Germans to purchase E-605 and commit suicide.

LEIDOLF, IRENE:
See "ANGELS OF DEATH"

LIPKE, JULIANE:
See "ANGEL MAKERS OF NAGYREV"

LUMBRERA, DIANA

A Texas native, Diana Lumbrera was seventeen years old when she married Lionel Garza in 1974. Their marriage was troubled almost from the start, but the quarreling Garzas made up frequently enough to produce three children in as many years. Daughter Melissa was born in 1975, Joanna in 1976, and their first son, Jose Lionel Lumbrera, in 1977.

Unfortunately, while Diana was adept at bearing children, she had no luck at keeping them alive. Joanna was the first to die, barely three months old when Diana brought her lifeless body to the community hospital in Bovina, Texas. According to Diana, the baby had experienced convulsions before she suddenly stopped breathing, and a pathologist's report blamed Joanna's death on "strangulation due to asphyxiation due to convulsive disorder." Under the circumstances, no autopsy was required.

Jose Lionel Lumbrera was two months old when Diana brought him to the Bovina emergency room on February 10, 1978. The baby had suddenly gone into convulsions and stopped breathing, she told physicians, but he was still alive when they reached the hospital. Resuscitation was successful, but doctors could find no apparent cause for the convulsions, and they sent Jose off to Lubbock's pediatric intensive care unit for observation. The baby's condition was listed as stable by February 13, when a 1:00

A.M. cardiac alarm brought a nurse to his room, in time to see Diana retreating from the crib. Jose seemed well enough that afternoon, when Diana phoned her husband to tell him the infant was dying. Her prophecy came true shortly after 6:30 P.M., when a nurse saw Diana run from the baby's room in tears; investigating, she found Jose cyanotic, and thirty minutes of CPR failed to revive him.

Less than eight months later, on October 2, Diana walked into the Bovina emergency room with daughter Melissa limp in her arms. The three-year-old was dead on arrival, Diana relating the familiar tale of unexplained convulsions followed by rapid death. An Amarillo pathologist's report ascribed Melissa's death to "asphyxia due to aspiration of stomach contents," and the case was closed.

Diana divorced her husband in 1979, but she was seldom without male companionship. Over the next seven years, beginning with daughter Melinda in 1980, she would bear three more children out of wedlock, each with a different father. None would live to see the inside of a kindergarten classroom, and even the children of Diana's relatives were not entirely safe.

On October 8, 1980, Diana went for a drive with six-week-old Ericka Aleman, the daughter of a cousin. Thirty minutes after setting out, they wound up at the local emergency room, Ericka already dead when Diana spilled out her now-familiar story of lethal convulsions. Incredibly, despite Lumbrera's four-year record of domestic tragedy, physicians saw no reason to suspect her of harming the child.

Daughter Melinda never made it as far as the hospital. On August 17, 1982, the two-year-old was pronounced dead at her mother's home, the cause officially listed as "acute heart failure due to increased taxation on a case of congenital heart disease." Once again, if physicians suspected foul play, they kept their doubts to themselves.

Fifteen months later, Diana bore another son, named Daniel. On March 25, 1984, he was treated by hospital physicians for an ear infection, with no apparent complications. Three days later he was back in the emergency room, dead on arrival, with the cause listed as "septicemia" — a fatal blood infection. Curiously, blood tests from his prior visit showed no evidence of septicemia, but the anomaly was dismissed as inexplicable.

In 1985, Diana pulled up stakes and moved to Garden City, Kansas. Impregnated by yet another boyfriend soon after her arrival, she delivered her third son, Jose Antonio, on February 21, 1986. The hardiest Lumbrera child, he managed to survive four years and three months in his mother's care, but Jose's time ran out in the spring of 1990. He was already dead when Diana carried him into a hospital emergency room on May 1... but this time her luck had run out.

The day before Jose's death, Diana had taken him to a local physician, citing her usual complaint of mysterious convulsions. The doctor could find no logical cause, but he wrote a prescription for antibiotics, which Diana never bothered to fill. In retrospect, authorities would say that this, like many other doctor's visits through the years, had been deliberately staged to lay the groundwork for a subsequent fatal attack.

This time around, hospital staffers called the police, and Detective James Hawkins questioned Diana at length, compiling a list of her previous children, along with the places and dates of their deaths. In Texas, authorities from Palmer, Lubbock, and Castro Counties launched new investigations, discovering that each of Diana's lost children had been insured for amounts between $3,000 and $5,000. (In Melissa's case a second insurance policy was purchased one day before she died.) Diana was the only person who observed the various convulsive episodes, and — with the exception of Jose Lionel — all were beyond help when Diana sought medical care.

Kansas authorities were first off the mark, with a murder indictment in Jose Antonio's death. In July 1990, a Parmer County, Texas, grand jury indicted Diana for first-degree murder in the cases of Joanna, Melinda, and Melissa. Lubbock County weighed in with charges stemming from Jose Lionel's death, and Castro County indicted Diana for Ericka Aleman's slaying on September 10.

Diana's murder trial in Garden City opened two weeks later, with any reference to the Texas killings barred. Diana's employer and an officer from her credit union were called to describe how she used false tales of misfortune — including a bout with leukemia for Jose and her own father's death in a nonexistent car wreck — to secure $850 in sympathy loans from the credit union. Prosecutors also noted that Jose Antonio was insured for $5,000 when he died, and Dr. Eva Vachel blamed the child's death on deliberate suffocation. Dr. William Eckert appeared for the defense, blaming the child's death on a massive viral infection. According to Eckert, Jose's heart, lungs, and liver were normal, revealing no evidence of murder. Prosecutors countered by noting that Eckert had never examined said organs, since they were removed during autopsy and never replaced in the corpse. Convicted of murder after less than an hour's deliberation, Diana was sentenced to life imprisonment, with a minimum of fifteen years inside before parole.

A few weeks later, Texas Rangers flew Diana back to Parmer County, where she faced three counts of murder, with a possible death sentence under a new serial-murder statute. In the interest of self-preservation, Diana pled guilty to Melissa's murder and accepted another life sentence, while charges were dropped in the cases of Melinda and Joanna. Lubbock County was next in line, handing down a third life sentence after Diana pled "no contest" — with no technical admission of guilt — to her first son's death. Castro County, in turn, waived prosecution on outstanding charges to save an estimated $50,000 in court costs. By June 1991, Diana was back in Kansas, officially beginning to serve her time. [See also: Johnson, Martha; Tinning, Marybeth; Tuggle, Debra; Turner, Lise; Woods, Martha]

LYLES, ANJETTE DONOVAN

Georgia born in 1925, Anjette Lyles was a popular restaurateur in Macon during the 1950s. She also had a taste for homicide, but managed to conceal that quirk from those around her. The police investigator handling her case described the four-time killer as "a nice woman" with "a nice smile and a good personality."

The restaurant she ran in Macon originally belonged to her father-in-law, Ben Lyles, Sr. Anjette's husband took over the business when his father died in 1945, but sold it off in 1951. Anjette bought it back after Ben Junior's sudden death, on January 25, 1952. She soon remarried, to commercial airline pilot Joe Neal Gabbert, but he died unexpectedly on December 2, 1955. With his death, Anjette reverted to her first married name, inviting mother-in-law Julia Lyles to share her home. Julia, in turn, became the family curse's third victim, dying suddenly on September 29, 1957.

In March 1958, Anjette's older daughter, nine-year-old Marcia Elaine, was hospitalized with a sudden, unexplained illness. Around the same time, two of Anjette's aunts in Cochran, Georgia, received a pair of anonymous letters. One read: "Please come at once. She's getting the same dose as the others. Please come at once." The aunts took this as a reference to Marcia Elaine, but police were skeptical, declining to investigate on the basis of such "sketchy" information. Marcia died on April 4, and no autopsy was performed.

The case took a turn for the weird days later, when a waitress at Anjette's restaurant fell suddenly ill. The woman noted that her bouts of nausea struck each time Anjette supplied her with a cup of coffee. Finally curious, police launched a full investigation, exhuming the four corpses on April 25. All contained arsenic, and Lyles was indicted on four counts of first-degree murder. In custody, she would say only that "I have committed no crime."

Police were still at a loss for a motive when they searched Anjette's home, seizing four bottles of arsenic-based ant poison and quantities of occult paraphernalia described by Sheriff James Wood as "voodoo equipment." Three of the poison bottles were empty, the fourth only half-full. Photos of an unidentified man were also retrieved from Anjette's stocking drawer, producing speculation that she may have had another lover waiting in the wings.

Detectives got their break with the discovery of the person who had helped Anjette forge several documents to profit from her crimes. The home she bought in April 1957 had been mortgaged three times over by year's end, and the rest of her finances were equally complex. Altogether, police reckoned that Lyles had reaped between $40,000 and $50,000 from the four murders.

Anjette was tried in October 1958 on one murder count, for poisoning Marcia Elaine. Witnesses recalled the defendant carrying bottles of poison in her purse on various occasions, and restaurant employee Carrie Jackson had watched Lyles prepare a pitcher of lemonade for Marcia while the girl was hospitalized. Before leaving the restaurant, Lyles had carried the pitcher and a brown paper bag into the washroom. (A similar bag was in evidence when Lyles carried buttermilk to her hospitalized mother-in-law.) Jackson also remembered Anjette's prediction that Marcia would die within a day or two of entering the hospital.

Jurors deliberated for an hour and a half before convicting Lyles of first-degree murder. She was sentenced to die, but a subsequent sanity hearing resulted in her 1960 transfer to Central State Hospital, in Milledgeville. Lyles died there, of natural causes, in December 1977.

MacDONALD, CAROL

Carol Tiedeman was the daughter of an affluent family in Mahwah, New Jersey, born in 1923. She graduated from Barnard College in 1944 and soon married Kenneth MacDonald, a former football star from Rutgers University. The newlyweds prospered financially, and their union produced four children: daughter Sharon in 1945; Bruce in 1947; Katherine in 1949; and Thomas in 1950. By 1953 they occupied a stylish home with an attached two-car garage, situated on an acre of land in an elite Mahwah suburb.

For all their apparent success, the marriage was troubled. Kenneth and Carol had undergone counseling for several years before they separated in February 1953, with Kenneth accusing his wife of adultery. Carol angrily denied the charge, but Kenneth was stubborn. In time, they quarreled over visitation rights, and Carol was reported as despondent over the impending divorce.

On the night of May 2, Carol made a series of telephone calls to her husband, her parents, her brother, and a New York newspaper. In the latter call, she asked how to "give a story," then rang off without delivering her news. Near midnight, she woke her children, dressed them in warm clothing over their pajamas, and led them to the garage, where they climbed into the family's station wagon. The fuel gauge registered close to empty when Carol started the engine, so she drove to a nearby gas station, filled the car's tank, and returned to the house.

There, she parked once more in the garage and kept the motor running as she closed the outer door. Carol left her children in the car while she stepped back inside the house, writing out six suicide notes. (Their content was never revealed, except to say that Carol hoped to "protect her children from disgrace.") Around 3 A.M., Carol returned to the garage and sat for awhile near the car. Abruptly, she changed her mind about killing the children, dragging all four from the vehicle, leaving three on the garage floor while she carried two-year-old Thomas back into the house.

It was already too late. The carbon monoxide had done its work, and all four children were dead when Carol phoned her brother again, at 6 A.M. on May 3. He summoned the police, who described Carol MacDonald as "distraught" at the time of her arrest. In custody, she told authorities that she had planned to kill herself, as well, but she had failed. Her only stated motive, echoing the several notes, was that she hoped to spare her victims "the disgrace" of a divorce.

MALCOLM, SARAH

Born in 1711, Sarah Malcolm was the daughter of an Irish merchant who fell on hard times in his native land. She moved to London as a young adult, working as a laundress before she was hired to keep house for 80-year-old Lydia Dunscomb, residing on Tanfield Court, in London's exclusive Inner Temple. It might have seemed a wonderful position to another girl from Sarah's circumstances... but she wanted more.

On February 4, 1733, Sarah strangled her employer, next turning on her fellow servants as potential witnesses. Elizabeth Harrison, age sixty, was likewise strangled, while Sarah slashed the throat of 16-year-old Ann Price. She began to loot the house of cash and other valuables, but her opportunity was lost when guests arrived for tea. They found the bodies, called police, and Sarah was arrested after stolen money and a bloodstained silver tankard were discovered in her room.

In custody, Sarah tried to blame two acquaintances — the Alexander brothers — for the triple murder, but they quickly surrendered and presented air-tight alibis. Convicted and sentenced to hang, Sarah was driven back to Tanfield Court in an open cart, on March 7, to mount a special scaffold erected at the scene of her crime. Following the execution, her corpse was dissected and her skeleton displayed for many years at the Cambridge Botanical Gardens.

MANSON "FAMILY"

In the past two decades, no fewer than a dozen full-length books have been published describing the criminal exploits of Charles Milles Manson and his bizarre "family," a transient commune-cult that included forty-odd members at its peak in the late 1960s. Despite Manson's blatant chauvinism, girls and young women flocked to him in droves between 1967 and '69, accepting the pint-sized ex-convict as a combination lover, father figure, and self-styled deity. Ironically, and in apparent defiance of Manson's male-dominant attitude, females typically outnumbered male "family" members two-to-one, emerging as leaders of the group after Manson was jailed for the last time in September 1969.

Born "no name Maddox" in Cincinnati, Ohio, on November 12, 1934, Manson was the illegitimate son of Kathleen Maddox, a 16-year-old prostitute. His surname was derived from one of Kathleen's many lovers, whom she briefly married, but it signified no blood connection. In 1936, Kathleen filed a paternity suit against one "Colonel Scott," of Ashland, Kentucky, winning the grand monthly sum of five dollars for child support. Scott instantly defaulted on the judgment and died in 1954, without ever acknowledging his son.

Manson's formative years were a non-stop nightmare of neglect and abuse. In 1939, with Kathleen serving five years for armed robbery, Charles was packed off to live with a sadistic uncle who constantly berated the boy as a "sissy," dressing him in girl's clothing for his first day of school in an effort to help Manson "act like a man." By 1947, Charles had begun a five-year trek through Indiana's juvenile detention system, reporting sexual abuse by guards and bunkmates alike. His adult arrests included federal charges of auto theft, cashing stolen checks, and transporting whores interstate. Finally paroled on March 21, 1967, over his own objections, Manson was drawn to San Francisco and the teeming Haight-Ashbury district.

It was the "Summer of Love," when thousands of young people flocked to the banner of drugs and "flower power," heeding Timothy Leary's advice to "tune in, turn on, drop out." The streets and crash pads overflowed with teenage runaways and drifters, seeking insight into the world and themselves. Behind the scenes, a small army of manipulators — gurus, outlaw bikers, pushers, pimps and Satanists — stood ready to squeeze a grim profit from the Age of Aquarius.

Bay Area "hippies" prided themselves on the motto "Never trust anyone over thirty," but 33-year-old Manson displayed a surprising charisma, attracting young dropouts from all strata of white society. His first recruit was Mary Theresa Brunner, a Wisconsin native and recent college graduate working in the library at U.C. Berkeley when she met Charlie, moving him into her small apartment without a second thought. A year later, she would bear him a son, christened Valentine Michael Manson, nicknamed "Pooh Bear" by the tribe.

Next on board was Lynnette Alice Fromme, a young redhead picked up in Venice, California, shortly after she was ousted from her family home. Manson dubbed her "Squeaky," introducing himself as "the God of fuck." His performance in that capacity was impressive enough to cinch Fromme's unflagging devotion, still fierce despite the passage of a quarter-century.

The transient collection of flower-waifs continued through 1967 and early 1968, Mary Brunner maintaining her job for awhile to keep Manson in drug money, listing her address with the federal parole board while he drifted up and down the coast at will. In July 1967, Manson was thumbing rides when he met Rev. Dean Moorhouse, recruiting the minister's daughter Ruth Ann (a.k.a. "Ouish") as another disciple. A year later Rev. Moorhouse was sentenced to prison on charges of furnishing LSD to a 13-year-old girl, but the "family" never missed him, drifting in a zany world of its own.

Patricia Krenwinkel met Manson in September 1967, while visiting a mutual friend in Manhattan Beach. The 18-year-old Sunday school teacher enjoyed swapping Biblical texts with Manson, enraptured to the point that she saw no contradiction in Charlie's description of himself as Jesus Christ and Satan. Two months later, in San Francisco, the "family" picked up Susan Denise Atkins, a 19-year-old San Jose native who had been on her own for four years, killing time with armed robbers, supporting herself with small-time drug deals and topless dancing gigs for Anton LaVey's Church of Satan. Around the same time, 13-year-old Diane ("Snake") Lake joined the "family" with her parents' wholehearted approval. By February 1968, the rootless clan included nubile youngsters Madaline ("Little Patty") Cottage, Nancy ("Brenda McCann") Pittman, and Ella Beth Sinder (a.k.a. "Yeller"). Catherine ("Gypsy") Share was Charlie's oldest disciple, at age twenty-seven. On April Fool's Day, the tribe was joined by Sandra Good, the 24-year-old daughter of a San Diego stockbroker. Six months later, Leslie Van Houten dropped in on the "family" at the Spahn movie ranch, near Los Angeles, and decided to stay.

Manson was collecting male disciples at the same time, notably Robert Beausoleil and Charles ("Tex") Watson, but females always formed the hard core of his "family," devoted to worship of Charlie, treating his every whim as a command from On High. On Manson's orders, they went out to scrounge for food in garbage dumpsters, peddled drugs, rehearsed guerilla warfare in the desert, and provided sex to any male selected by the "God of fuck." Along the way, the tribe rubbed shoulders with the Church of Satan, the Process Church of Final Judgment (worshipping Satan, Lucifer, and Jehovah simultaneously), the Circle Order of Dog Blood, and other bizarre cults. Manson grew obsessed with death and "Helter Skelter," his interpretation of a Beatles song predicting race war in America. In Manson's view, once "blackie" had been driven to the point of violence, helpless whites would be annihilated, leaving Manson and his "family" to rule the roost.

And so the violent deaths began.

On October 13, 1968, two women were found beaten and strangled to death near Ukiah, California. One, Nancy Warren, was the pregnant wife of a highway patrol officer. The other victim, Clida Delaney, was Warren's 64-year-old grandmother. The murders were ritualistic in nature, with thirty-six leather thongs wrapped around each victim's throat, and several members of the Manson "family"— including two later convicted of unrelated slayings — were visiting Ukiah at the time.

Two months later, on December 30, 17-year-old Marina Habe was abducted outside her West Hollywood home, her body recovered on New Year's Day, with multiple stab wounds in the neck and chest. Investigators learned that Habe was friendly with various "family" members, and police believe her ties with the Manson group led directly to her death.

On May 7, 1969, 64-year-old Darwin Scott-- the brother of Manson's alleged father — was hacked to death in his Ashland, Kentucky, apartment, pinned to the floor with a long butcher knife. Manson was out of touch with his California parole officer between May 22 and June 18, 1969, and an unidentified "LSD preacher from California" set up shop with several young women, in nearby Huntington, around the same time.

On July 17, 1969, 16-year-old Mark Walts disappeared while hitchhiking from Chatsworth, California, to the pier at Santa Monica, to do some fishing. His battered body, shot three times and possibly run over by a car, was found the next morning in Topanga Canyon. Walts was a frequent visitor to Manson's commune at the Spahn ranch, and the dead boy's brother publicly accused Manson of the murder, though no charges were filed.

Around the time of Walts' death, a "Jane Doe" corpse was discovered near Castaic, northeast of the Spahn ranch, tentatively identified from articles of clothing as Susan Scott, a "family" member once arrested with Susan Atkins and other Manson girls in Mendocino. Scott was living at the Spahn ranch when she dropped out of sight, and while the Castaic corpse remains technically unidentified, Susan has not been seen again.

In the month between July 27 and August 26, 1969, Manson's tribe slaughtered at least nine persons in Southern California. Musician Gary Hinman was the first to die, hacked to death in retaliation for a drug deal gone sour, "political" graffiti scrawled at the scene in his blood, as Manson tried to blame the crime on "blackie." On August 9, a Manson hit team raided the home of movie director Roman Polanski, butchering Polanski's wife — pregnant actress Sharon Tate — and four of her guests: Abigail Folger, Jay Sebring, Voytek Frykowski, and Steven Parent. The following night, Manson's "creepy crawlers" killed and mutilated another couple, Leno and Rosemary LaBianca, in their Los Angeles home.

An atmosphere of general panic gripped affluent L.A., the grisly crimes demonstrating that no one was safe. On August 16, sheriff's deputies raided the Spahn ranch, arresting Manson and company on various drug-related charges, but Charlie was back on the street by August 26. That night, he directed the murder of movie stuntman Donald "Shorty" Shea, a hanger-on who knew too much and was suspected of discussing "family" business with police.

Ironically, Manson's downfall came about through a relatively petty crime. On the night of September 18-19, 1969, members of the "family" burned a piece of road-grading equipment that was "obstructing" one of their desert dune buggy tracks. Arson investigators traced the evidence to Manson, and he was arrested again on October 12. A day later, Susan Atkins was picked up in Ontario, California, and she soon confided details of the Tate-LaBianca murders to cellmates in Los Angeles. Sweeping indictments followed, but even Manson's removal from circulation could not stop the killing.

On November 5, 1969, "family" member John ("Zero") Haught was shot and killed while "playing Russian roulette" in Venice, California. Eleven days later, another "Jane Doe" — tentatively identified as "family" associate Sherry Cooper — was found near the site where Marina Habe's body had been discovered in 1968. On November 21, Scientologists James Sharp, fifteen, and Doreen Gaul, nineteen, were found dead in a Los Angeles alley, stabbed more than fifty times each with a long-bladed knife. Investigators learned that Gaul had been a girlfriend of Bruce Davis, a "family" member subsequently convicted of first-degree murder in L.A.

And Manson's arm was long. Joel Pugh, husband of Sandra Good, flew to London in late 1968, accompanied by Bruce Davis. Their mission included the sale of some rare coins and the establishment of connections with a satanic order in Britain. Davis returned to the United States in April 1969, but Pugh lingered on. His body was found in a London hotel room on December 1, his throat slit with razor blades, his blood used to inscribe satanic "backwards writing" and "comic book drawings" on a nearby mirror.

Charged with the seven Tate-LaBianca murders, Manson and three of his female disciples — Susan Atkins, Patricia Krenwinkel, and Leslie Van Houten — went to trial in June 1970. A sideshow to the main event occurred three months later, when Ruth Moorhouse flew to Honolulu, attempting to murder prosecution witness Barbara Hoyt with a drugged hamburger. (Eight months pregnant at the time of her indictment, Moorhouse went into hiding, remaining at large until her arrest in October 1975.) The defense rested its case on November 19, and attorney Ronald Hughes disappeared eight days later, after he was driven to Sespe Hot Springs by two "family" associates called "James" and "Lauren." The lawyer's decomposing corpse was found in Sespe Creek five months later, around the time Manson and friends were convicted in L.A., sentenced to die on seven counts of first-degree murder.

Prosecutor Vincent Bugliosi believes that he has traced the fate of "James" and "Lauren," suspected of guilty knowledge in Hughes' death. On November 8, 1972, hikers found the body of 26-year-old James Willett, shotgunned and decapitated, in a shallow grave near Guerneville, California. Three days later, Willett's station wagon was spotted outside a house in Stockton, and police arrested two members of the Aryan Brotherhood inside, along with Nancy Pittman and two other Manson women. Lauren Willett, wife of James, was buried in the basement, and an initial tale of "Russian roulette" was dropped in April 1973, when four of the suspects pled guilty to murder charges.

Affiliation with the far-right Aryan Brotherhood was a deliberate Manson stratagem, to help protect Charlie from blacks in prison and promote his racist gospel on the street. On August 21, 1971, Mary Brunner and Catherine Share joined Aryan Brotherhood members in the robbery of an L.A. gun shop, shooting it out with police before they were captured. (In March 1973, all concerned were sentenced to long prison terms.) Two months later, on October 20, Aryan leader Kenneth Como escaped from the L.A. Hall of Justice, Sandra Good driving the getaway van until she crashed nearby and both were captured.

Meanwhile, the Manson trials continued in Los Angeles. Triggerman Tex Watson was convicted and sentenced to die for the Tate-LaBianca murders in 1971. Robert Beausoleil, Susan Atkins, and Mary Brunner were likewise sentenced for killing Gary Hinman, while Manson, Bruce Davis, and Steve Grogan were convicted in both the Hinman and Shea murders. As luck would have it, California's Supreme Court abolished the death penalty in February 1972, and all the "family" hackers are now technically eligible for parole.

In Manson's absence, Lynnette Fromme held the "family" reins, corresponding with Charlie in prison and spreading his gospel at large, forging new alliances with sundry cults and racist groups. In 1974, she headed up Charlie's new "Order of Rainbow," renaming the scattered faithful after colors. Atkins, Krenwinkel, and Van Houten declined to enlist, where upon "Squeaky" christened them "the Suckatash Sisters — Squash, Corn, and Bean." Atkins, for her part, was busy finding Jesus in her prison cell, penning a religious autobiography, describing herself as "born again."

Catherine Share was paroled in March 1975, on condition that she break all "family" ties, but Mary Brunner refused a similar offer, holding out awhile longer before she drifted into freedom and obscurity. Lynnette Fromme stole the headlines on September 4, 1975, when she pulled a gun on President Gerald Ford in Sacramento. Authorities disagree on whether or not she meant to kill Ford, but her trial jury had no doubts, convicting "Squeaky" of attempted assassination that November. On December 19, 1975, she was sentenced to a term of life imprisonment.

Not to be outdone, Sandra Good hit the headlines seven days after "Squeaky's" arrest, providing the Associated Press with a list of seventy politicians and businessmen marked for death on charges of polluting the environment. Good and cohort Susan Murphy, an ex-nurse, ran off copies of a letter threatening their chosen targets, signed by the "International People's Court of Retribution," trusting a friend to mail them. He went to the FBI instead, landing Good and Murphy in jail on extortion charges. Both were convicted in March 1976, sentenced to fifteen years in prison. A decade would pass before Good hit the streets again, still devoted to Manson, proclaiming his message of "peace and love" in tabloid interviews.

Charles Manson, meanwhile, remains a twisted celebrity of sorts, dancing and wisecracking with Geraldo Rivera, scowling through a series of hopeless parole interviews. Remnants of his off-beat "family" survive to the present day, members linked to groups promoting child pornography and sexual abuse, as well as rumored human sacrifice.

MAREK, MARTHE

A native of Vienna, this Austrian serial slayer was born in 1904, abandoned as an infant by her unknown parents, and adopted by a childless couple named Lowenstein. The family was poor by Viennese standards, and Marthe went to work in a dress shop at age fourteen. The following year, 1919, she caught the eye of 73-year-old Morris Fritsch, a wealthy department store owner, and Fritsch invited Marthe to become his ward. Reports differ on whether or not their arrangement included sex; we know only that Marthe was sent to expensive finishing schools in France and England, where she developed an enduring taste for the good life.

Back in Vienna, residing with Fritsch, Marthe met a young engineer named Emil Marek, beginning a secret affair. Fritsch died in 1920, leaving Marthe all his money and a stately home at Modling, but she unaccountably delayed her wedding to Marek for another four years. By that time, they had squandered most of Fritsch's savings and were shortly forced to sell the mansion. Always thinking, Marthe purchased an insurance policy on Emil, $10,000 payable in the event of a crippling accident.

Loss of a leg sounded just about right.

Young Emil Marek was as money-hungry as his bride. He eagerly agreed to stage an accident while "chopping wood," but at the first stroke of the ax he nearly fainted, writhing on the ground in agony. Marthe had to finish the job herself, and insurance adjustors became suspicious when Marek's physician found three separate cuts on his leg... a most peculiar accident indeed.

Both Mareks were charged with attempted fraud, but Marthe was not finished yet. She paid a male nurse to accuse the insurance company of bribing Emil's physician, then went public with her story and her "witness." The fraud charges were dropped, and while the Mareks were later convicted on a lesser charge of bribing the nurse, their insurance company still settled the claim with a payment of $3,000 — roughly enough to cover the costs of their various court dates and fines.

The couple relocated to Algiers, with Emil trying several business ventures, losing out with each in turn. The Mareks had two children by the time they came back to Vienna, looking for a way to change their luck. Marthe tried selling vegetables on the street, but it felt too much like work. Emil's sudden death, in July 1932, was blamed on "tuberculosis," and the insurance company paid off without complaint. Likewise with daughter Ingeborg, age seven, who followed her father into the ground a few weeks later. Young Peter Marek was lucky, for the moment, winding up in a boarding school instead of the morgue.

Marthe's next target was an aging aunt, Susanne Lowenstein, who invited her niece to move in as a full-time companion and nurse. The old lady soon died, with symptoms similar to Emil's, leaving Marthe her home and savings. Typically, the cash was soon gone, and Marthe had opened the house to boarders. One, an elderly woman named Kittenberger, collapsed and died under Marthe's roof, leaving $1,000 in life insurance to her landlady.

In 1937, Marthe tried a new insurance scam, removing valuable paintings from her home in the dead of night, storing them in a warehouse, and filing a burglary complaint. Ironically, Detective Ignatz Peters drew the case, and he remembered Marthe from his previous investigation of her husband's crippling "accident." Suspecting fraud, he tracked the paintings down and escorted Marthe to jail.

The door of Marthe's cell had barely slammed behind her when Mrs. Kittenberger's son approached police with the suspicion that his mother had been murdered. Exhumation proved him right, forensic experts reporting traces of the metallic poison thallium in Kittenberger's remains. On a hunch, Detective Peters ordered further tests on Emil Marek, daughter Ingeborg, and Susanne Lowenstein, with identical results. He also traced Peter Marek to a Viennese boarding school, where he lay deathly ill from thallium poisoning, but physicians managed to save the boy's life.

History had the last laugh on Marthe Marek. Adolf Hitler's *Anschluss* of March 1938 had restored capital punishment in Austria, and Marthe was sentenced to die on conviction of multiple murders. On December 6, 1938, she was beheaded with an ax in accordance with the new code of Nazi justice.

MARTIN, RHONDA BELLE

Mississippi born in 1907, Rhonda Martin was the daughter of a sawmill worker who moved his family to Mobile, Alabama, then left them in the lurch when Rhonda was twelve. She quit school three years later, helping her mother run a boarding house to pay the bills. That same year, Rhonda married one of the boarders, W.R. Alderman, but they divorced in 1926. She married her second husband, neighbor George Garrett, two years later, bearing him five children between 1930 and 1938.

Producing offspring was easy for Rhonda, but keeping them alive was something else. Four-year-old Mary Garrett was the first to go, in 1934, with Rhonda blaming her death on "pneumonia," calling her daughter an "afflicted" child who never walked or spoke. Three years later, on July 19, 1937, three-year-old Emogene followed her sister in death. Rhonda cited a "heart attack" as the cause, but Emogene's death certificate lists "accidental poisoning." Rhonda lost both her husband and one-year-old Judith in 1939, blaming their deaths on "pneumonia" and "jaundice," respectively. Six-year-old Ann Garrett fell prey to a lethal "throat disease" in 1940, while a "stomach disorder" claimed 11-year-old Ellyn on August 1, 1943. Rhonda's 60-year-old mother joined the casualty list a year later, her passing vaguely attributed to "infirmities."

With no surviving family to speak of, Rhonda found herself another husband. Talmadge Gibson worked as an attendant at the local V.A. hospital, but his bedside manner left something to be desired, and Rhonda divorced him after only five months. In 1949, she took another fling at matrimony, tying the knot with co-worker Claude Martin.

A widower with four children, Martin enjoyed life with Rhonda until February 1951, when he fell seriously ill with stomach cramps and vomiting. His death, in April, paid Rhonda $2,000 in life insurance, but she seemed to have little interest in cash. Her first expenditure, of some $400, was incurred when she moved Claude's first wife to a grave adjoining his, "because he would have wanted it that way."

Friends and family were stunned when Rhonda married her 21-year-old stepson, Ronald Martin, in December 1951. Aside from the 23-year age difference, their union was technically illegal under Alabama's incest statute. No one pressed the case in court, but Rhonda's three teenage stepdaughters were angry enough to leave home in protest. Ronald and Rhonda now had the house to themselves, but she continued brooding over the prospect of a forced annulment, her worst fears reinforced by steamy articles in "true confession" magazines.

In June 1955, Ronald was stricken with a painful stomach ailment. Rhonda blamed "ulcers," but physicians had their doubts, unable to confirm a diagnosis. Hospitalized for tests in October, Ronald was released in time to suffer a mysterious "nervous breakdown." Rhonda nursed him at home for several weeks, his condition steadily declining. Partial paralysis had set in by the time Ronald went back to the hospital, in December, and one of his doctors finally recognized the symptoms of arsenic poisoning. Strands of Ronald's hair were shipped off for testing, presumably to help diagnose an unspecified "nervous disorder."

The test results confirmed arsenic in Ronald's system, and his life was saved, though the partial paralysis proved irreversible. Exhumation and testing of Claude Martin's body revealed enough arsenic to kill several men, and Rhonda was arrested for murder on March 9, 1956. After three days of stubborn denial, she cracked on March 12, confessing that she poisoned Ronald and six of her eight suspected murder victims.

As explained by Rhonda in her conversations with detectives, the murders began with daughter Emogene in 1937. Rhonda had spiked the child's milk with poison "on the spur of the moment" and watched her die in agony. Husband George was dosed with poisoned whiskey over several days, until he finally collapsed. Rhonda's other acknowledged victims included daughters Ann and Ellyn, her own mother, and Claude Martin. She informed police that she avoided capture for a period of eighteen years by never consulting the same doctor twice.

Despite the small insurance payoff on George and one forged Social Security check, police were at a loss to define Rhonda's motive. At last, in lieu of seeming ignorant, they described their prisoner as suffering from a "severe complex that no one wanted her around and this led to the poison murders." In theory, at least, Rhonda's childhood abandonment by her father induced her to kill those she loved. As for the choice of weapons, she was said to be "fascinated by the effects of the poison."

Convicted on the basis of her own confessions and sentenced to die, Rhonda Martin was electrocuted on October 11, 1957. She stands as the last woman executed in the state of Alabama.

MATAJKE, DOROTHY JEAN

A resident of Nevada, Iowa, Dorothy Matajke began working as a nurse's aide and professional companion for the elderly and ailing in the 1970s. It came as no surprise to anyone when several of her patients died, and there were no suggestions of foul play except where money was concerned. In 1973, Matajke was convicted of fraud and sentenced to five years in prison. She escaped in February 1974 and remained at large until 1980, when she was recaptured and returned to finish out her sentence. Despite the prison break, she won parole in 1983, serving less than the original five years.

Upon release, Matajke moved to Little Rock and picked up with her old profession as a live-in nurse. On March 24, 1985, she moved in with Paul Kinsey, seventy-two, and his wife Opal, age seventy-one. When Opal died on April 5, the cause was listed as a recently-diagnosed cancer. Paul Kinsey's health began deteriorating rapidly after his wife's death, but relatives attributed his lapse to grief and loneliness.

On September 9, 1986, Matajke acquired a new client, elderly Marion Doyle. Another cancer patient, Doyle survived nine days of nursing by Matajke, but her death was not ascribed to cancer. Rather, a police report suggested that the woman had committed suicide. A routine inventory, made by the executor of Doyle's estate, discovered several checks made out to Dorothy Matajke, totaling almost $4,000. There was something curious about Doyle's signature, and on a hunch, her body was exhumed for reexamination. Tissue samples showed sufficient drugs to cause a fatal overdose.

Meanwhile, Paul Kinsey's health continued to decline. The old man stubbornly refused to eat or take his medication, telling relatives that every meal or dose prepared by his "companion" left him deathly ill. Kinsey ordered Matajke out of his house on October 28, and three days later he was hospitalized in critical condition. Dorothy Matajke bullied her way past relatives and doctors to visit her ex-patient in the emergency room, and she was still by his side when detectives came to arrest her.

Initially, the "nurse" was charged with forgery and theft for looting Marion Doyle's bank account. Subsequent charges included felony possession of a firearm, with additional counts of forgery related to checks written on Paul Kinsey's account. A search of Matajke's home yielded mislabeled bottles of drugs and tranquilizers, along with three bottles of arsenic-based ant poison, and more serious charges were added.

On November 24, Matajke was accused of first-degree murder in the death of Marion Doyle and first-degree battery in the non-fatal poisoning of Paul Kinsey. Opal Kinsey's body was exhumed December 5, with the results of laboratory tests kept secret pending disposition of the standing charges. After Paul Kinsey died, on February 10, 1987, assault charges were replaced with another count of first-degree murder.

In June 1987, Matajke was convicted of Paul Kinsey's murder and sentenced to life. Two months later, in a negotiated plea bargain, she received another term of sixty years for killing Marion Doyle. Charges are pending in the case of Opal Kinsey, and new investigations are expected in the deaths of several patients "cared for" by Matajke in Iowa.

MAYER, STEPHANIJA: See "ANGELS OF DEATH"

McANINCH, ALMA MAY

A native of Spring Hill, Iowa, born in 1902, Alma May was barely eighteen years old when she married Gurness McAninch in 1920. Gurness tried his hand at farming for awhile, then drifted through a series of semi-skilled jobs that left the transient family perpetually short of cash. Near poverty did not prevent the couple from producing seven children, though. Their first son, Ray, was born in 1922, followed by Cora Belle in 1924, Gail (another boy) in 1926, Geraldine in 1927, Morris in 1931, Max in 1933, and Dickie in 1935. Alma was expecting their eighth child in December 1936, when the family moved into a five-room shack in Norwalk, Iowa.

Problems continued to haunt Alma's brood. Their home was wired for electricity, but they still used kerosene lamps to reduce expenses. In January 1937, Alma slipped on some ice and fell down, suffering a spontaneous miscarriage. "After that," a neighbor recalled, "Mrs. McAninch seemed to give up. She just sat and stared. Her children had to look after themselves. Often, when I would speak to her, Mrs. McAninch didn't seem to hear me. She wouldn't answer."

The children also noticed Alma's depression. On several occasions, she told 15-year-old Ray that she would gladly kill herself "if it wasn't for you kids." Arrested on minor charges that summer, Gurness was concerned enough to tell police of Alma's suicide threats. The sheriff visited their home and took away the family's shotgun. Later, in October, 11-year-old Gail borrowed a shotgun and ammunition from one of the neighbors. He meant to go hunting with Ray, but Alma took the gun and used up all the ammunition blasting cans in her back yard, as if for target practice.

On October 30, Ray borrowed six more shotgun shells from a neighbor, intent on tomorrow's hunting expedition. Gurness was jailed again that afternoon, for breaking and entering, but Alma took the news in stride. If anything, she almost seemed relieved. Neighbors remarked that she had never seemed happier. Ray and Gail, for their part, were confident enough to leave her alone with the younger children that night, while they went off to visit friends.

Sometime after eight o'clock, Alma made the rounds with her shotgun, killing each of her five younger children in their beds, with close-range blasts between the eyes. The sixth round was reserved for Alma, and she pressed the shotgun's muzzle to her forehead, making sure she would not miss.

Ray and Gail returned home around midnight and found the bodies, Alma with the shotgun cradled in her lifeless arms. A newspaper report said that, "The wound in each case was almost exactly similar — a hole just above the bridge of the nose, between the eyes, about the size of a silver dollar. The brain of each was blown to bits." A Bible occupied the kitchen table, open to the Book of Exodus, and Alma left a note addressed to Ray and Gail, containing instructions for disposal of the bodies. It read in part: "You will find us dead. Don't get excited. Tell Dad I sure want him to go straight for the boys' sake. I have stood all I can take and best to take the kids along. All that saves the boys is no more shells."

McGINNIS, VIRGINIA: See REARDEN, VIRGINIA

METYARD, SARAH and SARAH MORGAN

This 18th-century British mother-daughter team were milliners who habitually abused the young, female apprentices they obtained from a local parish workhouse. In an era of sweatshops when wages were low and long hours routine, the Metyards set a standard for brutality, beating and starving their workers, sometimes resorting to more creative punishments for real or imagined transgressions of some minor rule. It was not uncommon for girls in the Metyard household to be bound in awkward positions, so they could neither sit nor stand, sometimes remaining in a crouch for hours while their muscles cramped and their cries of pain went unanswered.

In 1788, one of the weaker girls died, and Sarah Morgan Metyard hid her body in the attic, telling boarders and co-workers that the missing girl had run away. As it happened, the dead girl's sister was also employed with the Metyards, and she refused to believe that her sibling would flee without saying goodbye. At length, her complaints grew too loud and she was murdered, stashed in the attic with her sister. When the bodies ripened and began to smell, they were dismembered and consigned to London's sewer system. Bits and pieces of the girls were later found, but in the climate of the times they were dismissed as the remains of a surgeon's dissection specimen thrown out with the trash.

Two years later, a new lodger named Rooker came to stay with the Metyards. Appalled by the cruelty he witnessed in their shop, Rooker also watched the two Sarah's quarreling bitterly, learning to sympathize with the daughter. In time, he suggested that Sarah Morgan Metyard leave home and come to live with him, in his native Ealing. She agreed and moved in with Rooker as his mistress, letting her tale of double murder slip out in an unguarded moment. Rooker urged her to tell the police, couching her story in terms that would put all the blame on her mother, and the younger Metyard finally agreed. As luck would have it, Sarah Morgan Metyard and her lover had overestimated the sensitivity of British jurors. Before year's end, mother and daughter had both been convicted of murder, and they were hanged together at Tyburn, in 1790.

MONAHAN, ANNIE

An industrious "black widow," Annie Monahan murdered three husbands and a niece for profit, but it took police in New Haven, Connecticut, more than a decade to prove their case in court. In her heyday, Monahan set a new standard for mercenary serial killers, wedding — and poisoning — two brothers from the same family.

Her first husband/victim was Joseph Pallman, whose death on November 20, 1906 was officially ascribed to "edema and pneumonia." Life insurance paid the princely sum of $400. By May of 1908, Annie was out of mourning and ready for another trip to the altar. This time, the unlucky groom was Joseph Monahan. Joe managed to survive for eighteen months, expiring from "alcoholic gastritis" on November 14, 1909.

In fact, Joseph's symptoms were vague enough that doctors suspected arsenic poisoning, but Monahan was embalmed before they got around to calling for post-mortem tests. In those days, arsenic was a prime ingredient in most embalming fluids, and the autopsy was canceled as a waste of time, since murder would have been impossible to prove. Once more, the life insurance paid.

Widow Monahan's next target was Jennie McNamee, age seventeen, a niece who had moved in with Annie when her parents died. Her symptoms were identical to Joseph Monahan's, and Annie played the role of caring nurse until her niece expired on March 7, 1913. Insurance adjustors discovered that Annie had insured her ward with several different companies, lying on various applications to purchase policies worth a total of $2,000. The resultant autopsy found "enough arsenic to kill three men," and relatives suddenly recalled Annie sending her nephew Frank — Jennie's younger brother — to purchase rat poison while his sister was ill.

By the time of her arrest on murder charges, Annie had executed another marital coup, wedding John Monahan, her former brother-in-law. With his bride in jail, John started having second thoughts about his new $400 life insurance policy, purchased at Annie's insistence, but his fears were calmed when Annie won release on grounds of "insufficient evidence."

In retrospect, he should have trusted his first instincts.

In October 1916, John Monahan fell suddenly ill, his physician unable to locate the cause. A second doctor was consulted, this time one who was aware of Annie's former legal problems and the rumors that surrounded her bizarre run of "bad luck." John was hospitalized, his condition monitored by a battery of physicians, but they were too late to save him, and he died in agony on June 12, 1917.

New Haven police were already tracking the case, aware that Annie had purchased arsenic prior to John's illness, and traces of poison were found in a vial of his medicine, seized from her home. An autopsy confirmed arsenic as the cause of death, and Annie was faced with a new murder charge. Convicted on February 13, 1919, she was sentenced to life and subsequently died in prison.

MONVOISIN, CATHERINE:

See "CHAMBRE ARDENTE AFFAIR"

MOORE, BLANCHE

Less than five years after the execution of serial poisoner Velma Barfield, residents of North Carolina were shocked to discover a new "black widow" in their midst. Like Barfield, the new suspect was a wife and mother, deeply religious by most accounts, a pillar of the community. And like her predecessor, she indulged a taste for easy money that would land her on death row.

A Tarheel native, born February 17, 1933, Blanche Kiser was the daughter of P.D. Kiser, a self-described "primitive" minister who drank heavily between sermons, sometimes enlisting young Blanche as a prostitute to pay off his gambling debts. She married young to escape the abuse, tying the knot with James Taylor, five years her senior, in May 1952. Their first daughter, Vanessa, was born in 1953, the same year that Blanche went to work as a checker at the Kroger supermarket in Burlington. Another child, Cindi, followed in 1959, her birth preceding Blanche's elevation to head cashier by a matter of weeks.

All was not well in the Taylor household, however. James was cut from the same cloth as P.D. Kiser, a hard-drinking compulsive gambler who sometimes disappeared for whole weekends, returning empty-handed with a lame excuse for where the family's money went. Blanche retaliated with a series of affairs at the supermarket, bedding her male supervisors, sparking violent arguments at home. In 1962, Blanche focused her romantic attention on 27-year-old Raymond Reid, lately arrived as Kroger's new assistant manager in Burlington, but he was married, with two young children. It took three years of determined flirtation for Blanche to land Raymond in bed, but she never lacked for male companionship in terms of one-night stands.

In September 1966, Blanche made a stab at reconciliation with her father, but his health took a turn for the worse soon after she arrived. Forgiving daughter that she was, Blanche lingered at his side and nursed him to the bitter end, his death attributed to a "heart attack triggered by chronic emphysema." Doctors managed to overlook symptoms — including violent stomach cramps, diarrhea, projectile vomiting, delirium, and a bright-blue face — which pointed to death by arsenic poisoning.

Two years later, in 1968, a near-fatal heart attack and belated conversion to Christianity persuaded James Taylor to clean up his act. He became, in Blanche's words, "the perfect husband and father," but the change did nothing to divert her ongoing love affair with Raymond Reid. Blanche's mother-in-law, Isla Taylor, was bedridden by mid-1970, and Blanche did her best to make the old woman comfortable. When Isla died, on November 25, 1970, doctors attributed her passing to natural causes. Once again, they missed the eyeballs that had turned a brilliant cobalt blue, along with quantities of undigested arsenic remaining in the woman's stomach.

Raymond Reid abandoned his wife and children in 1971, renting a small apartment and filing for divorce. Blanche made a daily routine of stopping by to cook Reid's breakfast, proclaiming him "helpless" without her. Word of their affair fanned out from Kroger to the town at large, and Reid, at least, assumed that they were moving toward a permanent relationship. His divorce was finalized in 1973, and the rest was up to Blanche.

In September 1970, James Taylor came down with the "flu," sporting symptoms that included diarrhea, swollen glands, a sore throat, hair loss, bloody stool and urine, painful blisters on his hands and feet. Hospitalized near the end of the month, he died on October 2, barely an hour after Blanche brought him some ice cream from home. Taylor left a modest estate, but Blanche soon purchased a new home in Burlington, fostering suspicions that she may have tapped the till at work.

It came as no surprise to anyone in Burlington when Blanche and Ray Reid started dating openly. They spoke of marriage, but the glad event was constantly postponed for one reason or another. Over time, in the words of an assistant D.A. assigned to her case, Blanche decided that Reid "wasn't good enough, she wanted to date someone better." At first, she seemed to set her sights on store manager Kevin Denton, but the flirtatious relationship soured over time, and climaxed when Blanche filed suit against Denton and Kroger in 1985, charging sexual harassment on the job. Denton was forced to resign under fire, and Kroger settled the case out of court two years later, with a lump-sum payment of $275,000.

Meanwhile, Blanche was busy elsewhere in her quest for easy cash.

On January 23, 1985, a mysterious fire broke out at her Burlington home. Blanche blamed a "pervert" for the blaze, and firemen confirmed arson as the cause, accepting her tale of a nameless man seen loitering around the property. Blanche collected "a little" fire insurance, investing the cash in a new mobile home. When fire razed the trailer a month later, she blamed "that pervert" again and collected another insurance check.

"Someone better" finally entered Blanche's life on Easter Sunday, 1985. A handsome divorcée at age fifty-one, Rev. Dwight Moore was the pastor of the Carolina United Church of Christ. Blanche introduced herself at the conclusion of an Easter sunrise service, returning to be "counseled" as her lawsuit with Kroger dragged on. Soon, they were meeting for meals on a casual basis, Blanche dropping hints to her friends that she just might marry "a preacherman" in the next year or so.

Raymond Reid was still on tap, anticipating marriage, but he had become an obstacle to Blanche in her pursuit of the ideal companion. In early 1986, he developed "shingles," a skin condition similar to the early effects of arsenical peripheral neuritis. By April, he was hospitalized for the first time with symptoms that included diarrhea, vomiting, and loss of feeling in his hands and feet. Ironically, physicians missed the classic warning signs of arsenic poisoning and diagnosed Reid as suffering from Guillain-Barre syndrome, a rarely-fatal disease with identical symptoms. Physicians ordered special tests for "heavy metals intoxication" on June 27, a urine scan revealing six times the normal amount of arsenic in Reid's system, but the test results got lost in a snarl of bureaucratic red tape and never reached his physician.

Reid's health would ebb and flow for the next three months, but Blanche was taking no chances. She helped him draw up a new will, naming herself as executor and beneficiary to one-third of Reid's estate, the rest to be divided up between his sons. On daily visits to the hospital, she brought him gifts of food including homemade pudding and milkshakes. Despite her loving care and the doctors' best efforts, Reid's condition declined to the point that he was shifted to intensive care on October 4, suffering from renal and respiratory failure. By the time he died, three days later, he had gained sixty pounds in retained body fluids, bloating so severely that his skin began to rip. Guillain-Barre syndrome took the blame for Raymond's death, Blanche dodging requests for an autopsy with reluctant assent from Reid's sons.

Dwight Moore escorted Blanche to Raymond's funeral, her grief assuaged by some $30,000 from Reid's estate, plus untold contents looted from his safe deposit box and a safe in his home. Before she finished with the family, Reid's sons kicked in another $45,797 from their father's life insurance, persuaded that Raymond "would have wanted" Blanche to have the cash.

After a decent period of mourning, Blanche and Rev. Moore decided it was time to tie the knot. Their wedding date was set for August 23, 1987, but Blanche was sidelined in the meantime, one breast surgically removed to halt the spread of cancer. Recovery took time, and they pushed the ceremony back to November 27, 1988. This time, three weeks before the wedding, Rev. Moore was stricken down with vomiting and diarrhea, two operations required to correct an "intestinal blockage." The aging love birds finally got it right on April 21, 1989, embarking on a honeymoon trek to Montclair, New Jersey, where Dwight's first grandchild had lately been born.

Homeward bound on April 26, Dwight collapsed after eating a pastry on the Cape May ferry. Rather than seek medical care in New Jersey, Blanche drove him back to Burlington, for two days of "nursing" at home. Admitted to Alamance County Hospital on April 28, Moore took a sudden turn for the worse after Blanche delivered some homemade soup. Physicians sent him home without a diagnosis or a cure, and Moore's condition worsened after his next meal. Blanche drove him to North Carolina Memorial Hospital, but that worthy institution refused to admit Moore without a written referral from Alamance County. Home again, Moore was close to death by April 30, retaining forty pounds of body fluids in the twenty-four hours before Blanche took him back to Alamance County Hospital. From there, he was passed on again to North Carolina Memorial, this time with the necessary paperwork. Blanche told Dwight's family he was "fine," simply hospitalized "to do some tests."

In fact, she was correct. A toxic screen was ordered by physicians at North Carolina Memorial, and the results, filed on May 13, were startling: Moore's body contained twenty times the lethal dose of arsenic — enough, quite literally, to kill a moose. Police were summoned, perking up their ears when they discovered Blanche's run of rotten luck that spanned the best part of a quarter-century. For his part, Rev. Moore rejected any suggestion that Blanche was to blame for his illness. Rather, Dwight insisted, he must have inhaled the poison while spraying his garden for pests.

Despite Moore's loyalty, Blanche was running out of luck. Questioned by police on June 6, she denied bringing any food to Raymond Reid when he was ill, a statement flatly contradicted by hospital staffers. Reid's body was exhumed for tests on June 13, and arsenic was found. Results were the same with James Taylor, and Blanche was arrested for first-degree murder on July 18, held in the Alamance County jail without bond. (Lesser traces of arsenic were also found in the bodies of Blanche's father and mother-in-law, but evidence was insufficient to support a murder charge in either case.)

Blanche's trial for the murder of Raymond Reid opened in Winston-Salem on October 21, 1990, the accused black widow defending herself with denials of any wrongdoing. The state buried her plea of innocence with fifty-three witnesses who recalled her daily trips to the hospital, bearing food for Reid as he lay dying, racked with pain. Jurors convicted Blanche of Reid's murder on November 14, coming back three days later with a recommendation of death. The judge made it official on January 18, 1991, when he sentenced Blanche to die by lethal injection. With automatic appeals in progress, no date has been set for trial in the death of James Taylor or the attempted murder of Dwight Moore.

MYRTEL, HERA:
See BESSARABO, MARIE-LOUISE

NEELLEY, JUDITH ANN

Born June 7, 1964, in Murfreesboro, Tennessee, Judith Adams was the third of five children. She was nine years old when her father died in a boozy motorcycle crash, barely fifteen when she met the man who would irrevocably change her life.

Alvin Haward Neelley was a Georgia native, known to friends and family as a childhood prankster, "always smiling." Rejected by the navy for a minor heart condition, Alvin tried his hand at marriage, but it didn't take. He left three children when he hit the road and drifted through a string of odd jobs, winding up in Tennessee. Eleven years Judith's senior, Neelley dazzled her with his "sophistication," and they eloped to Georgia in the fall of 1979.

They settled briefly in Kennesaw, but Alvin's job at a roadside market offered no hope for advancement. Soon, the lovers began to drift again, pulling small robberies and passing bad checks to support themselves on the road. Judith was five months pregnant when they were finally married in Ringgold, Georgia, on July 14, 1980. Their honeymoon was an aimless trek through Alabama, Florida, Louisiana, Texas, always winding back to Georgia when they tired of traveling.

On October 31, 1980, Judith robbed a woman at gunpoint in the parking lot of Rome's Riverbend Mall. Arrested ten days later, as she tried to bounce a rubber check, she steered police to the motel where Al sat waiting. Together, they faced one count of robbery and fifteen counts of forgery. Judith delivered twins on November 12, and five days later she was transferred to a juvenile facility, the Rome Youth Development Center. For his role in the crime spree, Alvin drew a five-year prison term.

The outlaw lovers kept in touch by mail while they were locked away, some of the letters warm and loving, others jealous and accusatory. Alvin accused Judith of bedding black guards at the YDC; she threatened death to his imaginary girlfriends on the street. Released from custody in November 1981, Judith had to wait another five months for Alvin's parole. In the meantime, she played mother to a pair of living dolls.

Money always seemed to be a problem for the transient lovers who saw themselves as latter-day outlaws. Sometimes, they called each other "Boney and Claude," a joking reference to Depression-era desperadoes Bonnie Parker and Clyde Barrow. On the highway, driving separate cars, they kept in touch with CB radios. Al Neelley called himself "The Nightrider," while Judith preferred "Lady Sundance." In case someone missed the point, she was glad to explain: "You know, like *Butch Cassidy and the Sundance Kid.*" The cars were bought with $1,800 Alvin pilfered from the first job he obtained upon release from jail.

And when the thrill of stealing paled, they turned to random violence for the hell of it.

On September 10, 1982, four shots were fired into the home of Ken Dooley, a teacher at the Rome YDC. The following night, a Molotov cocktail damaged the house occupied by another YDC staffer, Linda Adair. At 1:41 A.M. on September 12, a female caller told police in Rome that the attacks were linked to "sex abuse that I went through in the YDC." She did not leave her name, but operators taped the call as a matter of routine.

Two weeks later, on September 25, 13-year-old Lisa Millican was abducted from the same Riverbend mall where Judith had robbed her last victim in October 1980. A resident of Cedartown's home for neglected children, Lisa was enjoying a day's outing when she met Judith Neelley and was lured into Alvin's clutches. The couple held her prisoner for three days, repeatedly molesting her in seedy motel rooms while their own children looked on. Finally tiring of the game, Judith tried injecting their victim with liquid drain cleaner, but she kept hitting muscle instead of a vein, reducing Lisa's flesh to what a coroner would call "the consistency of anchovy paste." Still Lisa lived, in agony, and she was driven to Alabama's Little River Canyon, finished off with bullets after more injections failed to do the job. Back in Rome, Judith made several anonymous calls to police, directing them to the body, apparently unaware that her voice was being recorded for posterity.

Three days after Lisa's body was recovered, on October 3, 26-year-old John Hancock and his fiancée, 23-year-old Janice Chatman, were walking down Rome's Shorter Street when a flashy car pulled to the curb. Incredibly, when total stranger Judith Neelley asked them to a party, both agreed, climbing into her car for a drive to some nearby woods. En route, they played with Judith's children and eavesdropped on her CB conversation with "The Nightrider." Alvin was waiting when they reached their destination, but Hancock later fingered Judith as the one who drew a gun and marched him through the trees, shooting him once in the back and leaving him for dead. Janice Chatman, like the killer family, was gone without a trace when Hancock came around and staggered off in search of help.

Initially, police saw no connections in the string of recent crimes. That changed on October 12, with help from Linda Adair. The Hancock shooting had occurred near her home, and descriptions of the slender blond with two young children rang a bell. Adair supplied detectives with a snapshot of the Neelley twins, mug shots of Al and Judith quickly filling in the family album. Hancock recognized their faces in a photo lineup; so did two young women earlier approached by Judith on the street, both wise enough to turn her invitation down.

Police got a break on October 14, when the Neelleys were arrested for check fraud in Judith's hometown of Murfreesboro. Alvin initially denied raping Lisa Millican, but he finally caved in. Even so, he contended, the crimes had been Judith's idea. She enjoyed rough sex with women, Alvin said, but the real turn-on was power — in this case, the literal power of life and death. Neelley fingered his wife for a minimum of eight murders, perhaps as many as fifteen, committed in her role as "enforcer" for an elusive white-slave ring. More to the point, he sketched and signed a map of rural Chattooga County, Georgia, where police found Janice Chatman's decomposing corpse.

The sketch sealed Alvin's fate in Georgia, but authorities in Alabama had no evidence to place him in the neighborhood of Little River Canyon. Indicted for murder and aggravated assault in the Chatman-Hancock case, Alvin pled guilty and was sentenced to a double term of life imprisonment. He would not testify in Alabama when his helpmate stood for trial.

And the wheels were already turning for Judith, across the border in DeKalb County. On December 17 she was denied youthful offender status, ordered to face trial as an adult on charges of first-degree murder, abduction with intent to harm, and abduction with intent to terrorize and sexually violate. It was a lethal combination, "special circumstances" that could send her off to the electric chair unless she beat the rap. Judith responded with a dual plea of not guilty and not guilty by reason of insanity, her trial set for March 7, 1983. Psychiatrists found her competent and legally sane, despite some evidence of "situational depression" and a vague personality disorder — "either of the passive-aggressive or dependent type."

Dependency, in fact, would be the key to Judith's defense, painting herself as a battered wife who followed Alvin's every command in fear of her life. Alabama detectives countered with descriptions of Judith as "one mean bitch" who "liked scaring people, dominating them."

Judith's trial opened in Fort Payne on schedule, with the defendant spending three days on the witness stand. Predictably, she blamed her husband for everything, reciting a three-year litany of rapes and beatings. To each and every charge, the answer for her motive was the same: "Because Al told me to."

Alvin's first wife, Jo Ann Browning, also spoke for the defense, describing a similar pattern of spousal abuse, but her testimony was muddled and contradictory. At one point, she told the court she had never divorced Alvin; moments later, she reversed herself, explaining that she had married Alvin before divorcing her first husband. Altogether, Browning's performance left much to be desired.

Jurors retired briefly before convicting Judith on all counts, but they were sympathetic enough to recommend life imprisonment over death. Judge Randall Cole disagreed, pronouncing a sentence of death on April 18, 1983. At eighteen, Judith Neelley became the youngest resident of Alabama's death row.

Police were still intrigued by Alvin's tale of other homicides, and while they found four Georgia cases still unsolved, between December 1981 and June of 1982, no evidence connected either Neelley to the crimes. In August 1984, a young woman in Murfreesboro identified newspaper photos of Judith as the same "Casey" who lured her to a motel in October 1982, there pulling a gun and joining her husband in an all-night marathon of sexual assault. Between rapes, "Casey" had boasted of numerous murders, but again, no further evidence was found.

Judith Neelley's motion for a new trial was denied on September 6, 1983, and her conviction was later affirmed on appeal. At this writing, she remains in prison, awaiting execution.

NEWMAN, SARAH JANE

A Pennsylvania native, Sarah Newman was eight years old when her family migrated to Texas, in 1821. She married the first of her six husbands at age thirteen, but his name has disappeared from history — much like the man himself. When questioned by her neighbors, Sarah simply said her man had gone to fight marauding Indians and never came back home. In those days, it seemed probable enough, and no one questioned Sarah's second marriage, to Jesse Robinson, in 1838. Nor, seemingly, were they surprised when Robinson bailed out in 1843, branding his wife a "common scold" who sometimes tried to settle their domestic arguments with a revolver.

At that, Robinson was the lucky one, a lone survivor among Sarah's half-dozen spouses. Her next choice, a few months after Robinson's departure, was George Skull, a horse trader from Goliad. The new Mrs. Skull — called "Sally" by her friends — soon earned a reputation for her temper, and she cut a dashing figure on the streets of Goliad, a six-gun and a bullwhip dangling from her belt. George later disappeared, but no one could be certain of the date. He was presumed dead in due course, but Sarah stubbornly refused to share the details with her neighbors.

Husband number four, John Doyle, had no luck keeping Sarah satisfied. They wed in 1852, but she was soon involved in a tempestuous affair with bandit Juan Cortina, up from Mexico. The shame of it drove John to drink, and liquor was the leading suspect when he drowned in the Nueces River, some months later. Even so, a local whispering campaign claimed Sarah had drowned John in a barrel of whiskey, afterward dropping his body in the river to simulate an accident.

At the height of the Civil War, Sarah came home to Goliad with husband number five. She introduced him as "Mr. Watkins," but he wasn't around long enough for neighbors to learn his first name. The newlyweds were off in Corpus Christi when Sarah shot and killed her groom. The sheriff bought her tale of firing blind at "an intruder" in the dead of night, but once again the rumor mill was working overtime. In Goliad, malicious gossips claimed that Mr. Watkins had been shot because he had the gall to rouse his wife from sleep against her will.

The final act of Sarah's long domestic tragedy played out in 1867. Married for the sixth time, to one William Harsdoff, she embarked at once with her new husband on a combination honeymoon and livestock-buying trip to Mexico. Neither was seen again, and while a traveler along the same road found a woman's decomposing body some weeks later, no link with the missing newlyweds was ever proved.

NICKELL, STELLA MAUDINE

In late September 1982, seven Illinois residents died mysteriously after ingesting capsules of Tylenol aspirin-free pain medication. Police discovered that the capsules had been spiked with cyanide and then returned to stores where they were purchased by unwitting victims. The spate of random, apparently motiveless murders remains unsolved today, its legacy a whole new list of regulations dealing with tamper-proof products and packaging. The deaths in Illinois were bad enough, but in the four years after their occurrence, no one knew that a determined would-be killer had been studying the crimes from 1,500 miles away, intent on making history repeat itself.

A native of Portland, Oregon, born in 1944, Stella Nickell grew up poor and married young, bearing her first child — daughter Cynthia — at age sixteen. In her twenties, she was convicted on charges of child abuse, fraud, and forgery, but the experience did nothing to curb her appetite for easy money. At age thirty-seven, in Auburn, Washington, she married Bruce Nickell, a part-time janitor and recovering alcoholic. Nickell had little to offer his bride, on the surface, but Stella saw potential others might have overlooked. They settled in a run-down trailer park, and Stella spent the next five years plotting her husband's death.

The trick was making it look like an accident, and Stella had a brainstorm in her second year of marriage, when the unsolved "Tylenol murders" made headlines from coast to coast. The plan seemed fool-proof, but she left nothing to chance, devoting the next three years to a detailed study of poisons, shopping for the perfect formula. Finally, late in 1985, she purchased a $40,000 life insurance policy on husband Bruce, complete with a double-indemnity clause that would pay off $176,000 in the event of accidental death.

On June 5, 1986, Bruce Nickell collapsed at home, after taking a dose of Excedrin to combat a headache. Rushed to a hospital in nearby Seattle, he died hours later, but physicians missed the cyanide coursing through his system, attributing his death to pulmonary emphysema. It wasn't the diagnosis Stella had hoped for, but her luck changed six days later, when 40-year-old Auburn resident Susan Snow swallowed an Excedrin capsule and died on the spot. This time, King County's medical examiner named poison as the cause of death, and Stella called police to voice her doubts about the diagnosis in her husband's case.

Detectives visited the trailer park and bagged two bottles of Excedrin for examination at their lab. A number of the capsules had been laced with cyanide, as in the case of Susan Snow, and new toxicology tests confirmed poison as Nickell's cause of death. A frantic search of local retail outlets turned up two bottles of Anacin 3 with poisoned capsules inside, and FBI agents entered the case under terms of the new Consumer Products Tampering Act, passed in the wake of Chicago's Tylenol scare.

Suspicion focused on Stella Nickell from the beginning. For starters, it appeared that only five bottles of medicine had been poisoned, two of those recovered from Stella's home; when Stella reported buying the bottles at two different stores, a month apart, G-men pronounced the story "virtually impossible." After police examined her husband's insurance policy, Stella first refused, then failed, a polygraph exam. Investigators also found her fingerprints on several library books about poisons, but reading is hardly a crime.

Authorities waited eighteen months for their big break, and it finally came from an unexpected source. Stella's daughter, Cynthia Hamilton, called police in January 1988, reporting that her mother had planned Bruce Nickell's murder almost from the day of their wedding. Cynthia had taken the conversations with a grain of salt until her stepfather died; a day later, Stella had called her to say: "I know what you're thinking, and the answer is 'no'."

Arrested on federal charges including five counts of violating the Consumer Products Tampering Act and two counts of causing death by tampering with consumer products, Stella Nickell went to trial in Seattle during April 1988. As prosecutors reconstructed the crime, Stella first poisoned the capsules she had in her home, trusting doctors to find traces of cyanide in her husband's body and issue a decree of accidental death. When that failed, she rushed out to poison more capsules at random, leaving bottles in three Auburn stores, biding her time until a total stranger's death gave her the opportunity to call police. Cynthia Hamilton provided the most damning testimony against her mother, Stella's defense attorney firing back with charges of a frame-up, branding Cynthia as a liar intent on claiming the $300,000 reward offered by a consortium of drug companies for a solution to the case. (In fact, the reward was divided among nine recipients, with Cynthia receiving $250,000 in the fall of 1990.)

Seattle jurors dismissed the frame-up theory, returning a five-count guilty verdict on May 8, 1988. Inspired to kill her husband by the Illinois Tylenol scare, Stella thus became the first defendant convicted under the new law spawned by that case. At sentencing, Judge William Dwyer cited her "exceptional callousness and cruelty," handing down twin 90-year sentences for each death, plus three concurrent 10-year sentences on separate counts of tampering with consumer products. Barring discipline infractions, Stella Nickell will be eligible for parole at age seventy-four, in the year 2018.

NOLLEN, ELSIE

Iowa born in 1907, Elsie Jones was barely sixteen years old when she married Albert Nollen, an alcoholic wife-beater six years her senior. They settled on a farm fifteen miles from Denison, where Albert worked as a tenant farmer, and six children arrived in due course — Orvin in 1926, Wilbert in 1927, Pauline in 1930, Carl in 1931, Leona in 1933, and Farly in 1935. By the summer of 1937, Elsie had reached her wit's end with the constant cycle of abuse, rural isolation, and the compelling demands of her brood.

On Saturday evening, August 28, Elsie quarreled with Albert over his desire to go out drinking. She rode with him to Denison at 6 P.M., hoping that her presence in the car would cut Al's boozing short, but she gave up in disgust at eleven o'clock and drove home alone. Back at the farmhouse, Elsie removed a hose from her washing machine, attached it to the car's exhaust pipe, and ran it into the nearest bedroom. That done, she sealed the farmhouse windows, started up the car, and went inside to join her sleeping children.

It was after 2 A.M. when Albert Nollen left the bar and found his car missing. He caught a ride home with neighbor Jack Schile, arriving at half-past two o'clock. Inside the house, Elsie and her six children lay dead from carbon monoxide poisoning. Some of the children had kicked their pajamas off as they died; others had stumbled out of their bedrooms before they collapsed. Elsie left a six-page suicide note, which read in part:

> I have tried and tried to live a decent life and raise my kids up right so they would be decent... But they have a father that does not care for them or me either. He don't know any better... Albert was awfully good to me when he wasn't drinking. I couldn't ask for a better husband.
>
> But oh, he sure was awful when he got drunk!... He has beat me up lots of times and I always forgot about that just because I loved him and wanted to live with him... Now today he got drunk. I never said much to him because I knew it would just be a fight again... I am doing this business because I can see that this family is not going to be raised up right and I think it is a shame to let them grow up and live such a life... I have lots to tell but I'm getting tired. I hope Albert will be happier when he is rid of us... Oh, my, such a life.

A special order for caskets was required before the Nollen family could be buried on August 31, since tiny Denison did not possess a large enough supply.

NORRIS, MELISSA

A young housewife in Gaithersburg, Maryland, Melissa Norris was dressing her infant son for a Palm Sunday service at Christian Tabernacle Church, in March 1976, when she lapsed into a religious "vision" and glimpsed a demon "possessing" her child. Intent on rescuing the baby, Melissa began whipping him, babbling phrases from the church's exorcism ritual, until the child stopped crying and went limp. Joyce Pope, a visitor who watched the beating without protest, suddenly became alarmed and called for help, but the infant died en route to a local hospital.

Jailed on murder charges, Melissa pled not guilty by reason of insanity. In support of that plea, she confessed to setting a fire that killed her mother and younger brother, years before. On another occasion, Melissa said, she had tried to strangle her grandmother and a friend from school. Independent witnesses testified that on the day before the fatal beating, Melissa had described herself to friends as "Christ reborn."

A judge accepted Melissa's insanity plea in August 1976, but psychiatrists agreed that she was presently rational. In spite of her obvious guilt, Norris was released on the spot, with no requirement for counseling or future supervision. Joyce Pope was not so fortunate: convicted on two counts of child abuse, she served eighteen months of a 14-year sentence, with psychiatric counseling required upon release from prison.

O'DONOHUE, MAUREEN

A native of Bellsville, Ontario, born in 1930, Maureen Upper was trained as a nurse at St. Michael's Hospital, in Toronto, and obtained her license in 1951. A short time later, she married Toronto attorney Melville O'Donohue, establishing a home which one neighbor described as "a house filled with love and happiness." Four daughters joined the family over time — Maureen born in 1953, Eileen in 1954, Katherine in 1955, and Mary-Jo in May 1957.

Three months after Mary-Jo's birth, in August, Maureen was hospitalized in Toronto for treatment of a "nervous breakdown." Discharged in late September, she continued psychiatric therapy as an outpatient. Neighbors were generally unaware of her worsening mental problems, though some regarded Maureen as a "perfectionist," noting that she fired a series of housekeepers for failing to meet her own high standards.

Shortly after 10 A.M. on November 11, 1957, Maureen took a roll of strong parcel twine and fashioned four nooses, suspended from a basement ceiling beam. Leading her children downstairs, she methodically hanged them in order of age, beginning with daughter Maureen and winding up with Mary-Jo. That done, she telephoned her husband, and while she made no mention of the murders, Melville sensed that something was wrong. He promptly called a neighbor, Mrs. Turner, asking her to go next door and check for any trouble in the house.

Maureen met her neighbor at the door, sobbing hysterically. Mrs. Turner made a hasty search and found the four girls hanging in the basement, cutting them down before she summoned police and an ambulance. Mary-Jo was revived at the scene, but her sisters were already dead. In the confusion of the moment, Maureen wandered out of the house and made her way to a nearby Catholic church. Police found her there and arrested her on murder charges. Days later, on the advice of two psychiatrists, Maureen was found incompetent for trial, and committed to a psychiatric hospital for an indefinite term.

OLAH, SUSANNAH:
See "ANGEL MAKERS OF AGYREV"

OLIVE, MARLENE

Terra Linda, in California's Marin County, is a middle-class suburb of San Francisco, the kind of bedroom community where mid-level executives find sanctuary after business hours. It presents a smooth, conservative facade, immortalized on celluloid when *American Graffiti* was filmed in the neighborhood during 1973. Two years later, that facade would shatter to reveal a hidden realm of angry, disaffected youth, hard drugs, black magic, kinky sex... and murder.

Marlene Olive would never know her biological parents, identified years later as a wealthy Norfolk, Virginia, teenager and a Scandinavian sailor on leave from his ship. Born on January 15, 1959, she was adopted the following day by James and Naomi Olive, desperate for a child after fourteen years of marriage. James was a doting father from day one, but friends describe Naomi as adopting "a very clinical approach to motherhood." Marlene would lack for nothing but affection in the years ahead, her relationship with Naomi degenerating over time from mere indifference to outright hatred.

The summer after Marlene's adoption, James lost his life savings in a failed business venture. He soon found a new job with Tenneco, serving the oil company in Ecuador, and while he loved the change of scene, Naomi hated it, becoming a paranoid recluse, drinking heavily, sometimes accusing James of mythical affairs. In 1964, Naomi was diagnosed as a "schizoid personality with paranoid features," and young Marlene was being shaped in her adoptive mother's image. As one acquaintance said of Naomi, "She either smothered Marlene or ignored her."

Back in the States by 1965, the family still moved frequently, James pursuing work in the petroleum industry. Marlene developed sundry allergies and was forced to undergo sporadic kidney dialysis treatments. At age ten, while playing in her father's study, she discovered her adoption papers. James and Naomi admitted the obvious, but they claimed Marlene's mother had died in a car wreck soon after delivering her child. Marlene, for her part, began to doubt Naomi's love, brooding over the identity of her "other mommy."

In the spring of 1973, Jim Olive's business brought the family to Terra Linda, where they purchased a house on Hibiscus Way. Naomi was her old, reclusive self, chain-smoking, holding four-way conversations with the "voices" in her head. With Marlene's adoption revealed, their arguments became more frequent and bitter. Naomi denounced her daughter as a "guttersnipe" and "no-good swine," the daughter of a "whore;" on more than one occasion, she paraded nude around the living room, grinding her hips and "holding her snatch" to simulate the presumed behavior of Marlene's true mother. Marlene lashed back by calling Naomi a "bitch" and a "crazy lady" who "lays around like a pig drinking all day." Enraged, the girl would gnaw her own right arm in anger, developing layers of scar tissue over time. Some of their screaming rows would end with Marlene locked inside the bathroom, while Naomi cursed and hammered on the door.

Marlene's chaotic home life inevitably took its toll outside the house. In ninth grade, she was arrested for shoplifting at a local mall, released to James after a stern lecture. Her grades took a nose dive, and Marlene began gobbling pills for her "nerves," obsessing over "heavy metal" music, dressing as a self-styled "glitter chick." By the summer of 1974, she was dating a teenage "warlock" who widened her horizons with marijuana and black magic rituals. He also introduced Marlene to sex, confirming Naomi's predictions when she caught the youngsters coupling in her house. At summer's end, the young man dumped Marlene, recalling that "she wanted to cling and I didn't want to be clung to." In her private hours, Marlene began to turn out morbid poetry, including this example:

no one stops
to step into my life
and those in it have long ago
fallen asleep.
I have been empty for so long.

That autumn, Marlene met 19-year-old Chuck Riley while tripping on LSD at the home of a mutual friend. An obese, slow-witted youth who tipped the scales at 340 pounds by age sixteen, Riley's achievements were limited to fast driving and fair marksmanship. Immersed in drugs by the time he dropped out of high school, Chuck supplemented his income from menial jobs by peddling dope to his peers. The drug trade brought him marginal acceptance, but he was still a virgin on the day he met Marlene and fell in love with her on sight.

To Riley, the drug-tripping teen displayed "a kind of innocence." She struck him as "the most beautiful girl in the world," and he dogged her tracks on campus, courting her with free marijuana and boundless adulation. Within a week of their first double date, he wrote Marlene a note reading:

"I am happy happy happy happy. In love love love love. Do with me what you will."

In time, Marlene would do exactly that.

At first, though, she remained aloof from Chuck. He gave up smoking, purchased better clothes, and worked off sixty pounds to make himself presentable. Marlene, meanwhile, was caught up in a nonstop whirl of drugs and kinky sex. She dabbled in witchcraft and carried a card in her purse, identifying herself as a "High Priestess of the Satanic Church." That winter, when she made a list of possible careers, her favored choices ranged from music and foreign affairs to "groupie," "massage lady," and "hooker."

By Christmas 1974, Marlene was obsessed with the notion of killing her mother, perhaps both parents, but her friends shrugged the diatribes off as "normal teenage talk." Chuck Riley seemed to have potential, with his presumed underworld connections, and Marlene took full advantage of his inexperience, using sex to control his every move. She encouraged Chuck to dress in black and check in several times a day, by telephone. When they made love, she sometimes ordered him to "rape" her, ripping off her clothes. Soon, they graduated into sadomasochism, Marlene masturbating with bottles, a gun barrel, even the blade of Chuck's hunting knife. From time to time, she brought a girlfriend home to play and made Chuck's adolescent fantasies come true.

On March 26, 1975, Marlene and Chuck were arrested for grand larceny, climaxing a shoplifting spree that had netted some $6,000 worth of merchandise in three weeks. In April, stopped for a traffic violation, they were jailed again after patrolmen found drugs and a sawed-off shotgun in Riley's car. Marlene explained the five-inch kitchen knife in her purse by saying she carried it "to sharpen colored pencils," and while police were skeptical, her father bought the story, taking steps to separate Marlene from her "undesirable" friends. Finally, in June, Naomi Olive signed her own death warrant by threatening to have Marlene locked up in juvenile hall for the summer.

On June 21, Marlene contrived to go shopping with her father, while Naomi stayed home. In their absence, Chuck Riley crept into the house, armed with a hammer and a .22-caliber pistol. Finding Naomi in bed, he bludgeoned her until the claw hammer stuck in her skull, gushing blood when he ripped it free. Still she lived, and Chuck ran to the kitchen for a steak knife, stabbing her repeatedly in the chest. He was trying to finish the job with a pillow pressed over her face when James and Marlene returned from the store, to discover the murder in progress.

As later described to police, James Olive found his wife near death, Chuck standing blood-drenched in her bedroom, and he grabbed the steak knife from the nightstand, rushing toward the youthful hulk. It felt like self-defense, therefore, when Chuck pulled out his gun and pumped four bullets into Olive's chest. Marlene surveyed the murder scene and focused on a portrait of herself above the bed, now streaked with blood. "Curse that bitch!" she raged. "Getting her blood all over my picture!"

With the deed accomplished, Chuck and Marlene went off to visit friends, ate dinner out, and wound up at a drive-in movie. Later, close to dawn, they drove the corpses to a rural party site and placed them in an open fire pit, soaking them with gasoline and setting them on fire. At 10:00 A.M. on Sunday, members of the fire department got a call from bikers and came out to douse the blaze, but their report dismissed the charred remains as "a deer carcass."

Back in Terra Linda, Marlene had a girlfriend move into her house, confessing the double murder before they settled down to some three-way bedroom action with Riley. A bad case of nerves had set in by June 26, Marlene cursing Chuck for killing her father along with Naomi, but they patched it up in time for a nocturnal tour of San Francisco nude bars. Driving home that night, Marlene fellated Chuck, then masturbated by crouching over the gear shift until his car nearly stalled.

By June 28, Jim Olive's business partner was openly worried, his numerous phone calls unanswered. Dropping by the house that Saturday, he rang the bell in vain, then pressed his nose against a window and beheld "an ungodly mess." Fearing robbery, he summoned police to the scene, but officers had departed before Marlene came home. She found their urgent note and paid a visit to the station house, believing she could cope with any questions that arose.

At first, she told detectives that her parents had gone to Lake Tahoe for a short vacation; she could not explain their failure to return. By Sunday morning, she admitted one or both of them were dead, but even then she managed to confuse and contradict herself at every turn. In one account, she said Naomi murdered James and fled the scene for parts unknown. A second version turned that story upside-down, with James the killer and Naomi as the corpse. On further consideration, she decided both parents were dead, murdered and carried away by a burglar... no, a hit man... or was it a group of Hell's Angels?

Finally, her imagination exhausted, Marlene directed police to the fire pit. On June 30, the blackened "deer carcass" was identified as human, detectives already homing in on Chuck Riley. They arrested Chuck and searched his home on July 1, seizing evidence that included three gasoline cans and a stack of letters from Marlene. One, written from jail and still unopened, told Riley: "I have no guilt feelings at all about my folks. NONE. NEITHER SHOULD YOU. *Relax.*" In custody, Chuck confessed the double slaying, committed, as he said, "Because Marlene told me to."

On July 10, the lovers were charged with two counts of first-degree murder, and a psychiatric evaluation was ordered for Marlene. Hospital staffers found her competent for trial but "very troubled," a judgment that left her eligible for the death penalty if tried as an adult. Riley, meanwhile, had few options left, Marlene denouncing him as "a madman" who murdered her parents on impulse, holding her a virtual prisoner over the next week, subject to his warped desires.

Marlene told the same fairy tale under oath, at her "fitness" hearing in September 1975, with mixed results. The presiding judge refused to send her up for trial as an adult, but he ruled that Marlene "did encourage, instigate, aide, abet and act as accomplice in the homicides of her parents." Under prevailing law, she was delivered to the California Youth Authority for confinement and rehabilitation, with mandatory release scheduled no later than her twenty-first birthday.

In fact, Marlene served less than four years before she was freed in 1979. Chuck Riley, meanwhile, was convicted of first-degree murder and condemned to the gas chamber, his sentence commuted to life imprisonment in 1977. Marlene settled in Hollywood after parole, graduating from grass and downers to speed and heroin. At last report, she was supporting herself and her habit as a prostitute... thus fulfilling one of her early career predictions.

PAPIN, CHRISTINE and LEA

Despite a six-year difference in their ages, French sisters Christine and Lea Papin were described by a psychiatrist as "Siamese souls," one incapable of functioning without the other. In fact, there were times when the younger Lea seemed barely able to function at all, losing even the power of coherent speech. Together, though, they managed to perform their duties as domestic servants — and, on one grim night in February 1933, they tried their hands at murder.

Christine and Lea, twenty-eight and twenty-two respectively, had found employment as a team in the Lancelin household, in the provincial town of Le Mans. The family they served consisted of a retired attorney, his wife, and their daughter Genevieve. Monsieur Lancelin was, by all accounts, easy to please, but his wife and daughter were more inclined to criticize the help in no uncertain terms. A trace of dust, a wrinkle in the linen, anything at all could spark a tirade.

On the day they lodged their last complaint, the subject was a faulty iron, "repaired" two days before, which shorted out and plunged the household into darkness. When the Lancelins descended on their servants in a fit of rage, all hell broke loose.

Monsieur Lancelin, meanwhile, was killing time at his club, returning home with his brother-in-law at 6:45 P.M. They found the doors locked, windows dark, except for one faint light that emanated from an attic occupied by Lea and Christine. That light, in turn, was suddenly extinguished at the sound of Lancelin and his companion knocking on the door. Confused, the men retreated, noting that the attic light came on again before they traveled half a block. Returning to the house, they knocked again... and watched the light wink out.

Police were summoned, and they forced a window, following their flashlight beams inside. They tried the lights, without result, and no one answered to their calls. An officer began to climb the stairs, then froze as he beheld a scene of carnage on the second-story landing.

From all appearances, a desperate battle had been fought there, Madame Lancelin and her daughter the clear losers. Both women were dead, battered almost beyond recognition, the landing's carpet blood-soaked, squelching underfoot. Beyond their death wounds, though, both women had been cruelly mutilated. Underneath their skirts, pale legs were notched with gashes from a knife, the way French bakers notch their loaves. Fingernails had been ripped from both victims, and one of Genevieve's teeth protruded from her scalp. A severed eye — her mother's — ogled the remains from several feet away.

Police continued to the attic, where a faint glow shone beneath the door. On barging in, they found the Papin sisters huddled in a single bed, a candle burning on the nightstand. They had scrubbed themselves and cleaned their murder tools — a kitchen knife, a hammer, and a pewter mug. Christine, wide-eyed, confessed the crime at once; her sister moaned and whimpered, never managing to find her voice.

In custody, Christine reported holy visions, but her guards were unimpressed. The sisters went to trial in August, troops with bayonets on hand for crowd control. Christine portrayed the murders as a form of mini-revolution, sparked by what they had endured from their employers over time. A defense attorney referred to "colossal doubts on their sanity," while the governor of a nearby asylum suggested the sisters were lesbians. Jurors dismissed Christine's visions as a scam, and she was sentenced to die, beheaded on schedule in February 1934. Lea Papin, as a "follower," was sentenced to ten years in prison and twenty years of municipal exile.

PARKER, BONNIE

The queen of America's Depression-era desperadoes was born October 1, 1910, at Rowena, Texas, the middle of three children sired by a hardworking bricklayer. She was four years old when her father died, and Bonnie's mother moved the family to Cement City in search of work. Blond and feisty, something of an exhibitionist from her Sunday school singing debut, Bonnie was recalled as "an adorable child" by her teachers in Cement City. At age sixteen, she married Roy Thornton, her high school sweetheart, and had his name tattooed on her thigh. The relationship was stormy, Thornton walking out on his bride three times between August 1927 and his final exit that December. By 1929 he was serving five years in prison for robbery, and Bonnie was living with her mother in Dallas, working at a diner to make ends meet. The diner folded in November 1929, and Bonnie was visiting a girlfriend in West Dallas two months later, when she met a sweet-talking charmer named Clyde Chestnut Barrow.

Born March 24, 1909, Barrow was the son of a Teleco, Texas, tenant farmer, fifth in a brood that would finally include eight children. He loved guns from childhood, starting with homemade toys and working his way up to the real thing, developing an early reputation as a crack shot. He quit school in the fifth grade, trying his hand at odd jobs before the family abandoned farming and moved to Dallas in 1922. By that time, Clyde and older brother Ivan — known as "Buck" — had agreed that work was for suckers, a necessary evil at the best of times. Theft was so much easier... and it was fun!

Bonnie Parker would later write, in a famous poem, that she "once knew Clyde when he was honest and upright and clean." In fact, Clyde had his first brush with the law four years before they met, in 1926, when he "forgot" to return a rented car. When police came calling, he fled on foot, bullets whistling around his head, but charges were dropped in deference to his youth. That December, Buck took the blame and the jail time when both brothers were arrested for stealing turkeys, but it was Clyde's second fall, the beginning of a reputation that would hound him to his grave.

Buck served a week for the turkey caper, and Clyde was waiting when he got out, anxious to pick up where they left off. Accomplice Frank Clause joined them for a long series of burglaries and auto thefts, climaxed by Buck's capture following a Denton, Texas, robbery in October 1929. Clyde escaped on that occasion, but authorities in Waco and Sherman were dogging his tracks, anxious to discuss the presence of his fingerprints on several looted safes and stolen cars.

By all accounts, it was love at first sight for Bonnie and Clyde. At four foot nine and ninety pounds, Bonnie was a living doll, one of the few women in Texas who literally looked up to Barrow's runty five foot four. Clyde's sister Nell would later call Bonnie "the answer to a sister's prayer for a wife for a best-loved brother." They were at her mother's home in Dallas, "mooning on the couch" one night in early February 1930, when police arrived with paperwork for Clyde's arrest. Transferred to Waco on March 2, he was convicted on seven felony counts, sentenced to two years in prison with twelve years on probation.

On March 8, 1930, brother Buck escaped from the Texas state prison at Huntsville. Three days later, Bonnie smuggled a .38 revolver into the Waco jail, taped to her thigh, and Clyde made an unscheduled departure with cellmate William Turner. They lasted seven days before a team of railroad bulls arrested them in Middleton, Ohio, and a routine check of fingerprints revealed that they were fugitives from justice. Back in Texas, Clyde was stunned to hear his sentence altered: he would have to serve all fourteen years.

Transferred to Huntsville on April 21, Clyde initially corresponded with his "wife" on an almost daily basis. By the summer of 1931, though, Bonnie's letters had begun to taper off, finally stopping altogether. She was dating other men in Dallas, doing her best to forget about Clyde. Brother Buck, meanwhile, had married a preacher's daughter named Blanche on July 1, 1931, and she nagged him into surrendering at Huntsville on December 27.

By that time, Clyde had seen enough of prison. His mother was working overtime, pestering the governor with pleas for Clyde's release, but Barrow was short on patience. In January 1932, seeking to escape a prison work detail, Clyde chopped two toes from his right foot with an ax. It was a futile gesture, though; his mother's work paid off in the form of a pardon on February 2, and Clyde came home on crutches. Bonnie dumped her new boyfriend the night Clyde turned up on her doorstep, but their true reunion was delayed until late March, when Barrow returned to Dallas from a short-lived job in Massachusetts. The lovers left Dallas together on March 20, 1932, and Bonnie was jailed in Kaufman, Texas, two days later. There had been a stolen car, a high-speed chase, and Clyde had left her in the lurch, escaping on foot while Bonnie was handcuffed and caged. It was in the Kaufman lockup that she penned her first epic poem, "The Story of Suicide Sal," recounting the emotions of a woman in prison, abandoned by her gangster boyfriend.

> If he had returned to me sometime,
> though he hadn't a cent to give,
> I'd forget all this hell that he's caused
> me,
> And love him as long as I live.

Clyde was busy, meanwhile, raising money the best way he knew. On March 25, he teamed with hoodlum Raymond Hamilton to rob the Sims Oil Company in Dallas. (Various accounts place Bonnie behind the wheel of the getaway car, though she spent that day and most of the next three months in jail.) A month later, on April 27, 65-year-old John Bucher was shot and killed in the robbery of his gas station at Hillsboro, Texas; a witness identified Clyde Barrow and Ray Hamilton as the bandits. On May 5, Clyde and Frank Clause staged a series of holdups in Lufkin, identified after the fact by two kidnap victims.

The Kaufman grand jury was sympathetic toward young Bonnie Parker, voting a "no-bill" on June 17, 1932. She returned to her mother's home in Dallas, lingering there till the end of the month, when she left to "visit a friend" in Wichita Falls. In fact, she was reunited with

Clyde, her jailhouse bitterness forgotten, more than willing to live on the road, supported by ill-gotten gains.

On July 31, Barrow and Hamilton held up the Neuhoff Packing Company, in Dallas. Five days later, while Bonnie spent the night with her mother, Clyde and Ray drove across the border to Atoka, Oklahoma, for a barn dance. They were sharing a drink in the car when Sheriff C.G. Maxwell and Deputy Eugene Moore strolled over to ask a few questions. Gunfire erupted, killing Moore where he stood, and leaving Maxwell mortally wounded. The outlaws wrecked their car in flight, but stole a series of others to make their getaway, Clyde calling for Bonnie bright and early on the morning of August 12, at her mother's home.

From Dallas, they drove straight through to Carlsbad, New Mexico, where Bonnie had an aunt. They had barely parked the car when Sheriff Joe Johns happened by, noticed the out-of-state license plates, and dropped in to pay his respects. It was Bonnie who got the drop on Sheriff Johns, herding him into the car for a wild ride back to Texas, leaving him unharmed in San Antonio. The gang was spotted stealing a second car in Victoria, and shots were exchanged with police at a roadblock near Wharton, but the outlaws escaped with no casualties on either side.

It was all too much for Hamilton's nerves, and Clyde agreed to take him home — in this case, Michigan, where Raymond's father lived. They dropped him there September 1, and spent the next month touring Michigan, Missouri, and Kansas. Drifting back to Texas, they looted a grocery store in Sherman on October 8, killing 67-year-old Howard Hall when he tried to resist. Surviving witnesses blamed Bonnie for the shooting; to the bitter end, her family maintained that Clyde and Bonnie were in Kansas City when the crime occurred. (Ray Hamilton, meanwhile, had been arrested in Michigan and shipped back to Texas, where conviction on outstanding charges earned him a sentence of 263 years in prison.)

Stopping in Dallas for a Halloween visit with family, Clyde recruited new accomplices in the persons of Hollis Hale and Frank Hardy, rolling on to Missouri for a month of small-time heists. The nadir of their sojourn in the Show-Me State came on November 30, when they stole the grand total of $115 dollars from an Orongo bank, barely escaping in the hail of gunfire from a civilian posse.

The close call and pitiful rewards were too much for Hale and Hardy, bandits who never lived up to their names. Back in Dallas on December 2, Bonnie and Clyde were met by William Daniel Jones, a 17-year-old car thief and childhood playmate of Clyde's who begged to "go out" with the gang. Clyde agreed, and they blew their first score in three days, trying to steal a parked car in Temple, Texas. Owner Doyle Johnson interrupted the thieves and was shot dead on the street. Bonnie blamed Jones for the shooting, while Jones would later blame Clyde — the first of many controversial incidents in which the truth has been forever lost to passing time.

Ray Hamilton was chafing at confinement on the Eastham farm by January 1933, dispatching pleas for help from Bonnie and Clyde. On January 6, with Jones, they dropped by the Dallas home of Raymond's sister, Lillie McBride, to discuss the prospects of a prison break. At that time, Lillie's home was known to cops and cons alike as an underworld "safe house," where fugitives could grab a home-cooked meal and rest in peace. This night, however, Lillie was in Eastham, visiting her brother, and police had occupied the house, expecting fugitive Odell Chandless.

What they got, instead, was Bonnie and Clyde.

The officers waited to spring their trap until Clyde had stepped up on the porch. It was sound strategy, but poorly executed, Deputy Malcolm Davis was killed as Clyde cut loose with a sawed-off shotgun, another officer wounded by flying glass. Jones covered Clyde's retreat with rifle fire, and the outlaws fled into Oklahoma, putting Ray's rescue on indefinite hold. Near the end of the month, in Springfield, Missouri, they kidnapped traffic officer Thomas Purcell, taking him on a 200-mile drive before they released him, unharmed.

Texas had a new governor in early 1933, and Miriam Ferguson celebrated her inauguration with a sweeping series of pardons for state prison inmates. One of those released, on March 22, was Buck Barrow. His wife hoped that Buck would "go straight," but family came first, and Buck soon met his brother in Arkansas, going on to make it a fivesome when the gang rented a small house in Joplin, Missouri.

In the interest of security, they used assumed names when they rented the cottage and paid their utility bills, a practice that soon aroused police suspicion. Armed with search warrants, a raiding party closed in on April 13, 1933, and a pitched battle broke out at the first glimpse of squad cars. Clyde and Jones were wounded in the shootout, but the whole gang managed to escape; behind them, Constable Wes Harryman and Detective Harry McGinnis lay dead in the driveway, riddled with bullets. Inside the house, police found money from a Springfield bank job, an arsenal of weapons, and Bonnie's ode to "Suicide Sal." They also discovered numerous snapshots of Bonnie, Clyde, and young Jones posing with weapons and getaway cars. One gag shot, of Bonnie packing a .38 and clenching a cigar between her teeth, would be published nationwide, advancing her reputation as a hard-bitten "gun moll."

A month after the Joplin shootout, on May 16, Bonnie and Clyde made their biggest score ever, taking an Okabena, Minnesota, bank for the grand total of $1,500. It was a close shave at that, another gauntlet of blazing guns outside as they raced for the city limits and freedom.

Near disaster overtook the gang on June 9, 1933, driving through the rainy night toward Erick, Oklahoma. A bridge was out near Wellington, and Clyde lost control of the car in a fiery crash, Bonnie suffering critical burns before she was pulled from the wreckage. Farmer Steve Pritchard stopped to help and found himself a hostage, Clyde and Jones moving Bonnie into Pritchard's home at gunpoint. A farmhand escaped in the confusion and police were on the way when someone — either Clyde or Jones — fired a panicky shot, drilling Pritchard's sister-in-law through the hand. Outside, the bandits kidnapped two patrolmen, used their car to flee the scene, and later left them tethered to a roadside tree.

Bonnie's condition was critical, with second- and third-degree burns over much of her body. On June 19, Clyde fetched her sister Billie from Dallas, wanting a relative on hand if Bonnie died. Four days later, running short of cash, Buck and William Jones set out to rob two Piggly-Wiggly stores in Fayetteville. Returning from the double heist, they met Marshal H.D. Humphrey and Deputy A.M. Salyars on the highway, exchanging shots that left Humphrey mortally wounded.

On July 8, running short of guns and ammunition, the Barrow gang held up a National Guard armory at Enid, Oklahoma, loading their cars with automatic weapons and other hardware. Ten days later, they robbed three gas stations in Fort Dodge, Iowa, driving on to the Red Crown Cabin Camp near Platte City, Missouri. Police were on alert for roving bands of strangers in those days, and suspicion brought a full-scale raiding party to the Red Crown Cabins on July 18. Police moved in behind an armored car, with tear gas and machine guns, and the gang fought back ferociously, wounding three officers before they escaped in two cars. This time it was a costly victory, Blanche blinded in one eye by a splinter of glass, Buck drilled through the head by a bullet that left him delirious, weak from loss of blood.

Next morning, a civilian posse tracked the fugitives to an abandoned amusement park between Dexter and Redfield, Iowa. Both cars were disabled in the first barrage of gunfire, Buck and Blanche captured after Clyde's older brother absorbed six more bullets. (He would die, still raving in delirium, on July 29.) Bonnie, Clyde, and Jones were also wounded, but they slipped through hostile lines in the confusion and were able to escape.

It was enough for William Jones. He stuck with Clyde and Bonnie through the early days of autumn, finally drifting back to Dallas. The police were waiting for him, copies of the Joplin snapshots all they needed to convict him as a member of the "Bloody Barrow" gang. With the electric chair in front of him, Jones did the best he could to save himself, dictating a 28-page confession that described his time with Clyde and Bonnie as a "living hell." According to Jones, he was shackled in chains or "unconscious" during most of the gang's major crimes, occasionally being forced to shoot at the police — unwillingly, of course — on pain of death if he refused. To make the story even more bizarre, Jones spoke at length about the sex life of the Barrow gang, describing how both Clyde and Bonnie used him constantly, exhausting Jones with their excessive and perverse desires.

Clyde Barrow never held the rambling fairy tale against his one time friend, expecting Jones to lie if it would save him from the chair. Two generations of reporters, though, have taken Jones' statement as their gospel, overlooking its absurdities, the total lack of evidence supporting any single charge. Author John Toland swallowed the story whole in 1963, his otherwise exemplary book, *The Dillinger Days*, accepting "blue-eyed country boy" Jones as the one infallibly honest member of the Barrow gang. Lew Louderback added a new twist in 1968, falsely describing Ray Hamilton as Bonnie's lover before she met Clyde, hinting that Ray's addition to the gang helped satisfy her "insatiable appetite for sex." Historian Carl Sifakis continued the trend in 1982, describing the union of Bonnie and Clyde as collaboration between "a homosexual and a near nymphomaniac." Movies, from 1967 to 1992, have been slightly kinder to the outlaw couple, painting Clyde as "straight" but impotent until the last weeks of his life — another claim for which there is no shred of evidence.

On January 16, 1934, Clyde finally came to Ray Hamilton's rescue. Pistols were stashed along the country road where Hamilton's work crew was chopping weeds, and when the shooting started, Clyde and Bonnie sprang from cover, laying down a screen of fire to cover the escape. Two guards were wounded in the melee; one of them, Maj. Joseph Crowson, died four days later, adding a new murder charge to the list. In addition to Hamilton, the break brought a new member — Louisiana native Henry Methvyn — to the gang. It seemed like a good idea at the time.

In Texas, the Eastham prison break sparked new demands for the capture or death of Bonnie and Clyde. Texas Ranger Frank Hamer, killer of sixty-five outlaws in face-to-face showdowns, was assigned on February 10 to track the fugitives across state lines and bring them back dead or alive. His trek would last 102 days, Hamer assisted much of the time by an old schoolmate of Clyde's, Deputy Ted Hinton. In the end, they would employ a combination of detective work and treachery to bag their prey.

On Easter Sunday 1934, the Barrow gang was idling at a highway rest stop outside Grapevine, Texas, when motorcycle officers E.B. Wheeler and H.D. Murphy rolled onto the scene. When the smoke cleared, both patrolmen were dead, riddled with bullets in the gangs' most controversial shooting. Newspaper reports (and Henry Methvyn) describe Bonnie standing over the prostrate victims, pumping bullets into their corpses and kicking them for good measure. Clyde's sister blamed Methvyn for the shooting, claiming he confessed the double murder in her presence. Clyde, ironically, would later blame Ray Hamilton, dispatching a letter to lawmen — signed with a thumbprint — that called Hamilton a "yellow punk," urging detectives to "Ask his girlfriend how they spent Easter." Ray, for his part, always claimed that he had left the gang in February, on another trip to Michigan.

Five days after the Easter killings, on April 6, Constable Cal Campbell was shot dead in a confrontation with the Barrow gang near Commerce, Oklahoma; police chief Perry Boyd was wounded in the shooting, later testifying that Bonnie, Clyde, and Methvyn all fired shots during the brief engagement. It was this incident that encouraged Methvyn to leave the gang in mid-April, catching a train back to his father's home in Louisiana.

Manhunters, meantime, had identified the new member of Clyde's gang, tracing his roots to the Pelican State. Father Ivan Methvyn lived in a tumble-down shack between Gibsland and Arcadia. He was poor but reasonable, listening attentively as lawmen spelled out his options. Cooperation meant life for his son; refusal meant a bullet in the head, or worse, a date with the electric chair.

The noose was tightening. Ray Hamilton was jailed on April 26, after robbing a bank at Lewisville, Texas. On May 19, police arrested Bonnie's sister Billie as the Grapevine shooter, indicating that a female killer was suspected well before Henry Methvyn issued his self-serving confession. (Billie was later released for lack of evidence.) In Louisiana, the trackers knew Ivan

Methvyn was expecting a visit from Bonnie and Clyde. He had agreed to bait their trap if Henry got a pardon from the state of Texas, and the deal was made.

On May 23, 1934, Bonnie and Clyde were approaching Methvyn's home when they saw Ivan's truck at the side of the road, one tire apparently flat. They pulled over to help, Clyde munching a sandwich and driving in his socks. Across the road, Frank Hamer, Ted Hinton, and four other lawmen sat behind Browning automatic rifles, surrounded by at least a dozen extra shotguns and pistols.

Like so much else about the story of these outlaw lovers, their final moments remain clouded by gunsmoke and conflicting stories. Were they offered a chance to surrender? Knowing Bonnie and Clyde, does it matter? An estimated 167 bullets ripped through their car in a matter of seconds, dozens piercing each body before they could reach the shotgun or pistol they carried. A search of the car revealed three BARs, twelve pistols, and 2,000 rounds of spare ammunition.

Bonnie Parker had anticipated the moment in her second epic poem, "The Story of Bonnie and Clyde."

Some day they'll go down together;
they'll bury them side by side;

To few it'll be grief—
To the law a relief—
But it's death for Bonnie and Clyde.

She was right on target, except for the funeral arrangements. Both outlaws were returned to Dallas, but they were buried separately — Bonnie in the Parker family plot, and Clyde beside his brother Buck. It hardly mattered to the legend, which had already taken on a life of its own.

How many men did Bonnie Parker kill? Eyewitness testimony — some of it admittedly dubious — linked her to at least three fatal shootings, and she was present as a willing accomplice to six more. Her general deportment between March 1930 and May 1934 belies family descriptions of the simple country girl who was "deathly afraid of guns." Her sex life aside, it is clear that Bonnie accepted the outlaw life and mentally prepared herself for the day when she would fall before "a sub-gun's rat-tat-tat."

Ray Hamilton was sentenced to die for the January murder of Joseph Crowson; in July 1934 he escaped from the death house but was swiftly recaptured, keeping his date with the chair on May 10, 1935. Henry Methvyn got his Texas pardon as promised, but Oklahoma was less forgiving. Convicted of Cal Campbell's murder, Henry was sentenced to die, his penalty later commuted to life imprisonment. Paroled in 1942, he lasted six more years before the boozy evening when a freight train flattened him, a short walk from his rural home.

PASOS, MARIE

A New York native, born in 1894, Marie Pasos gave no outward indication of dissatisfaction with her husband Jose, seven years her senior. Their union produced six children in a dozen years: daughter Celia in 1916; Beatrice in 1918; Joseph in 1919; Felicia in 1925; George in 1926; and Alfred in 1928. By that time, the family was mired in poverty despite Jose's working two jobs, their New York City apartment nearly bare of furniture. On the day Marie finally snapped, the total contents of her kitchen larder included a half-loaf of bread and a handful of vegetables.

Jose Pasos left for his night job as usual on Thursday, February 14, 1929. A short time later, with the children in bed, Marie turned on every gas jet in the small apartment. Unsatisfied with the flow of deadly fumes, she partially dismantled the stove to speed things up. It was shortly after 7 A.M. on Friday when a neighbor came for Jose at work, reporting that gas was leaking from his apartment and the door was jammed. Jose rushed home, broke down the door, and found all seven members of his family dead. Marie left no suicide note, authorities speculating that poverty had driven the mother of six to lethal desperation.

PEARCEY, MARY ELEANOR

A resident of North London's Kentish Town district, born in 1866, Mary Pearcey was busy juggling two lovers at age twenty-four. Charles Creighton paid her bills, but she reserved her true devotion for a handsome neighbor, furniture mover Frank Hogg. Trapped in what he described as a loveless "shotgun" marriage, Hogg could only spare stolen moments for Mary, spending most nights at home with his wife and 18-month-old daughter. Mary dropped in to visit the family now and again, but Phoebe Hogg remained cool to her guest, increasingly suspicious. It was a tense situation for Mary, and she finally decided that something had to give.

On October 24, 1890, neighbors saw Phoebe Hogg leave her home in Kentish Town, pushing her daughter's stroller toward Mary's house. Mother and child never returned, but Mary was seen with the same stroller later that day, struggling with what appeared to be a heavy load. Frank's sister Clara paid a call on Mary after dark, inquiring after Phoebe's whereabouts, but Mary pleaded ignorance.

A few hours later, Phoebe Hogg was found on Crossfield Road, in Hampstead, her throat slashed from ear to ear. It was morning before searchers found her child, apparently smothered, discarded on a rubbish heap near Finchley Road. The missing pram, with bloodstained cushions, had been dumped a mile from where the infant's body lay.

Suspicion fell on Mary from the start, and officers from Scotland Yard arrived to question her at home. She puzzled them by playing the piano while they toured her house, a search that turned up broken glass and furniture, extensive bloodstains, plus a gory cleaver and a pair of bloodstained kitchen knives. When asked about the signs of carnage, Mary sang her answer: "I was killing mice, killing mice, killing mice!"

Detectives didn't buy it, and a prosecutor would describe her odd behavior as the groundwork for a lame insanity defense. A body search by female officers revealed that Mary's underclothes were also soaked with blood, though she displayed no wounds. A neighbor suddenly remembered screams from Mary's home, around the estimated time of Phoebe's death, and Mary was jailed pending trial on a double murder charge.

As prosecutors pieced the crime together, Mary had invited Phoebe and her child to visit, stunning Phoebe with a blow before she slit the hapless woman's throat. The infant was alive when Mary dumped her adult victim in the pram, but she had suffocated under Phoebe's corpse. Convicted and sentenced to die, Mary arranged for Frank Hogg to receive a visitor's pass to the hanging. She mounted the scaffold on December 23, 1890. Her last words to the hangman: "The sentence is just, but the evidence was false."

PEETE, LOUISE

Born Lofie Louise Preslar, in Bienville, Louisiana, one of America's leading "black widows" was the daughter of a socially prominent newspaper publisher. She attended the best private schools in New Orleans, where she became notorious for her sexual escapades. Expelled from a posh finishing school, Louise went home to Bienville and settled down to the business of pleasure.

In 1903, she married Henry Bosley, a traveling salesman, joining him on the road. Working Dallas, Texas, in the summer of 1906, Henry caught his wife in bed with a local oilman and, grief-stricken, killed himself two days later. Louise sold Henry's belongings and moved to Shreveport, where she worked as a prostitute until she could afford a trip to Boston.

The dramatic change of scene meant little to Louise. Her trade was still the same, and as a hooker making house calls, she became a favorite with the local gentry. On the side, she also pilfered jewelry from the absent wives of wealthy clients, selling off the pieces that she did not choose to keep. In time, she pushed her luck too far and was discovered. Threatened with exposure, she retired to Waco, Texas, where she wooed and won Joe Appel, wildcat oil man, best known for the diamonds that studded his rings, belt buckle, even the buttons of his clothing.

One week after Joe first met Louise, he was discovered dead, a bullet in his skull, his diamonds missing. Called before a special grand jury, Louise admitted shooting Appel down — in "self-defense." The oil man tried to rape her, she maintained, and she was forced to act accordingly. The missing jewels forgotten, members of the jury openly applauded as they set her free.

By 1913, running out of luck and ready cash in Dallas, Louise married local hotel clerk Harry Faurote. It was primarily a marriage of convenience — hers — and flagrant adultery on the part of his bride soon drove Faurote to hang himself in the hotel basement.

In 1915, moving on to Denver, Louise married Richard Peete, a door-to-door salesman. She bore him a daughter in 1916, but Peete's meager income did not measure up to her standards, and she took off alone four years later, winding up in Los Angeles. There, while shopping for a house to rent, Louise met mining executive Jacob Denton. Denton had a house to rent, but he was soon persuaded to retain the property himself, acquiring Louise as a live-in companion. After several weeks of torrid sex, Louise asked Denton to marry her, but he refused.

It was a fatal error.

Smiling through rejection, Louise ordered Denton's caretaker to dump a ton of earth in the basement, where she planned to "raise mushrooms" — Denton's favorite delicacy — as a treat for her lover. No mushrooms had sprouted by the time Denton disappeared, on May 30, 1920, but Louise had numerous explanations for curious callers. First, she told all comers that her man had quarreled with "a Spanish-looking woman," who became enraged and chopped off his arm with a sword. Although he managed to survive, she said, poor Jacob was embarrassed by his handicap, and so had gone into seclusion! Pressed by Denton's lawyer, she revised the story to incorporate an amputated leg; the missing businessman was scheduled to return once he was comfortable with an artificial limb.

Incredibly, these tales kept everyone at bay for several months, while "Mrs. Denton" threw a string of lavish parties in her absent lover's home. It was September by the time that Denton's lawyer grew suspicious, calling on police to search the house. An hour's spade work turned up Denton's body in the basement, with a bullet in his head. Detectives started hunting for Louise and traced her back to Denver, where she had resumed a life of wedded bliss with Richard Peete.

Convicted on a murder charge in January 1921, Louise was sentenced to a term of life imprisonment. In the beginning, Richard corresponded faithfully, but absence failed to make Louise's heart grow fonder of the man she left behind. In 1924, when several of his letters went unanswered, Peete committed suicide.

San Quentin's warden, Clinton Duffy, once described Louise Peete as projecting "an air of innocent sweetness which masked a heart of ice." It was reported that she liked to boast about the lovers she had driven to their deaths, and she especially cherished Richard's suicide, as proof that even prison walls could not contain her fatal charm. In 1933, Louise was transferred from San Quentin to the prison at Tehachapi, and six years later, on her tenth attempt to win parole, she was released from custody.

Her ultimate release was due, in no small part, to intercession from a social worker, Margaret Logan, and her husband Arthur. Paroled to the care of a Mrs. Latham, in Los Angeles, Louise was allowed to take the name "Anna Lee" after her favorite movie star. She found employment at a serviceman's canteen in World War II; in 1942, an elderly female co-worker vanished inexplicably, her home discovered in a state of disarray. Detectives called on "Anna Lee," the missing woman's closest friend, and they were told the old woman had died of injuries suffered in a fall. In what may only be described as monumental negligence, they bought the story, never bothering to check out "Anna's" background or obtain a death certificate.

The kindly Mrs. Latham died in 1943, and Louise was paroled to the Logans. She married elderly bank manager Lee Judson in May 1944, and on May 30, Margaret Logan vanished without a trace, Louise telling Margaret's aged husband that his wife was in the hospital, unable to receive visitors. By late June, Louise had persuaded the authorities that Arthur Logan was insane; he was committed to a state hospital, where he died six months later. With typical lack of feeling, Louise donated his body to a medical school for dissection.

Louise moved into the Logan home with Judson, but all was not well in the household. In short order, her husband discovered a bullet hole in one wall, a suspicious mound of earth in the garden, and an insurance policy naming Louise as Margaret Logan's sole beneficiary. Still he said nothing, and it remained for Louise, herself, to unravel the web of deception.

By December 1944, Louise's parole officer had grown suspicious of the regular reports, submitted over Margaret Logan's shaky signature, that contained such glowing praise for their charge. Police invaded the Logan home shortly before Christmas, prompting Lee Judson to voice his suspicions at last. Margaret Logan's body was unearthed in the garden, whereupon Louise offered another of her patented fables. In this story, decrepit Arthur Logan had gone suddenly berserk, beating his wife to death in a maniacal rage. Terrified of attracting suspicion due to her background, Louise had buried the corpse and stalled for a month before having Arthur committed to the asylum.

Louise was charged with Margaret Logan's murder, her husband booked as an accessory. Acquitted on January 12, 1945, Judson took his own life the next day, leaping from the thirteenth floor of a Los Angeles office building. Louise, it was observed, seemed pleased with his reaction to their separation. Convicted of first-degree murder by a jury that included eleven women, Louise was this time sentenced to die. Her appeals failed, and she was executed in San Quentin's gas chamber on April 11, 1947.

POPOVA, MADAME

A prolific poisoner who undertook her work as much from sympathy as for the minor fees she charged, Madame Popova was an advocate of women's liberation long before the cause was recognized. A native of Samara, Russia, she was so distressed by the travail of peasant wives held "captive" by their brutish husbands that she volunteered an inexpensive, lethal remedy. For thirty years before her ultimate arrest, in March 1909, she ran a small disposal service for her female neighbors, picking up spare change and executing her commissions with dispatch. A client, suddenly remorseful, turned her in to the police, and Madame Popova confessed to "liberating" some 300 wives in her career. In custody, she boasted of the fact that she "did excellent work in freeing unhappy wives from their tyrants." In her own defense, Madame Popova told her captors she had never killed a woman. Czarist soldiers saved her from a mob that sought to burn her at the stake, and she was unrepentant as she stood before the firing squad. [See also: "Angel Makers of Nagyrev"]

POTTER, MARGARET

Peculiar mystery surrounds the case of Margaret Potter, accused of burning four victims to death in 1977. Despite national publicity surrounding the crime and her arrest, including mention in the *New York Times*, Potter has seemingly "disappeared" from official records, and the outcome of her case remains in doubt.

There is no question regarding the basic events of August 4, 1977. At 5:36 A.M., firefighters in Redondo Beach, California, responded to calls reporting an uncontrolled blaze at the two-story Potter household. They arrived too late to save 40-year-old Robert Potter, his seven-year-old son Bobby, eight-year-old daughter Judy, and an overnight guest, eight-year-old Melinda O'Brien. All apparently died in their beds, from a combination of burns and smoke inhalation. Twenty-year-old Randy Potter was listed in critical condition at Torrance Memorial Hospital's burn ward, while sister Cathy, age sixteen, escaped from the house without injury. Likewise unharmed was 39-year-old Margaret Potter, Robert's second wife and step-mother to his four children.

Police were instantly suspicious, grilling Margaret for several hours, finally announcing her arrest on suspicion of murder that afternoon. No immediate motive was suggested, detectives informing the *Los Angeles Times* that it would take "several days" to fit the last puzzle pieces in place.

And there, incredibly, the story ends. From the time of her arrest on August 4, Margaret Potter seems, in the words of one researcher, to "drop off the face of the earth." No further mention of her case appears in newspapers, around Los Angeles or nationwide. To date, police and fire department spokesmen have ignored the author's correspondence seeking further information on this troubling case. [See also: "Black Widow Murders" — Cleveland, Ohio]

POWELL, TINA MARIE: See FOSTER, LAFONDA

PUENTE, DOROTHEA MONTALVO

Born in 1959 and raised in an orphanage, Dorothea Puente claimed a total of four marriages, from which police were able to document two divorces. Her only child, a daughter, was put up for adoption at birth, finally meeting her mother — whom she described as a woman with "no real personality" — for the first time in 1986. Eight years earlier, Puente had been diagnosed as suffering from "chronic undifferentiated schizophrenia," a condition that sometimes produces delusions. Neighbors recall her fascination with acting, including boasts of nonexistent starring roles as "the evil woman" in various feature films. On the side, Puente billed herself as a "holistic doctor," but she earned her income, after 1978, from operating a boarding house in Sacramento, California.

In 1982, Puente was convicted of drugging and robbing strangers she met in various taverns, serving two and a half years in prison before she returned to her rooming house. She spent hours working in the garden, and neighbors described her as "very protective of her lawn." As one told reporters, "If somebody walked on her lawn, she'd cuss them in language that would make a sailor blush."

In 1986, Puente approached social worker Peggy Nickerson with an offer of quality lodgings for elderly persons on fixed incomes. Referring to Puente as "the best the system had to offer," Nickerson sent her nineteen clients over the next two years, growing concerned when some of them dropped out of sight. In May 1988, when neighbors complained of a sickly-sweet smell in her yard, Puente blamed the aroma on applications of "fish emulsion." "We couldn't stand it," one resident recalled. "There was a sick smell in the air, and there were lots of flies in the area."

On November 7, 1988, police dropped by the rooming house to check on tenant Bert Montoya, last seen in August. Briefly satisfied with Puente's explanation that Montoya had gone home to Mexico, officers returned with shovels five days later, after Peggy Nickerson reported one of her clients as missing.

The first corpse was unearthed on November 11, with two more recovered the following day. Puente disappeared that afternoon, before she could be taken into custody, and officers kept digging in her absence. By November 14, police had seven bodies in hand, and tenant John McCauley, fifty-nine, was charged as an accomplice in the murders. (He was later freed, for lack of evidence.) Detectives shook their heads in wonder as they realized that they were only blocks away from where another clutch of corpses had been excavated, at the home of killer Morris Solomon, in April 1987.

No more bodies were discovered at the rooming house, but officers believed there might be other victims, all the same. "We are getting a large number of calls from people with relatives who have stayed here," a police spokesman announced. "There are a lot more than seven names." In fact, as many as twenty-five former tenants were missing, and police had no I.D. on any of the seven corpses. (At least one had been decapitated, feet and hands removed, to prevent identification.) Detectives believe Puente murdered her tenants in a scheme to obtain their Social Security checks.

On November 17, Puente was traced to Los Angeles, fingered by a new acquaintance she met in a bar. Introducing herself as "Donna Johansson," she displayed an unusual interest in the man's disability income, offering to move in with him and "fix Thanksgiving dinner" on short acquaintance. Held without bond, she faced indictment on seven counts of murder, with the investigation still open. Two more counts of murder were added in subsequent weeks.

By December 10, 1988, Sacramento authorities had identified four of the victims unearthed at the Puente rooming house. Fingerprints and X-rays indicated that the four were 55-year-old Ben Fink, 52-year-old Alvaro Montoya, 65-year-old Dorothy Miller, and 65-year-old Vera Martin. One male victim and two females from the rooming house remained unidentified, while police added an eighth victim — a middle-aged male, found January 1, 1986, in a wooden box beside the Sacramento River — to the list of Puente's victims. Legal maneuvers delayed the opening of Puente's murder trial until February 9, 1993, with testimony expected to last from six to ten months.

QUINN, JANE

Awakened by a gunshot in the pre-dawn hours of November 2, 1911, John Miller scrambled out of bed and rushed to the apartment of his landlord, from where the sound had emanated. On arrival at the scene, he found John Quinn, the landlord, lying in his bed, blood streaming from a fatal bullet wound. According to the dead man's wife, a prowler was responsible, though Miller saw no evidence of theft or any struggle. Jane Quinn declined to testify at the resulting inquest, and a Chicago coroner's jury deliberated for one hour before ordering her arrest on murder charges.

By that time, on November 10, police had learned a thing or two about the lethal Mrs. Quinn. They knew about her marriage to Canadian John MacDonald, in October 1883, and his subsequent death from "alcohol poisoning" on September 28, 1901. A short month later, at Bass Lake, Michigan, the grieving widow had married Warren Thorpe — and he had later been shot to death in circumstances similar to those surrounding the Chicago case. Another death in bed, this time involving Jane's own mother, had occurred soon after, in the house once occupied by Warren Thorpe.

The evidence was overwhelming, and Jane Quinn was speedily convicted at her trial on murder charges, sentenced to a term of life imprisonment. If nothing else, the verdict may have spared some future victims from the clutches of a bona fide "black widow."

RACHALS, TERRI EDEN MAPLES

In November 1985, administrators at Phoebe Putney Hospital, in Albany, Georgia, were alarmed by a sudden rash of cardiac arrests in the intensive care unit. A review of hospital records showed six suspicious deaths, with an equal number of near-misses, since late October, and police were quietly notified. Post-mortem examinations blamed the six deaths on injections of potassium chloride, and homicide investigators went to work on the case full-time.

The first apparent victim had been 68-year-old Milton Lucas, pronounced dead on October 19, 1985. Next up was Minnie Houck, age fifty-eight, lost on November 7. Three days later, 36-year-old Joe Irwin joined the list, and Robert Parker, also thirty-six, died on November 15. Andrew Daniels, age seventy-three, lost his struggle for life on November 24, and he was followed two days later by three-year-old Norris Morgan. Survivors included patients Sam Bentley, George Whiting, Frances Freeman, and Jack Stephens, all of whom had suffered one or more unexplained cardiac arrests in ICU.

By New Year's, authorities were confident of six victims, but there may have been more. Lee Creech, a 26-year-old jail inmate, had died under treatment on December 21, and detectives were suspicious of three or four other deaths, dating back to mid-August. By March 1986, their investigation had focused on a 24-year-old nurse, Terri Rachals, and on March 13 she confessed to injecting five patients with lethal doses of potassium chloride. Twelve days later, Rachals was indicted on six counts of murder and twenty counts of aggravated assault against nine surviving patients. Some had received multiple injections, with Creech and Parker holding the record at six and four jolts, respectively.

Defense attorneys described their client as "a girl with a horrible, horrible background." Born in 1962, Terri was two years old when her mother suffered a nervous breakdown, and her father gave her up for adoption to the Maples family. In 1973, she lost her adoptive mother to a massive stroke. Over the next five years, until she finally left home at age sixteen, Terri claimed she was repeatedly molested by her adoptive father (a charge that Jim Maples — himself a stroke victim and recovering alcoholic — staunchly denies). In spite of everything, Terri graduated from high school with honors and went on to become a registered nurse. In 1980, she married Roger Rachals, an Albany printer and victim of cerebral palsy, giving birth to their son four years later. Friends were stunned by Terri's arrest and confession, noting her exemplary work record and active membership in the Byne Memorial Baptist Church.

At trial, in September 1986, the prosecution contended that Rachals "felt like a second-class citizen all her life," desirous of "power and control" that she ultimately sought "on the dark side of the street," by murdering her patients. Reference was made to her confession, but Terri took the stand on September 23, recanting her statements, denying any memory of the attacks. On September 26, jurors returned a verdict of guilty but mentally ill on one count of aggravated assault, acquitting Rachals on all other charges. Members of the panel said that, while she may indeed have been responsible for several deaths, the prosecution simply had not proved its case. On October 1, Rachals was sentenced to a 17-year prison term, with three years of probation on release.

RAIES, JEAN

Economic competition between morticians in Geneva, Switzerland, inspired the serial murders committed by nurse Jean Raies. In 1880, after one undertaker tried to "scoop" the competition with a financial bounty on reports of local deaths, Nurse Raies saw an opportunity to line her pocket. Before year's end, she poisoned twelve of her patients, "selling" each in turn to the free-spending mortician. Arrested after the twelfth killing, she was convicted of multiple murder and spent the rest of her life in a Swiss prison.

RANSOM, FLORENCE

An attractive, 34-year-old widow residing in Piddington, England, Florence Ransom had been romantically involved with Walter Fisher for five years before he moved into her home in September 1939, deserting his wife and 19-year-old daughter in nearby Matfield. It was a victory of sorts, but not enough for Florence. Ten months later, on July 9, 1940, she turned up in Matfield armed with a shotgun, calling Dorothy and Freda Fisher from their home. Both women were dropped in their tracks, killed instantly by close-range shots, and Florence was reloading to shoot them again when their maid, Charlotte Saunders, came running to the sounds of gunfire. Another blast finished the maid, and Ransom fled, dropping one of her white leather gloves at the scene.

Police traced the glove, and neighbors in Matfield recalled Florence — a.k.a. "Mrs. Fisher" — lurking around the scene of the crime. Arrested for murder a week after the shootings, Ransom was convicted on November 12 and sentenced to die. A month later, Florence was judged insane and her sentence was commuted to life. She was promptly transferred to the prison asylum at Broadmoor, where she spent the rest of her life.

READ, MARY

An adventurous tomboy who dressed as a man most of her life, Mary Read was successful in duping the British navy and army alike, serving at various times on a man-of-war, in the infantry, and in the cavalry. She found romance on horseback in the latter service, resigning to marry one of her barracks mates, and the newlyweds settled in Holland, opening an inn called The Three Horseshoes, at Breda. When her husband died, Read went back into costume, shipping out aboard a Dutch merchant ship bound for the Caribbean.

En route to its destination, the vessel was captured by pirates under the command of "Calico Jack" Rackham and his lover, Anne Bonny. Surviving members of the Dutch crew were pressed into service aboard Rackham's ship, while Anne Bonny — "not altogether so reserved in point of chastity" — cast a lascivious eye on one of the prisoners. Leading Mary to her cabin, Bonny was removing "his" jacket when she froze, startled at the sight of female breasts.

The two young women became fast friends, Bonny protecting Read's secret from the rest of the crew. They hit stormy weather when Rackham grew jealous, threatening to kill Bonny's "boyfriend" before he was briefed on the scam. In time, Mary found herself drawn to another young pirate on board, whereupon "she suffered the discovery of her sex to be made by carelessly showing her breasts, which were very white." The young sailor liked what he saw, and they soon became lovers... but Mary's new man left much to be desired. A hopeless coward, he was so terrified by a shipmate's dueling challenge that Mary had to fight in his place, killing the brawny pirate with one thrust of her sword.

No one questioned Read's status with the crew from that point on, and she became a zealous buccaneer, ready to loot and kill with the rest. In October 1720, Rackham's crew was surprised by a British assault force while celebrating their latest prize. The raiders struck with swords and pistols, most of Rackham's crew retreating to the hold, where they refused to fight. Anne Bonny stood her ground with Mary Read to face the enemy, Read turning on her shipmates with a brace of pistols, shouting "Come up you bastards, and fight like men!" When they refused to move, she shot two pirates, killing one, before she was subdued by the authorities.

At trial, a witness said of Read and Bonny that "the two cursed and swore with the best of the males, and never cringed from murder." Both were among the six pirates sentenced to die on various charges, along with Calico Jack and three of his men. When the judge rhetorically asked for reasons why they should not be hanged, both women rose and said in unison, "We plead our bellies!"

Startled to discover both were pregnant, the court stayed execution until after their children were born. Fate had other plans for Mary Read, however, and she contracted a fatal illness in prison, dying from natural causes in December 1720. [See also: Bonny, Anne]

REARDEN, VIRGINIA

In July 1987, Louisville attorney Steve Keeney was approached by a female member of his church, seeking legal advice. The woman had been trying for three months to collect a $2,500 life insurance payment on her daughter, killed in a California rock-climbing accident, but the insurance company was stalling without explanation. Keeney was moved by the woman's obvious grief and near-poverty, agreeing to help if he could. At the time, there was nothing to suggest that he would soon be matching wits with an industrious "black widow" and her homicidal brood.

The facts of the case seemed simple enough, at first glance. Deana Wild, age twenty-one, had been visiting Big Sur with friends — Virginia McGinnis and her husband Billy Joe — when she ventured too close to the edge of a cliff and plunged to her death on April 2, 1987. Virginia's son by a previous marriage, James Coates, had also been present, and all three agreed that Deana's fall was a tragic accident. So, apparently, did the Monterey County sheriff and coroner's office. Investigating officers were casual enough about the case that they refrained from taking any on-site photographs, accepting Virginia's assurance that she would give them her snapshots, taken moments before the event. In fact, Virginia lied to the police and sent the photos to Deana's mother, where they gathered dust for several months before eventually coming back to haunt her.

In the meantime, there were other photographs that troubled Keeney, pictures taken at Deana's autopsy which showed bruised hands and broken fingernails, as if the girl was clinging for her life before the final plunge. Keeney knew that Deana was married, separated from her seafaring husband of two years but hoping for a reconciliation, yet the death certificate listed her as "single." Interviews with passersby revealed that Virginia McGinnis had furnished conflicting accounts within minutes of Deana's fall: in one story, she described Deana as the daughter of a close friend; in another, the dead girl became Virginia's prospective daughter-in-law. More to the point, Keeney learned that Virginia had purchased a $35,000 life insurance policy on Deana the day before she died, listing Joe Coates as first beneficiary, herself as the second.

The case was beginning to smell, but assembling crucial evidence takes time. By March 1988, Keeney was nearing the deadline for a wrongful death suit, under California's prevailing statute of limitations, and authorities in Monterey County refused to file criminal charges on grounds of insufficient evidence. Increasingly frustrated, the Kentucky lawyer went back to work.

He learned that Deana had married Jay Wild in 1985, following her navy husband west to San Diego. Long separations had taken their toll by late 1986, and the couple was living apart, but Deana still had hopes of making the marriage work. The McGinnis family had befriended her, nagging her to move in with them, and she finally agreed, though she would tell her sister that the tribe was "sort of weird." In fact, she didn't know the half of it.

Keeney's research traced Virginia back to her roots in Ithaca, New York, where she was born in 1932. She reportedly met her first husband, Richard Coates, while he was helping fight the fire that destroyed her father's well-insured barn. Virginia bore him two sons, but she was more interested in collecting fire insurance payments, and Coates finally divorced her when he tired of blazes breaking out around the house.

Taking the divorce in stride, Virginia moved in with her father... and *his* house soon burned, providing another infusion of cash. In fact, Virginia rarely occupied a home that didn't burn, and all of them were well insured. On one occasion, in California, she had the nerve to reject an insurance company's offer of $85,000 for restoration of a partially burned house; within the week, a second fire leveled the damaged structure, and Virginia collected $147,000 with no questions asked!

Nor were her schemes restricted to the realm of fire insurance. Back in 1972, three-year-old Cynthia Coates had "accidentally hanged herself" with baling twine in Louisville, Kentucky. Authorities were never sure exactly how the child managed to reach an eight-foot rafter in the barn, but Virginia cut the body down before they arrived, and a coroner's report described the death as accidental. Cynthia's life insurance policy paid off on schedule.

Two years later, Virginia's second husband — Bud Rearden — was stricken with cancer. Virginia persuaded physicians that she was a nurse, fully qualified to inject his various medicines. Hospital records document one incident where Bud received a double dose of powerful painkillers, but he managed to survive. The night he passed away, Virginia gave her children money for a night out on the town, and they returned to find him dead. She cleaned the body, waived an autopsy, and collected Bud's insurance when cancer was listed as the cause of death.

Virginia had divorced her latest husband in the wake of Deana's fall, reverting to the Rearden surname, living with her sons by Richard Coates. It was an odd choice for a name, considering the lack of empathy she felt for dear, departed Bud. In fact, Virginia had not spoken to a single member of his family in almost fourteen years. Her sons had problems of their own, plea-bargaining on separate murder counts, and James spent most of his time behind bars on various felony charges.

Keeney filed his wrongful death suit with days to spare, twice serving subpoenas on Rearden, but she refused to appear or even respond. In her absence, the court filed a no-fault judgment of wrongful death against her, and Rearden was ordered to pay Deana's family $250,000 plus interest. Still there was no reply from the suspected killer, and Keeney persuaded San Diego officers to consider a murder charge, based on the fact that Deana's life insurance policy was purchased in their county.

By that time, autopsy reports had found traces of a strong anti-depressant drug, amitriptyline, in Deana's remains. Known to cause drowsiness and disorientation, the drug was never prescribed for Wild, but it had been for Billy McGinnis, five weeks before the Big Sur "accident." And then, there were Virginia's photos, several snaps of young Deana perched on rocks and smiling for the camera, another of her moving toward the cliff's edge with McGinnis, Billy's arm around her shoulders.

Virginia Rearden and her ex-husband were charged with first-degree murder, conspiracy to commit murder, forgery and insurance fraud; McGinnis later died of AIDS before he faced his day in court. Joe Coates, serving time on an unrelated conviction, was not indicted, but he tried to help his mother on the witness stand. In fact, Joe told the court, he *was* engaged to Deana on the day she died. They had picked out a ring, but Joe had no receipt and he could not remember what it looked like, much less where it was. On top of his amnesia, Joey's wedding plans had been kept secret from his friends, the woman he was married to in 1987, and the several others he was bedding regularly at the time.

The jury didn't buy it, voting to convict Rearden on all counts with a finding of "special circumstances" — in this case, murder for profit — that left her open to a possible death sentence. Her trial judge was inclined toward mercy, though, and on March 30, 1992, he sentenced Virginia to a prison term of life without parole.

RENCZI, VERA

Born to affluent parents at Bucharest, in the early 1900s, Vera Renczi had already displayed a precocious interest in sex by age ten, when her family moved to Berkerekul. At age fifteen, she was found in the dormitory of a boy's school at midnight, and Vera afterward eloped with several lovers, coming home each time when she grew tired of their attentions. It was fine for Vera to desert a paramour, but none must ever try to turn the tables, as she had begun to demonstrate possessiveness that bordered on the pathological.

Vera's first husband was a wealthy businessman, many years her senior, and she bore a son before he disappeared one day, without a trace. Declaring that her man had left without a word of explanation, Vera passed a year in mourning, finally reporting "news" of her husband's recent death in a car crash.

Vera soon remarried, to a younger man, but he was flagrantly unfaithful, vanishing a few months later on what Vera described as "a long journey." Another year passed before she announced the receipt of a letter, penned by her spouse, declaring his intent of leaving her forever.

Vera Renczi would not wed again, but she had many lovers — thirty-two in all — as years went by. They never seemed to stay around for long, and none were ever seen again once they "abandoned" Vera, but she always had an explanation for her neighbors... and another lover waiting in the wings. Police became involved when Vera's last paramour was reported missing by the wife he left at home; a search of Renczi's basement turned up thirty-five zinc coffins, with the bodies of her missing husbands, son, and lovers tucked away inside.

Detained on murder charges, Vera made a full confession, stating that she killed her husbands and her lovers off with arsenic when they began to stray, sometimes arranging for a romantic "last supper" to climax a tryst. Her son's demise had been a different story, brought about by threats of blackmail when he stumbled on the basement crypt by accident. Some evenings, Vera said, she liked to sit among the coffins in an armchair and enjoy the company of her adoring beaus. Convicted on the basis of her own confession, Vera drew a term of life and subsequently died in prison.

RENDALL, MARTHA

Australia's most sadistic murderess never married, but she managed to acquire a family all the same. By 1906, Martha Rendall was settled with carpenter Thomas Morris and his five children from a previous relationship, insisting that the children call her "Mother," whipping them for trivial infractions of her strict behavior code. Neighbors frequently remarked on Martha's harsh code of discipline, but none were anxious to interfere in another family's private business.

Matters went from bad to worse in 1907, when two of Tom Morris's daughters were stricken with sore throats. A doctor prescribed medicinal throat swabs, but the treatment — as administered by Martha — seemed more painful than the disease. Screams and anguished sobbing echoed from the Morris home for weeks before Anne died on July 28, with the cause of death diagnosed as diphtheria. When Olive Morris died three months later, the symptoms and diagnosis were identical. Fourteen-year-old Arthur Morris joined the casualty list on October 6, 1908, following more of Martha's throat-swabbing treatment, and while doctors were growing suspicious, an autopsy revealed no evidence of foul play. Again, the cause of death was listed as diphtheria.

Young George Morris was taking no chances when he began to suffer sore throat symptoms in April 1909. He ran away from home in lieu of letting Martha nurse him, and police were called to bring him back. Beginning with a canvass of the neighborhood, investigators heard their first reports of brutal discipline within the Morris family. With three children dead and a fourth missing, neighbors finally agreed to share their suspicions with authorities.

Court orders were obtained for exhumation of the three dead Morris children, and new autopsies yielded startling results. In place of the prescribed throat medicine, Martha Rendall had been "treating" her young patients with hydrochloric acid, killing them slowly, leaving burns that mimicked the typical inflammation of diphtheria.

Martha and her husband were both held on three counts of murder. At trial, evidence showed that Rendall had first dosed the children with acid-laced beverages, producing the sore throats which she afterwards swabbed with more acid. Tom Morris was acquitted of all charges by the jury, while Martha was convicted and condemned to die. Her execution, on October 6, 1909, marked the last time that a woman was hanged in Western Australia.

ROBACZYNSKI, MARY ROSE

On August 18, 1978, registered nurse Mary Robaczynski was indicted on charges of murdering four terminal patients at Maryland General Hospital, in Baltimore. The charges resulted from a four-month investigation, launched by police after hospital administrators reported "suspicious" deaths in the intensive care unit. Robaczynski, a 1975 graduate of Maryland General's nursing program, employed in ICU until March 8, 1978, surrendered voluntarily and was released by the court on her own recognizance.

According to authorities, the victims included three women and one man, whose life-support systems were unlawfully disconnected between December 1977 and March 1978, with 48-year-old Harry Gessner killed on Robaczynski's last day of employment. Colleagues described Robaczynski as an open advocate of euthanasia who freely admitted pulling the plug on selected "gorks" — hospital slang for "God only really knows" — in an effort to end their suffering.

Robaczynski's trial opened on February 25, 1979, with the defense contending that it is not murder to disconnect life-support machinery from a patient who may already be dead. On March 20, with the jury deadlocked 10-to-2 in favor of acquittal, a mistrial was declared. Nine days later, charges were dismissed in return for Robaczynski's promise to surrender her nursing license and refrain from practicing anywhere inside the United States.

ROBINSON, SARAH JANE

Irish-born Sarah Tennant emigrated to Boston with her family in the late 1860s. Wed to an American named Robinson, she bore him eight children through the years, five of them stillborn. When her husband died of a "mysterious disease" in 1882, his life insurance paid off promptly, ignoring remarkable similarities with the recent death of Sarah's landlord.

The widow's sister, Mrs. Arthur Freeman, was the next to die, with Sarah nursing her to the bitter end. More insurance payments arrived, and a grieving Art Freeman moved in with his sister-in-law, bringing his two children to share Sarah's hospitality.

Uncannily, the run of miserable luck continued. Freeman died within two months of changing his address. Two of Sarah's surviving children, William and Lizzie, were the next in line, followed swiftly by seven-year-old Thomas Freeman. Life insurance policies paid off for each in turn, but company adjusters had long since discarded their belief in coincidence. Exhumations were ordered, and arsenic was found.

Convicted at her first trial, Sarah won a reversal on appeal, but a new trial brought the identical verdict, and she was sentenced to die. A fresh appeal reduced her penalty to life imprisonment, and Sarah was still confined at the time of her death, in 1905.

ROEDER, MICHAELA

A native of West Germany, born in 1950, Michaela Roeder fulfilled her life's ambition of helping others when she became a nursing sister at St. Peter's Hospital, in the Ruhr valley town of Wuppertal-Barmen. No problems were recorded in the early years of her employment at St. Peter's, but by 1988 Michaela's colleagues had begun to call her the "Angel of Death," a facetious reference to the unusual number of patients who died in her care. To be sure, Roeder was assigned to the intensive-care unit, her patients arriving in critical condition to start with, but gallows humor gave way to outright suspicion in 1989, when nurse Stefan Judick saw Roeder inject a cancer patient with what proved to be a lethal dose of potassium chloride.

Booked on murder charges, Roeder sat in jail while police exhumed the corpses of some recent patients. New autopsies revealed that seventeen of the dead had received injections of clonidine — a drug that lowers blood pressure — without a doctor's orders. In several cases, the clonidine injections were combined with chloride of kalium, a drug designed to paralyze the heart.

In custody, Roeder confessed to killing ten patients, telling police "I just wanted to put an end to the agony these people were suffering." A review of medical records, however, suggested that some of her victims had been on the road to recovery, looking forward to their discharge from the hospital. In at least one case, that of 77-year-old Gertrud Horch, Roeder's action seemed to be a matter of personal convenience. Mrs. Horch was killed, the prosecution said, so that Michaela could enjoy a soccer match between West Germany and Italy.

Prosecutor Karl-Herman Majorowsky told jurors that Roeder "killed for satisfaction and as an exhibition of power. She enjoyed making decisions about who was to live and who wasn't. She considered herself the master over life and death." That opinion was supported by Roeder's own diary, including an entry which noted that her lethal ministration "worked splendidly" on a 94-year-old man suffering from a broken leg. Convicted on murder charges, Roeder received the maximum penalty of life imprisonment.

ROWNEY, MARGARET

A young widow in Van Nuys, California, Margaret Rowney had given birth to four children between 1943 and 1947. Her husband's premature death left Margaret emotionally devastated, but relatives and neighbors denied any warning of the tragic events of December 14, 1950. That evening, Rowney dressed her children in pajamas and loaded them into the family station wagon, driving aimlessly for awhile before she parked beneath a giant oak tree, some 300 yards from a Hollywood movie set. There, she rigged a hose from the car's exhaust pipe to her window and left the motor running. Margaret was dead when a passerby noticed the car; huddled lifeless in the back were seven-year-old Peggy, five-year-old George, four-year-old Guy, and three-year-old Thomas. Rowney left no suicide note, and authorities blamed her action on some unspecified mental illness.

SACH, AMELIA, and WALTERS, ANNIE

English born in 1873, Amelia Sach appeared to be a kindly soul who doted over children. So concerned was she about their welfare that she opened up a "nursing home" in East Finchley, London, catering to unwed mothers in their hour of need. Sach's clients were recruited through an advertisement in the papers.

> ACCOUCHEMENT: Before and during, skilled nursing. Home comforts. Baby can remain.

That final sentence was the clincher, with Amelia promising to make arrangements for "adoption"... if an extra fee of twenty-five or fifty pounds was paid. In fact, the infants were delivered to her simple-minded sidekick, Annie Walters, for disposal, generally dispatched with chlorodyne, their tiny corpses cast off in the Thames or buried in convenient garbage dumps.

In 1902, Amelia gave Walters the child of an unwed mother named Galley, instructing her to dispose of the baby as always. Ignoring the order, Annie took the infant home "for company," surprising her landlord (who was also a policeman). Walters explained that she was keeping the child as a favor to some friends who lived in Kensington, but she appeared confused. While chatting with the landlord's wife, Annie referred to the baby as "a dear little girl," but the landlady, having recently changed the child's diaper, knew it to be a boy.

When Annie's tiny roommate died, a few days later, inconvenient questions were delayed in deference to her grief. The tears seemed real enough, but two months later she produced another infant, this one also dying "accidentally" in its sleep. Interrogation of their suspect led detectives to the nursing home, and both women were sentenced to die on conviction of multiple murders.

As their hangman, H.A. Pierrepoint, noted in his diary: "These two women were baby farmers of the worst kind and were both repulsive in type. They had literally to be carried to the scaffold and protested to the end against their sentences." [See also: "Baby Farming"; Dean, Williamina; Dyer, Amelia; Waters, Margaret; Young, Lila]

SCIERI, ANTOINETTE

Little is known of Antoinette Scieri's early life, aside from the fact that she was born in Italy and emigrated to France as a child. In the early days of World War I, she worked at a casualty clearing station in Doullens, there beginning a long life of crime. She stole cash and jewelry from the wounded, also forging signatures on letters to their families, requesting money through the mail. Jailed for the theft of an officer's paybook in 1915, she was released the following year.

Celebrating her freedom, Antoinette married an Italian soldier named Salmon, bearing him two children before he discovered her flagrant infidelity and left her flat. Next, she took up with an alcoholic brute named Joseph Rossignol, who beat her regularly. Several times she had him jailed on charges of assault, but they were always reconciled. She bore another child, outside of wedlock, and in 1920 they moved to the village of St. Gilles, in southern France. Billing herself as "Nurse Scieri," Antoinette began shopping for elderly patients who needed her care... at a price.

With Nurse Scieri on the scene, St. Gilles experienced a rash of sudden deaths among the elderly and ailing. Antoinette lost five patients before the murder machine hit high gear, in December 1924, and from that point there was no turning back. On December 11, a 58-year-old spinster named Drouard died in Scieri's care. Christmas Eve saw the death of Madame Lachapelle, her final convulsions ascribed to "ptomaine poisoning." When Lachapelle's husband collapsed two days later, Antoinette blamed a heart attack, and a friendly physician agreed.

Joe Rossignol welcomed the new year in typical fashion, mauling his common-law wife in a drunken rage, but this time he had gone too far. When Antoinette served up a bowl of mussels, Rossignol consumed them greedily — and died two hours later. According to the testimony at her trial, Scieri watched his death throes, then went out to celebrate her freedom with a drunken orgy.

Nurse Scieri's next patients were Marie Martin, sixty-seven, and her sister, Madame Doyer. When Antoinette prepared a pot of coffee, Madame Doyer found it bitter, pouring hers down the sink when the nurse's back was turned. Martin drank hers down and shortly died, a circumstance that started ripples of suspicion in St. Gilles.

The last to die was Madame Gouan-Criquet, an ailing septuagenarian whose health declined rapidly under Antoinette's "nursing." The victim's husband notified police of his suspicions, and a bottle was found beneath the dead woman's bed, containing a mixture of ether and the herbicide pyralion. The bodies of Joe Rossignol and several other victims were exhumed for autopsy, all found to contain huge doses of pyralion.

In custody, Scieri openly confessed her crimes and tried to implicate a neighbor, who was later cleared by the police. On April 27, 1926, she was condemned to die upon conviction for a dozen homicides, the judge informing her: "You have been called a monster, but that expression is not strong enough. You are debauched. You are possessed of all the vices. You are also a drunkard, vicious, and a hypocrite. You have no shame. I do not believe judicial history contains the records of many criminals of your type."

Scieri shrugged and laughed as sentence was pronounced, aware that there had been no execution of a woman in France since the end of World War I. As expected, her sentence was soon commuted to life imprisonment, and she subsequently died in jail.

SEEGRIST, SYLVIA

Dubbed "Ms. Rambo" by the press, Sylvia Seegrist is nearly unique in the annals of feminine crime. With Priscilla Ford, she is one of only two female multiple killers in history to target total strangers in a public place. More to the point, she is the *only* female killer (so far) to adopt the typically "masculine" tactic of shooting random targets in broad daylight, at a crowded shopping mall.

Seegrist was a native Pennsylvanian, born in 1960. Her seemingly normal life took a sudden turn for the bizarre at age fifteen, with a series of erratic, violent incidents spanning the next ten years. Sylvia was hospitalized for psychiatric treatment a dozen times in that decade, all without apparent result. In 1981, a stabbing put her away for four months, but she emerged from the state hospital with her rage and delusions intact.

On October 30, 1985, Sylvia dressed herself in military-style fatigues, loaded a .22-caliber semiautomatic rifle, and filled her pockets with spare ammunition. She drove from her home in Crum Lynne to Springfield, a Philadelphia suburb in Delaware County, parking near the entrance of the Springfield Mall around 4 P.M. Emerging from her car, she opened fire on customers outside the mall, wounding several before she made her way inside, still firing. Seegrist was approaching Kinney's Shoes when she was tackled from behind by John Loufler, a volunteer fireman from Media, Pennsylvania. Other patrons grappled for the gun and finally disarmed her, holding Sylvia until police arrived.

In her wake, she left two victims dead and eight wounded. A two-year-old boy and a 64-

year-old man were killed outright; wounded survivors ranged in age from seventeen to sixty-seven years. The oldest of the wounded, an elderly physician from Springfield, subsequently died from gunshot wounds to the head and abdomen.

Seegrist was charged with three counts of first-degree murder, seven counts of attempted murder, plus one count each of possessing an unregistered firearm and possessing an instrument of crime. Arraigned before Judge Joseph DiPietro at the county seat in Media, Seegrist told the magistrate, "Hurry up, man. You know I'm guilty. Kill me on the spot."

As it happened, matters were not so simple. Psychiatric tests were ordered by the court, state physicians pronounced Seegrist unfit to participate in her own defense. On December 12, she was declared incompetent for trial and returned to a secure facility for treatment. Six months later, her condition had improved enough for Sylvia to face her day in court. Jurors convicted her across the board on June 27, 1986, returning a verdict of guilty but mentally ill on all counts. On October 31, a year and a day since her shooting spree, she was sentenced to three consecutive terms of life imprisonment. Defense attorneys asked for a "glimmer of hope" that Sylvia might be released if she responded to therapy, but Judge Robert Kelly rejected the plea, voicing an opinion that "she should not be put back on the street."

SHERMAN, LYDIA

Born Lydia Danbury in 1825, America's "Queen Poisoner" was the daughter of a butcher in New Brunswick, New Jersey. Lydia's mother died when the child was barely one year old, and she lost her father eight years later, moving on to live with other relatives. Working as a seamstress by age sixteen, she soon met blacksmith Ed Struck, and they were married in 1845. Their union produced six children, and Ed attempted to better his lot by taking a job with the New York City Police Department, but he was fired in 1863 on an accusation of cowardice, for refusing to break up a street brawl.

Alcohol eased the pangs of disgrace, but it did nothing to improve Ed's temper around the house. Lydia endured his abuse for awhile, but her patience was wearing thin, and she finally poisoned Struck on May 26, 1864. Alcoholism was blamed for his death, and Ed's life insurance left the family with a $5,000 nest egg, but Lydia was loathe to split the money seven ways. By May of 1866, convenient "illness" had disposed of all six children, ranging in age from nine months to eighteen years, a strategic move to Connecticut preventing New York authorities from noting Lydia's remarkable run of "bad luck."

In 1868, residing at New Haven, Connecticut, Lydia married elderly farmer Dennis Hurlburt. The aging groom didn't last long, and Lydia had gone through his money by April 1870, when she found work as a housekeeper in Derby, employed by wealthy Nelson Horatio Sherman. A widower with two children, Sherman was smitten by Lydia, and they soon tied the knot. His children, baby Frank and 14-year-old daughter Addie, were dead by year's end, but Sherman survived until May 12, 1871, when Lydia finished him off with a cup of poisoned cocoa.

Sherman's family doctor was suspicious, and Lydia fled to New York while arrangements were made for an autopsy. Physicians at Yale University found arsenic in Nelson's remains, and Lydia was extradited to Connecticut for trial. Jurors deliberated a brief fifty minutes before convicting her of second-degree murder, and she was sentenced to life imprisonment.

In January 1873, prison officials reported Lydia's confession to seven murders, specifically excluding Sherman and two of her own children. The others, she thought at the time, "would be better off dead." Lydia briefly escaped from custody in 1878, but was soon recaptured. She died of cancer at Wethersfield Prison on May 16, 1879.

SHOAF, MAMIE SHEY

By the spring of 1929, Mamie Shoaf had been married for nearly two decades. Her husband, Carey, worked for a lumber company in Lebanon, Kentucky, but his take-home pay was barely adequate to feed their seven children, ranging in age from two to seventeen years. Mamie made no secret of her mounting dissatisfaction at home. On May 23, she told a relative that she would not "go through another day like this."

She was true to her word.

On May 24, Mamie took her three youngest children — two-year-old Tom, seven-year-old Ina, and 11-year-old Catherine — to a local cemetery, where she slashed their throats with a knife. When all three lay dead, she cut her own throat, collapsing on the ground near their bodies. A short time later, passers-by followed the sound of her moans to the massacre site, but Mamie died from loss of blood before help arrived.

SIMS, PAULA MARIE

A native of Freeman, Missouri, born May 21, 1959, Paula Blew was the youngest of three children in a family marred by tragedy. Her older brother, Dennis, was subject to disabling seizures from age three, when he survived a critical bout of the measles, and Paula formed an intimate — some say unnatural — bond with her brother Randy at an early age. Seven years old when her family moved to La Plata, 200 miles northwest of St. Louis, Paula is recalled by friends and neighbors from her early childhood as "an ordinary kid." By age fifteen, though, she was using drugs and drinking, trusting birth control pills to keep her "safe" on dates, earning a reputation as one who liked to "party and get high."

On April 10, 1976, Paula was riding with brother Randy in a "borrowed" car, when Randy lost control and crashed the vehicle. He was dead at the scene, but Paula survived with severe facial injuries. An official report from the Missouri Highway Patrol lists "drinking and drugs" as contributing factors to the accident. At the crash site, a La Plata traffic officer remarked to highway patrolmen that he had once caught Randy and Paula having sex in a car, but the officer later refused to confirm his statement, and no other evidence of incest in the family has been documented.

A month after Randy's death, the Blew family moved to Wood River, Illinois, across the Mississippi River from St. Louis. They bought a comfortable house in suburban Cottage Hills, and Paula graduated from Civic Memorial High School, at nearby Bethalto, in 1977. She got her first job, at a local supermarket, the following year. Employees remember her as quiet, generally aloof, but she also possessed an unpredictable temper. One cashier remains convinced that Paula was the vandal who slashed his tires following an argument on the job.

Randy's death had reversed the free-wheeling trend of Paula's social life, but she began dating Robert Sims in 1980, and they were married on May 2, 1981. A resident of Alton, Illinois, Sims had been a navy seaman when he married his first wife in 1974, subsequently filing for divorce on charges of "extreme and repeated mental cruelty." In November 1979, Sims pled guilty to misdemeanor shoplifting and paid a $115 fine, but that appeared to be the full extent of his conflict with the law.

The newlyweds began their married life in Alton. Paula kept her job at the supermarket until December 1983, when she was fired for "discounting" — that is, undercharging friends for food and other items. A month later, Robert and Paula moved to Brighton, Illinois, purchasing a ranch-style home outside of town, well back from the road on a deep wooded lot. With trees all around and a pond in their own back yard, it seemed the perfect spot to raise a family.

Paula's first child — named Loralei after a favorite song from the rock group Queen — was born on June 5, 1986. Twelve days later, in a bizarre twist of fate, Paula reported the infant stolen from her home. According to her statement, Paula had been watching television when she saw a strange man coming downstairs, from the second floor. He was approximately six feet tall, wore dark clothes and a mask across his face, while brandishing a pistol. The intruder ordered Paula to the floor, face-down, and some five minutes passed before she heard the front door slam. She ran to check her baby, found the crib deserted, and immediately called police. Investigators found the screen door neatly cut, as if someone had reached inside to slip the latch; they also noted that the house appeared immaculate, with nothing out of place.

When no trace of Loralei had been found by June 20, Robert and Paula agreed to polygraph tests, with results indicating that both parents had lied on every question dealing with their daughter's disappearance. Four days later, police searched the Sims residence, finding traces of marijuana and fifteen Polaroid snapshots of Paula, posing nude at different stages of her recent pregnancy. Police dogs found an infant's skeletal remains in the woods, 150 feet from Paula's home, the bones scattered by predators, and subsequent genetic tests established a 97% probability that the child was Paula's daughter.

Authorities were openly skeptical of Paula's tale, by this time. FBI agents called the kidnapping story "totally unbelievable," flatly accusing Robert and Paula of killing their own child, but the parents remained steadfast in denial. Called before a local grand jury on March 12, 1987, both claimed their Fifth Amendment rights on advice from counsel, and no indictments were issued. Six months later, on September 8, a coroner's jury officially closed the case, noting that advanced decomposition ruled out any specific cause of death.

Meanwhile, in January 1987, Robert and Paula had moved back to Alton. Their second child, a son, was born there on February 1, 1988, named Randall after Paula's late, lamented brother. Another girl, Heather, followed in March 1989, and this one lasted all of six weeks before tragedy struck.

On the night of April 29, 1989, police were summoned to the Sims home in Alton, to investigate a second kidnapping. Robert had returned from work at 11:12 P.M., he said, to find Paula unconscious on the kitchen floor, Heather missing from her crib. As Paula reconstructed the event, she had been taking out the trash, around 10:30, when a gunman in a ski mask appeared from nowhere, ordered her back in the house, and clubbed her unconscious on the kitchen threshold. Detectives noted that both parents seemed oddly calm, and they were frankly shocked when Paula told her husband "My son's alright; that's all that matters." Robert's silent nod of agreement was almost as chilling as Paula's words. Physicians were unable to explain Paula's lack of any bruises or other marks consistent with a stunning blow to the head.

Four days later, on May 3, a motorist found Heather Sims in a trash can at a highway rest stop in St. Charles County, Missouri. The infant had been smothered and refrigerated after death, her tiny corpse sequestered in a plastic garbage bag. On May 4, a search of the Sims house retrieved similar garbage bags from the kitchen, while a blond human hair was found in the basement freezer owned by Paula's parents. Under grilling by the FBI, Robert Sims admitted that his wife "could have" taken Heather to her parents' home on April 29, while they were out of town. He left the interview expressing concern for his son, stating that he "had to believe" Paula was involved in Heather's death. Juvenile authorities shared that concern, and Randy Sims was taken into protective custody on May 5, 1989.

Within days, Robert and Paula had become the focus of bitter animosity in Alton. (A typical joke in the tense community listed SIMS as an acronym for "Sudden Infant Murder Syndrome.") Paula was indicted for first-degree murder on July 10, arrested the same day and held without bond. At a preliminary hearing four days later, testimony on the death of her first child was permitted to establish an apparent pattern of criminal behavior.

A change of venue transferred Paula's case to Peoria, Illinois, where the trial opened on January 8, 1990. Jurors convicted her of Heather's murder on January 27, but the same panel found unspecified mitigating factors that precluded a sentence of death. On February 1, Paula Sims was sentenced to a prison term of life without parole. No charges can be filed in Loralei's case without a specified cause of death, and no clear-cut motive has been suggested for the murder of either child.

Days after Paula's sentencing, Robert Sims flunked another polygraph test, authorities insisting he had knowledge of the second murder, even if they could not prove direct participation. On April 23, 1990, an Illinois court granted Sims permanent custody of his son, and he filed for divorce three months later. In his last jailhouse visit with Paula, Robert announced his intention of having her name removed from the family headstone in Alton.

"SKULL, SALLY": See NEWMAN, SARAH JANE

SOLIS, MAGDALENA

Magdalena Solis got her start in crime as a common prostitute, working the streets of Monterey, Mexico, while brother Eleazor served as her pimp. Their life style was far from affluent, and Magdalena was ready to try something new when they met the Hernandez brothers in 1962.

Cayetano and Santos Hernandez were con men with a sexual twist. They had organized a private fertility cult in rural Yerba Buena, recruiting gullible peasants with a promise of divine rewards in exchange for personal "sacrifice." Money was acceptable, of course, but sex would do if their disciples came up short, Santos servicing the women while his homosexual brother dealt with the men. It worked for several months, but now their flock was getting anxious, wondering aloud when their reward would be revealed. A few more days, or weeks at most, and the Hernandez brothers reckoned they would have a minor revolution on their hands.

The plot was relatively simple: Magdalena and her brother would appear in Yerba Buena, posing as the god and goddess of the cult. Their every word would be accepted by the superstitious peasants as divine commands, and they would have their pick of partners from the congregation, in addition to the cash donations they received.

Incredibly, it worked... but only for awhile. More time went by, and still the drop-in deities produced no treasure for the faithful. When her acolytes began complaining, Magdalena chose the two most vocal dissidents as human sacrifices. On her orders, they were bound to wooden crosses, stoned and hacked to death, their blood collected for a grim "communion" ritual.

Aside from silencing her critics, the sadistic ceremony triggered something dark and deadly in the back of Magdalena's mind. She found that she enjoyed the power of life and death, incorporating human sacrifice as a regular part of the cult's expanding repertoire. Six more of her disciples were handpicked for execution over the next few weeks, including Magdalena's lesbian lover, marked for death when she began sharing her favors with Santos Hernandez. On that occasion, to balance the card, a male victim was chosen to join the female "sinner," his heart carved out while he writhed on the cross.

Unknown to Magdalena and her drones, the latest double murder had been witnessed by a 14-year-old boy who ran to the police in Yerba Buena. Officer Martinez followed his young witness back to the murder site, and neither one of them was ever seen again. In time, a squad of federales was dispatched to find the missing constable, discovering his mutilated corpse.

It was a relatively simple task to track the cult from there, back to the cave where Magdalena and her followers were hiding out. Three officers were wounded in the ensuing shootout, on June 2, 1963, with Santos Hernandez killed by return fire before Magdalena surrendered her troops. Cayetano Hernandez was missing, slain and buried by a jealous disciple several days after the murder of Officer Hernandez.

The mass trial opened on June 13, with Magdalena, her brother, and twelve of their followers convicted on multiple murder charges. In the absence of capital punishment, all concerned were sentenced to 30-year prison terms and promptly forgotten. A quarter-century would pass before another death cult — this one even more deadly, led by another self-styled witch — was uncovered in the state of Tamaulipas, plucking victims off the street for purposes of human sacrifice. [See also: Aldrete, Sarah]

SORENSON, DELLA

A native of rural Nebraska, born in 1897, Della Sorenson married her first husband, Joe Weldam, in 1915, settling on his farm near St. Libory. Their union produced two children, but motherhood chafed on Della's nerves. In fact, *everything* seemed to irritate her; trivial slights or imagined grievances magnified in Della's mind to the status of a blood feud.

But Della didn't get mad; she got even.

The first to feel her wrath, however indirectly, was Della's sister-in-law, Mrs. Cooper. The source of their quarrel remains obscure, Mrs. Cooper recalling merely that Della seemed upset by Cooper's refusal to attend Della's church. For Della, though, the matter was more serious. "Mrs. Cooper always was running down my reputation," she later told police, "and to get even with her, I decided to kill three of her children."

At first, she settled for one. Mrs. Cooper dropped by for a visit on July 23, 1918, bringing her 13-month-old daughter Viola along for the ride, and Della was ready with a piece of poisoned candy for the child. Viola was dead before day's end, briefly satisfying Della's appetite for revenge.

The next to die was Della's mother-in-law, Wilhelmina Weldam, living with Joe and Della when she was poisoned in July 1920. Five years later, Della would inform police that she killed Wilhelmina because the old woman "was feeble and childish and a burden on my hands, and I wanted her out of the way."

Barely three months later, on September 7, Della poisoned her own daughter, three-year-old Minnie, in what she described to police as a mercy killing. "She ate and tore the clothes off the bed," Della said, "put her hands on the hot stove, could not talk and suffered terribly, so to relieve her suffering I put some of this poison into a glass of water, which I gave her. She died in a very short time. Soon as the child died I had a feeling of elation and happiness; then after thinking of what I had done, I had a feeling of fear and tried to hide what I had done." She was successful for the moment, and the cause of Minnie's death was listed as St. Vitus' dance.

By this time, Della Sorenson was on a roll. On September 20, she killed husband Joe with some poison purchased at a local hardware store. "We had a quarrel, a bad quarrel one day," she later told detectives. "I had it in for him. After he died and I came to, I was sorry for what I had done and wished I had never done it."

Della's sorrow had apparently worn off by February 1921, when she married Emmanuel Sorenson after a two-week courtship. The newlyweds settled in Dannebrog, Nebraska, where Della bore two more children, but domestic duties never kept her from nursing a grudge. Mrs. Cooper came to visit on August 20, 1922, and Della murdered four-month-old Clifford with another piece of poisoned candy. Still unsuspecting, Mrs. Cooper returned with her daughter Bessie in October, but this time Della's poisoned bread and butter failed to kill. "Every time I gave poison to one of Mrs. Cooper's children," Della later explained, "I said to myself, 'Now I am going to get even with you.'"

Four months later, on February 13, 1923, Della killed her youngest child. Baby Delia was nursing when Della dribbled some poison into her mouth. As later described to police, "She only lived a couple of hours after that." The infant was killed, in Della's words, "because it made me nervous and irritable and because it was not feeling very good and was continually fussing and crying." With a nod to irony, Sorenson poisoned Delia on her first birthday.

A short week later, one of Della's friends, Christina Brook, dropped by for a visit, bringing her new daughter Ruth. The child was eighteen days old on February 20, when Della slipped poison into her mouth, with fatal results. Looking back on the crime, Della claimed she "felt sorry" for Ruth, describing the infant as a victim of maternal neglect. Doctors blamed Ruth's death on "acute indigestion with exposure to cold contributing."

Next, Della plotted to kill another of her own children, three-year-old Margaret Weldam. Her plan was foiled when Margaret refused to drink her poison-laced medicine, so Della gave it to husband Emmanuel instead, hoping Ruth would thereby change her mind. In fact, the girl remained stubborn, and Emmanuel survived the child-sized dose of poison. Later, Della spiked his supper following an argument, but still her husband clung to life.

By this time, gossip had begun to circulate in Dannebrog, concerning Della's run of rotten luck. Authorities resolved to act on the next suspicious case, but Della kept them waiting until February 1925, when neighbor Mrs. Knott dropped in to visit with her year-old daughter Lillian. True to form, Della fed the child a piece of poisoned candy, but Lillian survived the resulting illness. Three days later, Della visited the Knotts at home, bringing poisoned cookies for Lillian and her three-year-old brother Lyle. Again, both children managed to survive, and a suspicious family doctor had their vomit analyzed. The test results showed poison, and Della Sorenson was jailed on April 17.

In custody, she admitted poisoning the Knotts children because "Their father stole my wine and I felt like I wanted to get even with him." Her confession spelled out a long series of murders and murder attempts, along with her apparent motive. "I had feelings which would steal over me at times," she said, "forcing me to destroy and kill. I felt funny and happy. I like to attend funerals. I'm happy when someone is dying." Sorenson's list of future victims included the long-suffering Mrs. Cooper and Della's stepmother, Mrs. Sidel, who had objected to Della's first marriage in 1915.

A sanity hearing was convened the day after Della's arrest. Dr. Fast, superintendent of the state asylum at Hastings, described Sorenson as suffering from dementia praecox — an obsolete term for schizophrenia that translates, literally, to "losing one's mind prematurely." A panel of physicians judged Della to be a "paranoiac victim" and a dangerous "imbecile," with the mind of a seven- or eight-year-old child. She was committed to the state asylum on April 20, with criminal charges dismissed.

SOULAKIOTIS, MARIAM

A Greek native, born in 1900, Mariam Soulakiotis was twenty-three years old when she left her job on a factory assembly line to work full-time for a new splinter group of the Greek Orthodox Church. Based on the Mount of Pines, outside the village of Keratea, the new Calendarist sect was led by 65-year-old Father Matthew, lately resigned from the mother church in protest over doctrinal changes. New recruits were trickling in to join the cult, but Mariam quickly emerged as a standout, described by one acquaintance as a young woman who "spoke glibly and managed to give her words an air of authority. She was certainly prepared to work, and she had a shrewd head on her young shoulders. She was comely for a peasant, not tall, but had a pair of eyes that could be passionate about something or someone."

In short order, Mariam had virtual control of the cult, directing construction of a monastery and other buildings, fending off complaints from male disciples with support from the reclusive Father Matthew. Graduating rapidly from "Sister" to "Mother" Mariam, Soulakiotis was named as heir to the cult when Father Matthew died in 1939. His will also gave her title to the cult's property and buildings, a circumstance that triggered unexpected greed in Mother Mariam.

From 1940 onward, Mariam launched an intensive recruiting campaign for the cult, dispatching monks and nuns throughout Greece to enlist new members. Before embarking on their pilgrimage, evangelists were instructed to concentrate on female recruits, preferably women of property who would donate their worldly goods to the cult in return for spiritual peace. At least 500 prospects heard the call by 1950, signing over their cash and other property to Mother Mariam when they joined the cult, but the worst was yet to come.

Aside from swindling her disciples, Mariam dominated every aspect of their lives, cutting off contact with relatives, caging some like animals, resorting to starvation, flogging, and torture to purge new recruits of their "demons." No doctors were permitted on the grounds, and many recruits who entered the commune were never seen again. A mother from Thebes joined the cult with her four adult daughters; all five were dead within six months of their arrival on the Mount of Pines. Nocturnal passers-by reported screams and moaning from the compound. One night, two drunken villagers scaled the fence and found an elderly woman chained to a wall, but she declined their help and the intruders kept their observation to themselves.

In March 1950, a resident of Athens wrote to the public prosecutor, complaining that Mother Mariam — now billing herself as "Popess" — had stripped the correspondent's mother of her cash and other property. Police launched an investigation, discovering that 177 Calendarists, ranging in age from twenty to eighty years, had died at the commune since 1940. Mariam's nuns insisted that the high death rate prevailed "because so many of those who came to us were old," but police had a different view. They found that female recruits typically signed over all worldly belongings in hopes of becoming "the brides of Christ in the next world." Refusal to sign the cult contract resulted in new arrivals being chained in cells, starved, beaten and otherwise tortured until they submitted.

Ironically, immediate submission to the Popess was no guarantee of protection. Those who signed their goods over willingly were subjected to a strict regimen of fasting, endless prayer, and back-breaking manual labor. Total silence was also enforced in the commune, with violators forced to kiss Miriam's feet before they were kicked and beaten into unconsciousness. One of the dead was 22-year-old Ileana Spirides, an American of Greek descent who vanished after traveling from Toledo, Ohio, to join the cult.

No murder charges were ever filed against Soulakiotis or her nuns, but Mariam was tried and convicted of illegally detaining a child in 1951, and sentenced to two years in prison. New felony charges, filed in 1953, brought the Popess an additional sentence of fourteen years.

SPARA, HIERONYMA

In 1659, a delegation of priests approached Pope Alexander VII in Rome, regaling the pontiff with a problem they deemed serious enough to abrogate the confidentiality of the confessional. In recent months, several Italian wives had confessed to poisoning their husbands, a breach of domestic etiquette shocking enough that the Pope, in turn, relayed the information to civil authorities.

Investigators traced the string of murders to a small feminist cult, organized by elderly Hieronyma Spara. A self-styled witch and seller of homemade perfumes, Spara led her disciples in worship of the goddess Diana, selling lethal doses of poison to those who were tired of their husbands. She was arrested after a female spy infiltrated the cult and purchased poison for the express purpose of killing her spouse.

Under torture, the "witch" confessed to multiple murders — the final number was never established — and named her disciples for authorities. Spara was publicly humiliated, along with her chief accomplice — "La Gratiosa" — and three of her paying clients, after which the five were hanged on charges of murder and witchcraft. Thirty other cultists were released from custody after being flogged through the streets in scanty attire. [See also: "Angel Makers of Nagyrev"; Popova, Madame]

SPENCER, BRENDA

A problem child from a broken home, born in 1963, Brenda Spencer lived with her father in San Diego after her parents divorced. An early drug abuser, habitual truant and thief, she thrived on violent television shows. Her favorite "toy" was the BB gun she used for killing birds and breaking windows at the Cleveland Elementary School, directly opposite her home. Incredibly, despite her antisocial attitudes and criminal behavior, Brenda's father bought her a .22-caliber semi-automatic rifle and 500 rounds of ammunition as a Christmas gift in 1978.

Brenda wasted no time in planning her next escapade, shifting equipment into the garage, and digging a hideout tunnel in her back yard. Throughout the week of January 22, Brenda told her closest friends that she was planning to "do something to get on TV." They didn't ask, and she held back the details, banking on surprise.

On Monday morning, January 29, Brenda lay in wait as Principal Burton Wragg opened Cleveland Elementary's gates for a group of waiting children. Suddenly, from Brenda's house, the sound of rifle fire rang out. Her first shots killed Wragg where he stood and also snuffed the life of Michael Suchar, a custodian. For twenty minutes Brenda blazed away, wounding a 30-year-old police officer and nine children between the ages of six and twelve. Six more hours would pass before she surrendered, talking to police and newsmen on the phone, her home under siege.

"I just started shooting," Brenda explained, as if it were the most natural thing in the world. "That's it. I just did it for the fun of it. I just don't like Mondays. I did this because it's a way to cheer up the day. Nobody likes Mondays."

In custody, Brenda was charged with two counts of murder and multiple counts of aggravated assault. A change of venue moved her trial north to Santa Ana, in Orange County, but jurors there were far from sympathetic. Convicted on both murder counts and one charge of assault, Brenda received concurrent prison terms of twenty-five years to life (for murder) and forty-eight years (for assault with a deadly weapon). Her flippant comments to the media inspired a punk-rock song, "I Don't Like Mondays," recorded by the Boomtown Rats.

STAGER, BARBARA

At 6:00 A.M. on February 1, 1988, police were summoned to the home of Russell Stager III in Durham, North Carolina. Barbara Stager led officers to the master bedroom where her husband, a popular baseball coach at Durham High School, lay unconscious, bleeding profusely from a bullet wound to the head. A .25-caliber semi-automatic pistol was found on the bed near his body. Barbara theorized that the gun had somehow gone off beneath her husband's pillow, but the bullet had passed *downward* through his skull.

Russ Stager was still alive when paramedics reached the scene, but his fate was sealed. Six hours later, despite the best efforts of trauma surgeons, he died at Duke University Medical Center, where his wife was employed as a secretary. At one point, while she waited for word of Stager's condition, Barbara was heard to blurt out, "Forgive me, I didn't mean to do it."

The remark was curious in itself, and police became suspicious when they learned that Stager's first husband, 30-year-old Larry Ford, had died under similar circumstances ten years earlier, in Randolph County. Ford had been a salesman, and Barbara reported that he was suffering from a groin injury on the night of March 22, 1978, tossing and turning to the point that she decided to sleep downstairs, on the couch. Moments later, she was roused by the sound of a shot and found him sprawled in the bedroom, mortally wounded. Police discovered a .25-caliber pistol on the floor beside the bed, purchased by Barbara the previous day for "self-protection." Ford's death was initially listed as accidental, but tests revealed no powder residue on his hands to suggest he had fired the gun. Reclassified as homicide, the case remained open, with no charges filed.

Barbara had collected almost $120,000 in life insurance on Ford, moving back to her native Durham where she met and married Russ Stager. Stager, in turn, was insured to the tune of nearly $156,000, a "coincidence" that only increased official doubts about the widow's story. More to the point, Stager himself had apparently been suspicious of Barbara. Shortly before his death, the coach had told his first wife, "This sounds crazy, but if anything should ever happen to me, please check it out. I'm beginning to have doubts about her first husband's death."

It would have been easy to dismiss the ex-wife's statement as a product of jealousy or spite, but Russ Stager had also committed his doubts about Barbara to tape. In April 1989, a Durham student gave police a tape cassette he had found in the high school locker room, soon after Stager's death. He had forgotten about the tape and never played it until that day, when he was startled to hear Stager's voice. Police listened intently as their victim spoke from beyond the grave, listing his doubts about Barbara and concerns for his own safety.

In his taped recitation, Russ Stager described catching Barbara "making out in a car" with some unidentified man on the day of her grandmother's funeral. Other comments related to vanishing credit card bills, forged checks, and Barbara's alleged embezzlement of funds from various employers. Stager speculated on his wife's complicity in Larry Ford's death, and described her strange habit of waking him in the middle of the night, feeding him pills that left him with nagging headaches. On one occasion, he had squirreled the pills away and had them analyzed, discovering that they were sleeping pills. "I really hope that I'm being paranoid about all the stuff that's going on," Stager concluded on tape, "but I really wonder."

So did the authorities. By this time, detectives had listed a total of thirty-three similarities between the deaths of Larry Ford and Russell Stager. Both men had been "accidentally" shot to death during normal sleeping hours. In each case, the weapon was a .25-caliber pistol purchased by Barbara Stager for purposes of "self-defense," although she told Durham detectives she was terrified of guns. At each shooting scene, police found the guns pointing at the victims, but ejected cartridges were found in unlikely places, as if the shots had been fired from a different angle. Both victims were military reserve officers with extensive firearms training, thus reducing the chances of a fatal accident. In each case, Barbara was the last person to see her late husbands alive... and the chief beneficiary of their estates.

With the tape in evidence, Barbara Stager was indicted for first-degree murder on April 19, 1989. Her trial opened on May 1 and lasted for two weeks. On May 17, jurors deliberated for fifty minutes before returning a guilty verdict; two days later, they recommended death as her punishment. Authorities in Randolph County, North Carolina, reopened the case of Larry Ford in June 1989, but no additional charges have been filed at this writing.

TANNENBAUM, GLORIA

A peculiar chapter of Colorado's criminal history was closed on March 9, 1971, with the announcement that Gloria Tannenbaum, suspect in two deaths and one disappearance, had died in the state mental hospital at Pueblo. A suicide note was found at her bedside, and authorities concluded she had somehow managed to ingest a dose of cyanide — the same poison allegedly used to kill two of her victims in 1969.

Gloria Tannenbaum's publicized troubles began after Dr. Thomas Riha, 40-year-old professor of Russian history at Colorado University, vanished from his home near the Boulder campus on March 14, 1969. Within a short time, Tannenbaum was charged, both in Boulder and in Denver, with four separate felony counts involving illegal disposal of Riha's property. Prior to her trial on one charge — that of forging his name on a $300 check — Gloria was pronounced insane by court psychiatrists and confined to the state hospital until such time as she recovered sufficiently to participate in her own defense.

In confinement, Tannenbaum boasted of influential contacts and hinted at "secret assignments" performed on behalf of intelligence agencies. Outside her narrow world, the search for Dr. Riha's body yielded no results, but homicide detectives now suspected Gloria in two more deaths. A couple of her neighbors, 78-year-old Gustav Ingwerson and Barbara Egbert, fifty-one, had recently died of apparent cyanide poisoning. There was insufficient evidence for indictment, but police believed that Gloria had murdered both, perhaps because they had possessed some information on the Riha case.

The deaths and disappearance are officially unsolved, but Gloria appears to have claimed the last word on the case for herself. "It doesn't matter really," she wrote to her attorney on the last night of her life, "but I will tell you this. I didn't do Tom or Gus or Barb in. I went nuts with hurt over losing them. Everything that has made me feel good about myself has been taken away. Life is very cheap."

TERRELL, BOBBIE SUE

A native of tiny Woodlawn, Illinois, the future "death angel" of Florida grew up overweight, myopic, and painfully shy. Her seven siblings included four brothers afflicted with muscular dystrophy, two of whom would die from the disease before Bobbie Sue reached her mid-thirties. Above-average grades in school were countered by an outspoken religious fervor that amused or embarrassed Bobbie's classmates. Only in church did she shine, playing the organ for Sunday services, displaying a fine singing voice.

Graduating high school in 1973, Bobbie Sue was doubtless influenced by family illness in her choice of a nursing career. By 1976, she was a registered nurse, ready to take her place in the medical community. Married to Danny Dudley a short time later, Bobbie was despondent at learning she could not bear children. The couple adopted a son, but their marriage collapsed when the boy was hospitalized for a drug overdose. Dudley accused his wife of feeding the child tranquilizers prescribed for her own schizophrenia, a charge that led to Bobbie being stripped of custody in the divorce.

Alone again, Bobbie Sue's health and mental state swiftly declined. In short order, she was hospitalized five times — for fibroid stomach tumors, for a hysterectomy and removal of her ovaries, for surgery on a broken arm that failed to heal properly, for gall bladder problems, for ulcers and pneumonia. Bobbie voluntarily committed herself to a state mental hospital, spending more than a year under psychiatric treatment. On release, she held several short-term nursing jobs before she was hired to work at Hillview Manor, a rest home in Greenville, Illinois.

It wasn't long before the staff at Hillview Manor started to record bizarre events surrounding Bobbie Sue. She fainted frequently on duty, with no apparent cause, and twice she slashed her own vagina with a pair of scissors. The second wound required emergency surgery at Barnes Hospital, in St. Louis, where Bobbie told a counselor she stabbed herself in rage and frustration over her own infertility.

Discharged from her job at the rest home, Bobbie Sue moved to St. Petersburg in July 1984, obtaining a Florida nursing license that August. Drifting from job to job in the Tampa Bay area, she was still dogged by mysterious ailments, including a bout of rectal bleeding that led to an emergency colostomy. In spite of everything, October found Bobbie employed as a shift supervisor at St. Petersburg's North Horizon Health Center, assigned to work from 11 P.M. to 7 A.M.

With Bobbie Sue in charge, the late-night "graveyard shift" soon lived up to its sinister nickname. Aggie Marsh, age ninety-seven, was the first to die, on November 13, 1984. Advanced age made her death seem commonplace, but eyebrows were raised a few days later, when 94-year-old Anna Larson nearly died from an insulin overdose. The riddle: Mrs. Larson was not diabetic, and insulin was kept in a locked cabinet, with Nurse Dudley holding the only key.

And the grim toll continued. On November 23, 85-year-old Leathy McKnight died from an insulin overdose on Dudley's shift; the same night, an unexplained fire broke out in a hospital linen closet, with arson suspected. Two more patients, 79-year-old Mary Cartwright and 85-year-old Stella Bradham, died on the night of November 25. The next day, a Monday dubbed "The Holocaust" by worried staffers, five more patients died in quick succession.

Matters went from bad to worse after that, including an anonymous call to the rest home, a woman's voice whispering that five patients had been murdered in their beds. Police were summoned to North Horizon in the pre-dawn hours of November 27, finding Nurse Dudley with a stab wound in her side. Bobbie Sue blamed a prowler for the assault, and detectives were further concerned by reports of twelve patient deaths in the past thirteen days.

A full-scale investigation was launched, leading to Bobbie Sue's December dismissal "for the good of the facility." When Bobbie filed a $22,000 claim for workmen's compensation based on her stabbing, the hospital countered with psychiatric reports branding Dudley a "borderline schizophrenic" who suffered from Munchausen's syndrome (a mental condition characterized by self-inflicted wounds and false claims of illness). Reports of Bobbie's Illinois self-mutilations were obtained, and her claim was rejected.

On January 31, 1985, Dudley entered a Pinellas County hospital for medical and psychiatric treatment. By this time, she was already a prime suspect in several deaths at North Horizon, and detectives had obtained exhumation orders for nine patients — including bodies buried in Wisconsin, Pennsylvania, and Texas. Bobbie Sue was still hospitalized on February 12, when Florida's Department of Professional Regulation issued an emergency order suspending her nurse's license. DPR spokesmen further asked the state's Board of Nursing for a permanent revocation order, calling Dudley "an immediate, serious danger to the public health, safety, and welfare."

Bobbie Sue demanded a formal hearing, and while waiting for her day in court, she married 38-year-old Ron Terrell, a plumber from Tampa. Matrimony failed to do the trick where Bobbie's mental problems were concerned, and she soon found herself in another mental ward, this time committed against her will. She was still inside when the Board of Nursing announced a five-year suspension of her license, with reinstatement conditional upon successful psychiatric treatment.

Licensing became the least of Bobbie's problems on March 17, when she was formally charged with attempting to murder Anna Larson in November 1984. Arresting officers found the Dudleys living in a roadside tent, recently evicted from their small apartment, but a search of the former residence still turned up sufficient evidence to support indictments on four counts of first-degree murder. Bobbie Sue was held without bond pending trial in the deaths of Aggie Marsh, Leathy McKnight, Stella Bradham, and Mary Cartwright.

That trial was scheduled to begin on October 20, 1985, but legal maneuvers and psychiatric tests repeatedly postponed the date. At last, in February 1988, Bobbie Sue pled guilty to reduced charges of second-degree murder and was sentenced to a combined term of sixty-five years in prison.

TINNING, MARYBETH ROE

For a devoted mother, Marybeth Tinning seemed to have no luck at all in raising children. In the thirteen years from 1972 to 1985, she lost nine infants in Schenectady, New York. Police would later charge that eight of those were slain deliberately, for motives so bizarre they challenge credibility.

The first to go was daughter Jennifer, a mere eight days old when she died on January 3, 1972. An autopsy listed the cause of death as acute meningitis, and since the baby never left St. Clare's Hospital after her birth, authorities consider her death the only case above suspicion. We may never know what psychic shock waves were triggered in Marybeth Tinning's mind by the death of her newborn daughter, but more of her children soon joined the casualty list.

Less than three weeks later, on January 20, two-year-old Joseph Tinning, Jr., was pronounced dead on arrival at Ellis Hospital, in Schenectady. Doctors blamed his death on a viral infection and "seizure disorder," but no autopsy was performed to verify those findings. Four-year-old Barbara Tinning died six weeks later, on March 20, and autopsy surgeons, lacking an obvious cause of death, attributed her passing to "cardiac arrest." Barbara's death was the first reported to police, but officers closed their file on the case after a brief consultation with hospital physicians.

And the deaths continued.

When two-week-old Timothy died at Ellis Hospital, doctors were once more unable to determine a cause, tossing the case into the grab-bag of Sudden Infant Death Syndrome (SIDS). On September 2, 1975, Nathan Tinning died at the age of five months, an autopsy blaming his case on "pulmonary edema." SIDS was the culprit again on February 2, 1979, when Mary Tinning died six months short of her third birthday, while no cause was ever determined in the death of three-month-old Jonathan, on March 24, 1980. Three-year-old Michael Tinning was still in the process of being adopted when he was rushed to St. Clare's Hospital on August 2, 1981. Physicians could not save his life, and while they viewed his passing with a "high level of suspicion," the cause of death was still listed as bronchial pneumonia.

The real questions began on December 20, 1985, when three-month-old Tammi Lynne Tinning was found unconscious in bed, blood staining her pillow. Rushed to St. Clare's Hospital, she was beyond help, and while doctors ascribed her death to SIDS, they also telephoned the state police. An investigation led to Marybeth Tinning's arrest on February 4, 1986, after she confessed to pressing a pillow over Tammi Lynne's face when the child "fussed and cried." In custody, she also confessed to murdering Timothy and Nathan, but staunchly denied killing any of the others. "I smothered them with a pillow," she told detectives, "because I'm not a good mother."

In fact, psychiatrists decided, the problem ran deeper than that. Marybeth Tinning was diagnosed as suffering from a condition called "Munchausen's syndrome by proxy," in which those responsible for the care of children, invalids and the like sometimes seek attention by harming their charges. Friends and relatives recalled Marybeth preening at funerals, basking in the spotlight of sympathy, playing her role of grieving mother to the hilt. It was suggested that the outpouring of condolence following the first baby's death, in 1972, had become addictive, driving Marybeth to kill one child after another in pursuit of the sympathy "fixes" she craved.

On July 17, 1987, Tinning was convicted of second-degree murder in Tammi Lynne's death, jurors acquitting her of "deliberately" killing the child, blaming her for a lesser degree of homicide through her "depraved indifference to human life." It was a compromise verdict — more grudging sympathy for Marybeth — but it carried a prison sentence of twenty years to life. Husband Joseph Tinning seemed bewildered by the whole affair. In newspaper interviews, he admitted occasional suspicion of his wife, but had managed to push it aside. "You have to trust your wife," he said. "She has her things to do, and as long as she gets them done, you don't ask questions." [See also: Johnson, Martha; Lumbrera, Diana; Turner, Lise; Tuggle, Debra; Woods, Martha]

TOFFANIA

History has a selective memory. Notorious events and individuals are seldom recognized before they do their worst, and afterward, their origins are often lost beyond recall. Such is the case with "La Toffania," recalled as one of Europe's most prolific murderers, with an estimated 600 victims spanning half a century. Her proper name is lost forever, with the details of her early life, but there is still enough to place her in the foremost ranks of killers, male or female.

An Italian native, born in 1653, Toffania spun her web from Naples, brewing and dispensing an arsenic-based potion known as "aqua toffania," in honor of its creator. At seventeen, Toffania dispatched her first victim, variously described as a husband or male relative, in Palermo. The experiment was so successful that she turned to poisoning as a career, supplying deadly doses for a price to clients — mostly women — who were anxious to dispose of mates or pesky lovers. In time, her fame and poison spread to France, Spain, even England, packaged as "Manna of St. Nicholas of Bari," a reputed lotion for the skin. Toffania advised her female clients that the poison could produce immediate results or slow, protracted death, depending on the dose, and she was said to recommend the latter for sadistic entertainment.

Ironically, some of Toffania's customers came to her in the honest belief that they were buying a cure-all medicine, said to flow periodically from the tomb of St. Nicholas. Misguided male clients were urged to drink the elixir themselves, while women were advised to dose their ailing menfolk without delay. Students of the case suggest that Toffania's choice of profession was motivated more by a hatred of men than by simple greed, a theory supported by the fact that few — if any — of her documented victims were female.

By 1719, Neapolitan husbands were dying off at such a rate that the Viceroy of Naples launched a personal investigation, picking up on local rumors and tracing them back to the source. Toffania, at age sixty-six, was known as the leader of a militant feminist group, believed to plot against men in secret, nocturnal gatherings. It was further noted that death inevitably followed a purchase of "aqua toffania," and plans were laid to arrest the prime suspect.

Before that happened, though, Toffania's disciples tipped her off, and she found sanctuary in a nearby convent. Authorities were put off by the church until a rumor spread that La Toffania's loyal followers had spiked the cisterns that provided Naples with its drinking water. At that point, the Viceroy sent troops to invade the convent and carry Toffania back to Naples, where she was lodged in a dungeon.

The local archbishop was outraged, demanding Toffania's release, but the Viceroy responded by ringing the archbishop's palace with troops. This, in turn, brought threats of excommunication, but the archbishop stopped short of issuing the formal Bull of condemnation. Meanwhile, Toffania confessed under torture, and while her estimate of 600 victims may seem inflated, the average of twelve victims per year is not unreasonable.

In custody, Toffania was pleased to name her clients, and a number of Italian noblewomen were convicted of murder on the basis of her testimony. La Toffania herself was tried in 1723, convicted and sentenced to death by strangulation. Once the sentence had been carried out, as a final gesture of contempt, her corpse was tossed over the wall of the convent where she sought refuge in 1719.

TOPPAN, JANE

Born Nora Kelly in Boston, during 1854, Toppan lost her mother in infancy. Her father, a tailor, soon went insane and was confined to an asylum after he was found in his shop, trying to stitch his own eyelids together. His four daughters lived briefly with their paternal grandfather, before they were relegated to a local orphanage. Abner Toppan and his wife, from Lowell, Massachusetts, legally adopted Nora in 1859, changing her first name to Jane. The girl excelled in school and seemed completely normal prior to being jilted by her fiancée, years later. After that, she twice attempted suicide and suffered through a period of odd behavior that included efforts to predict the future through analysis of dreams. (A sister, Ellen, joined their father in the lunatic asylum after suffering a mental breakdown in her twenties.)

Briefly stabilizing during 1880, Jane signed on as a student nurse at a hospital in Cambridge, Massachusetts. Once again, she excelled in her class work, but supervisors and colleagues were disturbed by her obsession with autopsies. Dismissed after two patients died mysteriously in her care, she left the hospital without her certificate, forging the paperwork necessary to find work as a private nurse. Over the next two decades, she was hired by dozens of New England families, caring for the ill and elderly in several states, but few of Toppan's patients managed to survive her "special" treatment.

On July 4, 1901, an old friend, Mattie Davis, died under Jane's care at Cambridge, and Toppan accompanied the body home to Cataumet, Massachusetts, for burial. Retained as the family nurse by patriarch Alden Davis, Jane finished off his married daughter, Annie Gordon, on July 29. The old man's death, a few days later, was blamed on "a stroke," and his surviving daughter, Mary Gibbs, was pronounced dead on August 19. Mary's husband demanded an autopsy, and lethal doses of morphine were found in the three latest victims, but Jane was not finished yet. Before her arrest in Amherst, New Hampshire, on October 29, she fed a deadly "tonic" to her foster sister, Edna Bannister, and she was working on another patient when police cut short her medical career.

In custody, Toppan confessed to thirty-one murders, naming her victims, but students of the case believe her final tally falls somewhere between seventy and 100 victims. No accurate list of her hospital slayings was ever compiled, and various New England families avoided the scandal by refusing official requests for exhumations and autopsies. At trial, Jane's lawyer grudgingly conceded eleven murders, staking his hopes on a plea of insanity. Toppan cinched the case with her own testimony, telling the court: "That is my ambition, to have killed more people — more helpless people — than any man or woman who has ever lived."

Declared insane, Toppan was confined for life to the state asylum at Taunton, Massachusetts, where she died in August 1938, at age eighty-four. She was remembered by her keepers as a "quiet old lady" but older attendants recalled her smile as she beckoned them into her room. "Get some morphine, dearie," she would say, "and we'll go out on the ward. You and I will have a lot of fun watching them die."

TUGGLE, DEBRA SUE

The case of Debra Tuggle perfectly exemplifies how loopholes in "The System" may allow determined murderers to roam at large for years. As the rarest of felons — a black female serial killer of children — she fell through the cracks of a government network designed to protect those she preyed on, claiming at least five victims before she was brought to a semblance of justice. Sadly, even when her crimes had been revealed, the very agencies that should have stopped her killing spree a decade earlier were more concerned with bad publicity than human lives.

With twenty-twenty hindsight, it is easy to declare that Debra Tuggle never should have been allowed to have a child, much less the five she ultimately bore to different fathers in eleven years. She clearly lacked the temperament for motherhood, but there was something else at work in Tuggle's mind as well, beyond mere rage or boredom with the drudgery of her maternal role. A dark and deadly "something" that compelled her to eliminate the very lives she brought into the world.

Debra's first child, William Henry, saw the light of day in 1972. Eighteen months later, he had a half-brother, Thomas Bates, and the pressure was mounting on Debra, pushing her over the edge. Both children died suddenly in 1974, Thomas barely two months old, William three months short of his second birthday. Physicians in Debra's home town of Little Rock, Arkansas, were sympathetic to the grieving mother's plight. In the absence of physical symptoms, they blamed William's death on pneumonia, listing Thomas as a victims of Sudden Infant Death Syndrome, (SIDS).

A third son, Ronald Johnson, was nine months old when he suddenly stopped breathing, in 1976. Again, Debra's public display of grief was convincing; once again, SIDS was blamed for the death. Two years later, Tuggle shot herself in the abdomen, an apparent suicide attempt, and was briefly committed to a state mental hospital for treatment. The doctors there pronounced her "cured," and she was on the street in time to bear and kill her fourth child — Terranz Tuggle — at Malvern, Arkansas, in 1979. As far as Malvern's finest could determine, it was one more SIDS-related death.

For all her aversion to children, Debra seemed to enjoy men and sex. Gravitating back to Little Rock, she met George Paxton, ten years her senior, on a blind date. They hit it off at once, and by early 1982 Paxton had asked Tuggle to share his home. If anyone asked, she was there to care for Paxton's three children, but Debra's duties were not limited to housekeeping. By the spring of 1983, she would herself be carrying a Paxton child.

But first, she had an urge to thin the herd.

On June 23, 1982, Paxton was out at the movies when Debra had him paged at the theater, sobbing out the news that his daughter, two-year-old Tomekia, was dead. She had no explanation, and the hospital required none. It was stretching credibility to blame SIDS for the passing of a child Tomekia's age, but stranger things have happened in the world of pediatric medicine. Case closed.

Almost.

The news that she was pregnant, in the spring of 1983, knocked Debra for a loop. That May, she tried to give herself a coathanger abortion, but she bungled the attempt. George Paxton's family doctor tried to have her booked for psychiatric treatment by the state, but his petition was denied. A healthy girl, G'Joy Paxton, was born in October 1983... but Debra's time was swiftly running out.

It took an employee of the state health department, Dr. Alexander Merrill, to finally see through Tuggle's long-running "bad luck," in November 1983. Merrill was the first to analyze a list of unrelated victim surnames, recognizing that a single woman had been linked to five child deaths within a decade. Pulaski County's coroner, Steve Nawojczyk, was interested, and so were the police. On March 20, 1984, Debra was jailed on four counts of first-degree murder; Terranz Tuggle's case, in Malvern, remained "open." Two days later, the court set her bond at a prohibitive $750,000.

Little Rock physicians and Arkansas public health officials were quick to absolve themselves of any negligence in Tuggle's case. Debra's children each had different fathers, after all... and besides, her explanations of the sudden deaths were "credible." In retrospect, we know that "normal" SIDS does not haunt any given family, claiming the lives of child after child, but Arkansas doctors appeared to be learning their craft by trial and error.

In custody, Tuggle admitted pressing a pillow over Tomekia's face to "stop her crying" while Debra watched television. She held the pillow in place for some two minutes, with the desired result, but claimed she still "didn't think Tomekia was dead." Only later — presumably when her program was finished — did the murderess realize her "mistake."

Skeptical jurors convicted Tuggle of first-degree murder on September 18, 1984, but they dredged up sympathy enough to recommend the statutory minimum sentence of ten years in prison. Sentenced accordingly, Debra still faced one more trial, on charges of murdering her first three sons. Conviction on those charges could bring a death sentence... but Tuggle's luck had finally begun to change.

On December 7, 1984, Circuit Judge Floyd Lofton dismissed all three outstanding murder counts. There was no scientific evidence to indicate a homicide in Ronald Johnson's death, the judge declared, and state law barred the prosecution from using Tuggle's conviction on an identical crime to make the case. As far as Thomas Bates and William Henry were concerned, Judge Lofton ruled that the statute of limitations had run out on their deaths after ten years of official inaction. Prosecutors vowed to appeal the ruling, but their efforts were fruitless, leaving Tuggle with the prospect of mandatory release at age thirty-six, in 1994.

Dr. Merrill, meanwhile, had established a system for tracking suspicious SIDS deaths in Arkansas. He was hot on the trail of another sinister case — four deaths in one family — when his superiors fired him in January 1985. Officially, Merrill was canned for airing "unwarranted criticism" of state health officials. In his mind, the doctor had been punished for "making waves" and exposing the foibles of a negligent bureaucracy.

No motive was advanced by prosecutors in the Tuggle case, but her behavior — including the bungled suicide — points toward another case of "Munchausen's syndrome by proxy," in which unstable mothers or other caregivers deliberately harm their charges, thriving on the resultant sympathy and attention. Assuming that Tuggle serves her full sentence and hits the street with child-bearing years still ahead, only prolonged, intensive therapy will prevent her tragedy from being repeated with new, helpless victims. [See also: Johnson, Martha; Lumbrera, Diana; Tinning, Marybeth; Turner, Lise; Woods, Martha]

TURK, GENENE JONES

In February 1983, a special grand jury convened in San Antonio, Texas, investigating the "suspicious" deaths of forty-seven children at Bexar County's Medical Center Hospital over the past four years. A similar probe in neighboring Kerr County was focused upon the hospitalization of eight infants who developed respiratory problems during treatment at a local clinic. One of those children had also died, and authorities were concerned over allegations that deaths in both counties were caused by deliberate administration of muscle-relaxing drugs.

Genene Jones, a 32-year-old licensed vocational nurse, was one of three former hospital employees subpoenaed by both grand juries. With nurse Deborah Saltenfuss, Jones had resigned from Medical Center Hospital in March 1982, moving on to a job at the Kerr County clinic run by another subpoenaed witness, Dr. Kathleen Holland. By the time the grand juries convened, Jones and Holland had both been named as defendants in a lawsuit filed by the parents of 15-month-old Chelsea McClellan, lost en route to the hospital after treatment at Holland's clinic, in September 1982.

An ex-beautician, Jones had entered nursing in 1977, working at several hospitals around San Antonio over the next five years. In early 1982, she followed Dr. Holland in the move to private practice, but her performance at the clinic left much to be desired. In August and September 1982, seven children suffered mysterious seizures while visiting Dr. Holland's office, their cases arousing suspicion at Kerr County's Sipp Peterson Hospital, where they were transferred for treatment. Jones was fired from her job on September 26, after "finding" a bottle of succinylincholine reported "lost" three weeks earlier, the rubber top pocked with needle marks.

(In retrospect, Dr. Holland's choice of nurses seemed peculiar, at the very least. Her depositions, filed with the authorities, maintain that hospital administrators had "indirectly cautioned" her against hiring Jones, describing

Genene as a possible suspect in hospital pediatric deaths dating back to October 1981. Three separate investigations were conducted at Bexar County's hospital between November 1981 and February 1983, all without cracking the string of mysterious deaths.)

From all appearances, murder allegations were less troubling to Jones than persistent rumors of lesbianism. Her response to the whispering campaign was a surprise marriage to 19-year-old Garron Ray Turk, a high school senior and recent co-worker at a San Angelo nursing home. Genene's new name also provided a brief respite from hostile publicity, but authorities knew where to find her when the time was right.

On May 26, 1983, Genene was indicted on two counts of murder in Kerr County, charged with injecting lethal doses of a muscle-relaxant and another unknown drug to deliberately cause Chelsea McClellan's death. Additional charges of injury were filed in the cases of six other children, all reportedly injected with drugs including succinylincholine during their visits to the Holland clinic. Facing a maximum sentence of 99 years in prison, Jones was held in lieu of $225,000 bond.

Six months later, on November 21, Genene was indicted in San Antonio, on charges of injuring four-week-old Rolando Santos by injecting him with heparin, an anticoagulant, in January 1982. Santos had been undergoing treatment for pneumonia when he suffered "spontaneous" hemorrhaging, but physicians managed to save his life. Their probe continuing, authorities named Jones as a suspect in at least ten infant deaths at Bexar County's pediatric ward.

Genene's murder trial opened in Georgetown, Texas, on January 15, 1984, with prosecutors introducing an ego motive. The defendant allegedly sought to become a hero or "miracle-worker" by "saving" children in life-and-death crises of her own creation, sometimes failing to revive her tiny victims. Nurses from Bexar County also recalled Genene's plan to promote a pediatric intensive care unit in San Antonio, ostensibly by raising the number of seriously ill children. "They're out there," she once told a colleague. "All you have to do is find them."

Jurors deliberated for three hours before convicting Jones of murder on February 15, fixing her penalty at 99 years in prison. Eight months later, on October 24, she was convicted of injuring Rolando Santos in San Antonio, sentenced to a concurrent term of sixty years. Suspected in at least ten other homicides, Jones was spared further prosecution when Bexar County hospital administrators shredded 9,000 pounds of pharmaceutical records in March 1984, destroying numerous pieces of evidence then under subpoena by the local grand jury.

TURNER, LISE JANE

Megan Turner was eleven weeks old on January 11, 1980, when her mother rushed her to a hospital emergency ward in Christchurch, New Zealand. The child had inexplicably stopped breathing, Lise Turner said, and help arrived too late to save her life. Physicians could not specify a cause of death, and so they blamed the tragedy on SIDS — the Sudden Infant Death Syndrome that strikes certain newborns without warning or apparent cause.

Lise Turner's second child, daughter Cheney Louise, was born on January 31, 1982. Seven weeks later, on March 15, a visiting neighbor found the baby dead in her crib, the blanket stained with blood from Cheney's mouth. Again, no cause of death was ascertained. Again, physicians put the blame on SIDS.

Lise Turner would have no more children, but bad luck continued to haunt her, stretching out a lethal hand to others in her company. Nine months after Cheney's death, in October 1982, four-month-old Catherine Packer was left with Lise while her mother went shopping. Mrs. Packer returned to find her child vomiting, bleeding from the mouth, but hospital physicians saved her life. At first, Catherine seemed to recover with no ill effects, but the strange attacks were repeated over the next six months, always occurring when Lise Turner came to call. Catherine's mother finally saw through the "coincidence" when Lise joined her on a visit to the hospital, her appearance prompting tearful screams from Catherine as she cowered in her bed. Turner was henceforth barred from the

Packer residence, but no charges were filed... and there were always more children around.

Katrina Hall, five weeks old, was stricken with vomiting and labored breathing in Lise's care, but she recovered in the hospital and suffered no more ill effects. Eight-month-old Michael Tinnion was less fortunate, found dead while Turner baby-sat, with sticky fluid seeping from his nose and mouth. This time, physicians diagnosed asphyxiation as the cause of death, prompting police to reexamine other cases from their files.

In November 1984, Lise Turner stood trial in the High Court of Christchurch, charged with three counts of murder and two counts of attempted murder. Prosecutors referred to four other attacks, on children unnamed in the indictments, but the evidence on file was bad enough. No motive was advanced, though Lise's crimes are strongly reminiscent of several American killers — all diagnosed as suffering from "Munchausen's syndrome by proxy." Convicted on all counts, Turner was sentenced to life imprisonment for murder, plus five years on each of the attempted murder counts. [See also: Johnson, Martha; Lumbrera, Diana; Tinning, Marybeth; Tuggle, Debra; Woods, Martha]

URDANIVIA, RUTH

A native of Allentown, Pennsylvania, born in 1918, Ruth Strawbridge graduated from Allentown High School at age seventeen. Her senior yearbook described her as the "strong, silent type... silent but wise." Those qualities were evident when Ruth moved to San Francisco and found employment as a clerk in the local FBI field office. She was still working there in the latter months of World War II, when she met and married Peruvian diplomat Jose Urdanivia.

The couple remained in San Francisco for several years, and Ruth bore two children there: Christina in 1947 and Ruth Lucille in 1949. Two more children, Louis and Marie, were born in 1950 and 1952 respectively, while the family was residing in Peru. A fifth and last child, daughter Carol, was born in Washington, D.C., where Jose served as second secretary at the Peruvian Embassy from 1954 to 1957.

Washington was a veritable Wonderland for Ruth Urdanivia. With her charming husband, she became well known in diplomatic circles, numbering Presidents Truman and Eisenhower among the luminaries she met at various affairs of state. In 1957, Jose was promoted to first secretary at the embassy, further honored a short time later with the assignment to serve as Peru's consul-general in Yokohama. He was boarding a flight to Japan, in November 1957, when disaster struck and he collapsed on the spot, dead at age forty-two from a massive heart attack.

By January 1958, Ruth was back in Allentown, sharing a five-room apartment with her children. Money was an immediate problem, Ruth discovering that the wives of foreign diplomats are ineligible for Social Security benefits. Jose's pension amounted to $50 per month, and while embassy employees took up a collection of some $2,000 for Ruth, she claimed that only $250 reached her hands.

For all that, the Urdanivias appeared to be a model family, the children popular in school, well dressed and courteous. Ruth found a clerking job at Hess Brothers, earning $200 a month, which left $120 after each month's rent. Her application for welfare was rejected on the grounds that Ruth earned $3.80 more per month than the permissible maximum for a Pennsylvania mother with five children. Things seemed to be looking up for Ruth on October 12, 1959, when she took a new job at Sacred Heart Hospital, and she scheduled an appointment for October 16 to purchase a home in the Allentown suburbs. As it happened, she would never keep that date with her realtor.

On Tuesday night, October 14, Ruth fed her children a lethal dose of barbiturate tablets dissolved in orange juice. She swallowed twenty-five tablets herself, but somehow survived, waking from a stupor on the morning of October 20 to find her children's bodies decomposing in their beds. Amazed to find herself alive, she broke a glass and cut her wrists, inflicting only superficial wounds. Next, she lay down near the kitchen stove and turned the gas jets on, remaining there until the smell of gas alarmed her neighbors and the caretaker was summoned to investigate.

Against all odds, Ruth lived. Hospitalized under police guard, she confessed to killing the children because she was "tired of seeing my children living in a pigsty and eating inferior food." In fact, detectives found her home tidy, with plentiful food on hand, but Ruth stuck by her story. "I went everywhere to get help," she said, "but couldn't get any. No one wanted to help a widow. I did it. I know it's a sin. If only I could have gone with them. The children are now with their father. I'm sorry I didn't finish the job so I could be with them too."

Despite repeated suicide threats, psychiatrists found Ruth sane and competent for trial. Charged with one count of murder, in the death of her oldest child, Ruth went to trial in April 1960. Jury selection was under way when Ruth changed her plea, against counsel's advice, and pled guilty to second-degree murder of all five children. A panel of three judges accepted that plea on April 7, sentencing Ruth to five concurrent indefinite terms in state prison. Paroled in January 1967, Urdanivia was last reported "doing well" as a hospital clerk in central Pennsylvania.

URSINUS,
SOPHIE CHARLOTTE ELIZABETH

The daughter of an Austrian diplomat, Sophie Weingarten was born in 1760. At age nineteen, she married elderly Privy Councilor Ursinus, of Berlin, a loveless union arranged by her parents. Ursinus ignored his wife's steamy affair with a young Dutch officer named Rogay, and it came to a bad end with Rogay's premature death from "consumption." Sophie's husband was the next to go, on September 11, 1800, and maiden aunt Christina Witte followed on January 23, 1801.

In fact, while doctors suspected nothing, all had been poisoned by Sophie. Rogay had planned to leave her for another woman, while the murders of Ursinus and her aunt were strictly business, carried out for the inheritance she would receive. The chink in Sophie's armor was a servant by the name of Klein, who knew the details of her crimes. When she suspected him of planning to desert her, Sophie started dosing Klein with poison, but he recognized the symptoms and was quick enough to save himself, repaying her treachery with a full statement to the police.

Detectives called on Sophie's villa, near Berlin, interrupting a game of whist when they served the warrant for her arrest. In custody, she admitted poisoning Klein, bestowing a generous pension upon her aggrieved servant. A jury later convicted her of killing Christina Witte, and Sophie was sentenced to life imprisonment.

Not that incarceration meant hardship, by any means. Transported to the prison at Glatz, on the Silesian frontier, Sophie was lodged in a deluxe suite of rooms normally reserved for the warden. Comfortable furniture was provided, along with servants to wait on the guests at Sophie's frequent dinner parties. Money was no problem, since the court allowed Sophie to keep both her husband's estate *and* her inheritance from Aunt Christina. Given the run of the prison, she entertained lavishly until her death on April 4, 1836. Sophie was laid to rest with great pomp in Glatz cemetery, serenaded by a children's choir while clergymen lined up to praise her generosity. If anyone recalled her victims, they refrained from mentioning such awkward matters at the graveside service.

VAN HOUTEN,
LESLIE:
See MANSON "FAMILY"

VAN VALKENBURGH,
ELIZABETH

A resident of Fulton, New York, Elizabeth Van Valkenburgh poisoned two husbands by spiking their tea with arsenic. Her second victim, John Van Valkenburgh, died in March 1845, and police were instantly suspicious of the grim "coincidence." In custody, Elizabeth confessed both murders, stating that she killed her husbands as a means of coping with their severe alcoholism. It was an extreme remedy, of course, but she admitted that "I always had a very ungovernable temper." Convicted and sentenced to die for her crimes, Elizabeth was hanged on January 24, 1846.

VELTEN, MARIA

A classic "black widow," Maria Velten spent twenty years killing her loved ones around Kempten, West Germany, before she was finally arrested at age sixty-seven. Her father was the first to die, in 1963, followed by an elderly aunt in 1970. Under questioning, Velten would describe the early poisonings as murders of convenience, with her victims being ill and she unable to provide the necessary care. From that point on, a profit motive would prevail, with Velten killing off two husbands — in 1976 and '78 — along with a well-to-do boyfriend in 1980. Arrested in August 1983, she was convicted on the basis of her own confession and was sentenced to a term of life imprisonment.

VERMILYEA, LOUISE

A "black widow" whose activities spanned the turn of the century, Louise Vermilyea came to grief when greed exceeded her discretion and she started reaching out to prey upon acquaintances, instead of relatives. At that, it took the death of a policeman in Chicago to alert authorities and raise suspicion over the peculiar fates experienced by several husbands, family members, and associates.

The officer in question, Arthur Bisonette, age twenty-six, had been a boarder in Vermilyea's home when he fell ill and died in late October 1911. Homicide detectives grew suspicious after speaking to Bisonette's father, who also reported stomach pains after dining with his son at the boarding house. Louise Vermilyea, he recalled, had sprinkled "white pepper" over his food before it was served. An autopsy on Bisonette discovered arsenic, and Louise was taken into custody pending exhumation of other suspected victims.

The string of homicides apparently began in 1893, when Fred Brinkamp, Louise's first husband, died at his farm near Barrington, Illinois. He left his widow richer by $5,000, but at sixty years of age, Fred's death wasn't considered cause for any undue comment.

Soon, two daughters by the marriage — Cora Brinkamp, eight years old, and Florence, nearly five — were also dead. In January 1906, Lillian Brinkamp, Fred's 26-year-old granddaughter, died in Chicago, stricken by "acute nephritis." It began to seem that members of the Brinkamp tribe had stumbled on a previously undiscovered family curse.

Louise remarried, meanwhile, to one Charles Vermilyea, fifty-nine. By 1909 he was dead, another victim of sudden illness, leaving his widow $1,000 in cash. Harry Vermilyea, a stepson, dropped dead in Chicago after he quarreled with Louise over the sale of a house at Crystal Lake, ten miles north of Chicago in McHenry County. Once again, coincidence was blamed.

In 1910, Louise inherited $1,200 on the death of Frank Brinkamp, her 23-year-old son from her first marriage. On his death bed, Brinkamp informed his fiancée, Elizabeth Nolan, of belated suspicions involving his mother, declaring that he was "going the way dad did."

Temporarily short of relatives, Louise began to practice on acquaintances. The first to die was Jason Ruppert, a railroad fireman who became ill after dining with Louise on January 15, 1910. Two days later, he was dead, and others followed swiftly. Richard Smith, a train conductor, rented rooms in the Vermilyea household, but he should have eaten elsewhere. Sudden illness struck him down a short time prior to Arthur Bisonette's arrival on the scene, and other victims might have fallen over time, had not Louise allowed the older Bisonette to get away.

While motive in the later homicides was never clear, financial gain was obvious in the elimination of Vermilyea's husbands and assorted offspring. Undertaker E.N. Blocks, of

Barrington, recalled that Louise "actually seemed to enjoy working around bodies, and while I never employed her, for a couple of years I couldn't keep her out of the office. At every death she would seem to hear of it just as soon as I, and she would reach the house only a little behind me."

While under house arrest, Louise Vermilyea denigrated the official efforts to indict her for a string of ten known homicides. "They may go as far as they like," she said of police, "for I have nothing to fear. I simply have been unfortunate in having people dying around me." On the side, her tough facade was crumbling, and on November 4 detectives rushed her to the hospital, a victim of her own "white pepper." The authorities reported that Louise had been ingesting poison with her meals since she was first confined at home, October 28. On November 9, she was reported as being near death, with valvular heart problems adding their punch to the poison. By December 9, she had been stricken with paralysis, described by her physician as a permanent condition.

VILLEDA, ANA MARIA RUIZ

Residents of Matamoros, Mexico, were still discussing the murderous drug cult led by Adolfo Constanzo and "Godmother" Sarah Aldrete when a new horror was visited upon their community, in 1991. Within a two-month period, eight teenage girls were raped and strangled on the Tex-Mex border, their bodies discarded in the Rio Grande.

The first victim was found in late August, twenty miles upriver from Brownsville, near the small community of El Sabino. The naked, battered corpse would remain unidentified, but pathologists placed the victim somewhere in her teens, reporting that she had been raped, beaten, and finally strangled to death. Police in Mexico and Texas searched their missing persons files without a match.

Number two, another "Jane Doe," was fished out of the Rio Grande three days later. Autopsy results confirmed rape and strangulation, but police were unable to link the two cases without a positive victim I.D. Descriptions of the two dead women were broadcast on both sides of the border, but no one came forward to identify the girls. By the time a third victim was found, in September, residents of Brownsville and Matamoros were debating the possibility of a new murder cult in the neighborhood.

In late September, a 16-year-old girl approached Matamoros police to report a friend missing. Both girls came from San Luis Potosi, 500 miles south of Matamoros, and they had come to the border city in search of jobs. While idling in the Plaza Allende, they were approached by a woman who introduced herself as "Maria," offering to help them find employment. They could always work as maids in Matamoros, she explained, but if they wanted better money, they would have to learn some English and apply for work in the United States. Maria offered to assist them with their English lessons and obtain a pair of green cards for the girls. Both eagerly agreed, but they got separated when they went for their belongings, and the witness had not seen her friend or the helpful Maria again. Before contacting the police, she spent three days scouring Matamoros for clues, encountering one old man who warned her that "Maria" was a dangerous woman who often "did bad things" to unsuspecting girls.

A fourth victim, 15-year-old Orefelinda Castillo, was hauled from the river on October 12. She had been raped and strangled like the others, and police determined that she had been robbed of 40,000 pesos — the equivalent of $13.30.

The case broke four days later, when 17-year-old Alma Lilia Camacho presented herself to police in Matamoros, reporting that she had been held captive on an isolated ranch for the past ten days. Like the previous witness, she had come to town looking for work, and she had met the helpful "Maria" at Plaza Allende. The woman offered her a job tending children at El Ebanito, twenty miles from Matamoros, where she would receive English lessons in preparation for work across the border. Alma agreed to the offer and entered a car with Maria; the driver was a man who introduced himself to Alma as "Rudolfo."

Their destination proved to be an isolated shack on a communal farm. Alma was ushered inside and told to wait while Maria and Rudolfo went to finalize arrangements with her new employer. As they left, Maria locked the door, and Alma found that the windows were barred.

She also found that she was not alone. Orefelinda Castillo was there ahead of her, bruised and battered, apparently ill, complaining of starvation, beatings, and repeated rapes. Rudolfo had threatened her life after the last assault, and her fears were realized next morning, when the man returned and dragged Castillo from the hovel, never to return.

Alma determined to save herself by playing along with Rudolfo's demands, pretending to enjoy his crude advances, buying time. After several days, Rudolfo agreed to help her escape, accepting Alma's promise of a later rendezvous in Matamoros. He left the shack unlocked, as planned, but Alma ran to the police instead, and led a raiding party to the ranch.

The residents, identified by Alma as her captors, were 28-year-old Rudolfo Infante Jimenez and his girlfriend, 20-year-old Ana Maria Villeda. Both denied ever seeing Alma Camacho before, but Alma's description of the ten-by-fifteen shack was perfect in every detail, down to the dirty blue carpet and red blanket on the sagging metal cot. Nearby, manhunters found the violated body of 17-year-old Enriqueta Vega Rocha.

It was enough for an arrest, and the authorities ran a quick background check on their suspects. Both were Mexican natives, but Rudolfo Infante had become a naturalized U.S. citizen, abandoning his wife and two children in San Benito, Texas, under threat of an indictment for aggravated robbery. Ana Villeda hailed from the state of San Luis Potosi, and she had followed the path of her alleged victims, drifting to Matamoros in search of work. What she found, instead, was Rudolfo Infante.

Under questioning, Ana admitted luring nine young women to the ranch, but she insisted that robbery was the only motive. Rudolfo, she insisted, had raped and murdered eight of the victims on his own initiative, before Alma Camacho escaped. His attitude, as voiced to Ana, had been simple: "Why should I fool around with women who have had children when I can have virgins?"

Infante, for his part, told a different story. He confessed to "having an affair" with his second victim, but denied that any of the others were molested. All the killing had been done by Ana, he initially proclaimed, adjusting his story by October 19 to admit three killings of his own. The robberies were penny-ante all the way, their largest haul from any single victim totaling $17 in U.S. currency.

Prosecutors in the state of Tamaulipas were not dismayed by the conflicting stories from their suspects. Regardless of who did the actual killing, they said, both parties were equally guilty under law, and each was charged with eight counts of first-degree murder, plus eight counts of kidnapping. In the absence of capital punishment, Villeda and Infante faced a maximum sentence of forty years in prison.

"VOISIN, LA": See "CHAMBRE ARDENTE AFFAIR"

WADDINGHAM, DOROTHEA NANCY

Born in 1899, Dorothea Waddingham was a self-styled "nurse" who gained her limited experience while employed at a workhouse infirmary. Widowed by the death of husband Thomas Leech, she acquired a new lover in Ronald Sullivan, a hero of World War I whose battlefield prowess did not prevent Waddingham from dominating every aspect of his life. In fact, the lure of domination may have been his primary attraction to this homely, long-faced woman with buck teeth and bulging eyes.

In January 1935, Waddingham used her maiden name to open a "nursing home for aged and chronic cases" at Nottingham, England. Sullivan dealt with the grunt work, while Waddingham handled the nursing, their establishment soon accredited by the County Nursing Association. That august body also provided Dorothea with her first two patients, 89-year-old Mrs. Baguley (suffering from advanced senility) and her daughter Ada, age fifty (a victim of creeping paralysis). Mrs. Baguley was sufficiently impressed with Waddingham to change her will, leaving her entire estate — some 2,000 pounds in all — to Waddingham and Sullivan in return for their promise of perpetual care for both women.

The ink was barely dry on that document when Mrs. Baguley died, of "old age," on May 12, 1935. Her daughter lasted four months longer, collapsing with "a cerebral hemorrhage" on September 10. In Waddingham's professional opinion, Ada's stroke had been produced by eating too much chocolate. The nurse requested swift cremation, offering a purported letter from Ada Baguley, dated August 29, which concluded: "It is my wish to remain with Nurse and my last wish is that my relatives shall not know of my death."

That last provision was curious enough to raise suspicion in Dr. Cyril Banks, the medical officer required to approve cremations in Nottingham. Banks ordered a double autopsy, and high levels of morphine were discovered in both bodies. Handwriting analysts declared that Waddingham herself had penned Ada's last letter, and murder charges were filed. Ron Sullivan was briefly jailed, but evidence of Dorothea's dominating style secured his release with charges dropped.

Tried at Nottingham on February 4, 1936, Waddingham insisted that a Dr. Mansfield — signatory of the Baguley death certificates — had ordered morphine injections for both women before they died. Mansfield denied prescribing any drugs, and jurors convicted Waddingham on both counts, with a rare recommendation of mercy. The trial judge disagreed and sentenced her to hang, the order carried out on April 16, 1936.

WAGNER, WALTRAUD: See "ANGELS OF DEATH"

WALKUP, MARIE

An Arizona native, born in 1905, Marie Green was barely twenty when she met and married James Walkup, an army veteran who had moved to Flagstaff in the wake of World War I. His sterling military record served James well in business, paving the way for his election to the Coconino County Board of Supervisors and the Flagstaff Chamber of Commerce. Over time, Marie bore four children — Daniel in 1927, Rose Marie in 1929, John in 1935, and Elizabeth in 1936.

The only problem in their lives, by 1937, seemed to be Marie's affliction with a chronic intestinal ailment. Visiting her family physician on July 22, Marie was depressed, voicing a fear that her children had caught the unnamed disease. In fact, none displayed any symptoms, but Marie would not accept the doctor's reassurance. Later that night, with husband James away on business, Marie called her doctor's answering service, requesting a house call next morning. As it happened, he would never have to make the trip.

In the predawn hours of July 23, Marie Walkup moved through her darkened home, stabbing and strangling each of her children in turn. When all four were dead, she took a rifle from the closet and drove to a nearby golf course, still clad in her nightgown and robe. Lying down on the grass, she cocked the rifle, aimed it at herself, and pressed the trigger with her toe. Dawn was breaking when a caretaker found her corpse, and police were dispatched to her home.

There, investigators found the charnel house in perfect order. Coroner Max Miller told the press Marie had slaughtered her children "with such dispatch that not an object was out of place in the home. The children, their night clothes and bedding neatly arranged, were tucked into their beds as though asleep." Marie had left four notes, including one for her milkman, canceling the regular delivery. The note addressed to her husband read: "Because of my lack of discipline, the children are happier this way. Only grief would come to them. You are strong in faith, never doubting — mercy, mercy to my people. I loved you, and I have failed."

WALTERS, ANNIE: See SACH, AMELIA

WARDLAW SISTERS

Three daughters of a prominent Southern family, the Wardlaw sisters led a strange life of seclusion, dressing all in black, moving frequently from one Dixie town to another. Outwardly, they were the very picture of genteel Southern grace, but their rootless lifestyle disguised a sinister reality.

Virginia Wardlaw was the leader of the clan, a spinster graduate of Wellesley College who became a respected teacher. Sisters Caroline Wardlaw Martin and Mary Wardlaw Sneyd both married, but later left their husbands to live with Virginia. Along the way, they started to support themselves by killing relatives for life insurance.

The first known victim was Mary's son, John Sneyd, who burned to death in 1900, the "accident" paying his mother $12,000. Sister Caroline was next up at bat, reuniting with husband John Martin and moving to New York, where he soon died from "undetermined causes," his life insurance paying off to the tune of $10,000. With cash in hand, Caroline rejoined her sisters in Tennessee, where Virginia had lately been hired as the head of Soule College at Murfreesboro.

Target number three was Caroline's daughter, Oscey Martin, separated from her own husband, living with her mother and aunts. The sisters insured Oscey's life, then began starving her to death, finally drowning her in the bathtub when she overstayed her welcome. It was the last straw, and all three sisters were arrested for murder when they tried to cash in Oscey's life insurance policy.

A suspect in jail is one thing, however; conviction is another. Virginia Wardlaw cheated the state by starving herself to death in a jailhouse hunger strike, and Mary was acquitted at trial. Only Caroline was convicted of her daughter's slaying, subsequently ruled insane and committed to a Tennessee state hospital, where she died in 1913.

WASHINGTON, ANNETTE

Once employed by a home health care service on Long Island, New York, 28-year-old Annette Washington was discharged from her job in July 1986. A single mother with a nine-year-old son to feed, she was also supporting her boyfriend's drug habit on the side. Embittered by the loss of employment, she devised a scheme to solve both problems simultaneously, by the grim expedient of killing off her former patients.

Loretta O'Flaherty, age eighty-five, was the first to go, found dead in her Bronx apartment on August 8, 1986. Two kitchen knives had been employed to cut her throat before her flat was ransacked for cash and other valuables. Two weeks later, 68-year-old Edna Fumasoli was killed at her home, stabbed ninety times by a frenzied assailant.

Similarities in the two crimes led detectives to begin a background search for links between the victims. The name of Annette Washington surfaced in due course, and police learned that both victims had been terrified of robbery, establishing a "knocking code" to let them know a friend was at the door.

Suspecting that the victims' latest "friend" had been a Judas in disguise, authorities arrested Washington in mid-September and secured her confession to the crimes. Pleading guilty on two counts of murder, plus assault and weapons charges, she received a prison term of fifty years to life in July 1987. At this writing, her unnamed male accomplice is still at large.

WATERS, MARGARET

English born in 1835, Margaret Waters married and moved to Newfoundland in her early twenties, living quietly there without incident until her husband's untimely death. Back in Brixton by 1866, she opened a boarding house, assisted in the venture by her sister, Sarah Ellis. Business was slow, and before year's end, Margaret shifted directions to try her hand at the lethal trade of "baby farming."

Margaret lured prospective clients with newspaper ads promising "a good home with a mother's love and care" for "a respectable person wishing her child to be entirely adopted." Respondents met with "Mrs. Oliver" in a public place, negotiating fees in the general range of two to four pounds, but mother's love was sadly lacking under Margaret's roof. In fact, she pocketed the cash and kept the babies drugged with laudanum while they starved to death, too cruel or squeamish to dispatch them quickly. On the side, she turned an extra profit pawning baby clothes.

Police were hot on Margaret's trail by June of 1870, though they refused to say what tipped them off. A Sergeant Relph responded to her latest ad and got a letter back from "Mrs. Willis" that read: "The child would be well brought up and carefully educated, he would learn a good trade and be to us in all respects as our own. We have been married for several years but have no family. We are in a comfortable position, have a good business, and a home in every way to make a child happy. We are both very fond of children, and should you entrust your little one to our care, you may rely upon his receiving the love and care of a mother."

Sgt. Relph met Waters at a railroad station on June 10, trailing her home when she refused to give her address. A raiding party struck next morning, following their noses to a filthy bedroom where five infants lay huddled together, drugged with laudanum, on a urine-soaked couch. Five more, ranging in age from a few weeks to thirty months, were found in the back yard. Sarah Ellis claimed one child as her own, but Waters denied any knowledge of where the other nine came from or whose they might be.

In custody, Margaret soon dropped her charade of ignorance, admitting that she had been "in the business" for roughly four years. She estimated that forty children had passed through her hands in that time, but officers found ninety-two pawn tickets in her home, all issued to Waters for baby clothes. One of the infants found at her house was retrieved by a grandparent, the other nine winding up at a Brixton workhouse, where five died from the combined effects of drugs and malnutrition.

Once the case made tabloid headlines, several women got in touch with the police, admitting they had left their children in the baby farmer's care. Detectives also heard from Ellen O'Connor, once a servant for the sisters, who remembered buying laudanum on Margaret's orders and collecting letters addressed to Waters under various pseudonyms. When infants died, O'Connor said, her mistress dropped the bodies off at any point that seemed convenient — underneath a railroad bridge, perhaps, or on a garbage dump.

Margaret did her best to shield sister Sarah from prosecution, declaring that "I am the sinner and I must suffer," but authorities disagreed. Both sisters went on trial in September 1870, charged with one count of murdering an infant identified by its grandfather, Mr. Cowen. In court, Waters claimed that unsavory conditions in her home were much exaggerated by police. "The Cowen baby was a very fine child," she testified, "and I was much pleased with it, but it did not get on, whatever I did."

In fact, Margaret admitted that five babies had died in her care over time, aside from the five already known to police. Ellen O'Connor and another ex-servant recalled six "disappearances," leaving a minimum of nineteen children unaccounted for by Margaret's own tally. Jurors acquitted Sarah Ellis of the murder charge, but she later pled guilty to obtaining money by false pretenses and served eighteen months in prison. Waters, for her part, was convicted of murder and sentenced to hang. She mounted the gallows on October 11, 1870.

WEBER, JEANNE

Born in 1875, at a small fishing village in northern France, Jeanne Weber left home for Paris at age fourteen, working various menial jobs until her marriage in 1893. Her husband was a drunkard, and by 1905, with two of their three children lately deceased, Jeanne was also drinking heavily, residing in a seedy Paris tenement with her spouse and a seven-year-old son.

On March 2, 1905, Weber was baby-sitting for her sister-in-law, when one of the woman's two daughters — 18-month-old Georgette — suddenly "fell ill" and died. Strange bruises on her neck were ignored by the examining physician, and Jeanne was welcomed back to baby-sit on March 11. Two-year-old Suzanne did not survive the visit, but a doctor blamed the second death on unexplained "convulsions."

Weber was baby-sitting for her brother on March 25, when his daughter, seven-year-old Germaine, suffered a sudden attack of "choking," complete with red marks on her throat. The child survived that episode, but she was less fortunate the following day, when Aunt Jeanne returned. Diphtheria was blamed for her death — and for that of Weber's son, Marcel, just four days later. Once again, the tell-tale marks of strangulation were ignored.

On April 5, 1905, Weber invited two of her sisters-in-law to dinner, afterward remaining home with 10-year-old nephew Maurice while the other women went out shopping. They returned prematurely, to find Maurice gasping on the bed, his throat mottled with bruises, Jeanne standing over him with a crazed expression on her face. Charges were filed, and Weber's trial opened on January 29, 1906, with the prosecution alleging eight murders, including all three of Weber's own children and two others — Lucie Aleandre and Marcel Poyatos — who had died while in her care. It was alleged that Weber killed her son in March to throw suspicion off, but jurors were reluctant to believe the worst about a grieving mother, and Weber was acquitted on February 6.

Fourteen months later, on April 7, 1907, a physician from the town of Villedieu was summoned to the home of a peasant named Bavouzet. He was greeted at the door by a baby-sitter, "Madame Moulinet," who led him to the cot where nine-year-old Auguste Bavouzet lay dead, his throat badly bruised. The cause of death was listed as "convulsions," but the doctor changed his tune on May 4, when "Madame Moulinet" was identified as Jeanne Weber. Held over for trial, Weber was released in December, after a second autopsy blamed the boy's death on "typhoid."

Weber quickly dropped from sight, surfacing next as an orderly at a children's hospital in Faucombault, moving on from there to the Children's Home in Orgevile, run by friends who sought to "make up for the wrongs that justice has inflicted upon an innocent woman." Working as "Marie Lemoine," Weber had been on the job for less than a week when she was caught strangling a child in the home. Embarrassed by their own naiveté, the owners quietly dismissed her and the incident was covered up.

Back in Paris, Weber was arrested for vagrancy and briefly confined to the asylum at Nantere, but doctors there pronounced her sane and set her free. She drifted into prostitution, picking up a common-law husband along the way, and on May 8, 1908 the couple settled at an inn in Commercy. A short time later, Jeanne was found strangling the innkeeper's son, 10-year-old Marcel Poirot, with a bloody handkerchief. The father had to punch her in the face three times, with all his might, before she would release the lifeless body.

Held for trial on murder charges, Weber was declared insane on October 25, 1908, packed off to the asylum at Mareville. Credited with at least ten murders, she survived two years in captivity before manually strangling herself in 1910.

WILLIAMSON, STELLA

No one in the small town of Gallitzin, Pennsylvania, gave much thought to Stella Williamson in life. Unmarried and reclusive, seldom speaking even to her closest neighbors, it was clear that Stella loved her privacy. She made a regular appearance in her local church, but the parishioners knew nothing of her past and little of her present life, beyond the obvious. In 1975, one of Stella's legs was amputated, and she never quite recovered. She was seventy-six at the time of her death, in August 1980, and while the event seemed predictable, its aftermath would spark an uproar in Gallitzin.

Following the funeral, one of Stella's few acquaintances discovered a sealed envelope, marked for opening after her death. The letter within, written in 1960, directed police to the attic of Williamson's house, where an ancient trunk was opened to reveal the withered remains of five human infants. The tiny corpses were wrapped in newspapers from Johnstown, Pittsburgh, and New York City, with dates spanning the decade from 1923 to 1933. John Barron, coroner for Cambria County, reported that four of the infants were newborns, while one was older, perhaps by as much as eight months.

All things considered, there was little that authorities could do about the startling case. It was presumed that Williamson, a lifelong spinster by her own account, had born the children out of wedlock through the years, disposing of them as they came, and that she somehow felt compelled to save the pitiful remains. Details of the case reportedly were offered in her parting message to authorities, but none have been revealed. As Coroner Barron explained to the press, "Everybody involved is deceased. But we have to make sure the obvious is the truth. We have to make sure it's not a coverup."

WILSON, CATHERINE

A poisoner-for-profit, born at Boston, England, in 1822, Catherine Wilson kept a low profile for the first thirty-one years of her life. In 1853, she applied for a housekeeper's job at the home of a Boston widower named Mawer. Wilson billed herself as a widow, but no record exists of either a marriage or her husband's death. (If he existed, he may have been her first victim.) Mawer was generally healthy, except for sporadic gout attacks, which his doctor treated with colchium. As it happened, while helpful in small doses, colchium was lethal in larger amounts.

Wilson worked in the household for a year, impressing Mawer with her energy and dedication. They became great friends, with Mawer giving Wilson's tender care full credit for the late improvement in his gout. To show his gratitude, Mawer rewrote his will, naming Wilson as his only heir.

It was a fatal mistake.

Mawer died in October 1854, after ten days of diarrhea and projectile vomiting. Wilson put on a show of grief, and no one appeared to suspect her of poisoning Mawer, despite a nurse's comment that the patient's health declined each time his "good friend" served him tea.

Catherine's meager inheritance took her to London, where she rented rooms from landlady Maria Soames in 1855. She had picked up a live-in lover, one James Dixon, along the way, passing him off to Soames as her brother. Unknown to anyone, she also packed a large supply of colchium from Mawer's private stock.

Wilson soon grew tired of Dixon's heavy drinking, frequently accompanied by physical abuse, and she treated him to a fatal dose of colchium. She blamed "consumption" for his death, pleading with Dixon's physician to skip the autopsy, but the doctor persevered, discovering no evidence of tuberculosis. Even so, he missed the tell-tale signs of poison and attributed the patient's death to natural causes.

With Dixon out of the way, Catherine set her sights on her landlady's bank account. Maria Soames was not inclined to change her will, but she did make a series of loans to Catherine before Maria died at age fifty, in October 1856. An inquest was ordered, and Catherine began to hedge her bets, spreading a rumor that Soames had killed herself after being jilted by an anonymous lover. (When one acquaintance asked why Wilson did not stop Maria from imbibing poisoned brandy, Catherine replied, "It wasn't my business.") Somehow, the rumors failed to reach official ears, and autopsy results attributed Maria's death to "heart disease and peritonitis." As a parting shot, Wilson billed the dead woman's estate for ten pounds, presenting a forged promissory note to support her claim.

By 1859, Wilson was back in Boston, befriending a Mrs. Jackson and tapping her for loans. Her latest pigeon died four days after withdrawing 120 pounds from the bank, and while Wilson avoided suspicion, the money was never found.

Later in 1859, Catherine struck up a friendship with Ann Atkinson, an aunt of James Dixon's from Cumberland, in the north of England. Atkinson visited Catherine in London that fall, for a shopping excursion, but the trip was spoiled when Atkinson mysteriously lost her purse, with fifty-one pounds inside. A year later, in October 1860, Ann repeated the journey, bringing 120 pounds from home. She found Wilson short of cash, behind on her rent, but Catherine's problems were soon resolved in typical style.

Four days after Atkinson's arrival in London, her husband received a telegram from Wilson, telling him his wife was ill. He hurried south, but Ann was dead when he arrived, Catherine bedridden with grief. Physicians called for an autopsy, but Wilson persuaded Ann's husband to refuse them, citing Ann's last wish to avoid having her body "cut up." Sorting through Ann's effects, the grieving husband was surprised to find her penniless. He knew that she had brought 120 pounds from Cumberland, but Wilson had an answer for everything. Ann had been robbed on the train, she said, arriving with only a handful of coins to her name, embarrassed to tell her husband what had happened. Atkinson swallowed the story and took his wife home for burial, while Wilson spent the next week paying off her debts, flaunting a new diamond ring allegedly given to her by Ann as "a token of gratitude."

In the spring of 1862, Catherine ingratiated herself with Sarah Carnell, recently estranged from her husband. Wilson volunteered to serve as go-between, striving to effect a reconciliation, but she was more concerned with Sarah's money than her love life. Sarah soon fell ill, relying on Catherine as her nurse, but Wilson's "herbal tea" was too hot to handle. One sip had Sarah screaming, dashing her cup to the floor. By the time help arrived, the "tea" — sulfuric acid — had begun to scorch her sheets.

Police went looking for Wilson, but she fled to London, evading arrest for six weeks. In the interim, a number of her victims were exhumed and tested for poison, homicide investigators naming Catherine as a suspect in at least five murders, perhaps as many as seven.

Her first trial, though, was for the attempted murder of Sarah Carnell. Defense attorneys blamed a local chemist for confusing the prescription, and a jury bought it, voting for acquittal on September 25. Wilson left the courtroom smiling, but her troubles were not over yet. Arrested for murder days later, she was convicted and sentenced to die for killing Maria Soames. Catherine was hanged at London's Horsemonger Gaol on October 20, 1862, while a crowd of 20,000 gawkers cheered the spectacle. Her execution was the last public hanging of a female prisoner in London.

WILSON, ELIZABETH

A single mother's lot has never been easy, and it was all the more difficult in East Bradford, Pennsylvania, in the year 1785. Elizabeth Wilson's twins were barely ten weeks old when the impoverished woman found that she could not afford to feed them. The thought of seeking help eluded her, and she decided to murder the children rather than watch them starve, a crime for which she was swiftly arrested and sentenced to die. Elizabeth's brother prevailed on the governor to commute her sentence, but Alexander Morse would not invent the telegraph for another fifty-two years, and the message had to be carried from Philadelphia by hand. Sadly for Elizabeth, winter rains had turned the unpaved roads of Delaware County into a quagmire, retarding her brother's progress on horseback. He arrived too late to save her, reaching the prison at Chester twenty-three minutes after Elizabeth was hanged, on January 3, 1786.

WILSON, MARY ELIZABETH

A humble English maid, Mary Wilson was twenty-two years old when she met her first husband, laborer John Knowles, in 1913. Settling at Windy Hook, the newlyweds took in a lodger — chimney sweep John Russell — to help with expenses, and Russell was soon sharing Mary's bed while her husband went off to work. The strange affair would span four decades, but it ended badly... at least for the two men involved.

In the summer of 1956, John Knowles was stricken with a sudden illness, writhing through his final hours in a misery of stomach cramps and vomiting. John Russell lived to celebrate the new year, but his luck ran out a few weeks later. Symptoms were identical, and doctors tried in vain to save his life. Both deaths were written off to "natural causes," and Mary Wilson inherited the grand sum of forty-six pounds from her two lost loves.

In the summer of 1957, Mary met a retired real estate agent, 75-year-old Oliver Leonard. Mary's motive for pursuing the relationship was evident in her first question to a mutual friend: "Does the old bugger have any money?" The answer was affirmative, and they were married that September, at the Jarrow register office. The honeymoon ended thirteen days later, with a midnight call to neighbors that Mary's husband was dying. An autopsy blamed his death on myocardial degeneration and chronic nephritis, leaving the widow Leonard to collect another fifty pounds.

Ernest Wilson, a 75-year-old retired engineer, was recruiting prospective housekeepers when he caught Mary's eye. In short order, she turned the interview around, discovering that Wilson had a paid-up life insurance policy and 100 pounds banked with the local Cooperative Society. It was a fortune by Mary's standards, and she soon persuaded Wilson to propose.

At their wedding reception, Mary displayed a sharp eye for economy. "Save the left-over cakes," she told her caterer. "They'll come in handy for the funeral." A short time later, she returned and told him, "Never mind those cakes. I may give this one an extension."

In fact, Wilson's time ran out on November 11, 1957, his passing marked by symptoms familiar from previous cases. Dr. William Wallace certified the cause as cardiovascular failure, but Mary's wedding jokes came back to haunt her. Pathologists examined Wilson's corpse, unearthing Oliver Leonard for good measure, and traces of phosphorous-based poison — common to various pesticides — were found in both victims.

Indicted on two counts of murder, Mary Wilson was tried at Leeds in March 1958. Attorney Rose Heilbron contended that Leonard and Wilson had each ingested the phosphorous voluntarily, as a cure for impotence, but judge and jury alike rejected the lame alibi. Convicted and sentenced to hang, Wilson saw her penalty commuted to life imprisonment on appeal. She survived three years in custody, at Holloway Prison, and died of natural causes in 1961.

WISE, MARTHA

A native of Medina County, Ohio, Martha Hasel was born in 1883, growing up on a farm with her parents and three brothers. One of her teachers described Martha as "the dullest child in school. She was even too dull to make trouble." Another recalled that "she was never able to learn anything," and a classmate remembered Martha "always crying and every time anyone spoke to her she would burst into tears." On the side, she held protracted conversations with imaginary "friends."

In 1906, Martha married farmer Albert Wise, bearing him five children through the years. One died in infancy, but that left four young mouths to feed, with money constantly in short supply. When Albert died in 1923, it came as a relief of sorts, a small insurance payment granting Martha the first leisure time of her life. She began to go for long walks in the woods, sometimes at night, accompanied by the childhood friends whom no one else could see.

In time, the "friendly" voices started whispering of death.

On November 24, 1924, Martha purchased arsenic at a local drug store, dropping by her parents' home to spike the kitchen water bucket. Martha's mother, 69-year-old Sophia Hasel, died on December 13, stricken with stomach cramps and violent diarrhea. Two of Martha's brothers and several friends developed similar symptoms while visiting the Hasel home, but all survived.

In the wake of Sophia's death, Martha targeted her aunt and uncle, Fred and Lillie Gienke, who lived on a farm near Medina with their six children, ranging in age from nine to twenty-four. No one linked Martha's visits to the sudden illness which befell the Gienke clan at New Year's, 1925, with 53-year-old Lillie dying on January 4. Each time the other family members seemed to be recovering, Martha would drop by to chat, and their condition would decline. Fred Gienke died on February 8, at age fifty-nine, and the children were farmed out to neighbors, one son winding up in Martha's care.

Police launched their investigation on February 12, ruling out botulism and other natural causes before they settled on arsenic poisoning. Even then, they were far from solving the case, as no poison was found at the Gienke farm, and the family seemed to have no enemies. Prosecutor Joseph Seymour described himself as "at sea" on March 12, telling newsmen that "Administration of the poison appears to have been accidental or the work of a moron." Days later, notified of Sophia Hasel's similar death, Seymour changed his tune. This time, he told the press, "I fully believe the deaths and illness of other members of the family can be laid to the hands of a crazed person." But who?

A week after Seymour's second statement to the press, he received an anonymous letter. It read: "I just want to make a suggestion — see if you can find out if there was ill feeling between Martha Wise and Lillie Gienke. I know something of the treachery of this Martha Hasel Wise and also her craftiness to evade suspicion. She is what you might call a moron. Could it be to get rid of her mother and get the property and of Lillie for suspecting her. She claimed to have been made sick too, but that may be a lie too."

Martha was pulled in for questioning, and she swiftly confessed to poisoning both families — a total of sixteen persons, including sundry visitors, of whom three died. (Four of the Gienke children were described in later press reports as "crippled for life.") She also spoke of stealing jewelry from friends and relatives, along with burning down three local barns, the first a year before her husband died. "I like fires," Martha explained. "They were red and bright, and I loved to see the flames shooting up into the sky."

Her explanation for the poisonings was even more bizarre. "It was the devil who told me to do it," Martha said. "He came to me while I was working in the fields. He followed me everywhere." Joe Seymour agreed with psychiatrists that Martha was suffering from "mental dementia," but he went ahead with prosecution all the same, her trial for the murder of Lillie Gienke beginning on May 4, 1925.

By then, sensational headlines were billing Martha as the "Borgia of America." Lillie Gienke's body was the only one exhumed, and arsenic was found in the remains. Several prosecution witnesses were wheeled into court on hospital gurneys, still suffering from the effects of poisoning, and their condition doubtless swayed the jury toward conviction. Martha's lawyer, meanwhile, plumped for an insanity defense, presenting witnesses to the effect that Martha suffered "fits" and sometimes crawled around on all fours, "barking like a dog." Jurors were skeptical, deliberating for barely an hour on May 13 before they convicted Martha of first-degree murder, with a recommendation of mercy. Sentenced to life imprisonment, she subsequently died in custody.

WOOD, CATHERINE: See GRAHAM, GWENDOLYN

WOODS, MARTHA

An Army wife who followed her husband around the country, from one military base to the next, Martha Woods also suffered from the bizarre mental illness dubbed "Munchausen's syndrome by proxy." Victims of this rare condition are driven to seek attention or sympathy by fabricating ailments for their loved ones, sometimes inflicting deliberate harm to support their claims of mysterious illness. In this case, the quirk cost seven children their lives.

Martha's victims included three of her own children, a nephew, a niece, a neighbor's child, and the son she adopted when targets grew scarce. The cross-country killing spree lasted most of a quarter-century, from 1946 to 1969. Geography was Martha's friend, preventing medical practitioners in various locations from connecting her several crimes, until her luck ran out at last in Baltimore.

Martha's pattern was always the same, involving a rush to the nearest hospital with an unconscious baby in her arms. Each time, the infant was alone in Martha's care when it abruptly, inexplicably "stopped breathing." The children were revived, sent home with Woods, but they inevitably suffered more attacks within a span of hours or days. Altogether, police calculated in hindsight, nine children had suffered a total of twenty-seven life-threatening respiratory attacks, with seven resulting in death. The first six deaths were listed as "natural," though symptoms were consistent with deliberate suffocation.

Aside from her penchant for smothering infants, Woods also displayed the typical Munchausen's trait of pathological lying. Following the adoption of daughter Judy, she complained of threats from the girl's real parents. They had turned up on her doorstep, Martha claimed, demanding their daughter back, threatening her life when she refused. Faceless strangers were circling her home in a car at odd hours, and someone had tried to burn the house. In fact, Army CID agents found flammable liquid splashed on one wall of Martha's home, but they suspected her of staging the scene herself. Judy's biological parents were miles away, in another state, and officers finally dismissed the whole story as an elaborate hoax.

Time ran out for Woods in Baltimore, when authorities finally turned up evidence of murder in the death of her adopted son, seven-month-old Paul. Intensive psychiatric testing found her sane and fit for trial. The judge admitted evidence from other deaths to prove the case on Paul, and Martha was convicted after five months of testimony, and sentenced to life imprisonment on one count of first-degree murder. [See also: Johnson, Martha; Lumbrera, Diana; Tinning, Marybeth; Tuggle, Debra; Turner, Lise]

WRIGHT, BLANCHE

America's first identified hitwoman was a native of New York City, born to an alcoholic mother in 1959, sexually abused by a series of men from age seven. One of Blanche Wright's foster fathers died of a heart attack while trying to rape her, but others would not be put off. Growing up in the crime-ridden Bronx, it was not unexpected that she forged a life outside the law, but her descent into multiple murder was a case of follow-the-leader... in this case, the man she loved.

Robert Young was a career criminal and mental case whose rap sheet included multiple charges of rape and homicide. In 1974, interrupted while burglarizing a nurse's apartment, he shot the woman dead and sodomized her corpse before he left the flat. A short time later, jailed on charges of sodomizing an 11-year-old girl, Young ran out of luck when police searched his home and discovered the pistol used in the nurse's murder. Conviction earned him a sentence of eighteen years, and he was packed off to the Matteawan State Hospital for the Criminally Insane. Young met Blanche Wright after he escaped from the asylum in a mass breakout, in May 1977. It was love of a sort at first sight, and Blanche was willing to follow her man anywhere.

On January 21, 1980, a young black woman came knocking at the door of drug dealer Felipe Rodriguez, in the Bronx's Bedford Park district. She asked to buy dope, but when Rodriguez opened the door, a male companion leaped into view, brandishing a pistol with a silencer attached. The couple forced their way inside, shoved Rodriguez to the floor, and cuffed his hands behind his back. Felipe's common-law wife, Martha Navas, made the mistake of pleading for his life, receiving three shots in the head for her trouble. Next, the black man shot Felipe in the head, before settling down to loot the apartment of $8,000 in cash and drugs. Neighbor Luis Martin came knocking, concerned about the racket from next door, and he was shot dead on the threshold, his pockets rifled for money. The killers fled after shooting Rodriguez once more, but he managed to survive his wounds. Martha Navas and Luis Martin were not so fortunate.

Two weeks later, dealer Marshall Howells was leaving his Mount Kisco apartment with bodyguard Sam Nevins when a young black couple approached them on the street. At first, the strangers resembled any other pair of lovers, holding hands and whispering between themselves, but then the young man drew a gun and fired point-blank at Howells. His pistol jammed on the second shot, and Nevins had a chance to return fire, pumping a bullet into the black man's chest. At that, the woman pulled a gun of her own and sent Nevins running for cover. Her companion was already dead, but Howells showed signs of life, and the young woman took time to finish him off with a shot to the head.

Police surveyed the contents of the slain assassin's pockets, coming up with I.D. in the name of "Joseph Morales," residing at a nonexistent address. Four days later, a woman calling herself "Lupe Ocasio," the dead man's aunt, stepped forward to claim his body and personal effects, requesting that the corpse be sent to a Bronx mortuary near her home. By that time, fingerprints had identified the shooter as fugitive Robert Young, and detectives were hot on the trail of his female accomplice.

Officers called at the address of Young's "aunt," and 21-year-old Blanche Wright answered the door, introducing herself as a neighbor. She matched the female killer's description in all respects, and a search of her apartment soon revealed the pistol used to murder Marshall Howells. Under questioning, she admitted the contract killing, inspired by Howells' failure to pay off on a recent drug deal. Blanche also confessed her role in the Rodriguez massacre and the November 1979 murder of drug dealer Carlos Medina. In each case, she claimed, Robert Young had forced her to help him against her will.

Wright's murder trial was postponed due to pregnancy, convened after the birth of her child. Jurors were unimpressed by her claims of coercion, and she was convicted on all counts. The trial judge handed down a sentence of eighteen years to life for the Howells murder, with an additional fifteen years to life in the Navas-Martin homicides.

WRIGHT, JEANNE ANNE

A New Jersey welfare mother, born in 1958, Jeanne Wright dropped out of high school when she became pregnant with the first of her four illegitimate children. Boyfriend Emilio Andujar admitted paternity in three of Jeanne's pregnancies, but he did little or nothing to support the children, leaving Wright to live with her parents in a low-income housing project. Overcrowding in the small apartment forced her to move with her brood in 1983, and Andujar became increasingly abusive, threatening to seize custody of the children. Wright was diagnosed as suffering from chronic depression and a borderline personality disorder, but no one saw the problem as deserving intervention.

In October 1983, Jeanne's food stamps were cut off by the state, and her welfare check arrived two weeks late. On November 10, Wright took her children to the Cooper River, picking out a secluded spot where she could "hide and think." Concluding that the children would be "better off dead," she waited several hours, lulling them to sleep before she dropped all four into the swift-moving current. The first corpse surfaced on November 27, little Jonathan Wright discovered two months short of his third birthday.

Indicted on four counts of murder, Jeanne Wright pled guilty across the board on February 21, 1984. Two months later, on April 19, she was sentenced to four concurrent terms of life imprisonment.

WUORNOS, AILEEN CAROL

She has been heralded in tabloid headlines and on television talk shows as America's "first female serial killer." In fact, Aileen Wuornos is neither the first nor the worst, although she did display a curiously "masculine" tendency to prey on strangers of the opposite sex. Suspected of at least seven murders, sentenced to die in four of the six cases she confessed to police, Wuornos still maintains that some or all of her admitted killings were performed in self-defense, resisting violent assaults by men whom she solicited while working as a prostitute. Ironically, information uncovered by investigative journalists in November 1992 suggests that in one case, at least, her story may well be true.

America's future media monster was born Aileen Pittman in Rochester, Michigan, on February 29, 1956. Her teenage parents separated months before she was born, father Leo Pittman moving on to serve time in Kansas and Michigan mental hospitals as a deranged child-molester. Mother Diane recalls Aileen and her older brother Keith as "crying, unhappy babies," and their racket prompted her to leave them with her parents in early 1960. On March 18 of that year, maternal grandparents Lauri and Britta Wuornos legally adopted the children as their own.

Aileen's childhood showed little improvement from there. At age six, she suffered scarring facial burns while she and Keith were setting fires with lighter fluid. Aileen later told police that she had sex with Keith at an early age, but acquaintances doubt the story and Keith is unable to speak for himself, having died of throat cancer in 1976. At any rate, Aileen was clearly having sex with *someone*, for she turned up pregnant in her fourteenth year, delivering her son at a Detroit maternity home on March 23, 1971. Grandmother Britta died on July 7, and while her death was blamed on liver failure, Diane Pratt suspected her father of murder, claiming he threatened to kill Aileen and Keith if they were not removed from his home.

In fact, they became wards of the court, Aileen soon dropping out of school to work the streets full-time, earning her way as a teenage hooker, drifting across country as the spirit moved her. In May 1974, using the alias "Sandra Kretsch," she was jailed in Jefferson County, Colorado, for disorderly conduct, drunk driving, and firing a .22-caliber pistol from a moving vehicle. Additional charges of failure to appear were filed when she skipped town ahead of her trial. Back in Michigan on July 13, 1976, Aileen was arrested in Antrim County for simple assault and disturbing the peace, after she lobbed a cue ball at a bartender's head. Outstanding warrants from Troy, Michigan, were also served on charges of driving without a license and consuming alcohol in a motor vehicle. On August 4, Aileen settled her debt to society with a $105 fine.

The money came, at least indirectly, from her brother. Keith's death, on July 17, 1976, surprised her with a life insurance payment of $10,000, squandered within two months on luxuries including a new car, which Aileen promptly wrecked. In late September, broke again, she hitched a ride to Florida, anxious to sample a warmer climate, hoping to practice her trade in the sun. It was a change of scene, but Aileen's attitude was still the same, and she inevitably faced more trouble with the law.

On May 20, 1981, Wuornos was arrested in Edgewater, Florida, for armed robbery of a convenience store. Sentenced to prison on May 4, 1982, she was released thirteen months later, on June 30, 1983. Her next arrest, on May 1, 1984, was for trying to pass forged checks at a bank in Key West. On November 30, 1985, named as a suspect in the theft of a pistol and ammunition in Pasco County, Aileen borrowed the alias "Lori Grody" from an aunt in Michigan. Eleven days later, the Florida Highway Patrol cited "Grody" for driving without a valid license. On January 4, 1986, Aileen was arrested in Miami under her own name, charged with auto theft, resisting arrest, and obstruction by false information; police found a 38-caliber revolver and a box of ammunition in the stolen car. On June 2, 1986, Volusia County deputies detained "Lori Grody" for questioning after a male companion accused her of pulling a gun in his car and demanding $200; in spite of her denials, Aileen was carrying spare ammunition on her person, and a .22 pistol was found beneath the passenger's seat she occupied. A week later, using the new alias of "Susan Blahovec," she was ticketed for speeding in Jefferson County, Florida. The citation includes a telling observation: "Attitude poor. Thinks she's above the law."

A few days after the Jefferson County incident, Aileen met lesbian Tyria Moore in a Daytona gay bar. They soon became lovers, and while the passion faded in a year or so, they remained close friends and traveling companions, more or less inseparable for the next four years. On July 4, 1987, police in Daytona Beach detained "Tina Moore" and "Susan Blahovec" for questioning, on suspicion of slugging a man with a beer bottle. "Blahovec" was alone on December 18, when highway patrolmen cited her for walking on the interstate and possessing a suspended driver's license. Once again, the citation noted "Attitude POOR," and "Susan" proved it over the next two months, with threatening letters mailed to the circuit court clerk on January 11 and February 9, 1988.

A month later, Wuornos was trying a new approach and a new alias. On March 12, 1988, "Cammie Marsh Green" accused a Daytona Beach bus driver of assault, claiming he pushed her off the bus following an argument; Tyria

Moore was listed as a witness to the incident. On July 23, a Daytona Beach landlord accused Moore and "Susan Blahovec" of vandalizing their apartment, ripping out carpets and painting the walls dark brown without his approval. In November 1988, "Susan Blahovec" launched a six-day campaign of threatening calls against a Zephyr Hills supermarket, following an altercation over lottery tickets.

By 1989, Aileen's demeanor was increasingly erratic and belligerent. Never one to take an insult lightly, she now went out of her way to provoke confrontations, seldom traveling without a loaded pistol in her purse. She worked the bars and truck stops, thumbing rides to snag a trick when all else failed, supplementing her prostitute's income with theft when she could. Increasingly, with Moore, she talked about the many troubles in her life, a yearning for revenge.

Richard Mallory, a 51-year-old electrician from Palm Harbor, was last seen alive by coworkers on November 30, 1989. His car was found abandoned at Ormond Beach, in Volusia County, the next day, his wallet and personal papers scattered nearby, along with several condoms and a half-empty bottle of vodka. On December 13, his fully-dressed corpse was found in the woods northwest of Daytona Beach, shot three times in the chest with a .22 pistol. Police searching for a motive in the murder learned that Mallory had been divorced five times, earning himself a reputation as a "heavy drinker" who was "very paranoid" and "very much into porno and the topless-bar scene." A former employee described him as "mental," but police came up empty in their search for a criminal record. They could find "nothing dirty" on the victim, finally concluding he was "just paranoid and pussy-crazy."

The investigation was stalled at that point on June 1, 1990, when a nude "John Doe" victim was found, shot six times with a .22 and dumped in the woods forty miles north of Tampa. By June 7, the corpse had been identified from dental records as 43-year-old David Spears, last seen leaving his Sarasota workplace on May 19. Spears had planned to visit his ex-wife in Orlando that afternoon, but he never made it. Ironically, his boss had spotted the dead man's missing pickup truck on May 25, parked along I-75 south of Gainesville, but there the trail went cold.

By the time Spears was identified, a third victim had already been found. Charles Carskaddon, age forty, was a part-time rodeo worker from Booneville, Missouri, missing since May 31. He had vanished somewhere along I-75, en route from Booneville to meet his fiancée in Tampa, his naked corpse found thirty miles south of the Spears murder site on June 6. Carskaddon had been shot nine times with a .22-caliber weapon, suggesting a pattern to officers who still resisted the notion of a serial killer at large. On June 7, Carskaddon's car was found in Marion County, a .45 automatic and various personal items listed as stolen from the vehicle.

Peter Siems, a 65-year-old merchant seaman turned missionary, was last seen on June 7, 1990, when he left his Jupiter, Florida, home to visit relatives in Arkansas. Siems never arrived, and a missing-person report was filed with police on June 22. No trace of the man had been found by July 4, when his car was wrecked and abandoned in Orange Springs, Florida. Witnesses described the vehicle's occupants as two women, one blonde and one brunette, providing police sketch artists with a likeness of each. The blonde was injured, bleeding, and a bloody palmprint was lifted from the vehicle's trunk.

Eugene Burress, age fifty, left the Ocala sausage factory where he worked to make his normal delivery rounds on July 30, 1990. A missing-person report was filed when he had not returned by 2:00 A.M. the next day, and his delivery van was found two hours later. On August 4, his fully-dressed body was found by a family picnicking in the Ocala National Forest. Burress had been shot twice with a .22-caliber pistol, in the back and chest. Nearby, police found his credit cards, clipboard, business receipts, and an empty cash bag from a local bank.

Fifty-six-year-old Dick Humphreys was a retired Alabama police chief, lately employed by the Florida Department of Health and Rehabilitative Services to investigate child abuse claims in Ocala. His wife reported him missing when he failed to return home from work on the night of September 11, 1990, and Humphreys was found the next day in an undeveloped subdivision, shot seven times with a .22 pistol, his pants pockets turned inside-out. On September 19, his car was found abandoned, stripped of license plates, behind a defunct service station in Live Oak. Impounded on September 25, the car was not traced to Humphreys until October 13, the same day his discarded badge and other personal belongings were found in Lake County, seventy miles southeast of the murder scene.

Victim number seven was 60-year-old Walter Antonio, a truck driver from Merritt Island who doubled as a reserve police officer for Brevard County. Found in the woods northwest of Cross City, on November 19, 1990, he had been shot three times in the back and once in the head. Antonio was nude except for socks, his clothes later found in a remote area of neighboring Taylor County. His car, meanwhile, was found back in Brevard County on November 24. Police determined that Antonio's killer had stolen a distinctive gold ring, along with his badge, nightstick, handcuffs, and flashlight.

By that time, journalists had noted the obvious pattern detectives were reluctant to accept, and media exposure forced authorities to go public with their suspect sketches on November 30, 1990. Over the next three weeks, police received four calls identifying the nameless women as Tyria Moore and "Lee Blahovec." Their movements were traced through motel receipts, detectives learning that "Blahovec" also liked to call herself "Lori Grody" and "Cammie Marsh Greene." Fingerprint comparisons did the rest, naming "Blahovec/Grody/Greene" as Aileen Wuornos, placing her at the scene where Peter Siems's car was wrecked in July, but it still remained for officers to track the women down.

Meanwhile, "Cammie Greene" was busy pawning items stolen from her victims, pocketing some extra cash. On December 6, she pawned Richard Mallory's camera and radar detector in Daytona, moving on to Ormond Beach with a box of tools stolen from David Spears. (She also left a thumbprint behind in Ormond Beach, identical to that of "Lori Grody.") The next day, in Volusia County, "Greene" pawned Walter Antonio's ring, later identified by his fiancée and the jeweler who sized it.

With mug shots and a list of names in hand, it was a relatively simple matter to trace Aileen Wuornos, though her rootless lifestyle delayed the arrest for another month. On January 9, 1991, she was seized at the Last Resort, a biker bar in Harbor Oaks, detained on outstanding warrants for "Lori Grody" while police finished building their murder case. A day later, Tyria Moore was traced to her sister's home in Pennsylvania, where she agreed to help police. Back in Florida, detectives arranged a series of telephone conversations between Moore and Wuornos, Tyria begging Aileen to confess for Moore's sake, to spare her from prosecution as an accomplice. One conversation led police to a storage warehouse Aileen had rented, a search revealing tools stolen from David Spears, the nightstick taken from Walter Antonio, another camera and electric razor belonging to Richard Mallory.

On January 16, 1991, Wuornos summoned detectives and confessed six killings, all allegedly performed in self-defense. She denied killing Peter Siems, whose body was still missing, and likewise disclaimed any link to the murder of a "John Doe" victim shot to death with a .22-caliber weapon in Brooks County, Georgia, found in an advanced state of decay on May 5, 1990. (No charges were filed in that case.) "I shot 'em 'cause to me it was like a self-defending thing," she told police, "because I felt if I didn't shoot 'em and I didn't kill 'em, first of all... if they survived, my ass would be gettin' in trouble for attempted murder, so I'm up shit's creek on that one anyway, and if I didn't kill 'em, you know, of course, I mean I *had* to kill 'em... or, it's like retaliation, too. It's like, 'You bastards, you were going to hurt me.'"

Within two weeks of her arrest, Aileen and her attorney had sold movie rights to her story. At the same time, three top investigators on her case retained their own lawyer to field offers from Hollywood, cringing with embarrassment when their unseemly haste to profit on the case was publicly revealed. In self-defense, the officers maintained that they were moved to sell their version of the case by "pure intentions," planning to put the money in "a victim's fund." To a man, they denounced exposure of their scheme as the malicious work of brother officers, driven by their jealousy at being cut out of the deal.

A bizarre sideshow to the pending murder trial began in late January 1991, with the appearance of Arlene Pralle as Aileen's chief advocate. A 44-year-old rancher's wife and "born-again" Christian, Pralle advised Wuornos in her first letter to prison that "Jesus told me to write you." Soon, they were having daily telephone conversations at Pralle's expense, Arlene arranging interviews for Wuornos and herself, becoming a fixture on tabloid talk shows from coast to coast. In Pralle's words, their relationship was "a soul binding. We're like Jonathan and David in the Bible. It's as though part of me is trapped in jail with her. We always know what the other is feeling and thinking. I just wish I was Houdini. I would get her out of there. If there was a way, I would do it, and we could go and be vagabonds forever." Instead, Pralle did the next best thing, legally adopting Wuornos as her "daughter."

Aileen's trial for the murder of Richard Mallory opened on January 13, 1992. Eleven days later, Wuornos took the stand as the only defense witness, repeating her tale of violent rape and beating at Mallory's hands, insisting that she shot him dead in self-defense, using her pistol only after he threatened her life. With no hard evidence to support her claim, jurors rejected the story, deliberating a mere ninety minutes before they convicted Aileen of first-degree murder on January 27. "I'm innocent!" she shouted, when the verdict was announced. "I was raped! I hope you get raped! Scumbags of America!" The jury recommended death on January 29, and the following day Aileen was formally sentenced to die. In April, she pled guilty to the murders of victims Burress, Humphreys, and Spears, with a second death sentence delivered on May 7, 1992.

Around the same time, Aileen offered to show police where the corpse of Peter Siems was hidden, near Beaufort, South Carolina. Authorities flew her to the Piedmont State, but nothing was found at the designated site, Daytona police insisting that Wuornos created the ruse to get a free vacation from jail. They speculate that Siems was dumped in a swamp near I-95, north of Jacksonville, but his body has never been found.

The Wuornos case took an ironic twist on November 10, 1992, with reporter Michele Gillen's revelations on "Dateline NBC." Thus far, Aileen's defenders and Florida prosecutors alike had failed to unearth any criminal record for Richard Mallory that would substantiate Aileen's claim of rape and assault. In the official view, Mallory was "clean," if somewhat "paranoid and pussy-crazy." Gillen, though, had no apparent difficulty finding out that Mallory had served ten years for violent rape in another state, facts easily obtained by checking his name through the FBI's computer network.

"The fascinating part about this," Gillen said, "is here is a woman who for the past year has been screaming that she didn't get a fair trial and that everyone was rushing to make a TV movie about her — and in reality that comes true." (The first TV movie depicting Aileen aired on a rival network one week to the day after Gillen's report.) Even so, Gillen stopped short of calling for Aileen's release. "She's a sick woman who blew those men away," Gillen declared, "but that's no reason for the state to say, 'She's confessed to killing men, we don't have to do our homework.'"

YOUNG, LILA GLADYS

Lila Coolen was the daughter of devout Seventh-Day Adventist parents, born at Fox Point, Nova Scotia, in 1899. At age twenty-six, she met and married William Peach Young, an Oregon native transplanted to New Brunswick, where he aspired to the role of an Adventist "medical missionary" without benefit of ordination or medical training. Soon after their marriage, with Lila expecting the first of five children, the Youngs moved to Chicago, where William was licensed as a chiropractor in December 1927. Two months later, they moved back to Nova Scotia, opening the Life and Health Sanitarium in East Chester, forty miles southwest of Halifax.

Lila entered service as a professional midwife, and their establishment was soon rechristened the Ideal Maternity Home and Sanitarium, with William acting as the superintendent and Lila as managing director. Clients flocked to the "home" in response to newspaper advertisements that read:

> IDEAL MATERNITY HOME "Mothers Refuge" also department for girls. NO PUBLICITY INFANTS home in connection. Write for literature. East Chester, N.S.

Brochures for the home promised to shield "Expectant Mothers from gossip," but every service has its price. Married women seeking refuge with the Youngs paid an average of $75 each for delivery and two weeks of convalescence in the early days of operation, but unwed mothers, frightened of scandal, faced a stiffer price. The Youngs demanded an average $100 or $200 in advance for room and board, delivery of the infant, and arranging subsequent adoption, plus another $12 for diapers and supplies, with an average two-dollar weekly maintenance fee for warehousing infants between delivery and adoption. If a baby died at the home, the mother was charged $20 for a funeral — performed by the Youngs' handyman at a standing rate of fifty cents per corpse, with white pine butterboxes standing in for coffins.

In short, it was the classic "baby farming" racket, elevated to an art form. Girls without the ready cash in hand were sometimes allowed to work off their debts at the home, thus providing the Youngs with a steady stream of unpaid domestic help. Medical care was another realm open to shortcuts, with Lila and William each billing themselves as "doctors" on their letterheads. In fact, Lila delivered the babies herself, while William knelt at the bedside in prayer, but some clients saw a more ruthless side of the Youngs, complaining of Lila's rough — even brutal — handling. "She was physically immense," one client recalled. "She had an overwhelming presence and a great sense of power. She could strike terror into people. No one dared challenge her."

In short order, the Ideal Maternity Home became a virtual baby factory, hosting scores of unwed mothers averaging age seventeen. Between 1928 and 1935, Lila reported 148 births and twelve infant deaths at the home — a mortality rate of 8.1% that nearly tripled Nova Scotia's 3.1% average. On March 4, 1936, Lila and William were charged with two counts of manslaughter in the January deaths of Eva Nieforth and her newborn child, allegedly caused by negligence and unsanitary conditions at the home. Both were acquitted at a three-day trial in May 1936, but the Royal Canadian Mounted Police adopted a policy of investigating each reported death at the home in years to come.

One problem, of course, was the issue of *un*reported infant deaths. Handyman Glen Shatford would later admit burying between 100 and 125 babies in a field owned by Lila's parents near Fox Point, adjoining the Adventist cemetery. "We buried them in rows," he said, "so it was easy to see how many there were." In a typical case, recalled by Shatford from April 1938, an unnamed infant lay in the Youngs' tool shed for five days, covered by a box, before it was driven to Fox Point for burial. A motive for the surreptitious disposal may be found in Lila's standard charge of $300 to board a baby "for the rest of its natural life." Some were farmed out to a neighbor who cared for their needs at three dollars a week, while others reached the end of their "natural lives" in record time. Some adoption "rejects" — including children of mixed race or those with physical defects — were reportedly starved to death on a diet of water and molasses.

For all the money paid to Lila and her husband by their pregnant clients, the Youngs made their greatest profit from adoptive parents, charging an average of $800 to $1,000 per infant in the 1930s, escalating to an average $5,000 per head during World War II. In the 1940s, Ideal Maternity earned $60,000 per year from its live-in clients, including a special $50 fee from any mother who specified adoptive parents of a particular religion. On the flip side, Lila and William banked at least $3.5 million from the "adoption" — i.e. sale — of infants between 1937 and 1947. One client who changed her mind in 1946 and sought to get her child back was told the boy had already been placed for adoption, but he might be retrieved... if the mother could come up with $10,000 in cash.

By 1943, the Youngs were housing seventy infants on any given day. Their original cottage had grown to a sprawling complex of fifty-four rooms, fourteen bathrooms, and multiple nurseries, valued at $40,000 with no outstanding mortgage. Clients could reserve private or semiprivate rooms, if they were put off by the thought of sleeping on a common ward. Business was so good, in fact, that Lila began to brag... and thereby caused herself no end of grief.

Public health officials had been watching the Youngs for a decade, but they found their first concrete evidence of neglect in 1945, inspectors reporting squalid conditions, swarming flies and filthy bedding, some infants weighing 50% of the norm for their age. Lila fired back with charges of harassment, but her time was running out. A new amendment to the Maternity Boarding House Act of 1940 broadened licensing requirements to incorporated companies, and the Youngs' license application was swiftly rejected, Ideal Maternity ordered shut down in November 1945.

It was not that simple to close a multimillion-dollar business, of course, and the Youngs continued to operate without a license while their case was on appeal. U.S. Immigration officers joined the chorus of complaints in early 1946, citing evidence that Lila had smuggled black market babies into the States. In March, the Youngs were arraigned on eight counts including violation of the Maternity Boarding House Act and practicing medicine without a license, but their conviction on three counts, on March 27, resulted in a piddling fine of $150. On June 5, 1946, they were convicted of illegally selling babies to four American couples, fined a total of $428.90. William, drinking heavily by now, was later convicted of perjury based on his testimony at the June trial, but babies were still being born at Ideal Maternity in early 1947.

The end, when it came, was as much a result of Lila's arrogance as any official action. Fuming at media coverage of her case, she filed a $25,000 libel suit against the local newspaper, thereby opening the floodgates of damning testimony from all sides. Jurors dismissed her suit after brief deliberation, and the trial exposed her operation for the brutal, mercenary sham it was. Ideal Maternity was closed before year's end, the Youngs bankrupt and debt-ridden, finally selling off their property and moving to Quebec. The "home," scheduled for conversion into a resort hotel, burned to the ground on September 23, 1962. Cancer had claimed William's life by year's end, and Lila died of leukemia in 1967, after moving back to Nova Scotia. Her tombstone bears the legend: "Till We Meet Again." [See also: "Baby Farming;" Dean, Williamina; Dyer, Amelia; Sach, Amelia; Waters, Margaret]

ZWANZIGER, ANNA MARIA

A native of Nuremberg, Germany, Anna Schonleben was born in 1760, the daughter of a successful innkeeper. She married young, to a self-styled attorney named Zwanziger, but her shining knight turned out to be a drunken bully, leaving her saddled with debts when he drank himself into the grave. Described in one report as "ugly, stunted, without attractions of face, figure, speech... this misshapen woman whom some people likened to a toad," Anna tried to recoup her losses by selling candy and toys, but her forays in business repeatedly failed. At last, despondent, she hired herself out as a domestic servant, traveling widely through Germany and Austria, narrowly avoiding capture for the theft of an employer's diamond ring.

By 1806, Anna was preoccupied with marriage, lacking only a prospective groom. She planned to find a wealthy, single boss and worm her way into his heart, becoming indispensable around the house and finally persuading Mr. Right to marry her.

Zwanziger's first target was a judge named Glaser, living in the town of Pegnitz, near Bayreuth. Anna mistook Judge Glaser for a widower, when in fact he was merely separated from his wife, looking forward to a reconciliation. Anna stepped in to play matchmaker, writing to Frau Glaser on the judge's behalf, urging her to come home. The Glasers were grateful, but their happiness was short-lived. Frau Glaser was barely back in the house before she fell gravely ill, stricken with stomach pains and vomiting that claimed her life after three days. Anna was expecting a proposal on the rebound, but Judge Glaser fired her instead, leaving her bitter and unemployed.

She moved on to the home of Judge Grohmann, nursing the 38-year-old bachelor through a painful attack of gout, but Anna seethed with anger at the announcement of his plan to marry a young, attractive woman. Arsenic canceled the wedding, and Zwanziger poisoned two of her fellow servants as a parting shot, but the domestics managed to survive.

Another judge, named Gebhard, was the next in line, hiring Anna to cook for himself, his pregnant wife, and their several children. With Anna in the kitchen, Mrs. Gebhard soon complained of stomach pains and bitter-tasting meals, but the judge ignored his wife's suspicions, seeming surprised when she died. Anna went on to poison two of Gebhard's servants, both of whom survived, but the judge gave her notice to leave after a "mistake with ingredients" nearly wiped out the guest list at a dinner party. On her last day of work, Anna spiked the noon meal with arsenic, one of Gebhard's queasy servants urging him to have the food analyzed. Gebhard did so, and the lab found arsenic, but he refrained from calling the police in fear of scandal. Anna would be gone when he got home that night, becoming someone else's problem.

Getting rid of her was not that simple, though. Before she left the house, Zwanziger fed the youngest Gebhard child a biscuit soaked in poisoned milk. The infant died, and Gebhard finally sent for the police. Detectives swept the house, discovering that Anna had been busy in her final hours under Gebhard's roof. Every container of salt, sugar, and coffee in the house had been liberally dosed with arsenic before she left. In her absence, autopsies found arsenic in the remains of Frau Glaser, along with Gebhard's wife and child.

By that time, Anna was back in Nuremburg, deluding herself that Judge Gebhard might give her a second chance. She wrote him several letters, alternately bullying and pleading, before police tracked her down and arrested her on October 18, 1809. Packets of arsenic were found in her pockets, but she staunchly denied any crime. Her trial dragged on for over a year, prolonged by a Bavarian statute requiring a confession to support any murder conviction. Finally, without warning, Anna broke down in court, sobbing, "Yes, I killed them all and would have killed more if I had the chance."

Anna was sentenced to die, beheaded with an ax in July 1811. In a final statement to her jailers she declared, "It is perhaps better for the community that I should die, as it would be impossible for me to give up the practice of poisoning people."

Bibliography

Adleman, Robert. *The Bloody Benders*. New York: Stein & Day, 1970.

Anderson, Chris, and Sharon McGehee. *Bodies Of Evidence*. New York: Lyle Stuart, 1991.

Anonymous. *Narrative And Confession Of Lucretia P. Cannon*. New York: n.p., 1841.

------. *The Poison Fiend!* Philadelphia: Barclay & Co., 1872.

------. *Truth Stranger Than Fiction: Lydia Sherman*. Philadelphia: T.R. Callenden, 1873.

Appleton, Arthur. *Mary Ann Cotton*. London: Michael Joseph, 1973.

Biondi, Ray, and Walt Hecox. *All His Father's Sins*. New York: Pocket Books, 1988.

Bishop, George. *Witness To Evil*. Los Angeles: Nash Publishing, 1971.

Blackburn, Daniel. *Human Harvest*. Los Angeles: Knightsbridge, 1990.

Boar, Roger, and Nigel Blundell. *The World's Most Infamous Murders*. New York: Exeter Books, 1983.

Brown, Wenzell. *Introduction To Murder*. New York: Greenberg, 1952.

Buck, Pearl. *The Honeymoon Killers*. London: Sphere Books, 1970.

Bugliosi, Vincent, and Curt Gentry. *Helter Skelter*. New York: Norton, 1974.

Cahill, Bette. *Butterbox Babies*. Toronto: McClelland-Bantam, 1992.

Christie, Trevor. *Etched In Arsenic*. Philadelphia: J.B. Lippincott, 1968.

Cook, Thomas. *Early Graves*. New York: Dutton, 1990.

De la Torre, Lillian. *The Truth About Belle Gunness*. New York: Gold Medal, 1955.

Deming, Richard. *Women: The New Criminals*. New York: Thomas Nelson, 1977.

Dunbar, Dorothy. *Blood In The Parlor*. New York: Barnes, 1964.

Ebon, Martin (ed). *The World's Weirdest Cults*. New York: New American Library, 1979.

Egginton, Joyce. *From Cradle To Grave*. New York: William Morrow, 1989.

Elkind, Peter. *The Death Shift*. New York: Viking, 1989.

Emmons, Nuel, and Charles Manson. *Manson In His Own Words*. New York: Grove, 1986.

Ewing, Charles. *Kids Who Kill*. Lexington, MA: Lexington Books, 1990.

Farr, Louise. *The Sunset Murders*. New York: Pocket Books, 1992.

Fortune, Jan. *The True Story Of Bonnie And Clyde*. New York: Signet, 1968.

Gaute, J.H.H., and Robin Odell. *Murder "Whatdunit."* London: Harrap, 1982.

----- and ------. *Murder Whereabouts*. London: Harrap, 1986.

------ and ------. *The New Murderers' Who's Who*. New York: International Polygonics, 1989.

Ginsburg, Philip. *Poisoned Blood*. New York: Warner, 1987.

Glaister, John. *The Power Of Poison*. New York: William Morrow, 1954.

Green, Jonathon. *The Greatest Criminals Of All Time*. New York: Stein & Day, 1982.

Gribble, Leonard. *The Hallmark Of Horror*. London: John Long, 1973.

------. *Sisters Of Cain*. London: John Long, 1972.

Gross, Kenneth. *The Alice Crimmins Case*. New York: Alfred A. Knopf, 1975.

Hardy, Allison. *Kate Bender, The Kansas Murderess*. Girard, KS: Haldeman-Julius, 1944.

Harrison, Fred. *Brady & Hindley*. London: Ashgrove Press, 1986.

Hartman, Mary. *Victorian Murderesses*. New York: Schocken Books, 1977.

Heppenstall, Rayner. *French Crime In The Romantic Age*. London: Hamish Hamilton, 1970.

Hickey, Eric. *Serial Murderers And Their Victims.* Pacific Grove, CA: Brooks/Cole Publishing Co., 1991.

Humes, Edward. *Buried Secrets.* New York: Dutton, 1991.

Hyde, H. Montgomery. *United In Crime.* New York: Roy, 1955.

James, John. *The Benders In Kansas.* Wichita: Kan-Okla Publishing, 1913.

Jones, Ann. *Women Who Kill.* New York: Holt, Rinehart and Winston, 1980.

Jones, Richard (ed). *Killer Couples.* Secaucus, NJ: Lyle Stuart, 1987.

Kilroy, Jim, and Bob Stewart. *Sacrifice.* Dallas: Word Publishing, 1990.

Kingston, Charles. *Remarkable Rouges.* London: John Lane, 1921.

Kuncl, Tom, and Paul Eisenstein. *Ladies Who Kill.* New York: Pinnacle, 1985.

Lambert, Richard. *When Justice Faltered.* London: Methuen, 1935.

Lane, Brian, and Wilfred Gregg. *The Encyclopedia Of Serial Killers.* London: Headline, 1992.

Langlois, Janet. *Belle Gunness.* Bloomington, IN: IU Press, 1985.

Levin, Jack, and James Fox. *Mass Murder.* New York: Plenum, 1985.

Levine, Richard. *Bad Blood.* New York: Random House, 1982.

Leyton, Elliott. *Sole Survivor.* Toronto: Seal Books, 1990.

Linedecker, Clifford. *HELL Ranch.* Austin, TX: Diamond Books, 1989.

------. *Serial Thrill Killers.* New York: Knightsbridge, 1990.

------. *Thrill Killers.* New York: Paperjacks, 1988.

------, and William Burt. *Nurses Who Kill.* New York: Pinnacle, 1990.

Livsey, Clara. *The Manson Women.* New York: Marek, 1980.

Louderback, Lew. *The Bad Ones.* New York: Fawcett, 1968.

Marchbanks, David. *The Moors Murders.* London: Frewin, 1966.

Markman, Ronald, and Dominick Bosco. *Alone With The Devil.* New York: Doubleday, 1989.

Master, R.E.L., and Eduard Lea. *Perverse Crimes In History.* New York: Julian, 1963.

McDonald, Robin. *Black Widow.* New York: St. Martin's, 1986.

McNally, Raymond. *Dracula Was A Woman.* New York: McGraw-Hill, 1983.

Mitchell, David. *Pirates, An Illustrated History.* New York: Dial Press, 1976.

Moore, Kelly, and Dan Reed. *Deadly Medicine.* New York: St. Martin's, 1988.

Mossiker, Frances. *The Affair Of The Poisons.* New York: Knopf, 1969.

Nash, Jay Robert. *Look For The Woman.* New York: Evans, 1981.

------. *Murder, America.* New York: Simon & Schuster, 1980.

------. *World Encyclopedia Of 20th Century Murder.* New York: Paragon House, 1992.

Newton, Michael. *Hunting Humans.* Port Townsend, WA: Loompanics Unlimited, 1990.

------. *Mass Murder.* New York: Garland, 1988.

------. *Raising Hell.* New York: Avon, 1993.

------. *Serial Slaughter.* Port Townsend, WA: Loompanics Unlimited, 1992.

------, and Judy Ann Newton. *The FBI Most Wanted.* New York: Garland, 1989.

O'Donnell, Bernard. *The World's Worst Women.* London: W.H. Allen, 1953.

O'Donnell, Elliott. *Women Bluebeards.* London: Stanley Paul, n.d.

Penrose, Valentine. *The Bloody Countess.* London: Calder & Boyars, 1970.

Plaidy, Jean. *A Triptych Of Poisoners.* London: Robert Hale, 1958.

Potter, J.D. *The Monsters Of The Moors.* New York: Ballantine, 1966.

Provost, Gary. *Across The Border.* New York: Pocket Books, 1989.

Quimby, Myron. *The Devil's Emissaries.* New York: Curtis Books, 1969.

Reinhardt, James. *The Psychology Of Strange Killers.* Springfield, IL: C.C. Thomas, 1962.

Remsburg, Bonnie. *Mom, Dad, Mike, And Pattie.* New York: Bantam, 1993.

Reynolds, Michael. *Dead Ends.* New York: Warner, 1992.

Reynolds, Richard. *Cry For War.* San Francisco: Squibob Press, 1987.

Ritchie, Jean. *Myra Hindley.* London: Angus & Robertson, 1988.

Sanders, Ed. *The Family.* New York: Dutton, 1971; Signet, 1989.

Schutze, Jim. *Cauldron Of Blood.* New York: Avon, 1989.

------. *Preacher's Girl.* New York: William Morrow, 1993.

Segrave, Kerry. *Women Serial And Mass Murderers.* Jefferson, NC: McFarland & Co., 1992.

Sereny, Gitta. *The Case Of Mary Bell.* London: Methuen, 1972.

Sifakis, Carl. *The Encyclopedia Of American Crime.* New York: Facts on File, 1982.

Sparrow, Gerald. *Women Who Murder.* London: Arthur Barker, Ltd., 1970.

Stokes, Hugh. *Madame De Brinvilliers.* London: Thomas Nelson, 1912.

Van Hoffman, Eric. *A Venom In The Blood.* New York: Donald I. Fine, 1990.

Watkins, Paul, and Guillermo Soledad. *My Life With Charles Manson.* New York: Bantam, 1979.

Weber, Don, and Charles Bosworth. *Precious Victims.* New York: Signet, 1991.

Williams, Emlyn. *Beyond Belief.* New York: Random House, 1967.

Williamson, W.H. *Annals Of Crime: Some Extraordinary Women.* New York: M. Evans, 1981.

Wilson, Colin, and Patricia Putnam. *The Encyclopedia Of Murder.* New York: Putnam, 1961.

------, and Donald Seaman. *The Encyclopedia Of Modern Murder, 1962-1982.* New York: Putnam, 1983.

------, and ------. *The Serial Killers.* New York: Carol, 1990.

Wilson, Patrick. *Murderess.* London: Joseph, 1971.

Wilson, Robert. *Devil's Disciples.* Poole, England: Javelin Books, 1986.

Wood, Walter (ed). *Survivors' Tales Of Famous Crimes.* London: Cassell, 1916.

Yerrington, J.M.W. *The Official Report Of The Trial Of Sarah Jane Robinson.* Boston: Wright & Potter, 1888.

York, Mary. *The Bender Tragedy.* Mankato, KS: George W. Neff, 1875.

Zierold, Norman. *Three Sisters In Black.* Boston: Little, Brown, 1968.